8 Barker

JONATHAN CAPE
PAPERBACK
JCP 9

THE MEN WHO RULED INDIA
THE FOUNDERS

D0941082

PHILIP WOODRUFF

The Men Who Ruled India
*
THE FOUNDERS

JONATHAN CAPE
THIRTY BEDFORD SQUARE LONDON

VOL. I THE FOUNDERS: FIRST PUBLISHED NOVEMBER 1953
THIS PAPERBACK EDITION FIRST PUBLISHED 1963

For copyright reasons, this
book may not be issued on
loan or otherwise except in
its original soft cover.

*Reprinted by Lithography in Great Britain
by Jarrold & Sons Ltd, Norwich*

CONTENTS

INTRODUCTION   11

PART I

Under the Moguls

1600-1751

I   THE FIRST SERVANT OF THE COMPANY   19
II   THE KING'S AMBASSADOR   30
III   THE GREAT MOGUL   37
IV   A JOURNEY FROM AGRA TO SURAT   48
V   THE ENGLISH HOUSE AT SURAT   53
VI   REBELLION AT BOMBAY   57
VII   MADRAS: THE ENLIGHTENED PRESIDENCY   64
VIII   JOB CHARNOCK   70
IX   WAR IN THE SOUTH   76
          1. The New Century   76
          2. The March to Arcot   81

PART II

The Revolution

1751-1798

I   THE REVOLUTION IN BENGAL   93
II   ONE OF THE WORST   104
III   SOME OF THE BEST   114
          1. Vansittart   114
          2. Verelst and the Supervisors   119
IV   WARREN HASTINGS   122
V   SIR JOHN SHORE AND THE LAND REVENUE   133
          1. John Shore   133
          2. The Revenue Controversy   136
          3. Reports from the Districts   139
          4. Some Questions Answered   143
VI   THE WORLD OF WILLIAM HICKEY   151
VII   A COUNTRY STATION   163
VIII   THE INDIA SHORE LEFT   172

7

CONTENTS

PART III

The Golden Age

1798-1858

I	MUNRO AND THE PEASANT SETTLEMENT	183
II	MALCOLM AND CENTRAL INDIA	198
III	ELPHINSTONE AND THE MARATHAS	212
IV	ACROSS INDIA	223
	1. With Heber	223
	2. With Jacquemont	233
V	BOMBAY	238
	1. Jonathan Duncan	238
	2. Mountstuart Elphinstone	240
	3. Boy Malcolm	244
VI	SOME EVILS ENDED	248
	1. Human Sacrifice	248
	2. Burning Widows	253
	3. Strangling Travellers	259
VII	METCALFE AND THE SUPREME POST	266
VIII	FORT WILLIAM AND HAILEYBURY	279
IX	THOMASON AND THE SETTLEMENT OF THE NORTH-WEST	287
	1. An Outspoken Service	287
	2. Robert Bird	292
	3. James Thomason	301
X	BEFORE THE DELUGE	306
XI	THE TITANS OF THE PUNJAB	324
	1. The First Sikh War and the Regency	324
	2. Edwardes and Bannu	330
	3. The Rule of the Titans	334
XII	THE MUTINY	344
	1. The Sepoy Army	344
	2. The Causes of the Great Mutiny	348
	3. The Savagery on both Sides	355
	4. The Civilian's Part in Hindustan	362
	5. The Civilian's Part in the Punjab	370
	EPILOGUE	379
	NOTES ON THE AUTHORITIES	382
	INDEX	389

MAPS

MOGUL INDIA 1608 — 25

REMNANTS OF THE MOGUL EMPIRE 1751 — 80

CLIVE AND ARCOT — 82

THE REVOLUTION IN BENGAL — 102

BEFORE WELLESLEY 1795 — 199

AFTER WELLESLEY 1805 — 201

AFTER THE MARATHA WARS — 203

AFTER DALHOUSIE — 339

To the Peoples of India and Pakistan
whose tranquillity was our care
and whose continuance
in the family of nations to which we belong
is our Memorial

INTRODUCTION

THERE comes a time in a man's life when he may well stand back and consider what he has built, planted, written or begotten and whether it was worth doing. If in such a mood the English — and by that I mean all those who speak English; Chaucer and Drake, Milton and Marlborough, Clive and Hastings, belong to us all — if the English look back on their varied history, the long connection with India will be an achievement that cannot be ignored.

It is too soon to say if it will last. But though the political structure may change to something unrecognizable, it is hard to believe that the impress of English ways of thinking will vanish altogether. And the achievement itself, whatever the future holds, is surely a matter for pride.

There are many ways of looking at it. The heart of one man will beat faster — though perhaps against his will — to remember how a handful of his countrymen mastered and ruled so many millions by the sword, by diplomacy, above all by a stubborn tenacity of purpose. To another, the main matter for pride will be that so few among so many had so slight a need for force, that so often the district officer really was at heart what the villagers called him in their petitions, the father and mother of his people. And to another again it will seem that the years of renunciation with which the story ends are the finest in the long record.

For more than three centuries the effort was sustained. It was an effort in which two parts combined, as brain and muscle join in the sweep of a scythe. There was the will of the people of England expressed imperfectly by the Crown, by Parliament, by the Court of Directors of the East India Company; at the other end, there were men in India who fought, won, governed, trained and handed over what they had made, sometimes in conscious disagreement with the will of England but in obedience to it at the last.

In the years between 1914 and 1940, India was a problem not yet solved that lay on England's conscience; now that one way or another, rightly or wrongly, it is India's problem not ours, we can begin to look back with detachment. And there are things which should be set down before they are forgotten, the smell of dust thirstily drinking the first rain, the spicy peppery smell of a grain-dealer's shop, the reek of mangoes, marigolds and lush vegetation when the sun breaks through the clouds in August and the earth steams, things too that fade more quickly such as the sound of men's voices in petition, the look on a man's face when he is found guilty, a peasant's emotion when a wrong has been put right.

This book is an account of the men who ruled India, whether they began as soldiers or civilians, written in the light of such memories as these. The scene is a mass of land the size of Europe; the period is three centuries and a half. There were something over four hundred districts in British India and a district officer in each. To write a history of the Indian Civil Service on the scale of Fortescue's History of the British Army would be the work of a lifetime. It is probably too soon for such a book as that; at any rate, this is not it. This is a rapid survey, while memory lives, of the surface only of the great mass of material that is available.

If the episode is considered as a whole, it lasts from 1600 to 1947. Within that stretch of time there are four — or possibly five — periods to be distinguished from each other. There is the beginning, when the servants of the Company were suppliants to the Mogul; then comes a time of transition, the brief startling score of years that left them masters of India; then the long stretch of a century and a half in which they administered the continent; finally the thirty years during which power was deliberately transferred. The long stretch of administration again may be thought of as two; at first, the sovereignty of Parliament was exercised through a corporation known as the Company; from 1858 onwards the Crown ruled direct. But the sovereignty of the Crown had been recognized fifty years earlier and the change was one of machinery more than spirit. I should have preferred to deal with the whole in one book and not to pause at the Mutiny, which is an interlude, an interruption to the main development. But the method I have used is against brevity.

To summarize and condense means almost inevitably to be abstract. I have tried instead to be concrete, to take one scene that illustrates a point and to dwell on that, passing mercilessly, though with regret, over many years and places before the next; it is a method less unfair to the reader than abstract comment though still unfair because it selects. But the men of whom I have tried to give an account have interested me so much that by the end of the Mutiny they have filled one book already. Even so, it deals with the revolution that gave them the mastery of India, the transformation of corrupt Nabobs into a body of men who boasted that 'no public service in the whole world can evince more integrity', the survey and settlement of the greater part of the continent, the reactionary outbreak of 1857, events of which each could easily have made a volume. The result has no claim to be a work of original scholarship; it is still less a work of reference, nor is it meant only for those who know India. It is meant for anyone who would like to know what sort of men carried out this one English achievement.

They were men who by the middle of the nineteenth century had brought peace to the country instead of anarchy, had mapped the fields and made lists of every man's rights and had made a beginning of the task of building roads, bridges and railways, of harnessing the rivers to irrigation. More important, they had associated Indians with them in their work and the greater part of the administration was carried out by Indians. But perhaps nothing the Company's servants did was of greater value in the end than their release in India of some gusts of that dry and searing wind, that bracing scepticism, which swept through Europe after the French Revolution and which in the milder climate of England had come to be associated with the name of Jeremy Bentham. It was a spirit which inquired sceptically whether an institution was defensible by human reason, whether it contributed to human happiness, and whether it was consistent with a respect for the value of human beings as individuals. It was a spirit which found much to question in India at a time when her own civilization had ceased to grow, when pity for human suffering seemed used up and finished. This alien breath provoked new life and indignant reaction; India began to grow again and her mind took on new vigour. Indians did not, as the English of the 'twenties and 'thirties had expected, accept the full doctrine of Christianity together with Western education but this side-wind from the main current of Christendom stirred their minds deeply and changed their conception of their own religion.

Here they are then, the civil servants of the Honourable East India Company, learning among their bolts of gingham and taffety that they must be diplomats, administrators and soldiers; thrown suddenly into positions where the opportunities for wealth and power were such as have been open to no men since the Roman Emperors asserted their control over the pro-consuls; abusing their power and then transforming themselves into a body of men 'minutely just, inflexibly upright', men as Lord Radcliffe has said, who were content to be themselves, who used power not for selfish ends but as they thought was right, men who 'after ruling millions of subjects, after commanding victorious armies, after dictating terms of peace at the gates of hostile capitals . . . return to their native land with no more than a decent competence'.

One aspect of the outlook, not of them all, but of the best of them, should be remembered. 'Whenever we are obliged to resign our sovereignty', wrote Munro, 'we should leave the natives so far improved from their connection with us, as to be capable of maintaining a free, or at least a regular, government among themselves', while Elphinstone, with still clearer insight, thought 'the most desirable death for us to die should be the improvement of the natives reaching such a pitch as would render it impossible for a foreign nation to retain the government. . . .'

To write of them as a class is inevitable because that is the way men think; but human beings do not really fit into classes. The rulers of India were men, quick with fleshly desire, lust for power, and all the miraculous diversity of man; humorous, solemn and unpredictable; adventurous, soaked in routine, timid and bold. Yet they have something in common. Nearly all of them — after the transformation — believe that the performance of duty is something good in itself; hardly one questions the value of his work. But he will do his work his own way. He is critical and sometimes contemptuous of authority. I have stressed this point again and again, the independence of these men, their detachment, their questioning spirit. But there is a contradictory tendency as well. Already in the 'forties and 'fifties, long before the Mutiny, there is apparent a hardening of the arteries, a greater readiness to take the whole business of British rule for granted. This was to be expected, an inevitable result of the growth of system.

The system began when Haileybury was founded in the first decade of the nineteenth century; it was still growing and hardening when the process was interrupted by the Mutiny. All through the nineteenth century, three Governors out of ten, an occasional Member of the Viceroy's Council, sometimes a Commander-in-Chief, a few judges — altogether between a dozen and a score of men in the highest posts — came to their appointments direct from England; but the majority of the government at the centre, almost the whole of the provincial governments, the officer at the head of each district, all belonged to a specially selected official class, never much more than a thousand strong, who were responsible not to the people they governed but — through the Company or direct — to Parliament in Westminster, seven thousand miles away, and who in fact governed in the light of what they themselves believed to be right.

The nearest parallels on anything like the same scale are the civil services of China under the Emperors and of the Ottoman Empire under Suleiman the Magnificent; the Romans had nothing comparable. But there is an ideal model for the Indian system, not consciously adopted and exactly followed, for that is not the way English minds work, but a model with which every English statesman in the nineteenth century was familiar. Plato pictured a state ruled by guardians, men specially chosen by their seniors in the service, trained in the use of their bodies and in the study of history, taught that they were a separate race from those they ruled, aloof, superior to the ties of marriage or fatherhood and to the attraction of gold, governing by the light of what they knew to be beautiful and good.

Nothing could be more foreign to what either Englishmen or Athenians have really liked; if the names of England and Athens are linked in men's minds with the idea of freedom, it is mainly because both liked to choose and control those who governed them. But the Athenians would not give the islands and colonies the freedom for which they had themselves fought at Salamis and Marathon, the English learnt only slowly the lessons of Yorktown and Saratoga. They did, however, learn in the end. They were moving all through the nineteenth century towards a society in which each individual had a right and a means to express his views and make them felt; cautiously, year by year, in the Reform Bills, in the Constitution of Canada, in the Repeal of the Combination Act, they pared away restrictions based on privilege and extended the circle within which men were free.

India too would one day be free; Macaulay said so, Queen Victoria said so, Gladstone said so. Munro, Elphinstone and Metcalfe felt in their bones that it must be so and it was the conscious will of England. But for the present it was guardianship India needed. And in fact it was to peace and unity rather than to freedom, that the effort in India was directed, to equal justice for all, roads, railways, canals, bridges. That was the mixture, very good for the child, to be given firmly and taken without fuss. And to give it, the means found to be best was a corps of men specially selected, brought up in a rigour of bodily hardship to which no other modern people have subjected their ruling class, trained by cold baths, cricket, and the history of Greece and Rome, a separate race from those they ruled, aloof, superior to bribery, discouraged from marriage until they were middle-aged, and then subjected to long separations. The merchants of the East India Company were there to hand; some memory of

Akbar's civil service survived; every decision was made by men who had been brought up on Plato. That was the triple parentage of the service.

Plato taught that the guardians of the state should not know their parents; the English did not go so far as that, but when they were eight years old the children from whom rulers were to be chosen were taken away from home for three-quarters of every year, taught not to mention their mothers or their own Christian names, brought up in the traditions of the Sparta which Plato had admired. And the children grew up to be true guardians; no other people in history can equal their record of disinterested guardianship. But guardians conserve their trust and seldom encourage change; it is not surprising that they were not always loved nor that in the end their wards outgrew their tutelage. What is surprising is that so often there was real warmth and affection between the district officer and the peasant, that the system was always much looser than it looked, that so much freedom was always left to the individual officer that the guardians fell in practice so far short of Platonic rigidity.

To one invincible prejudice which runs through the book I will confess in advance. It is a belief in the Christian doctrine that a man must be judged not by his worst so much as by his best, and in the end not even by his best but by what he aimed at. And so English rule in India is to be judged by the conscious will of England expressed in Parliament and by the aims of a good district officer, not by the nasty little atavistic impulses that came wriggling up from the subconscious when an official at the Treasury scored a departmental triumph over the India Office, when a merchant fixed something over an opulent lunch. 'Not what thou art, nor what thou hast been, does God consider, but what thou wouldst be.'

I am very grateful to the association of retired members of the Indian Civil Service who have made it possible for me to write this book. I must, however, explain that they have no responsibility for anything I have said. I made it clear before accepting the task that it would have to be a personal book and there is not a thought in it for which I can put the blame on anyone else. I am also most grateful to many people who have lent me letters, sent me manuscripts and described particular aspects of the subject in conversation. I have, I hope, acknowledged these debts in the notes; to all who have helped me I can only give my thanks and wish that the result could be less imperfect.

P. W.

THE FOUNDERS

I
UNDER THE MOGULS
1600-1751

CHAPTER I

WILLIAM HAWKINS

THE FIRST SERVANT OF THE COMPANY IN INDIA

ELIZABETH BY THE GRACE OF GOD QUEEN OF
England France and Ireland, Defender of the Faith, to all our
Officers, Ministers and Subjects . . . , Greeting

PRIDE rings in the formal words; you can hear the trumpets peal along the narrow city lanes. This is more than the charter of a company of merchants; it is an act of state, a move in the war with Spain. Trade is the object, but so long as Spain and Portugal claim a monopoly of the West Indies and the East, there is no trade without fighting and the business of the new company will not all of it be carried on in ledgers and account books.

That much they must have known when they met in the Founders' Hall on September 24th, 1599, to petition the Queen for their charter. But just how much they were founding, how much more than a trading company was the enterprise they were beginning, not one of them can have guessed. Nor is it clear three and a half centuries later, when the stir and movement of the tale end and only its effects remain.

Whereas our most dear and loving cousin, George Earl of Cumberland
and other our well-beloved subjects . . . have of our certain knowledge
been petitioners unto us for our Royal assent and license to be granted
unto them, that they, of their own Adventures, costs and charges,
as well for the honour of this our realm of England as for the increase
of our navigation and advancement of trade of merchandise . . . might
adventure and set forth one or more voyage, with convenient number
of Ships and Pinnaces, by way of traffic and merchandise to the East
Indies. . . .

For the honour of this our realm of England, for navigation, trade, merchandise, and because it was what they liked to do; that was why the bold eyes of the Queen's captains and merchants had roved East as well as West. They sought gold, fame and danger in every corner of the world they opened and devoured with such zest. They had been East already in ones and twos; they had found the Portuguese before them in India, the Dutch in the Spice Islands. Both treated the English as poachers. The Portuguese had the Pope's blessing; he had given them the Eastern seas, and for the moment they were the more formidable because their crown was one with Spain's. The Dutch had no blessing but the plain advantage of being first in the field, for they were not inclined to pay attention to the English claim that Drake had touched at Ternate on his way round the world and made a treaty with the King. The English were poachers, and sea poachers are at a disadvantage when they operate without a base ten thousand miles from home.

The Dutch were a nation of merchants; they had seen the chance when the English and the winds of heaven destroyed the Armada, and in their case there had been no need for delay while the city convinced the court. They had sent their ships at once and already they owned safe harbours and strong warehouses. The Portuguese had been in the East more than a hundred years. The English, third in the field, for the Danes were never a serious danger, petitioned the Queen for the same backing as their rivals. But in 1599 there were hopes of peace with Spain; the Queen would not imperil the negotiations by licensing trespass in the East; she kept her hand on the jesses. Next year, 1600, the hope of peace died; the time came and on the last day of the sixteenth century the Queen gave the Company their charter.

Know ye therefore ... that they ... shall be a body Corporate and Politic in deed and in name by the name of the Governor and Company of merchants of London trading into the East Indies. ...

Peaceful words enough, and no doubt the merchants of London would have liked nothing better than peaceful trade that brought home gold. Indeed, they said so. 'There is no intention,' they said when the sailors asked how prizes should be divided, 'there is no intention to make any attempt for reprisals but only to pursue the voyages in a merchantlike course.' But in the end they added that the commander should always do what he thought best and if without hazard to the voyage he should find himself with a prize on hand, why, he should make with the mariners what agreement they both thought fit. It was a far-sighted provision, for in practice there was never much peace about the business and from the first two voyages the profits were less from trade than from privateering. And to some of their servants this was perhaps not entirely a discouragement.

THE FIRST SERVANT OF THE COMPANY

When the First Voyage was fitted out in 1601, England was still at war with the joint crowns of Spain and Portugal. Portugal was strong along the coasts of India and this may be one reason why the first two voyages were not directed there. But the Elizabethan was not usually slow to dip his hand in a hornet's nest if there was anything to be got out of it. Spices were a more compelling reason; it was spices that made the big profits and India was not yet thought of as a market where spices could be bought or English goods sold.

This is a tale of men and doings in India: there is no place here for the first two voyages, the scurvy, the ships taken off Sumatra and Malacca, the treaty with the King of the Achins, the million pounds of pepper the first voyage brought home. It is not till the Third Voyage that India is mentioned in the instructions from the Governor and Company to their servants. This was in March 1607, by which time the war had come to an end with the Treaty of London, and there may have been some faint hope that the Portuguese would now be less strict gamekeepers than before. At any rate, India was now for the first time an object of the venture, though not even now the first.

The ships of the Third Voyage were the *Red Dragon* of seven hundred tons and the *Hector* of five hundred, with a pinnace, the *Consent*, of a hundred and fifteen, the company being two hundred and eighty merchants and mariners all told. The general of this fleet of cockle-shells was William Keeling and:

> we appoint and ordain our loving friend William Hawkins to be lieutenant of the ships and men and to take passage in the *Hector*.

The Governor and Company go on with instructions that prayers are to be said morning and evening:

> that all jointly may with reverence and humility pray unto Almighty God to bless and preserve them from all dangers in this long and tedious voyage.

There is to be no swearing or dicing, and:

> when you shall water and refresh your men you shall give them severe warning to behave themselves peaceably and civilly towards the people of that place . . . and use a discreet means in eating of fruit. . . .

The ships are to be kept clean, taking good example in this matter from the Dutch: at Mozambique, the chance is to be taken of buying some 'oliphauntes teeth', and at Socotra, two or three tons of aloes and some ambergris. At Socotra too a pilot is to be found for the passage to Aden, trade with this port being the first object of the venture. But if Socotra is not reached before the monsoon, Aden would have to be left out. 'If you come not to Socotra in convenient time, sail directly to Cambaya . . . where if you come about mid-September you may safely ride in the road.' In that case, the General was to go on to Bantam in the island of Java, William Hawkins staying at Surat to deliver King James I's letter to the King of that place.

The ships of the Third Voyage sailed with a reasonable store of provisions. They had bread for twenty-one months; ship beer for three months, strong beer for one month, cider for twelve months at a quart a day each man and wine for eight months at a pint; beef dry-salted, beef pickled, pork pickled, and three kinds of salt fish, besides meal, peas, beans and oatmeal. But whatever you took with you on such a voyage in the reign of James I, you must rely on replenishing with food and water somewhere; the coasts and islands where you might touch were many of them unknown and those that were known often hostile. Navigation was the merest guesswork and among the great Atlantic waves the ships were very small. Scurvy occurred on almost every voyage and sometimes attacked more than half the crew. Altogether, it was from no imaginary dangers that the ship's company were directed to pray for preservation.

The *Red Dragon* and the rest sailed from England in March 1607. They did not reach Table Bay till December, nor Socotra till April 1608, thirteen months from home. There was just time to get to Aden if they were lucky but their bad luck held and they were driven back by contrary winds. At last they gave up the idea of Aden; the general would go on to Bantam while Hawkins in the *Hector* made for Surat. He sailed from Socotra for the second time on August 4th and on August 24th, 1608, sixteen months from home, the *Hector* dropped anchor at the entrance to the river Tapti, the first ship to fly the English flag off the coast of India.

Hawkins sent messengers to the Governor and when after some delays he received encouraging assurances he went on shore himself, where 'after their barbarous manner I was kindly received'. But he could not see the Governor, who was, he suspected, drunk with opium. He had met, right from the start, the supreme indifference of the Mogul officials to trade. They simply were not interested in promoting commerce; not one exception appears. But each had a lively interest in avoiding the wrath or envy of his superior and in supplying the Emperor with what the Elizabethan merchant called toys, any presents that were novelties at the Court. The presents Hawkins had brought for Jahangir were confiscated; Mukarrab Khan, who was in charge of the customs of this part of the West Coast, would prefer to lay them before the Emperor himself.

Meanwhile Hawkins could get no answer when he sought permission to build a factory. By this he meant a warehouse for storing trade goods; the Portuguese, the Dutch, every European nation trading to India, had found that prices went up when a ship came in; if you wanted to buy pepper or indigo the only way to get it at a reasonable price was to keep a man on the spot who could bargain for it at harvest-time, when prices dropped, and store it till a ship came. So a factory was the first object of Hawkins's diplomacy; already it was clear that the first of the Company's servants in India must be diplomat before he could be trader. After a good deal of evasion Hawkins was told that only the Emperor could give permission; he must take the pains of two months' travel, go to Agra himself and beg for it there.

Meanwhile, there was a danger more active than Mogul apathy. Having emptied his ship of lead and iron and bought what goods he could for Bantam, Hawkins called Master Marlowe and all the company who were on shore — two boat loads — told them Master Marlowe was their commander, instructed them to return to the ship and sail to Bantam, and 'at last, seeing them embark themselves, bade them farewell'. But only next day, ten or twelve of them were back; they had escaped with difficulty, all the rest of the two boats' companies with the barks and goods being taken by the Portugals. How it happened is not very clear, but the English had apparently trusted in the peace and had been unwilling to fight until too late.

Hawkins sent a letter to the captain-major of the Portugals; the two kings, he said, were at peace, and he made no doubt that the king of Portugal would be pleased if the subjects and goods of His Majesty King James were delivered back. But at the receipt of this: 'the proud rascal braved so much, as the messenger told me, most vilely abusing His Majesty, terming him King of Fishermen and of an island of no import, and a fart for his commission, scorning to send me any answer'.

Hawkins replied in kind, sending a message by the captain of a Portuguese frigate that the 'great captain in abusing the King of

England is a base villain and a traitor to his king, and I will maintain it with my sword if he dare come on shore'. But the challenge had no effect; the goods and boats' crews were sent to Goa and Hawkins had to give them up for lost and send away the *Hector* for Bantam, leaving at Surat beside himself only William Finch, merchant, and two English servants. It was a decision that required courage, for now everything was against him. 'That dog Mukarrab Khan' had by now almost all of any value that Hawkins had brought with him and would give no better price than 'his own barbarous conscience afforded'. He was, Hawkins thought, plotting with the Jesuits to take his life as well as his goods, for neither of them wanted him to reach Agra. And the omens were adverse, for the first two Dutchmen to land at Surat had been handed over to the Portugals, taken to Goa and there executed.

'After the departure of my ship, I was so misused that it was insufferable, but so long as my ship was at the bar I was flattered withal. But howsoever, well used or ill, it was not for me to take thought for anything, although remaining in an heathen country, environed with so many enemies, who daily did nothing else but plot to murther me. . . .'

The first attempt was a quarrel, forced on him at the water's edge by three gallants with coats of buff down to their knees, their rapiers and pistols by their side, and some forty followers scattered behind them. Hawkins laid hand on his weapon but the fight was prevented by the Mogul captain; perhaps the Emperor had expressed a wish to see this stranger of a new people, for his officers clearly did not want to be held responsible for his death.

For some time, says Hawkins, 'I could not peep out of doors for fear of the Portugals, who in troops lay lurking in the byways to give me assault to murther me'. Once they came with thirty or forty men to attack his house, with friars to give them absolution, but he was warned, and having a strong house with good doors was able to repel the attack. All this time, William Finch was little help to him, for he was suffering from a bloody flux, an affliction that comes sooner or later to most newcomers to India. But at last things began to improve; Finch recovered, and the Governor forbade the Portugals to carry arms in the town. On February 1st, 1609, Hawkins felt able to start his journey to Agra.

He had engaged a troop of fifty Pathans, valiant horsemen, to protect him on the way. This turned out a wise precaution, for the Portugals had wrought with a friend of theirs, a Raja near whose

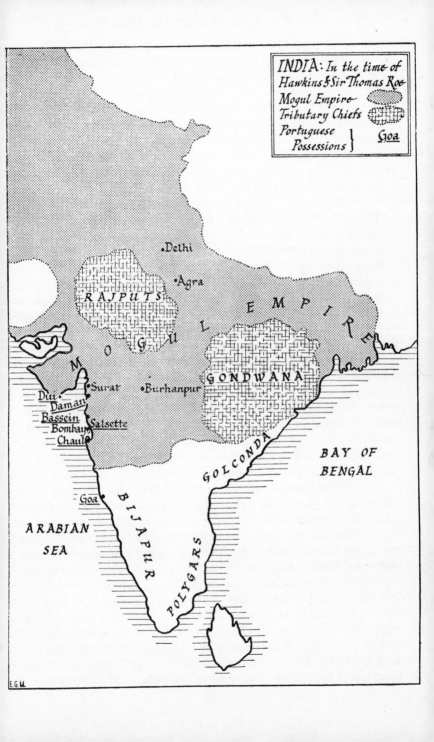

territories he must pass, to attack him. His party was too strong and he was allowed to pass, only to discover that his coachman had been hired to stab him and his interpreter to poison him. This arrangement turned out to be less prodigal than it appeared; only the coachman had been paid in advance and he alone had any serious intention of carrying out the deed. On February 18th, Hawkins arrived safely at Bramport, the name always used by the English for Burhanpur. They seem from the start to have been sturdily determined to stand as little nonsense as possible from Indian names. Here he stayed for a few days before going on his way towards Agra.

It is clear already that Hawkins was a direct and practical man, by no means given to refinements of fancy, and in any case sufficiently occupied with his own safety to have few thoughts to spare for the ways of villagers or the country through which he passed. He says nothing about either. But the road he saw on his journey when the first light came to show him the way — for he started early — is a road still to be found in every district of India. It is a road of earth, very broad, so that there is plenty of room to go round a bad patch in the rains. It is striped in the early morning light by long shadows where the wheels have worn deep ruts in the pearly dust; it is flanked on either side by an intermittent hedge of cactus and tall plumes of elephant grass. In these first minutes of the day the dust is still too moist with dew to rise high above the ground; all is still clear and sweet. There are lines of camels pulling tall carts like gipsy caravans, droves of patient little grey-white cattle and black sullen buffaloes going to graze, a peasant carrying his shoes on the end of his bamboo pole to save leather, a potter with his donkeys, traffic that will not change much in three hundred years.

Nor will the fields on either side of the road be very different then and now. In Hawkins's day as now there will be black partridges calling in the wheat and barley; the crops will be fresh and green, as high as the calf of a man's leg, heavy with dew. There will be grey partridges running in the tall pulse called *arhar* and among the little chick-pea known as *gram*. There will be blackbuck wandering between the plots of cotton and pepper; men will be beginning to cut into the squares of sugar-cane that still bristle with pike-heads as defiant as clusters of Spanish infantry. Only there will be more opium and poppy in Hawkins's day and near Agra there will be indigo. Since it is February they will be working the wells and, not long after the sun is up, Hawkins will hear an inconsequent little song, rising and falling in a recitative more like a lark's than a man's;

it is the song of the man who catches the great leather bag the bullocks have dragged up from the depths of the well, catches and swings it glistening over the watercourse to spill its cool glittering burden on the fields.

Hawkins left Bramport on March 2nd and reached Agra on April 16th. He was looking for a house 'in a very secret manner' when messengers came from the King who insisted on bringing him to the presence in such haste that, 'I could scarce obtain time to apparel myself in my best attire'. Not only this, but he had no presents worth the name, the infamous Mukarrab Khan having taken everything but a few rolls of cloth, and stout English woollens were not likely to appeal much to the Emperor.

However, Hawkins presented his letter. It was addressed to the great King of Surat, Ackbursha (meaning Akbar Shah who had of course died in 1605) requesting him to allow, 'our subjects to settle a factory there, like as we will do to yours if at any time it shall be requested of us . . .' It was translated from Portuguese or Spanish into Persian by a Jesuit father, with some unfavourable comments on its style. Hawkins at once took up the cudgels, explaining that the Portuguese were enemies of the English and could not be expected to act as impartial interpreters. In the course of the altercation he revealed his own knowledge of Turkish, for he had been a Levant merchant. Turkish was still the family, as opposed to the Court, language of the Mogul Emperors, and he was invited into the inner audience chamber. Here the King said that he had heard Mukarrab Khan had not dealt well with Hawkins, and having made fair promises for the future he wrote most strictly to Mukarrab Khan 'conjuring him to be none of his friend if he did not deal well with the English'.

Now began a long course of ups and downs. Jehangir was pleased to find an Englishman who could speak Turkish and he seems to have felt a personal liking for Hawkins, or perhaps he was amused by the novelty of hearing a man blurt out his thoughts with so little disguise. At any rate there came an invitation to stay at court as a resident ambassador and Hawkins was made a Commander of four hundred, a post in the imperial service that was nominally worth over three thousand pounds a year sterling. Not only this, not only the entrée nightly to the inner audience chamber, but:

'the King was very earnest with me to take a white maiden out of his palace; he would give her all things necessary with slaves and he would promise me she should turn Christian, and by this means my meats and drinks should be looked to and I should live without fear of the Jesuit's poison'. Hawkins, however, insisted that she must be a genuine Christian, none of your last-minute converts; so the King 'called to memory' a Christian Armenian, a daughter of one of Akbar's captains, and Hawkins married her.

This was extraordinary favour, but all the time the Portuguese were working against him, together with Mukarrab Khan and other envious courtiers. The order or *firman* to the Governor of Surat, permitting the English to build their factory, was sealed and dispatched but cancelled by a second that followed hard on the heels of the messenger; an English ship arrived with prospect of presents, hopes of mastiffs, greyhounds, suits of armour and trifles of glass, and the firman was drawn up afresh; but news came of a magnificent ruby at Goa which might be sent to Jehangir if he were friends with Portugal — but not with England — and again the order was cancelled. Mukarrab Khan falls from grace and English affairs look up, but during one of Jehangir's very occasional periods of abstinence and reform Hawkins comes to court smelling of drink, is sent home in disgrace and denied the entrée.

The stiff obstinacy that was the strength of his countrymen in war led Hawkins to one mistake that undid months of patience. It seemed, not for the first time, that all was at his feet; Mukarrab Khan had been summoned from Surat, degraded, and ordered to pay every man what he owed. He made Hawkins an offer, a far better offer than he had ever made before, in settlement for the goods he had taken. The offer was made through the Vizier, the Prime Minister, Asaf Khan, the greatest man in the kingdom. But it was not the full amount and Hawkins refused to be fobbed off or to accept Asaf Khan's advice. He never had another chance to get his money and, what was worse, made Asaf Khan his enemy.

Now gradually he fell from favour. Even after his disgrace he once more persuaded Jehangir to seal the order — 'so this time again I was afloat' — but the Jesuit secret service picked up the news and passed it to Mukarrab Khan, now forgiven and on his way to Goa on a mission of friendship. Back came his protest; it was no use talking to the Portuguese of friendship unless the Emperor would bar the English from his ports. The decree had not been delivered; Asaf Khan had seen to that. Now it was withdrawn and Hawkins was overthrown again. He was suffered no more to enter within the red rails, the place of honour near the King where all his time he had stood; his post of commander of four hundred was never formally withdrawn but it was easy for Asaf Khan to arrange that it should bring in no revenue. Hawkins made a last throw, complaining to the King of his treatment by the Minister and praying that either his post should be made a reality or he should be given leave to depart. The answer came coldly that he had leave. The first diplomatic mission of an Englishman in India was over.

CHAPTER II

THE KING'S AMBASSADOR

IT was the malice of the Portugals, as much as Mogul apathy or his own mishandling, that had caused Hawkins's failure. They were a people who, like the English, had come to India for trade and their history had followed a prophetic pattern. Met by the implacable antagonism of the Arab traders on the West Coast, they had made treaties with the Hindu Rajas of the Deccan and built forts to protect themselves. But they had been very chary of continental commitments. A hundred years before the English company was founded, Almeida, their first viceroy of the Indies, had written to Lisbon:

'the greater the number of fortresses you hold, the weaker will be your power; let all your forces be on the sea, because if we should not be powerful at sea (which may the Lord forbid) everything will at once be against us . . . Let it be known for certain that as long as you may be powerful at sea, you will hold India as yours, and if you do not possess this power, little will avail you a fortress on shore. . . .'

But by 1512, his successor Albuquerque was appointing in each fortress a governor to settle the disputes of each race, a Hindu for the Hindus, a Muslim for the Muslims, and to rule all a Portuguese Factor who was judge in suits between merchants of different nationalities. A very little later, at the request of the inhabitants of the country districts round Goa, he appointed Portuguese officers to collect the revenue and administer justice, each with a Hindu clerk and two hundred peons or footmen of the country. The trader had already found that diplomacy and war were not enough as defences for his trade; he must go one step further and administer the territory surrounding his fortress.

In the course of a century, the Portuguese effort had begun to exhaust itself. The burden of Empire was too great for so small a country so far from home; religious intolerance raised up enemies; the union of the Crown with Spain did not in the long run strengthen Portugal. Already power was slipping away to the Dutch in the Spice Islands and Malacca, but here in India the Portuguese were still thought invincible at sea. The Moguls did not challenge them, the Emperor being of the opinion that naval warfare was a degrading

pastime suitable only for Europeans; it was from the English that the
first shock to their supremacy was received, when in 1612 a Portuguese fleet attacked the English *Red Dragon* with the pinnace
Ozeander, where they lay before Surat.

'Here we remained trading until the 29th of November when the
same day, our ships lying in the mouth of the river of Surat, four Portugal galleons with a whole fleet of frigates came in sight of our two ships,
or rather one ship and a pinnace. Then our general in the *Dragon*
presently weighed anchor and worthily encouraged our men not to
fear them nor the greatness of their ships or fleet but to shew themselves true Englishmen; and so met their admiral and vice-admiral
and shot not one shoot till he came between them and then gave each
of them a broadside and a brave volley of shot which made them give
way and no more come near her that day . . .' And next day: 'The
fiery *Dragon* bestirring herself, in some three hours hot fight drove
three of the galleons on the sands and then the *Ozeander*, drawing
little water, danced the hay about them and so paid them that they
durst not show a man on their decks, killing and spoiling their men,
and battered their ships exceedingly. . . .'

This is the account of Nicholas Withington, an early servant of the
Company and something of a rogue. But there is no reason to doubt
his evidence here. The fight was renewed a few days later, when the
English were again greatly outnumbered, but 'the general weighed
anchor and with a brave resolution set on them, beating and spoiling
them in such fashion their whole defence was in flying away. . . .'

This victory of Captain Best's was the first blow to the Portuguese,
but even before this the English had shown that they were to be
feared at sea. After Hawkins's departure, Sir Henry Middleton,
already exasperated by the delays and vacillation of the Mogul
authorities, had at last been refused all leave to trade. He did not
stay to argue but sailed for the Red Sea where he took toll of the Surat
traders. This more brusque diplomacy was at first thought unlikely
to be good for trade, and it certainly provided Mukarrab Khan at
Agra with material for his far-sighted argument that the English were
a people to whom any concession would be immediately treated as a
stepping-stone to more. But it did dispose the Surat authorities for
the first time to regard the English as something more than petitioners; they had power to harm. Then came Best's brilliant defensive
action; now the thought was born that here at last was someone who
could be played off against the Portuguese. By 1614, Mukarrab Khan
was at war with the Portuguese and asking the English for help in

ships and artillery; in 1615 Downton, attacked again by a Portuguese armada and again greatly outnumbered, beat them off no less decisively than Best.

This meant a changed attitude that was undoubtedly a help to Sir Thomas Roe, King James's ambassador to the court of Jehangir. He was a man very different from Hawkins, no Turkey merchant ready to take an Armenian wife, but a gentleman, a courtier, a former Esquire of the Body to the Queen, a friend of Prince Henry and his sister Elizabeth of Bohemia . . . 'Th' eclipse and glory of her kind.' He was 'of a pregnant understanding, well spoken, learned, industrious and of a comely personage'. He was the first Ambassador, Hawkins and the others having been mere traders bearing letters; it was a distinction to which Sir Thomas attached importance.

It was on September 19th, 1615, that the first boats went ashore to tell the governor of Surat of the arrival of an Ambassador, an announcement at which the inhabitants openly laughed. A week passed in negotiations during which Roe insisted that an Ambassador was not by polite nations subjected to customs examination, while the Governor was equally firm that by the tradition of Surat he was. When this seemed to be settled, Sir Thomas landed and found the chief officers of Surat with about thirty companions sitting under an open tent. 'Coming almost to them and they not rising, I stayed and sent them word I would not come further if they sat still, whereupon they all rose and I entered the tent . . .' This was the keynote of all that followed; Roe was determined to assert the dignity of his master and was quite clear that Ambassadors took precedence of Governors; the Governor must visit him before he would visit the Governor. He succeeded in the end in getting his way; he had paradoxically an advantage because his master was distant by a year's sailing, while the Governor might at any moment be degraded or whipped because he had not done the right thing. The one vacillated and the other stood firm; Roe therefore won, so far at least as the visit was concerned. But there was delay and obstruction on every point and it was not till the last day of October that the Ambassador started for Agra.

He followed the same road as Hawkins, by Bramport, and at Agra events took a familiar course. The Emperor was delighted to see him and seemed pleased with his presents; he spoke to Roe at length and promised him much. But when it came to performance it was Asaf Khan who must draw up the document and hand it over. And Asaf Khan was the Vizier, the brother of Nur Mahal the Emperor's beloved wife, the most powerful man in the empire and one already offended by Hawkins. He could be relied on to add a condition that would be unacceptable to Sir Thomas. The English must promise on no account to molest the Portuguese if the latter wished to trade at Surat. But it had been the other way round, the Ambassador protested; it had been the Portuguese who had molested the English, and to promise not to attack would be humiliating unless their enemies agreed to a similar condition. It would also be dangerous, for the Portuguese might sail in peaceably, anchor among the English ships and then loose fireships upon them in the night.

The condition was dropped in the end and all seemed as if it would go well again. Roe drew up a Treaty between the two sovereigns, giving the English free leave to trade at any port in the Mogul empire, on the east coast as well as the west, also the privilege of paying customs once but thereafter no further dues or *octroi* on the same goods. But the Emperor could not be brought to sign a treaty; it did not seem fitting that he should bind himself, as though dealing with an equal, to any man, and certainly not to the king of an obscure and distant island of fishermen and wool merchants. A firman, an order to his officers, argued Asaf Khan, was quite sufficient, and it would be more suitable for Prince Khurram to give it than the Emperor since Surat lay in his viceroyalty. Prince Khurram, one day to rule as Shah Jahan, was Asaf Khan's son-in-law. Sir Thomas thought little of this; a firman, he knew, could be upset next day. There was no law here but the King's whim and thus no constancy. He wanted a treaty.

He was in India until February 17th, 1618, altogether nearly three years and a half, maintaining the whole time a front of indomitable firmness, in spite of a very mean provision of presents for the Emperor and his officials and in spite of the knowledge that King James was not very likely to back him up if he went in too deep. For him, as for Hawkins, there were many ups and downs. Jehangir was a man of varied tastes and moods; even when drunk he would dispute with pleasure the teachings of Jesus, Mohammad and Moses; he would spend hours playing with a gold whistle Hawkins gave him or examining the coach sent him by King James and with equal zest he would turn to the more invigorating pleasure of seeing criminals trampled to death by elephants. He clearly liked the Ambassador and to him was usually kind and considerate; again and again he appeared to be on the point of giving him all he wanted. Then Asaf Khan would slip in a clause or a proviso and all would be lost. The Emperor was consistent only in a profound lack of interest in commerce.

In the end, Roe did not get his treaty. It was a conception foreign to Mogul ideas; the Emperor issued orders, he did not bind himself. There was never really any hope of what Roe wanted. But he did succeed in preventing for three years the worst oppression and rapacity of the Surat authorities, he did get the servants of the Company a general permission to trade and by his courage and his steady stand on principle he raised the opinion in which the English were held. His chaplain, Terry, summed up his achievement well:

'There can be no dealing with this King upon very sure terms, for he will say and unsay, promise and deny. Yet we Englishmen did not at all suffer by that inconstancy of his, but there found a free trade, a peaceable residence and a very good esteem with that King and people.'

Sir Thomas Roe was a King's man not a Company's. He was the first to sound a note that a few of his countrymen, and rather more of his countrywomen, were to repeat during the three and a half centuries, conscientiously staying their course and doing their duty, but with no happiness in what they did.

'I shall be glad to do your Lordship service in England,' he writes to Lord Carew, 'for this is the dullest basest place that ever I saw and maketh me weary of speaking of it.'

He struck other notes too that were to be heard again:

'Assure you,' he wrote, 'I know these people are best treated with the sword in one hand and the Caducean in the other.'

And again, our only dependence is 'upon the same ground that we began and by which we subsist, fear'.

But he cannot always have felt that India was dull; no one could be wholly bored who looked into the future and analysed the present as Roe did. Almost in the words of Almeida, he wrote:

'A war and traffic are incompatible. By my consent, you shall no way engage yourselves but at sea, where you are like to gain as often as to lose. It is the beggaring of the Portugal, notwithstanding his many rich residences and territories, that he keeps soldiers that spend his gains . . . He never profited by the Indies since he defended them . . . Let this be received as a rule that if you will profit seek it at sea and in quiet trade.'

These men, Roe, Hawkins, Terry and their fellows, were Elizabethans. They knew nothing, when they left their small green island, of the Asia they would find, nothing but tales of men with their heads below their arms, of men with their eyes in the midst of their chests, the marvels that they had read of in Sir John de Mandeville, the tales with which Othello won his wife. It is no wonder that Hawkins gives lists of diamonds, rubies and elephant-trappings and compares the Mogul courtiers with nobles in Europe, saying that Khan signifies a Duke, that a commander of five thousand is a Marquis, comparisons that could hardly be more misleading. But Roe saw deeper; he begins a letter describing Mogul India with the one essential difference between English and Indian Kingship.

'They have no written law. The King by his own word ruleth.'

This verdict was true; it is useless to protest against it the learning of Muslim lawyers, for in the Emperor's dominions the Emperor's whim was law; it might change from minute to minute and no one would gainsay him. Muslim law ran only when the Emperor wished. And Roe saw too the next great difference between Europe and Asia, a difference flowing from the first; for the King, he wrote:

'is every man's heir, which maketh him rich and the country evil builded. The great men about him are not born noble but favourites raised; to whom . . . he assigneth so much land as is bound to maintain so many horses as a rent, each horse at five and twenty pound sterling by the year . . . but as they die . . . so it returneth to the King, like rivers to the sea.'

Another traveller, Bernier, saw this more clearly still:

'The Nobles of Hindustan,' he wrote, 'cannot be proprietors of land or enjoy an independent revenue, like the nobility of France and the other states of Christendom. Their incomes consist exclusively of pensions which the King grants or takes away according to his own will or pleasure.'

Bernier saw that this was the reason for the wholesale desertions when a new star rose. All turned on the Emperor's favour; no courtier had lands of his own he could retire to; none dared do anything else than flatter the Emperor while he reigned and desert him the moment things began to go wrong.

Hawkins and Roe were there in Agra, groping, against the blaze of jewels and brocaded stuff, the swaying of elephants loaded with gold, the strange ritual, the prayers, the salutations, the savage executions, groping for a truth they could understand and convey to Englishmen. Roe saw more truly than his successors, nearly two hundred years later, who turned those same 'raised favourites' into English landlords, but there was much he could not see. He and Hawkins both could see the Emperor at his beads about the break of day, and again, when his prayer was ended, showing himself to the people. They could see him a third time at noon, when he came forth from his women and till three o'clock 'sat watching pastimes and sports made by men and the fighting of beasts'. Then at three they would see him sitting in his seat royal, the shadows of the awnings sharp on the red sandstone of the pavement, 'with every man before him in his degree, ready to do justice, and beyond and in front the master hangman, with forty hangmen wearing on their heads a certain quilted cap different from all others, with a hatchet on their shoulders and others with all sorts of whips'; all this they could see, Jahangir reeling away to his sleeping quarters after his five cups of wine and his opium, Jahangir slaying his secretary with his own hand on a sudden fancy, ordering gallant men to grapple and buffet unarmed with a lion; but they could not see how the land was ruled nor how the tiller of the soil had his living.

But we, who are beyond space and time, who know that the men of his blood who follow Hawkins are to rule this Empire, who want to understand the tasks they will have to perform, we can rise high in the air till we see North to the Himalayas and South to the Deccan, East to Bengal and West to Kandahar, forward to Aurangzebe and back to Akbar. From so high much is dim, but we can see the shape of Akbar's empire and the beginnings of the crumbling and ruin into which it was to fall. We can see something of the greatness of Akbar, who built so much that the English were to buttress, strengthen and use as a foundation.

CHAPTER III

THE GREAT MOGUL

AKBAR was very great. In any company, at any time, he was a King. There is a bigness about everything he does, so that turning to him even from such characters as Elizabeth of England and Philip of Spain, there is a consciousness of a different scale, something larger, coarser, nearer to the earth, more elemental; it is like handling ducks' eggs after hens'. He is great in his bodily vigour and his passions, striking down and stunning with his bare fist a rebel who came sword in hand to murder him, leaping from the neck of one fighting elephant to another's; great in the energy that drove him to found cannon with his own hands, to interest himself in every craft; great in the spiritual restlessness that led him all his life to seek truth and refuse dogma. He was great even in his occasional cruelties, in his startling and far more frequent humanity, in his wide tolerance, based not on indifference but on deep interest in the faiths of men.

He was a foreigner. His mother tongue was a form of Turki, the language Timur had spoken on the banks of the Oxus; his state language was Persian, already heavily loaded with the Arabic of the Koran. Though he rejected its dogma his thought has the directness of Islam. He had had to fight for the throne and men who win empires by force are inclined to rely on force. But Akbar, for all his directness, saw something more than physical force. He tried to give India the unity she had nearly attained once under Asoka, and once again under the Gupta dynasty; his was the third attempt and the fourth was to be the British. He was not the man to be satisfied by the tip-and-run raids of his ancestors, cosmic in scale though they were. He meant to establish a lasting empire.

And he perceived at once the three things that were needed if his Empire was to be stable. A fair rent must be fixed for the peasant and a steady revenue for the treasury; the land must be ruled by men who were impartial and responsible to himself; and the Muslim must live at peace with the Hindu. He went some way towards succeeding in each of those three essentials; the English went further with two and failed in the last.

Besides Akbar, only Sher Shah among the Muslim rulers of

India saw that his Empire's first need was a solvent treasury and that in the end it must stand or fall by a peasantry to whom life was not intolerable and to whom cultivation offered some reward. Sher Shah had no time to go far; Akbar throughout the whole of his reign was experimenting with systems that would give his rule these foundations. His grasp of detail never slackened; he suggested new schemes, he directed and controlled them; his revenue minister was a servant who carried out the Emperor's policy, not an adviser to initiate.

When the English, two hundred years later, began to grope for clues that would lead to these same beginnings of good government, a treasury and a peasantry that were both stable, much of Akbar's work was obscured by wreckage. The English, puzzled by the strangeness of all they saw, felt with puzzled fingers for something they knew, something they could describe in English terms. They looked for the owner of the land, hoping for an English lord or squire of the eighteenth century, the father of his tenants, a patron of the arts, a justice of the peace. But the conception was misleading in India. In one sense, indeed, it is misleading to speak of the ownership of land anywhere; the man we call the owner is always to some extent a trustee, can hardly own land in the same sense as a table or a toothbrush. In Mogul India, where he could not sell, mortgage, or bequeath land, he had really only a right to till the soil or sometimes a right to collect the sovereign's rent.

It is easy and misleading to generalize; there were differences from province to province, from decade to decade; but it is true to say that what was most usual in Akbar's day was the village community, the brotherhood, who held the land of the village in common. Of the arable land, each shareholder held the right to cultivate a parcel, but, if he died without heir, his parcel reverted to the brotherhood and would be divided. There would be grazing-land too, and perhaps, if the village was lucky, woodland; here the share-holders had common rights of grazing and woodcutting, but they could not cultivate a piece of grazing-land without the permission both of the shareholders and of the King or his representative. There were infinite variations, but this may be called the norm, the simplest and most ancient shape of rural life; it is still to be found today. And there is no ownership here. The commune or brotherhood hold the land in trust for their descendants and certain manorial rights are reserved to the sovereign, to whom they must pay a share of the produce.

Rent to the sovereign, or perhaps it should be called tribute, the King's share, was paid traditionally by the simple method of sharing. At harvest, each man's grain was piled in heaps on the threshing floor of dried and polished mud. The grain stood in pale heaps beneath the blue sky, in the hot wind of early April. There has been no change here; you can still see the piles of grain, the stream of it pouring down to be sifted and winnowed by the wind, the cloth held to catch the chaff; you can still smell the dry smell of the grain and the piled straw, see the bullocks chewing the cud, the carts tilted up with the single shaft pointing to heaven. Three hundred years later, there are still villages where the grain is put in heaps, this for the landlord, that for the peasant. But no longer is there the first heap, from which a portion was found for the servants of the village, the accountant, the watchman, the scavenger, the washerman, the skinner, the weaver, the blacksmith, all the specialists who do not till, sow and milk. Their heap came first in Mogul days, then the King's heap, and last the peasant's.

Anyone can see at once that from the point of view of the treasury this was a very poor system. The treasurer did not know till long after the harvest how much grain there would be and though no doubt it would usually be possible to sell it to grain-dealers on the spot, there must have been times when there were heavy expenses on carting and loss by damp and mildew. With the more paying crops, sugar, cotton, indigo, poppy, collection must have been still more difficult and unsatisfactory. The juice of the poppy, for instance, is collected day by day.

It was a simple transition from sharing to the next stage, when the crop is estimated by eye before it is reaped and the King's share translated into money which the peasant has to pay when he reaps. But this too is cumbersome, because an expert has to look at each crop in each field, and it would be hard to think of an arrangement that lent itself more easily to corruption. So a third stage follows quickly; now the fields are measured and the peasant pays a fixed rent, according to what he sows, so much for every acre of wheat, less when he sows barley, more when he sows sugar-cane.

Of course the three stages did not succeed each other orderly and neatly everywhere; one went on by the side of the other; the old custom of heaps of grain continued into the twentieth century. But it was a sequence that was liable to occur. By Akbar's time the third stage had been reached in many areas and he spent much thought on improving it. Everyone, whatever the quality of his

39

land, had to pay one-third of what was assumed to be the average produce of an acre; in the case of wheat it was about eight and a half hundredweight of wheat for each acre on which wheat was grown. It would take two wretched little bullock-carts to carry it, more in the South, less in the Punjab where the cattle are bigger than round Agra. This was turned into cash on the basis of the prices at the moment in the imperial camp.

It was an arrangement that caused much distress. For one thing, it was hard on a man with poor land; for another, prices were much higher in the imperial camp than anywhere else in the country. In the tenth year of Akbar's reign, he changed over to local prices, and in the fifteenth year of the reign, another step was taken and the amount of the yield due was calculated separately for much smaller areas, each being perhaps a quarter the size of an English county. This was fairer to the peasant; in a poor county, his pile of wheat would be assessed at less than eight hundredweight. But the grain was still turned into cash at local rates which had to be sanctioned by the Emperor, a procedure so cumbrous that the revenue staff were in despair until Akbar himself suggested a way out. This last step was to fix in advance the price at which each kind of crop would be converted into cash. It was settled on an average of the prices for the previous ten years. Three hundred years ago, just as today, the value of an acre of barley was about two-thirds that of wheat while sugar-cane was double, and if a normal rotation of crops is assumed, the peasant of Akbar's day paid about twice as much in real value over a five-year period as he would have done in 1910. If he sowed wheat, what he paid to Akbar in rupees for an acre would have bought as much as seventeen or twenty rupees in 1910.

It was the beginning of a fair assessment, but there was a long way to go before reaching a yearly rent for each field based on the quality of the soil and on average prices in that district for the last thirty years. And there was still the method of collection to be decided.

There were many local variations — this can hardly be said too often — and it is misleading to speak as though there was one system over the whole Empire, or even two or three. But so long as this is remembered, it is true to say that there were two main kinds of territory owing allegiance to Akbar. Of one, the best example is Rajputana, where chiefs or petty kings, who had ruled before the Muslims came, acknowledged the suzerainty of the Emperor and paid him tribute. They were responsible in their own area for collecting the King's share of the grain, for keeping order and administering justice. It seems usually to have been Akbar's intention that in their own areas the chiefs should take the equivalent in cash of one-third of the probable crop, calculated in just the same way as in the area directly under himself.

In this territory of his own, the country directly conquered and administered, Akbar's usual way of getting in the rent was to put so many villages in the hands of an assignee, a member of the imperial service. It seemed to the Moguls a waste of administrative effort to collect money from the peasant and then pay it out again to various officials. Far better, it seemed to them, to settle what an official's pay should be, assign him an area that was estimated to yield the amount of his salary, and let him collect for himself.

The members of the imperial service were carefully graduated by rank and pay. Hawkins, it will be remembered, was a commander of four hundred horse and his pay was supposed to be more than £3000 a year. The salary of a commander of one thousand would have bought as much in Akbar's day as thirty thousand rupees a month in 1914, three times the pay of the Governor of the largest English province; a commander of five thousand received the equivalent of about one hundred thousand rupees a month in the currency of 1914, five times the pay of an English Viceroy.

It was a service in which there were no rules for entrance or promotion, no division of function. A man might go from the Treasury or the Revenue Office to command an army in the field, from control of the library to the imperial stables, from the administration of the gladiatorial games to be governor of a province. Official rank might be bestowed on a physician, a poet, a scholar, a performer on the flute or a barbarian merchant who happened to speak Turkish. Great prizes indeed there were, but no security; at any moment an official might be degraded, banished, tortured or executed, and at the last, the Emperor was every man's heir. All the same, and with all its insecurity, it was the only career open to an ambitious man and it attracted great ability from varied sources, Afghans, Persians, Moguls, Hindus, Georgians and Armenians all holding posts under Akbar.

Though it sounded a convenient method of administration, the system of assignments had grave disadvantages, both for the assignee and the peasant, and so in the long run for the State. The official was not supposed to hold too long an assignment to one tract; he might become too powerful and a danger to the throne if his local influence grew. There were constant changes of duty and the tract did not necessarily change with the post, but not much would be forthcoming from a tract near Lahore if the assignee was posted to Behar. At the doors of the revenue office one may suppose, then, that there were always officials anxious to arrange for their assignment to be moved nearer to the seat of their duties; there would be others who had been too long assigned to one tract, who knew they were due for transfer, and were anxious to avoid it; there would be others recently appointed who had not yet been assigned what Hawkins called 'their living'. There were popular areas, near Lahore or Agra, and remote tracts where only the most ruthless, energetic and courageous official could raise any income at all. Altogether a post in the revenue office must have had its opportunities, and it is easy to see why Hawkins found his command was not worth much when he had offended Asaf Khan.

Perhaps because of those opportunities, the organization of the revenue and pay offices was complex. Just how complex may be seen from the processes which had to be gone through before pay could be drawn by one of the few men entitled to a salary direct from the treasury. It is to be remembered that every appointment was classed as a command of so many horse.

'The appointment, having been made by the Emperor personally, would first be recorded in the diary, in which all his orders were entered. The diary having been checked and passed, an extract of the order was then made, signed by three officials, and handed over to the copying office, where an abridgement was prepared, signed by four officials, and then sealed by the Ministers of State. The abridgement then passed to the military office, which called for estimates and descriptive rolls of the troops to be furnished; when these were ready, a statement of salary was made out, and after being entered in the records of all sections of the office was sent on to the financial department. There an account was drawn up, and a report submitted to the Emperor, and on an allowance being formally sanctioned, a pay-certificate was drafted, and passed through the hands of the Finance Minister, the Commander-in-Chief, and the Military Accountant. This last officer prepared the final document, which required six signatures from three separate departments, and would at last be accepted by the Treasury as authority for payment of the salary.'

It seems from this likely that the Mogul official had to spend at least as much of his time on getting his living as he did on his duties. For even when he had got his assignment — and that, it must be repeated, was the most usual way of paying an official — even when he had besieged and mollified the revenue office, when he had been assigned a tract in an area that was reasonably accessible, neither mountain nor desert, where the soil was not too barren nor the inhabitants too perverse to make any thought of revenue out of the question — even then, he was faced with the labour of the collection. And this was not simple, for the population was less than in modern times and there was much land still uncultivated. There was more land than the people needed and the assessment was so high that there was not much inducement to cultivate at all; press him too hard and the peasant would run away. He could always find land to cultivate somewhere else; another assignee would be glad to see him come and no questions would be asked. According to his disposition, he might run away or join a robber band or sit listless in apathy and do nothing, leaving the land uncultivated. The collector of taxes might come to find the village deserted, like an empty hive where the bees were left no honey for the winter, the cells empty and the floor brown with dust.

This problem grew worse under Akbar's successors as the assessment grew more severe and central control weaker. One English traveller speaks of a governor who personally cut a peasant in two halves with his sword for failing to cultivate and sow a field. Here are Aurangzebe's instructions to his officers:

'At the beginning of the year inform yourself as far as possible about the condition of every peasant, and whether they are engaged in cultivation or are abstaining from it. If they have the means to cultivate, ply them with inducements and assurances of kindness, and show them any favour they may desire. But if it be found that, in spite of having means to cultivate, and of a favourable season, they are abstaining from cultivation, then you should urge and threaten them, and make use of force and the whip.'

Sher Shah, Akbar's predecessor, the only Emperor who before coming to the throne had experience of managing an assigned estate, had been even more decisive and explicit. If men did not pay their rent, it was rebellion; they were to be killed and their families enslaved. 'Eradicate and destroy them, that their wickedness and rebellion spread not to others,' he wrote.

It was justifiable by Islamic texts to take from the peasant all he could be made to pay, everything beyond the barest needs of his existence. Akbar, like a wise bee-master, realized that it was impolitic to take all the honey, and limited the amount to one-third. He alone tried to build up a body of civil servants who would make just collections. His successors eventually raised the King's share to one half and from the beginning abandoned all attempts to protect the peasant. In its final developments the system of assignment became one of merciless extortion and the attitude of the assignees exactly that put into their mouths by Bernier:

'Why should the neglected state of this land create uneasiness in our minds? and why should we expend our money and time to render it fruitful? We may be deprived of it in a single moment and our exertions would benefit neither ourselves nor our children. Let us draw from the soil all the money we can, though the peasant should starve or abscond and we should leave it, when commanded to quit, a dreary wilderness.'

That was the system in its last degradation, when the assignee had hardly any duty to perform and had become almost indistinguishable from the farmer of taxes. But even in Akbar's day, with his firm hand and watchful eye to restrain excesses, it was vicious and inefficient. He must have felt it so, for with many measures to control it he made one serious attempt at complete reform. He appointed Collectors who were paid a salary from the treasury and were responsible for realizing and paying in the full amount of revenue at which the tract was assessed.

They were unfortunate, for Todar Mal, one of Akbar's most brilliant officials and one of the very few Hindus in the imperial service who was not a Rajput, was transferred to a military command just as the scheme was put into force. It was Akbar's scheme but it had been worked out by Todar Mal. He was succeeded as Revenue Minister by his most jealous rival; Todar Mal came back from a successful war to find the scheme a failure. The collectors had no doubt many of them been corrupt, but even if they had been honest, they had been so under-staffed, so 'harried by futile correspondence', that they could hardly have collected even a fair assessment of one-third. But their tracts were not assessed on the actual yield but on what the revenue office thought they ought to produce. The Collectors were all in arrears; Todar Mal, exasperated that his rival should have spoiled in execution a scheme so brilliant in conception, began a rigorous audit.

'But the collectors were brought to account by Raja Todar Mal and many good men died from the severe beatings which were administered and from the tortures of the rack and pincers. So many died from protracted confinement in the prisons of the Revenue authorities that there was no need of executioner or swordsman and no one cared to find them graves or graveclothes.' The writer, an orthodox Muslim, is hostile to Akbar and to Todar Mal; there may be some exaggeration, but one may conclude that the inquiry was searching. Some collectors survived; they are heard of occasionally much later; but there was an end for the present of the idea that direct rule by collectors should replace the system of assignment.

Akbar's India was the North. His rule did not reach to the Deccan or the far South; here in the independent Muslim and Hindu kingdoms the peasant seems usually to have been worse off than in the North. In the place of official assignees there were usually farmers of taxes, men not even supposed to be governed by any motive but rapacity; in Golconda, the farms of taxes were annually put to auction, a system, as Moreland says, probably the most extortionate yet devised by man.

Akbar then had gone some way towards fixing a stable system of taxation; his peasants were better off than they were to be again for two centuries, until the English were over their worst and earliest mistakes. He was less successful with his civil service, but he does seem to have instilled the idea of a service in which creed was kept for a man's private life. He failed to set up a universal religion that Hindu and Muslim alike would join but he did achieve, not only in his court but among his people, not only in his lifetime but for some years after his death, a degree of imaginative tolerance hard to find in India today and certainly lacking in Elizabeth's England or Philip's Spain. Tom Coryat, the author of *Coryat's Crudities*, who walked from Aleppo through Persia and reached Agra in Roe's time, was something of a linguist. Hearing the Mullahs cry from the minarets Islam's profession of faith, he mounted a minaret himself and called aloud in Arabic: 'There is no God but God and Jesus his Son; Mohammad is an impostor.' Perhaps he failed to make himself understood; at any rate, no one molested him; it is hard to believe that a Muslim who had made as provocative a declaration on the steps of St. Paul's would not have suffered for it, however poor his pronunciation.

This was the India in which the first Englishmen found themselves. A brilliant court, profuse in display, for there was no point in saving for the Emperor; long processions of elephants with trappings of gold and silver, silks, jewels, servants, fans of peacock feathers, glowing carpets, horses from Persia and Arabia; it was not surprising that stories went to Europe of the wealth of India. And it was true that Akbar's revenue was many times that of Elizabeth. But a different tale would have gone back if it had been possible then to consider the true wealth of the country. There was little commerce or industry; it was a country of peasants. The peasant was taxed twice as heavily as in 1914 and he was worse off in real goods. He had fewer cooking pots, his wife had fewer ornaments; his credit was even worse and his reserves less. It has been calculated that as a rule he needed about half the proceeds of the holding for expenses, to replace bullocks and carts, for seed, to pay village officials and the like; if the King's share was one-third he was left with one-sixth to eat — in a good year.

But many years were not good and famine was endemic. It is only on the coastal strips that the monsoon can be relied on, and there were few years in the seventeenth century when it could be said that in no part of India was there a shortage of food. And a shortage very quickly became a famine. In a country depending on pack and draught animals for transport it would have been impossible to do much to alleviate a famine that was really widespread, even if anyone had tried. The animals bringing the grain would have to carry their own fodder, and if the journey was more than a very few days' march there would be no room for anything else. This was perhaps one reason why no one did try.

We in this generation have supped full with horror; for us horror need not be stressed. There are many descriptions of famine; one will do. It is Peter Mundy's; he is writing of a journey during the famine of 1631, which was one of the worst of the century.

'No less lamentable was it to see the poor people scraping on the dunghills for food, yea in the very excrements of beasts, as horses, oxen, etc., belonging to travellers, for grain that perchance might come undigested from them, and that with great greediness and strife among themselves, generally looking like anatomies with life, but scarce strength enough to remove themselves from under men's feet, many of them expiring, others new dead . . . From Surat to this place, all the highway was strowed with dead people, our noses never free from the stink of them, especially about towns; for they drag them out by the heels, stark naked, and all ages and sexes, till they are out of the gates, and there they are left, so that the way is half barred up . . .' And again: 'In this place, men and women were driven to that extremity by hunger that they sold their children for 12s. 6d., yea and to give them away to any that would take them . . .' And later he adds: 'Women were seen to roast their children; men travelling in the way were laid hold of to be eaten and having cut away much of his flesh, he was glad if he could get away and save his life, others killed outright and devoured. A man or woman no sooner dead but they were cut in pieces to be eaten.'

A people, then, who throughout India lived near to starvation, to whom in most areas famine was a reality which might mean cannibalism and slavery and was always close at hand; a people whose only refuge against oppression and extortion was flight, either to other land or to join the bands of thieves and marauders who wrung a scanty and dangerous living from the caravans of travellers; these were the people over whom the Moguls ruled.

It is not easy for honesty or pity to flourish at the court of absolutism anywhere, least of all where there is no permanence and 'the King is every man's heir'. No one need be surprised then that such growths are hard to find among Mogul courtiers and officials each of whom must keep himself in the King's favour if he is to live. But somehow, among the peasants, in the stony soil of fear, hunger and poverty, these virtues did survive; they lived on through the bad times of Maratha and Pindari raids and the Sikh fighting before the coming of Ranjit Singh; they were still to be found in the villages, if you went to look for them, three hundred years later, together with a warm hospitality and the dignity of people poor in material possessions but conscious of long ancestry. It is hard to understand how these things survived but they did.

To this India the English came soon after Akbar died, when his fabric still stood, proud and strong to the eye, but already beginning to rot. Here they began to trade; here, by the exercise of diplomacy and no little courage and tenacity, they began to spread. By 1623, four years after Roe's going, they had factories subordinate to the main establishment of Surat at Broach, Ahmedabad, Agra, Masulipatam and Bramport. It was a tiny beginning.

CHAPTER IV

A JOURNEY FROM AGRA TO SURAT

DURING the century that followed that first small beginning
made in India, the English in the island settled whether
King or Parliament should be ruler and then, looking abroad,
found themselves confronted on the continent by Louis instead of
Philip, by France instead of Spain, a new representative of the
principle of intolerant personal domination which they had shown
so effectively that they disliked. That power too they defeated and
confined within bounds. In the process, they found themselves,
with some surprise, allies of their old trade rivals the Dutch, whom
by the time the business of Louis was finished they had outstripped
and out-distanced. It was a century in which something was
achieved.

But it is depressing for a Western mind to turn in the same period
from Europe to India, not only because the degree of cruelty and
human misery is on the whole greater, but because there is no sign
of growth in any desirable or even definite direction. There is none
of that steady development of a principle or an institution by the
yearly addition of small practical changes which makes English
history and which in England gradually transformed society and
government. Instead there is a melancholy record of insurrection,
treachery and murder. The sons of each Emperor are rivals for the
throne; as their father grows older they begin to jockey for position
and before he is dead they are in arms against each other and against
him. The most able and unscrupulous imprisons, blinds or kills the
rest, as a queen bee stabs each young queen struggling out of her
cell. Each seems when enthroned eager only to eclipse the memory
of his father. If there was any principle of government at all among
the Moguls who followed Akbar it was:

'a concentration on a barren struggle to divide, rather than a
concerted effort to increase, the annual produce of the country'.

It is like reading of a land periodically devastated by hordes of
lemmings or locusts; it is like turning from the history of a coral
reef, in which every act and every death is a foundation, to the
depressing chronicle of a succession of castles built on the waste
sand of the sea-shore and each in turn inevitably destroyed by the
tide.

Outwardly, the Mogul Empire appeared firm enough except for a period of anarchy towards the end of each reign — indeed, Aurangzebe increased his dominions considerably — but inwardly the structure grew steadily weaker because Akbar's objects were neglected. Year by year the peasantry were more grievously oppressed; year by year the civil service became more corrupt; while from the accession of Aurangzebe onwards any chance of Muslim and Hindu becoming one people disappeared in a wave of savage intolerance. The poll-tax was re-imposed on unbelievers, temples were destroyed and idols were smashed. Of all Akbar's work, only his conquests and his empty buildings remained. But it was not till the death of Aurangzebe that the decay which had been long at work within the fabric appeared on the surface.

In this India the English wished to trade. They had, as we know, to contend with the enmity of the Portuguese and the Dutch, with whom their relations were confusing. In the first place, the men on the spot did not always know whether in Europe their countries were at war or peace, fast friends or sworn enemies. If they did know, they did not always consider themselves bound and were often ready to anticipate the next reversal of relations. Not only this, but during the first half of the century, the Dutch and English, bitter enemies in the further East, were in India usually ready to combine against the Portuguese, whom they hated for the cruelties of the Goa inquisition. Later, as the Dutch attained complete mastery in the Spice Islands while the Portuguese became less and less serious as rivals of anyone, the English and Portuguese drew together.

But whatever fierce little battles they had to fight with the Portuguese in the Persian Gulf or at Surat, whatever intrigues of their rivals they had to combat, the English had also to make their way with the Indian powers, and the servants of the Company had to learn something of India. They had learnt as soon as they came that they must be diplomats before they could be traders; they learnt more than that as, like the Portuguese before them but much more slowly, gradually and usually with reluctance, they began to administer and rule small numbers of Indians. Not because they liked it or chose it but because it was the only thing to do at the moment, they found themselves settling disputes, sometimes urging a peaceful settlement.

With many differences, there was much in their life that was to be familiar to those who came later, and already there were opportunities for that stubborn and unquestioning fidelity that in the years to come was to be their strength. Peter Mundy, for example, a Cornishman who signed on for five years only as a servant of the Company, made a journey in 1632 from Agra to Surat with 268 camels and 109 carts loaded with indigo and saltpetre. On the first day, he stepped into a small moving world of tents, men, bullocks and camels that in some degree every district officer was to know.

The danger from robbers was serious everywhere but particularly in Rajputana; Mundy was instructed to attach his caravan, with the hundred and seventy peons or footsoldiers he had for protection, to the troops of one Bakir Khan who was on his way to his new post as Governor of Gujerat. Many other merchants and travellers sought the same protection and it was a long straggling convoy.

'Never had caravan more need of assistance than this, considering the greatness of the charge, the length of the way, multitude and diversity of the worst sort of people in India to deal withal, but, last and worst, bound to keep company with troops with such a number of base cattle and carts that all that saw them held it impossible they should long hold out. Yet with all these hard conditions am I thrust out alone with little language, having nobody that I can trust or cares to take any pains to ease me to look after the company's goods, to help to compound the unreasonable demands of carters and camelers, to decide their quarrels and differences, to persuade them to reason, they being most commonly obstinately bent to do what they list, although to the Company's loss. . . .'

So Mundy wrote. About three weeks after the journey began, he notes in his diary that:

'Here the carters required fifty rupees per cart to supply themselves with oxen . . . every day we were afraid we should not hold out the next, nor never a day, night, nor scarce an hour but that one or other tells me there is such a cart broken and would know what I would enorder about it. Another comes after him and says that such a cart's wheel is in pieces. Another after him that the oxen of such a cart are tired and can go no further, and that one cart is gone another way and that another cart is two or three *kos* behind the rest. . . .'

This, as he says, was our continual life, until Bakir Khan and his troops took a road that neither the carts nor camels would face at all. Then at last, six weeks from Agra, the caravan was left with no protection but the hundred and seventy foot of the Company's own men, and from now on, instead of driving on the caravan relentlessly in order to keep up with the troops, the main task was to keep it together against the danger of robbers and to deal with another danger, perhaps only finely distinguishable, the demands of petty chiefs for blackmail. Feeling grew worse between camelers and carters; on April 11th 'the camelers and carters fell out about the way, the carts breaking into the files of the camels so that from words they fell to blows and wounds, the Jats, who had charge of the carts, having hurt one of the Baluches on the breast very dangerously. At our arrival at our halting-place, the Baluches and camelers would have revenged themselves but the Jats and carters came to meet them with their weapons and pieces charged, these being Hindus and the Baluches Muslims, there being upwards of 220 of each side. With much ado the matter was pacified for that time, but had they gone by the ears, it might have endangered much the Company's property. This is the effect of joining carts with camels and Jats with Baluches in one caravan. ...'

Here already is the voice of the wary and experienced administrator and indeed, some wariness was necessary. There were several men killed and several alarms of robbers, but no more carts lost of the Company's, though others with the caravan were pillaged. But when at Ahmedabad Mundy came up with Bakir Khan, he was refused audience, it being signified, in accordance with custom through a subordinate, that there were twenty thousand rupees to pay for the good will of the great man on the journey. In the end, 'fearing of some hard usage and seeing that there was no other remedy, we sent him, though to our griefs, four thousand rupees ...' and all was settled.

A dangerous land, in which a man must rely on himself and in which the English were still suppliants for favour. It was at first the custom for all foreign merchants, Arabs, Portuguese, Dutch or English, to petition for every journey, for every building, for all they did, but gradually they were allotted certain fields within which they could rule themselves. Sometimes their importunity won them a concession; now it would be a service done by an English physician to a great man's daughter; sometimes it was no more than that the governor was ready to save himself trouble.

It was no accident that later in most of India the English district officers were to be called Collectors, nor was it entirely due to the Company's commercial outlook. The title and the outlook it indicated came from the Moguls. To collect the revenue was the first duty of the Mogul official; to keep order and distribute justice were secondary functions to be executed with just sufficient vigour to maintain prestige and prevent rebellion. Merchants who complained that they had been robbed were apt to be told with some indignation that officials were there to collect revenue, not to dry-nurse people well able to afford retainers and protect themselves. Anyone who has set up house in India knows that even in the twentieth century he becomes at once the arbiter between gardener's wife and washerman's, between table-servant and cook. When there was no regular police system, anyone who employed servants or labour was still more certain to find himself an administrator in embryo.

The Hindu Rajas of the Deccan in the South were from the start only too glad to let foreigners govern themselves and their servants according to their own odd ways. The Moguls, however much inclined to suit their own convenience and do the same, were more concerned with prestige; they felt something derogatory to their own authority in the formal recognition of any other. But catch the Mogul in the right mood — as sooner or later you were sure to do if you went on long enough — and he would give what you wanted.

CHAPTER V

THE ENGLISH HOUSE AT SURAT

So gradually the English established themselves. In Surat, they were soon living a life of some formality. Here is the account of Albert de Mandelslo, a traveller from Holstein who visited Surat in 1638 and stayed at the house where the English merchants lived a collegiate and usually celibate life:

'In the evening, some merchants and others belonging to the President brought me from my chamber to supper into a great hall where the Minister [the Chaplain] with about a dozen merchants who kept me company, but the President and his Second supped not, out of fear of overcharging their stomachs, digestion being slowly performed by reason of the great heats . . . After supper, the Minister carried me into a great open gallery, where I found the President and his Second taking the coolness of the sea air. This was the place of our ordinary rendez-vous, where we met every night, to wit, the President, his Second, the principal Merchant, the Minister and myself; but the other merchants came not but when they were invited by the President. At dinner, he kept a great table of about fifteen or sixteen dishes of meat, besides the dessert.

'The respect and deference which the other merchants have for the President was very remarkable, as also the order which was there observed in all things, especially at Divine Service, which was said twice a day, in the morning at six, and at eight at night, and on Sundays thrice. No person in the house but had his particular function, and their certain hours assigned them as well for work as recreation . . . On Fridays after prayers, there was a particular assembly at which met with us three other merchants, who were of kin to the President . . . to make a commemoration and drink their wives' healths. . . .'

Mundy adds to this picture:

'In the house aforesaid dwelleth the President and Council, merchants and other factors, ordinarily to the number of ten or twelve, a Preacher and Surgeon, Steward, Attendants and other officers as cooks, bakers, and men of service, altogether to the number of twenty-five or twenty-six persons English.

'Our diet here for the most part is such as we have in England, fine bread of wheat, Beef, Mutton, Hens, pigeons dressed after our own manner by English cooks. Sometimes we have this country wild fowl, Antelopes and perchance wild boar; but ordinarily we have dopeage and rice, kedgeree, and pickled Mangoes.' [Dopeage seems to mean curry, being the English form of the Gujerati form of a Persian word.] 'Our strong drink is Rack [arrack], like strong water, next a kind of beer made of coarse sugar and other ingredients, pleasant to the taste and wholesome, but many times water. There is sometimes used a composition of Rack, water, sugar and juice of limes.'

Mandelslo also speaks of punch, 'a kind of drink consisting of aqua vitae, rosewater, juice of citrons and sugar'. But 'at our ordinary meetings every day we took only *thé* . . .' And Terry adds: 'That most ancient and innocent drink of the world, Water, is the common drink of East India'. On the whole, the scene is a good deal more temperate than it was to become.

Had these men not believed they were in the hands of God, they might have had some excuse for excessive drinking, for death was never far away. When Peter Mundy returned to Surat on May 25th, 1633, from his journey with Bakir Khan, he found only seven Englishmen alive out of twenty-one whom he had left there six months before, and of those seven, three more died before he finished writing up the last stage of his diary. This of course was the year of the great famine which was followed by much sickness; things cannot always have been as bad as that.

Life does not seem to have settled down into so formal a routine as at Surat in the English house at Agra, of which Mundy writes:

'The honourable company have a house wherein their servants reside . . . in the heart of the city, where we live after this country manner of meat, drink and apparel; our meat for the most part after the Custom of this place, sitting on the ground at our meat or discourse. The rooms in general covered with carpets with great round high cushions to lean on (this as well in public as in private). Our habit when we go abroad is a Shash [turban] on our heads, a white linen scarf over our shoulders, a fine white linen coat, a girdle to gird about us, breeches and shoes, our swords and daggers by our sides. Thus in the city. But when we go out of town, we have our bows and arrows at our saddle and a buckler hanging on our shoulders. However, we never stir a foot out of doors but on horseback, it being the custom of the city.'

Peter Mundy slides away as the stream slips smoothly by, but before he is quite out of sight over the stern, there is his love of gardens to be remembered, and particularly that at Surat, 'the neatest and costliest for its bigness in all the country hereabouts'. And he speaks for many of his countrymen when he writes of how in his journey:

'I saw that which I much longed for, a Spring which, issuing out of a little bank with a full and clear stream, ran into a little brook adjoining, whose green and pleasant banks represented unto my memory England's flourishing and fruitful soil. . . .'

The stream flows by and Mundy is back in England, with his admirable sketches of dancing-girls, processions, tombs and gardens, of a widow burned alive with her husband and pillars of dead men's heads. Business increases at the Surat factory and more settlements are started. By 1647 the English have twenty-three factories and settlements in India and ninety employees. But for forty years more, till 1687, Surat was still the headquarters, and so long as Surat was the headquarters the English were petitioners to the Mogul. All the same, progress was made. They acquired some prestige, not to mention a firman permitting them to trade duty free for twelve months, when Sir George Oxenden successfully defended the factory against 'that grand rebel Sivaji', first and greatest of the Mahratta freebooters, who seized and looted Surat in 1664. He came again in 1670 in Gerald Aungier's first year of office, and again the factory alone held out. But there was no great change in the factors' way of life; perhaps there was a little less leisure, certainly there was more intemperance; changes at home were reflected in India and the old certain faith in God's protection is not so manifest. There is an impatience of piety and some grumbles at the frequency of prayers, 'for in these hot countries, neither a man's spirit nor voice can hold touch with long duties'. But on the whole, it is not a very different life. Here is the account of Dr. Fryer, a surgeon in the Company's service, an exact observer, though over-discreet and something of a pedant:

'Here they live, in shipping time, in a continual hurly burly, the Banians presenting themselves from the hour of ten till noon, and then after noon at four till night, as if it were an Exchange in every row; below stairs, the packers and warehouse keepers, together with merchants bringing and receiving musters, make a mere Billingsgate, for if you make not a noise, they hardly think you intent on what you are doing.'

Dr. Fryer goes on to explain that Surat is the first station in India, the others being modelled on Surat 'in their several seignories', and that although the Company must confirm the appointment there is an established convention that the Second in Council at Surat is also

Deputy-Governor of Bombay and the Secretary at Surat Agent of Persia. But both prefer to remain at Surat, where, says Dr. Fryer darkly, 'consignments compensate those emoluments . . . after the rate of five in the hundred commission'.

'It would be too mean,' he goes on, 'to descend to indirect ways, which are chiefly managed by the Banians, the fittest tools for any deceitful undertaking; out of whom are made brokers for the Company and private persons, who are allowed two per cent on all bargains, beside what they squeeze secretly out of things bought; which cannot be well understood for want of knowledge of their language; which ignorance is safer than to hazard being poisoned for prying too nearly into their actions. Though the Company, to encourage young men in their service, maintain a master to learn them to write and read the language and an annuity to be annexed when they gain a perfection therein, which few attempt and fewer attain.'

No one could call Dr. Fryer a clear writer, even when he is not being archly discreet, but a meaning can be discerned; the officials take five per cent and the Banians two per cent, 'besides what can be squeezed'. And as to laziness in foreign languages, that was always a characteristic of the English.

He goes on to tell how when the President is in Surat there is a guard of English soldiers, consisting of a double file led by a Sergeant:

'The present Deputy has only forty Moor-men and a flag-man carrying St. George his colours swallow-tailed in silk, fastened to a silver partisan; with a small attendance of horse with silver bridles and furniture for the gentlemen of the house and coaches for Ladies and Council.

'The President besides these has a noise of trumpets and is carried himself in a palankeen, a horse of state led before him, a fan of ostriches' feathers to keep off the sun, as the Omrahs or nobles have . . . Besides these, every one according to his quality has his menial servants to wait on him in his chamber and follow him out. . . .'

Prayers at six; a morning of business; dinner, a little folding of the hands in sleep; in the afternoon, more business if a ship is in, but if not it is the custom to ride or drive abroad or stroll in the English garden. It sounds a tranquil picture enough, but for the President and Council crisis succeeded crisis with fair regularity, and many were of a kind to affect the life of the most junior writer. No sooner was Sivaji's second raid over than Bombay became an anxiety and there followed all the business of Pettit and Bowcher, Sir Josiah and Keigwin's Rebellion.

CHAPTER VI

REBELLION AT BOMBAY

THE island of Bombay, as everyone knows, was part of the dowry of Charles II's Portuguese queen in 1660. It was thus Crown property, not Company's. An imposing armament was sent to take possession but its leader, Sir Abraham Shipman, was met by the embarrassing news that the Portuguese Viceroy refused to hand over the island. Sir Abraham's orders were to protect the Portuguese against the Dutch, Portugal now being England's ally; he could hardly begin by turning them out of Bombay. He was a year from home, but went back for orders, landing a force on Anjidiv, an island near Surat, where most of the men died before he returned. He is to be remembered for his saying:

'The harbour of Bombay is the noblest that ever I see; the air healthful and is exceedingly well seated for trade, and would in two or three years undo Surat by bringing hither all the trade. For the merchants living at Surat are under a very great tyranny, their money being liable to be taken away when the Mogul or his governor pleaseth and their persons abused.'

It was not till 1665 that the Portuguese Viceroy, still protesting, handed over Bombay to the English crown. But Charles II did not like finding money for its maintenance; in 1668 he made it over to the Company in return for a large loan, it being 'in free and common soccage, as of the Manor of East Greenwich, on payment of the annual rent of £10 in gold on the 30th September each year'.

As Shipman had foreseen, trade came to Bombay instead of Surat, merchants of all races being anxious to settle in an island where they felt secure against confiscation of their goods, and many also hoping for refuge from the religious intolerance either of Aurangzebe or of the Portuguese. It was indeed tolerance that filled and built Bombay, tolerance, and in the first few years the wisdom of the English at Surat. Sir George Oxenden had successfully defended the English factory against Sivaji and with dignified yet conciliatory firmness had composed a minor war with the Moguls; he was succeeded in 1669 as President of Surat and Governor of Bombay by Gerald Aungier, a man even more energetic, far-sighted and able than himself.

It would have been easy for Aungier to make the mistake of trying to bolster up Surat and suppress the infant Bombay. If he needed persuasion as to the folly of such a course, it was provided in 1670 when Surat was raided by Sivaji a second time, the English factory again stoutly maintaining its virginity. Aungier saw the advantage of an island; on the mainland, he was at the mercy of Mogul and Maratha alike. He urged the Court of Directors to fortify Bombay and transfer the headquarters there. In the meantime, till the defences were complete, he stayed on in Surat as Governor of Bombay, where his Deputy ruled for him. By 1674, when the useful Dr. Fryer wrote his description, a good deal of progress had been made.

'The Government here now is English; the soldiers have martial law. The freemen, common; the chief arbitrator whereof is the President with his Council at Surat; under him is a justiciary and Court of Pleas with a committee for regulation of affairs and presenting all complaints.

'The President has a large commission and is Vice-Regis; he has a Council here also and a guard when he walks or rides abroad . . . He has his chaplains, physician, surgeon and domesticks; his linguist and mintmaster. At meals he has his trumpets usher in his courses and soft music at the table. If he move out of his chamber, the silver staves wait on him; if down stairs, the guard receive him; if he go abroad the Bandarines and Moors under two standards march before him . . . But for all this gallantry, I reckon they walk but in charnelhouses. . . .'

The justiciary was perhaps more versatile than learned in the law and was not even very consistent to any principles of its own. Captain Nicholls, the first judge, was a retired sea captain, a freeman of Bombay; he was removed from office for refusing to pay his debts. However, he soon took up his half-pike as captain of infantry, only to be again in trouble for an offence which 'we know not well how to put into such decent terms as may become us to your Honours'. He was succeeded by Old Gary, a person of ambiguous ancestry, equally fluent in Portuguese, Italian, Latin, French and English; he had been a successful courtier at the court of the Queen of Achin in Sumatra, and later a factor and merchant under the Company. He can hardly have been a good one, for he was retrenched in 1656, and it must have been mainly because he happened to be on the spot that he became Deputy Governor and for a short time Governor of the island under the King. He is described as of a mercurial temperament, and his justice certainly seems to have been unpredictable as summer lightning, for he

'condemned a man to be hanged on a Tuesday and the Man suffered according to sentence; but on the Friday after, the poor dead Fellow was ordered to be called before the court but would not comply with the summons'.

Even Dr. John St. John, Doctor of Laws, sent out from England to be judge, sentenced a man 'to lose all that he had in the world and a thousand pounds beside and to lie in prison at his own charges till the fine was paid'.

These last two stories come from Captain Alexander Hamilton, who is more of a gossip than a historian, but an impression remains that the procedure of the courts was informal. All the same, it was something to have a Chief Justice at all, and the town was growing rapidly. Dr. Fryer notes:

'The people that live here are a mixture of most of the neighbouring countries, most of them fugitives and vagabonds, no account being here taken of them; others perhaps invited here (and of them a great number) by the liberty granted them in their several religions, which here are solemnized with variety of fopperies . . . Of these, one among another, may be reckoned 60,000 souls; more by 50,000 than the Portugals ever could. For which number this Island is not able to find provisions, it being most of it a rock above water. . . .'

There is a good deal of shrewdness behind Fryer; he has seen the two essential things about Bombay in those early days. It was built on tolerance and it was dependent on the mainland for food. The mainland was held by the Marathas who were perpetually at war with the Moguls. The English wished to be neutral, but it was impossible to break with the Moguls, to whom Surat and the other factories were hostages; it was impossible to deny the harbour of Bombay to the Sidi, the Mogul admiral, who used it as a refuge during the monsoon. Everyone knew that the Sidi would promise the English to behave strictly as a neutral while in their harbour, but that in fact he would amuse himself by raids on the Maratha mainland all through the winter, as the English in the seventeenth and eighteenth centuries perversely called the monsoon. And it was obvious that sooner or later the Marathas would retaliate. It was as nice a problem in diplomacy as ever faced Savoy or Luxemburg, and except for one bad interlude the merchants made a reasonably good hand of it — with some friendly interposition by Divine Foresight.

They were not, on the other hand, always helped from London. This was the beginning of the reign in Leadenhall Street of Sir Josiah Child, of whom it has been well said:

'his appearance as a city merchant instead of as Emperor of China or the great Mogul seems an error of Providence'.

For twenty years he directed the affairs of the Company as though it were his private business, getting what he wanted by bribery, intrigue and sheer force of character. At this moment he was in his early or Little England period. He was a man who did nothing by halves; his simplest orders were dictated in terms of passion and high drama; he would use the language of Lear defying the storm in a letter about ordnance stores. Money had to be saved; he ordered that the defences should be left unfinished and the militia disbanded. To defend the island was a 'vain pompous insignificant course', that would have sacrificed all the trade of the North of India 'for a feather to be gazed at by the Poor Indians and Portuguese'. These orders were received when the Marathas had made up their minds to advance through Portuguese Salsette, cross to the island and there put an end to Bombay as a refuge for the Sidi.

This is not the place for the whole story of those exciting years. There are battles, forays, sieges and ambushes, now and for two hundred years more, that must be passed by because it would need not a book but a library to tell of them. There is no place here for the tale of the *Revenge*, who, emulous of her namesake a hundred years earlier, fought single-handed with twenty grabs and forty gallivats manned by Marathas and beat them from the mouth of Bombay harbour; no place for the imperious Sir Josiah's machinations for the defeat of his rival Papillon in Leadenhall Street and for the appointment as President in Surat of a man he was quite sure would do exactly what he was told. It is enough to say that Pettit, who seems to have been an able and honest man, a worthy though inferior successor to Aungier, was deliberately passed over and broken so that John Child, namesake but not brother of the autocrat, could take his place. Pettit and his friend Bowcher set up in Surat a business of their own; in the eyes of Child the Great of Leadenhall Street and Child the Less of Surat, they were interlopers and as good as pirates, but the Mogul Governor of Surat did not see it that way and as long as they kept out of Bombay and away from the Company's factory they were safe. They even got a firman from the Emperor permitting them to trade on the same terms as the Company. And Madam Bowcher — she is always Madam — held a salon in Surat where she delighted in saying the most atrocious things about Sir John Child. No one of course was allowed to visit them, but the salon continued and the things got round; the English have often deployed an unexpected talent for political warfare.

Pettit and Bowcher were an irritation, a chafing spot; worse, far worse, was the unreasonable attitude of the garrison of Bombay. Confronted by hordes of indignant and war-like Marathas on the mainland, their winter peace disturbed every year by the insolence of the Sidi's followers, both companies of infantry as well as the freemen and factors heard with sullen anger of the tempestuous cheeseparing of Sir Josiah. And the soldiers had a more compelling grievance, because their pay, inadequate enough to start with, was paid in a local copper coinage, implausibly known as budgerooks and dugonies, which did not pass current at all upon the mainland and in the island only at a rate much lower than that reckoned by the Company. The result was that every pay-day the soldier lost between twenty and thirty per cent of what was due to him.

At last the garrison resolved to have no more of the imperious Josiah, his namesake at Surat, or the Company. They confined Child's Deputy Governor, declared that the island had reverted to His Majesty Charles II, and in the King's name proclaimed as Governor Captain Keigwin, the commander of the two companies and the Militia. The proclamation went on that 'the intolerable extortions, oppressions, and unjust impositions that hath been for these five years past most rigorously exacted . . . by the English East India Company and their servants . . . with many other Sordid actions . . . hath occasioned God's just judgments to overtake them in the full careers of their pride and malice, avarice and injustice . . .' and much more to the same effect.

The Deputy Governor was treated with consideration, and indeed throughout the whole episode Keigwin behaved like a gentleman, keeping to his story that he was the King's governor and displaying a high courtesy that played Child the Less off the stage, even when he launched his most moving appeal.

'Oh, Johnny Thorburn,' writes Child, addressing the rebels' Attorney-General, Treasurer, Chief Justice, Accountant, Secretary and Captain-Lieutenant, 'Oh, Johnny Thorburn, thy Ingratitude is of deep dye! Come one, two or three of you and look on your Governor; I am the same that lived among you not long ago and then had wars with Sivaji Raja and great disturbances from the Portuguese yet protected you all with God's blessing.'

But the rebels were unmoved even by this, and resisted all the efforts of the Governor and his commissioners to cause dissension between leaders and followers, only surrendering a year later, as bloodlessly as they had rebelled, at the express command of Charles II, and to his emissary. In that year Keigwin, by firmly refusing to let him into the harbour, ended 'the Sidi's winter sports' without any of the evil consequences that had been feared. He also finished the fortifications, paid everyone his dues, and handed over the Treasury with as much in it as when he had taken it over, a display of competence which perhaps partly accounted for the licking of the lips with which Child had contemplated his end on the gallows and the regret with which he saw him go.

'Keigwin, that notorious naughty rascal,' he writes, aping the hyperbole of Josiah, 'is on board the *Charles II*, as impudent as hell, glorying in his roguery . . . it is ten thousand pities he should escape the halter. . . .'

The rebellion was an interlude, curiously English, a thoroughly healthy symptom; but it is clear by the time it is over that something has happened. The English are now established; they are a power, and secure in their island can ride out a storm on the mainland. Hear the changed voice of the great Josiah, no longer a Little Englander:

'It is our ambition for the honour of our King and Country and the good of Posterity, as well as this company, to make the English nation as formidable as the Dutch, or any other Europe nation are or ever were in India; but that cannot be done only in the form and with the method of merchants, without the political skill of making all fortified places repay their full charges and expenses.'

This was in 1685, a year after the Rebellion; two years later he writes:

'That which we promise ourselves in a most especial manner from our new President and Council is that they will establish Such a Polity of civil and military power and create and secure Such a large Revenue to maintain both as may be the foundation of a large, well-grounded, secure English dominion in India for all time to come.'

This must not be read in the light of after events; dominion *in* India, not *over* India, Josiah writes, and there is no reason to suppose he meant more than he said. Nor is it likely that this was much more representative of the thoughts of the councillors in Bombay than the retrenchment of five years earlier. But it is a long journey, all the same, from the humble petitions of William Hawkins and his fellows, to Bombay as it appears now to Indian eyes. Here is the narrative of Khafi Khan, an honest historian, who in 1694 was the agent of a commander of four thousand in the service of Aurangzebe. He had to ask the English for protection to a convoy, which, though it is not explicitly stated, must have been a sea convoy, and it is obviously with a distinct sense of his own courage that he enters what he regards as a nest of pirates. A Mogul ship had recently been taken by Englishmen, who were as a matter of fact really pirates and not the Company's servants at all, and some factors had been imprisoned in retaliation; Khafi Khan had some grounds for apprehension.

'When I entered the fortress, I observed that from the gate there was on each side of the road a line of youths, of twelve or fourteen years of age, well dressed and having excellent muskets on their shoulders. Every step I advanced, young men with sprouting beards, handsome and well-clothed, with fine muskets in their hands, were visible on every side. As I went onwards, I found Englishmen standing, with long beards, of similar age, and with the same accoutrements and dress. After that I saw musketeers, young men well dressed and arranged, drawn up in ranks. Further on, I saw Englishmen with white beards, clothed in brocade, with muskets on their shoulders, drawn up in two ranks and in perfect array. Next I saw some English children, handsome, and wearing pearls on the borders of their hats. In the same way, on both sides, as far as the door of the house where he abode, I found drawn up in ranks on both sides nearly seven thousand musketeers, dressed and accoutred as for a review.'

But if it seems that for the English on the West Coast the century has been one of achievement, all that has been done falls into perspective when judged by that most infallible of modern standards, the annual consumption of stationery. Here is the President sending home his yearly demand for the whole of India:

'The paper your Honours sent us this year appears very bad, appearing old decayed stuff that will not bear ink; we humbly desire your Honours will give order we have better paper for the future, and please to direct that we have no more ink sent us nor compasses and at the most six penknives a year and a dozen of black lead pencils with six ink-glasses.'

CHAPTER VII

MADRAS: THE ENLIGHTENED
PRESIDENCY

ON the West coast, the English won an uneasy independence
as soon as they had an island to defend; their ships became
something to be reckoned with, a force which neither Mogul
nor Maratha wished to see the firm ally of the other. But Bombay
was not the first piece of territory to be administered. In 1639, Mr.
Francis Day, Chief Factor of the Company's station at Armagon,
obtained from a descendant of the old Rajas of Vijayanagar the grant
of a strip of land on the coast of Coromandel, about six miles long
by one broad. Within this husk was a kernel, only about four hundred
yards by a hundred but defensible. The English built a wall and
within it a college for the factors and merchants, a house for the
Governor. This was the White Town; outside the walls but within
the six-mile strip, sprang up the Black Town. The whole was at first
called Sri Ranga Raja Patanam, later Chinna Patanam and at last
Madras Patanam.

This settlement was in many ways just like the others   Trade was
still the main object:

'And if our Dyers can attain to the dying of a perfect Coal Black,
pleasant grass greens and carnations, then send of each sort 2000
pieces with 100 pink colours. But if they be not perfect colours, send
but 100 of each for a trial. . . .'

As at Surat, life was still mainly collegiate, though by the end of
the century, there were breaches appearing in the old primitive rule.

'All our Merchants, Factors, Writers and apprentices are in the
several factories to live within the Company's house or Factory, save
only at the Fort (St. George at Madras) where we have a garrison
and the Town under our Government; the Agent and Council then
may permit such as they shall think fit to reside in our Town of
Madras patam. But not elsewhere.'

But there was a difference at Madras from the beginning which
persisted to the end, a leisurely self-sufficiency, and in the seventeenth
century there was also a way of being well ahead of the other Presidencies and sometimes of Europe. In the first place, this narrow strip
the English claimed from the first to hold in full sovereignty, though

the claim was not very logical in face of their payment of an annual tribute of twelve hundred pagodas, or about five hundred pounds sterling. But in practice there was no real doubt; the English maintained soldiers to defend the place and they punished criminals, two functions which in Europe were by now the attributes of a sovereign. Very soon after the English came, two men murdered 'a common whore for her jewels', throwing her body in the river; the Raja enjoined the English to deal with the murderers according to their own laws, and so, fearing that their town might become a resort of thieves and worse, the council did justice upon them and hanged them on a gibbet, reporting to London after the event. Eight months later they executed by shooting a Portuguese who had killed two of the Company's Indian soldiers.

Until 1670, only odd glimpses of Madras are to be caught; from then onwards, there is no longer any need to rely on travellers, the records being perhaps as complete as for any place or period before the twentieth century. The Council met at eight in the morning every Monday and Thursday; the pettiest matters were discussed and recorded and a copy of the diary sent to England every year with a letter of review. The whole system is clear to the eyes; we can see the Agent or Governor, with his Second in Council, the Book-keeper; his Third, the Warehouse-keeper, and his Fourth, the Customer or Customs Officer. The Agent's salary was three hundred pounds a year; his three Members of Council drew one hundred pounds, seventy and fifty respectively. Factors received something between forty and twenty, Writers ten pounds and Apprentices five.

In the White Town, the Agent himself was commander of the garrison, and was the supreme authority for law and order. In the case of an offence committed by a European, the Agent and his Council were the judges and a jury was empanelled. Justice in the Black Town was more summary, the Customer, or Fourth in Council, acting as Magistrate and condemning, flogging, fining or imprisoning at discretion, while the duty of keeping order and presenting offenders to the Magistrate fell to an Indian known as the Pedda Naik. He was paid, on the Mogul principle, by some free rice fields and permission to levy duties on rice, oil, fish and betel-nut.

The Restoration brought a charter permitting the Company to build fortifications, raise troops and make war on powers not Christian. With the increase in authority came a succession of Governors who seem to have been usually men of a fierce vigour. Sir Edward Winter in 1665 experienced feelings that many officials have known but controlled; indignant at being superseded, he arrested his successor for high treason, another member of Council being killed by the soldiers in the course of the altercation. Winter must have had the support of most of the factors and soldiers, for he prolonged his tenure of office by three years and like Keigwin only surrendered to overwhelming force sent from England to subdue him. Langhorn, Master, Yale, Pitt — all were men of character with a certain contempt for the opinion of anyone else.

Here is an account of Madras and its Governor in 1674 by the observant Dr. Fryer:

'The Agent here is Sir William Langhorn, a gentleman of indefatigable industry and worth. He is Superintendent over all the Factories on the Coast of Coromandel, as far as the Bay of Bengala, and up Huygly river, . . . as far as Patna. He has his Mint and privilege of coining . . . Moreover he has his Justiciaries, to give sentence, but not on life and death to the King's liege people of England, though over the rest they may. His personal guard consists of three hundred or four hundred Blacks, besides a band of fifteen hundred men ready on summons. He never goes abroad without fifes, drums, trumpets and a flag with two balls in a red field, accompanied with his Council and Factors on horseback with their Ladies in palenkeens. . . .'

The business of life and death is confusing. The Court of Directors seem very soon to have cut down the powers assumed on the spot, and for a long time the Governor and Council were allowed to hang Europeans only for piracy, a restriction the more energetic Governors evaded by a free interpretation of the term. Piracy, they held, meant crossing a piece of water while in possession of property for which no strict account could be given. There is the well-known story of how Governor Elihu Yale, whose name survives in the university, hanged his English groom, one Cross, for piracy, he having taken a ride on his master's horse without permission and stayed away two nights. Cross must have forded the Koum to get out of the White Town and so qualified technically for the punishment; in England of course he could have been hanged for stealing a horse. But the power to hang Indians was claimed from the first and exercised with no tiresome restrictions.

It is the more surprising to find that as early as 1680 the Governor of Madras forbade the burning of a Hindu widow. And there are frequent resolutions regarding the slave trade:

'Monday, 18th September, 1683. There being great number of slaves yearly exported from this place, to the great grievance of many persons whose children are very commonly privily stolen away from them by those who are constant traders in this way, the Agent and Council, considering the scandal that might accrue to the Government and the great loss that many parents may undergo by such actions, have ordered that no more slaves be sent off the shore again.'

'Monday, 13th November, 1683. An order in English, Portuguese, Gentoo [i.e. Tamil] and Malabar, for the preventing the transportation of this country people by sea and making them slaves in other countries. . . .'

It is partly because it means a loss of wealth that the slave trade is forbidden, but there is more to it than that and the grief of the parents is several times mentioned in the proclamation. Here is a responsiveness to public opinion and a social conscience more developed than in England; it is to be a century and a half before Westminster forbids the slave trade. It is clear that it was not the fact of slavery to which exception was taken but the cruelty of transportation; there was no objection to keeping slaves in Madras; another entry reads:

'Thursday, 29th September, 1687: We do now order that Mr. Fraser, who being Land Customer has the best opportunity for it, do buy forty young sound slaves for the Right Honourable Company and dispose them to the several Mussoola boats . . .' [used for landing in the surf of Madras].

By 1685, the doctrine of sovereignty was stated explicitly and in all its lack of logic by Sir Josiah, now quite recovered from his Little England period; his style grows chaster as his imagination warms to the imperial theme. He is directing the President how to deal with an appeal by the King of Golconda for help against the Mogul Emperor — an appeal which must surely have been answered by circumstance if not in writing long before Leadenhall Street knew of it.

'For the King of Golconda's writing to you, you may acquaint him in a decent and friendly manner that we are none of his subjects, wherein we would have you be guided by the old Proverb "suaviter in modo, fortiter in re". But if nevertheless he pretend to any dominion over your city, you may, when you are in good condition, tell him in plain terms that we own him for our good friend, ally and confederate, and sovereign and lord paramount of all that country, excepting the small territory belonging to Madras of which we claim the sovereignty and will maintain and defend against all persons and

govern by our own laws, without any appeal to any prince or potentate whatsoever, except our Sovereign Lord the King, paying unto
him, the King of Golconda, our agreed tribute of 1200 pagodas per
annum. And if ever he break with you upon these terms, we require
you to defend yourselves by arms and from that time renounce paying
him any more tribute. . . .'

A sovereign territory, for whose maintenance and defence it was by
no means enough to provide men skilled only in measuring cloth and
casting up accounts; here is the Court of Directors — and that is to
say the superb Josiah — admonishing the President and his Council
on an occasion when some of them at least might have been expected
to feel some disappointment:

'Let none of you think much or grudge at the speedy advancement
of Mr. Higginson. We do not do it out of any partiality for him, . . .
but sincerely as we apprehend for the public good; knowing him to
be a man of learning and competently well read in ancient histories
of the Greeks and Latins, which, with a good stock of natural parts,
only can render a man fit for Government and Political science,
martial prudence, and other requisites for ruling over a great city.
This, we say, with some experience of the world and knowledge of
the laws and customs of nations, can alone qualify men for such a
Government, and for treaties of peace or war, or commerce with
foreign Princes. It is not being bred a boy in India or studying long
there and speaking the language, understanding critically the trade
of the place, that is sufficient to fit a man for such a command as the
Second of Fort St. George. . . .'

It was to be some time before those thoughts were accepted by
everyone. Sir Josiah was undoubtedly a great man; here is another
project of his which did not mature very rapidly:

'If you could contrive a form of corporation to be established, of
the Natives mixed with some English freemen, . . . some public use
might be made thereof; and we might give the members some privileges and pre-eminencies by Charter under our seal . . .; and we might
make a public advantage of them, without abating essentially any part
of our dominion when we please to exert it. And . . . your people
would more willingly and liberally disburse five shillings towards the
public good, being taxed by themselves, than sixpence imposed by
our despotical power. . . .'

This is the voice of a statesman; it is a long time since the defence
of Bombay was 'a feather for the poor Indian to gaze on'. But indeed,
as early as 1683 the Court of Directors had written:

'... we would have you to strengthen and fortify our Fort and Town by Degrees, that it may be terrible against the assault of any Indian Prince and the Dutch power of India ... But we must needs desire you so to contrive your business (but with all gentleness) that the inhabitants may pay the full charge of all repairs and fortifications, who do live easier under our Government than under any Government in Asia, or indeed under any Government in the known part of the world'.

This led to a crisis of a kind that was to become familiar. A house-tax was proposed, 'of three fanams a year for a small house, six for a middle size house and nine for a great house'. Nine fanams would be rather less than two shillings. The inhabitants, however, stopped all work and presented a petition to the Council, recounting the past benefits they had received and protesting against the tax: the President and Council reasoned with them, but

'... they continued very obstinate and declared themselves unwilling and unable to pay ...; it would breed a custom and they feared it would be increased hereafter ... After which they were one by one asked whether they would leave the town and make war upon us or submit to our orders and governments; to which they every one answered they would submit, but on a sudden all at once denied what they had said, and that they would not pay, do what we would to them; which forced us to cause the drum to beat and declare our resolution that we would execute our orders, declared to them yesterday by beat of drum, of pulling down their houses, selling their lands and banishing them the place. Which, when they perceived us so much in earnest, at last submitted. ...'

That was a dilemma with which perhaps every young district officer has been faced in one form or another. Reason tells him that those heart-rending protestations cannot be true; he must harden his heart and not be made a fool of; but all the same there is a whisper of doubt in his ear and it does not cease until the moment of release and relief when at last the rebels submit and all things are at peace and quiet.

CHAPTER VIII

JOB CHARNOCK

MADRAS was the first of the three Presidencies to claim sovereignty, and the first to be chartered — in 1687 — as a Municipal Corporation with a Mayor's Court. If its President and Council were also the first to develop some sense of responsibility to the people they ruled, it was perhaps partly due to their comparative security. Madras had till 1688 no more formidable neighbour than the King of Golconda; but Bombay was menaced by the Marathas, while Calcutta was in the heart of the richest province of the Mogul Empire.

The Portuguese as usual had been first in Bengal. But they incurred the anger of Shah Jehan because they not unreasonably held aloof when he rose in arms against his father Jahangir. Once Shah Jehan was firmly on the throne he took his revenge, driving the Portuguese out of Hooghly, massacring the men and carrying off the women. The English crept joyfully into the perilous vacancy thus created.

In 1640, the skill of the Company's physician, Dr. Boughton, won them further privileges. There was soon well established at Hooghly a Bay Council, subordinate to the Agent and Council at Madras, having jurisdiction over factories at Balasore, Cossimbazar, Patna, Dacca and Singhiya. Their letters and records are preserved and there are the private journals of Streynsham Master and William Hedges. Master had been employed as a young man on the West Coast; he had been back in England for two years and a half when in 1675 he was selected as a fit and able person to restore order to the settlements on the East Coast. In these the Company suspected, with some justice, that there was not only inattention to business but a good deal of private trade carried on either openly or, what was worse, through interlopers or pirates.

Master was a good choice, for he was a born administrator, exact and thorough, painstaking and energetic. He began at once a series of tours up the Madras coast and into Bengal and at station after station composed quarrels, went through the accounts, drew up gradation lists of the Company's servants in order of seniority, inspected warehouses and buildings, gave orders for repairs and made regulations for the future, only to find on his next visit that much of the work had to be done again. He had been perhaps a trifle too impatient with those less able and energetic than himself; he was a little too fond of his own way; this, and his being attended on his 'progress (as we may call it) with such a princely train and charge' were made excuses in Leadenhall Street for his dismissal, the truth, one may suspect, being simply that he was too able and too masterful.

In 1680, a year that will do as well as another, the English in Bengal may be observed to display many of the less pleasant aspects of petty officialdom. There are quarrels about precedence and transfers; Charnock refuses to keep the books as Second at Hooghly and insists on the place that is his due; Hervey is rebuked for taking too long on his journey from Hooghly to Patna; there is the unsavoury business of Thomas, the warehouse-keeper and Third at Hooghly, who 'having been some time distracted in his wits' becomes really mad and says the most unpleasant things about his wife's liking for Vincent, the First in Council. But behind the quarrels and the pettiness of office is always the relationship with the Moguls, in which there is usually a hint of menace.

Aurangzebe had restored the poll-tax on unbelievers and this had to be compounded for. Presents to the Viceroy of Bengal and his subordinates are a continual trouble; the Viceroy expects a present and so does his *diwan* or Prime Minister; there is also the Emperor's diwan, an official from the central revenue office who since the days of Akbar and Todar Mal has accompanied every Viceroy. There is the Governor and his minister at Dacca; in Bihar there is another Viceroy and another hierarchy. And they all have clerks. Persian horses were a favourite present in Bengal, cordial waters in Madras; there is a list of acceptable presents thoughtfully sent by the Emperor's Minister, as a child before a birthday writes to a favourite aunt, which includes:

'Boxes with clockwork; China screens with clockwork, both painted and with images; images and junks that go with clockwork. . . .

'Europe fusees; one or two small field pieces, guns, etc., will not be amiss. . . .'

Elephants and horses are mentioned *en passant* but:

'Good pieces of Ambergrease will do extremely well . . .' and

'Clocks and watches that strike or have chimes you must by all means send. . . .'

This was for the Emperor; in Bengal, however, rupees would usually do extremely well. But the treatment was habit-forming; the dose had to be not only repeated but increased if the symptoms were not to recur. By an expenditure of fifty thousand rupees, an order had been obtained from the Emperor permitting the Company to trade on terms which would end all difficulties but, needless to say, when the order came it could be interpreted by local officials in a sense quite different from that intended by the English, and it continued to be necessary to give presents as before. In Patna, there was some question of whether an outgoing Viceroy should receive a present as well as his successor; Peacock, the Chief of the Factory, and Meverell, his Third, were seized, forced to walk through the town bare-headed and bare-footed and subjected to many other indignities before they paid up and were released.

The position was really intolerable; the Emperor's order, obtained at so much expense of money, time and trouble, was valueless; there was really nothing for it but sooner or later to convince the Mogul that it was worth being friendly with the English. The dispute dragged on, with arguments about customs, poll-tax and presents; at last came the inevitable open breach. Job Charnock, now First in the Bay Council, assumed the rank of lieutenant-colonel, which was his automatically in time of war, and defended a part of the modern Calcutta with some amateur skill and a remarkable display of military tenacity in the face of much stronger forces. After one or two rebuffs, he scored a minor tactical victory and made a truce; then, seizing the chance to do with a good grace what he would soon have been forced to do with no grace at all, he withdrew to an island at the mouth of the Hooghly, where he soon had to stand a second siege.

Charnock is a man who for some reason has touched the imagination of English and Indian alike. Here is an Indian account of his withdrawal:

'Mr. Chanak, with great indignation, prepared to fight; but as he had a very small force and only one vessel was present at the time, while the Moguls had assembled in great number, he saw no advantage in taking any hostile measure against them and was obliged to weigh anchor. He had a burning-glass in his ship, with which, by concentrating the sun's rays, he burnt the river face of the city as far as Chandarnagar. With a view to avenge this injury, the army commander wrote to the police-station at Makhua with orders to stop the vessel. The police officer accordingly prepared an iron chain, each link of which was twenty pounds in weight . . . The chain being extended across the river, the vessel was intercepted, but Mr. Chanak cut through the chain with a European sword and went on his way. . . .'

Sir Josiah was not the man to put up with insult and humiliation; he declared war on the Mogul Emperor, perhaps the richest and most powerful monarch in the world, and sent six companies of infantry and ten armed vessels under Captain Heath to conquer India. Their operations were made more difficult by instructions to sail up the Ganges and take Chittagong and by the reluctance of Captain Heath to accept Charnock's assurance that Chittagong was at the mouth of another river nearly two hundred miles away and strategically quite beside the point. At last the remains of the expedition, with Charnock and his factors on board, fell back on Madras; now the war began to be waged as it should have been and now the Mogul began to feel the effect of sea power. Sir Josiah's geography might be shaky but he had a remarkable grasp of the essential. Here are his comments when Aurangzebe reduced the King of Golconda and moved forward into the Carnatic:

'The subjects of the Mogul cannot bear a war with the English for twelve months together, without starving and dying by thousands for want of work to purchase rice; not singly for want of our trade but because by our war we obstruct their trade with all the Eastern nations, which is ten times as much as ours and all European nations put together. Therefore we conclude Fort St. George is now much more worth and secure to us than ever it was in the mean King of Golconda's time, for he had little at sea for us to revenge ourselves upon, but now if new injuries should be offered us, we have a fat enemy to deal with, from whom something is to be got to bear our charges. . . .'

He was right; the upshot is told in the minutes of the Fort St. George Council for Monday, October 7th, 1689 and more romantically by Nawab Muhabbat Khan, recounter of the burning-glass story:

'In those days the Emperor Aurangzebe was . . . straitened . . . for provisions, and his camp was reduced to starvation. Upon this, the Chief of the Factory in the Carnatic sent vessels laden with grain, showing great consideration for the throne . . . The Emperor was much pleased . . . and the royal orders were issued, exempting the ships of the Company from custom duties, . . . and giving permission for the establishment of factories in Bengal. . . .'

Job Charnock came back in triumph and founded a city that was to become one of the largest in the world. He was the rougher kind of Company's servant; he was not a man of good birth and education like Streynsham Master or Gerald Aungier, nor can he be credited

73

with any great foresight or imagination. But he catches the fancy, he sticks in the memory, perhaps from something in the harsh syllables of his name but perhaps more truly because of the silent stubborn obstinacy that seems to have been his strength, as it was his country-men's. Master and the Madras Council wished to make him Second at Hooghly when he thought he should be First at Cossimbazar. He said little but stuck to his guns, refused to take over the books at Hooghly for months on end and got his way.

With the same doggedness he refused to pay unjust claims at Patna, defended himself with a few men against the Mogul thousands, endured the ignorance and indecision of Heath. And to his stubborn-ness he added a touch of the picturesque. Everyone has heard of how he rescued from the flames a Brahman widow of transcendent loveli-ness, lived with her happily for fourteen years, set up a magnificent tomb over her body and sacrificed a cock there every year on the anniversary of her death. It is not a Brahman practice to sacrifice cocks, but, as the husband of a Brahman widow, Charnock could hardly be expected to be particularly orthodox in his paganism. He died in 1693, having 'reigned more absolutely than a Rajah, only he wanted much of their humanity'.

The seventeenth century ended then with all three Presidencies established. For the Mogul Empire it had not been a century of progress or achievement; Aurangzebe had extended his dominions but his intolerance had hastened the collapse of his dynasty. The English in India, however, might well have looked back with some complacency. In the first years after 1608 they had been a colony of traders, begging for the right to exist in Surat on sufferance; now the Governors of Madras and Bombay live in regal state with a navy, a standing army, a militia, judges and a mint. The servants of the Com-pany are still mainly concerned with kerseys and calicoes; it is trade they are after. But already they are experienced in the diplomacy of the East; they are learning to be administrators in a small way, and every man among them is an occasional soldier.

Gone are the days when they petitioned against the employment of gentlemen and begged that they might be allowed to consort with those of their own degree. There have been men among them of imagination, foresight and restraint; in almost any society Oxenden, Aungier and Master would have shone. Others, such as Pitt and Charnock, excel by the force of a stubborn gusto for mastery; there is a plentiful supply of men with the fierce valour of Sir Edward Winter, James Keigwin or Captain Minchin of the *Revenge*. Idleness and folly no doubt are there in plenty, and much technical dishonesty, for you will not get incorruptibility for ten pounds a year. But most of it is the sanctioned dishonesty of the East, the commission that does not go beyond what is customary and which no one thinks matter for reproach. It was certainly no worse among the English in India than in Whitehall, where Sir Josiah squared King, Court and Parliament for £80,000 and 'by his great annual presents could command both at Court and in Westminster Hall what he pleased'.

They are quarrelsome, no one can deny it; a hot-tempered, full-blooded generation who eat too much meat for the climate and drink too much arrack punch and too much of the livery flavoursome wines of Spain and the Canaries. But the quarrels vanish and the ranks close when they are faced by Mogul or Portuguese and already they display, when compared with those who surround them, the qualities that are to put this empire in their hands — a stubborn fidelity to each other and, within reasonable commercial limits, to the Company; an obstinate tenacity of purpose; discipline; a preference on the whole for keeping their word. Above all, there is among them a fair number of that rare sub-species of man through whose character shines the sharp blade of decision, the steel of leadership.

CHAPTER IX

WAR IN THE SOUTH

1. THE NEW CENTURY

DURING the first half of the eighteenth century, there was no great change in the way the English lived in India. Then, at the mid of the century, the wind blew, as it was to blow again a hundred years later, a sharp and sudden blast that changed the face of nature. But in the meantime, says Hamilton:

'Most gentlemen and ladies in Bengal live both splendidly and pleasantly, the forenoons being dedicated to business and after dinner to rest, and in the evening to recreate themselves in chaises or palankeens in the fields, or to gardens, or by water in their budgeroes, which is a convenient boat that goes swiftly by the force of oars. On the river sometimes there is the diversion of fishing or fowling or both; and before night they make friendly visits to one another. . . .'

It was as well to live splendidly and pleasantly while you could, for Hamilton writes elsewhere:

'The Company has a pretty good hospital at Calcutta, where many go in to undergo the penance of physic but few come out to give account of its operation . . .' And again:

'One year I was there and there were reckoned in August about twelve hundred English, . . . and before the beginning of January there were four hundred and sixty burials registered in the clerk's book of mortality. . . .'

Promotion, it will be seen, was likely to be swifter than the Company's time-scale provided for. There had been no more apprentices since 1695; the newcomer now usually began as a Writer on £10 a year, and could expect to rise to Factor on £20 in three or four years. In the gradation list for Masulipatam in 1676 there are eight Writers, none with five years' service. There is only one Factor; his pay is £20 and he 'came out a Factor' just four years ago. There is one Merchant, with five years' service and £30 a year and six Senior Merchants in this list; fourteen years is the longest service recorded among them, and apart from the Agent, who came out only last year, the youngest has six years' service. It is much the same story in the gradation list for the Bay, though there is one Senior Merchant, Job Charnock, with eighteen years to his credit.

Governors and Agents seem often to have come in direct, not up the scale of promotion. We have seen the case of Higginson, learned in Greek and Roman history; Master was another, but the most outstanding was Thomas Pitt, who for years had been the chief rival of the Company, a private merchant daring to trade in defiance of their monopoly, a rank interloper, 'no better than a pirate' (wrote Hedges), 'a fellow of a haughty, huffying, daring temper'. At last he became such a nuisance that the Court of Directors made him Governor of Madras. He made a very good one too and would be remembered for that even if he was not also memorable for begetting a line of Prime Ministers.

The young Writer then had to look forward to three or four years of drudgery, if he lived so long. He was forbidden, throughout his service, to take part in private trade outside India; the rules about internal trade varied at different periods and were seldom observed. Whatever the rules, in his first year or two the Writer probably lacked either the capital or the knowledge needed. On the other hand, he had no inevitable expenses. He ate and boarded free; he had no long list of servants to pay, for in addition to his salary he had an allowance from the Company that was meant to cover the payments he must incur.

'The Company's allowance is eight pagodas twenty-three fanams [that is, about three pounds ten shillings] a month, out of which the money paid for servant's wages, washing, candles and many other necessaries belonging to housekeeping together with the dearness and scarcity of provisions makes it as much as ever we can do to live upon that allowance. . . .'

This is part of a letter from a young gentleman in the Company's civil service, Robert Clive, to his father. He had to pay for his passage out and his keep on the voyage; he had also to furnish his rooms on arrival and buy clothes. It is clear that a young man who had no private means would feel very sharply the need for an outfit allowance and would find it hard not to run into debt — and the Company were very hard on debt. But sooner or later he would find a means to start in private trade and then he would be rich before long.

It is easy now to say that the Company should have paid their servants a better salary. But it has to be remembered that throughout the seventeenth century, the Company was the target for bitter attacks on the score that, by exporting bullion, the Court of Directors were draining the country of its wealth. Indeed, in the *Dictionary of National Biography*, Sir Josiah Child is labelled a writer on political economy; so he was, but his writings were strictly practical; his pamphlets were directed at those who attacked the Company. He wrote to defend a monopoly and the right of the monopolists and no one else to export bullion; he was led to doctrines that ended the economic theories of the century and fathered the Free Trade of a hundred years later. Meanwhile, outgoings had to be kept down.

A second company was founded in 1696, mainly as a revolt of the City against the autocratic ways of Sir Josiah. It must have meant a fierce increase in competition for a year or two and until a truce was made in 1698, life in India must have been less leisurely. The two companies agreed in 1702 to combine, their servants ruling alternately in an uneasy condominium; then in 1709 they united and the incident was over. It seems to have caused more talk in London than in India; the tavern songs of Queen Anne's reign are full of it.

There was not much change in the life the English led, but two events which made a small showing on the map were important. In 1690, the Marathas sold the English as much land as would fall within random shot of a cannon fired from Cuddalore; the largest cannon in the Presidency was fetched at once and Fort St. David founded. And in 1698 the Mogul, scared by an insurrection in Bengal, gave the English leave to fortify Calcutta and granted them in three villages the right to collect the King's share of the produce and to administer justice.

No sovereignty was claimed here. The English Company simply became a *Zamindar*, or landholder in Bengal; it is a term to be used with care, for it means something different in other parts of India and particularly in the Punjab. In Bengal it seems to have been used loosely for any intermediary with a right to collect the King's share, whether he was hereditary chief, Mogul official, or mercenary farmer of taxes. One of the English merchants became the Zamindar; here is the description of his own functions by Mr. Holwell (later of the Black Hole), who held the post from 1752 to 1756:

'The Zamindar acts in a double capacity . . . , the one as Superintendent and Collector of your Revenues, the other as Judge of . . . a tribunal for all matters both civil and criminal, wherein the natives only, subjects of the Mogul are concerned. He tried in a summary way, had the power of the lash, fine, and imprisonment; he determined all matters of *meum* and *tuum*; and in all criminal cases proceeded to sentence and punishment immediately after hearing, except when the crime (as murder) requires the lash to be inflicted until death, in which case he suspends execution of the sentence until the facts and evidence are laid before the President and his confirmation of the sentence obtained. . . .'

It is not pleasant to find that even in that age, callous to death and suffering though most men were, even so far from home, Englishmen should have whipped murderers to death because they had no legal power to hang them. A palate nice in horrors is required to discriminate between this and the Mogul custom in the same circumstances, which was to mutilate and leave to die.

That they had become zamindars made no real difference to the relations of the English with the Moguls. It is true that in 1701, Governor Beard of Calcutta felt himself strong enough to defy the Emperor Aurangzebe, stopping the sailing of all Mogul ships with the remark that he could not always be giving way to every little rascal. But the embassy to Delhi of John Surman and Edward Stephenson, which lasted from 1715 to 1717, showed that since the time of Sir Thomas Roe the only thing that had really changed was the Emperor's power. The dull round of bribery and intrigue, into favour and out again, procrastination, evasion and deceit — all that was unchanged; only the Emperor was weaker, his Viceroys stronger, their whims no longer liable to reversal if his ear could be reached. And in Bengal, the tale of the Viceroys and their governors is the familiar sequence of idle debauchee alternating with merciless tyrant — though one can detect a hint of individuality in the tyrant who, to make recalcitrants pay their arrears of land revenue, 'compelled them to put on loose trousers, into which were introduced live cats'. Orders of exemption from Delhi were not only expensive to obtain but useless when received. Continual appeasement was a main duty for the Agent in the Bay and his successor the Governor of Fort William.

Meanwhile, the face of India is a melancholy sight. It has been well described, and for once it is permissible to let oneself drift on the strong tide of Macaulay's rhetoric. Every schoolboy knows the brilliant passage in which he compares India after the death of Aurangzebe with 'the wide dominion of the Franks' after the death of Charlemagne who

'was scarcely interred when the imbecility and disputes of his descendants began to bring contempt on themselves and destruction on their subjects. . . .'

while in the forty years that followed the death of Aurangzebe:

'A succession of nominal sovereigns, sunk in indolence and debauchery, sauntered away life in secluded palaces, chewing bang, fondling concubines, and listening to buffoons. A succession of

REMNANTS OF THE
MOGUL EMPIRE
1751
Controlled from Delhi
Virtually Independent

AFGHANS

RAJPUTS

OUDH

BEHAR

BENGAL

MARATHAS

NIZAM'S
DOMINIONS

ARABIAN
SEA

BAY OF
BENGAL

MYSORE

COCHIN

E.G.M.

ferocious invaders descended through the western passes to prey on the defenceless wealth of Hindostan ... and every corner of the wide Empire learned to tremble at the mighty name of the Marathas ... Wherever their kettle-drums were heard, the peasant threw his bag of rice on his shoulder, hid his small savings in his girdle, and fled with his wife and children to the mountains or the jungles, to the milder neighbourhood of the hyaena and the tiger.'

There is seldom any doubt about what Macaulay means, and it is a delight to roll his sentences over the tongue even when he is misleading, but here he is not, and he is exactly right when he goes on:

'Wherever the Viceroys of the Mogul retained authority they became sovereigns. They might still acknowledge in words the superiority of the house of Tamerlane; as a Count of Flanders or a Duke of Burgundy might have acknowledged the superiority of the most helpless driveller among the later Carlovingians. In truth however they were no longer lieutenants removable at pleasure but independent hereditary princes.'

What is almost as important for the English who are to come later, this tendency to become hereditary and independent spread downwards; wherever he could, the collector of the King's share of the produce of the soil turned his official assignment or his commerical contract into a hereditary chieftainship.

2. THE MARCH TO ARCOT

It was in these conditions of growing chaos that war began in the South, an incident in that Hundred and Thirty Years' War with the French which occupied the English intermittently from the accession of William of Orange to the downfall of Napoleon. It is a war that for the general reader is apt to be both dull and confusing. The numbers of French and English are very small and the loss from disease high, so that the arrival of ships from Europe with five hundred fresh soldiers for either nation is usually enough to sway the balance completely to their advantage: the Indian troops on either side were seldom emotionally committed one way or the other and so were usually ready to change sides with the swing of the tide. The result is an uneasy see-saw of apparently overwhelming victory and calamity which has none of the mounting excitement of the campaigns from Torres Viedras to Salamanca, or of the triple hammer-blows of Blenheim, Ramillies and Oudenarde. What is even more fatal to dramatic tension, the Indian chiefs who are nominally the principals can hardly be distinguished from each other. Scarcely any indication of character is to be discerned, except in one man, Chanda Sahib, the French candidate for the throne of the Carnatic, a prince of unusual intellectual attainments, who during a varied and adventurous life displays a certain nobility in defeat, a swashbuckling aptitude for getting out of awkward situations, a *panache* that he did not lose until the last wretched scene when he was miserably slaughtered on the very spot where sixteen years before he had deceived a widowed Queen by a false oath taken on a bogus Koran.

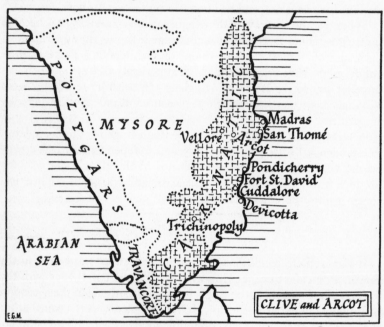

But some understanding of at least a part of the War in the South we must have, because we need to know the background against which the English lived in India and because it is now that the march of events begins to put the Empire into English hands, it is now that the will, the daring, and the energy of a few men in the service of the Company knit together into something stronger than themselves, a cable that tows them on into the tremendous sweep of the effort to impose peace and unity on India by domination.

War broke out between France and England in 1743; the news reached India in 1744. There is no room here to follow the ups and downs of war's fortune in Madras, the courage and resolution of

Hinde, Agent at Fort St. David, the military ability of Stringer Lawrence, the father of the Indian Army. It must be enough to say that the first period, of open war, was indecisive, with the advantage slightly to the French; peace was signed in Europe and a period followed in which Dupleix, the French governor, a man who as a diplomatist and an organizer of victory had something of the restless genius of Napoleon, tried to make himself master of Southern India by putting his candidates on two thrones, that of the Nizam or Viceroy of the Deccan and that of his nominal vassal, the Nawab of the Carnatic or of Arcot.

There was peace in Europe between France and England but in India there could be no peace short of complete victory for Dupleix. Each nation supported its own puppets. A time came when both Dupleix's candidates were enthroned. The English claimant to the Carnatic, Mohammad Ali, with some English soldiers, was besieged and heavily outnumbered at Trichinopoly. It seemed only a matter of time before Mohammad Ali and the whole force with him surrendered; there would be an end then of all pretence; the English would have no Nawab to fight for and they would have nothing to do but submit to the mercy of Dupleix.

It was now that a suggestion was put forward by Robert Clive, the young gentleman in the Company's civil service already mentioned, now for the second time turned temporary soldier. Now was the time, he believed, to relieve the pressure on Trichinopoly by marching to attack Arcot, the capital of the Carnatic. The town was not strongly held and its new ruler, Chanda Sahib, the French candidate, could hardly stand by and see it lost. It was a suggestion of which the direct results lasted two hundred years and the indirect may last as long again; the decision to adopt it will stand comparison with that to bring back fighters from France in 1940, to send armour to Egypt in 1941. Anyone might have thought of it, but no one else did; few would have had the courage or foresight to adopt it; not many besides Clive would have carried it out.

Anyone might have thought of it; it was the strategy of the march to Blenheim, of Jackson's march to Mannassas Junction, of the expeditions to the Dardanelles and Gallipoli. Instead of sending more strength to the maelstrom where it is expected and where it will meet strength, a thrust is launched at a tender point where it is not expected. The enemy must hastily withdraw strength from the maelstrom to counter the thrust; now it is he who anxiously wonders where the next blow will fall and you who grimly plan it.

Anyone can think of such a plan, but it takes faith in the future to find the men and decide that the thing shall be done. Fortunately Mr. Thomas Saunders who was now President at Fort St. David was a man worthy to be War Minister to anyone. If Dupleix was a Napoleon, lacking only the not unimportant gift of winning battles, Saunders was a Pitt or Churchill in miniature. He was surrounded by enemies; the whole continental background was in hostile hands; at Trichinopoly Chanda Sahib's troops outnumbered Mohammad Ali's by ten to one, while the English were two to the French three and, what was worse, were in poor spirits. But Saunders perceived the valour, the leadership, and the genius of Clive, a man not yet 26, a Writer who had been a subaltern for a short time and later a quarter-master, now re-commissioned as a Captain. He heard Clive's plan and accepted all the deadly risk involved; with the unanimous support of his Council he scraped together for Clive's march every man that could be raised, leaving himself only a hundred English soldiers at Fort St. David and fifty at Madras. For the expeditionary force there were two hundred English and three hundred sepoys, with eight officers, six of whom had never seen action. Of these six, four were young men in the civil service of the Company who were now commissioned for the first time. They had three field pieces for their artillery; a siege train of two eighteen-pounders was sent after them later.

The expedition marched from Madras on August 26th, 1751; on the 31st Clive was within ten miles of Arcot, which was garrisoned by a force of about eleven hundred men. But the news that the English 'had marched with unconcern through a violent storm of thunder lightning and rain, gave the garrison so high an opinion of the fortitude of the approaching enemy that they instantly abandoned the fort'.

'We marched,' wrote an English sergeant, 'without opposition through the town amidst a million Spectators, whose looks betrayed them traitors, notwithstanding their pretended friendship and dirty presents. We then took possession of the fort. . . .'

The fort stood in the middle of the town, whose inhabitants had been impressed as much by the omens with which the arrival of the English was marked as by the fortitude of the troops in disregarding them; now came the surprise of favourable treatment and a scrupulous respect for property. They decided that they were neutral and would take no part in what was to follow; they kept to this resolution even when the garrison seemed most at a disadvantage.

Clive, no sooner in Arcot than he was besieged, began by a number of sorties, intended partly to keep the enemy at a distance but still more to impress them with the fighting spirit of his troops. But by calling in men from neighbouring towns the enemy increased steadily in numbers till from the eleven hundred of the original garrison they had become over three thousand; they were so strong in the surrounding country that, when the time came to bring in the two eighteen-pounders, it was necessary for all the garrison to go out and escort them, leaving only thirty English and fifty sepoys in the fort. 'The number of our men would not admit of even sentries upon the proper posts round the walls, so that we were obliged to divide into parties and keep moving round. The enemy did little else but pop at us from the houses on the side of the ditch, by which we had one or two wounded, till about two o'clock when a great number of horse and foot came up close to the gate and were received by all the fire we had and some Grenades, which put them into confusion and obliged them to retire.' The enemy had decided to neglect the convoy and do all they could to take the fort. They made a second attack soon after the first, on the opposite side of the fort, but 'we were apprised of the place they intended to attack by the hideous shouts and noise they made'. They were driven off; eighty men held a wall a mile long against three thousand; the two eighteen-pounders were brought in.

But by now, the thrust at Arcot was beginning to have the effect intended. Four thousand of Chanda Sahib's best troops left Trichinopoly and were joined on the march by reinforcements of French from Pondicherry; being now considerably more than ten to Clive's one, the enemy proceeded to occupy the town whose houses clustered beneath the walls of the fort. Clive chose this moment, the last before a regular siege should close down upon him, to make a fierce sally with every man he could. It was expensive; he lost two of his officers and fifteen Europeans, but both sides had been shown how the English could fight and that was worth many men.

Another two thousand men joined the enemy, making their total about ten thousand, of whom a hundred and fifty were French. Clive had a hundred and twenty English and two hundred sepoys fit for duty. Here is the sergeant's account of how the siege closed grimly down:

'24th September. The enemy now in possession of the town hindered all manner of supplies of provisions, cut off the communication for the waters coming into the fort, and we had nothing before

our eyes but the dismal prospect of either being starved out by block-
ade or being obliged to stand a storm in case of their bringing battering cannon to make a breach, which the unshaken fortitude of our
officers made us cheerfully resolve upon rather than meanly submit to
any terms could be proposed us. Great was the disadvantages we
laboured under from the malsituation and condition of the fort. The
town houses close to the walls, the ditch in many places easily fordable
and in some dry. The walls in many places tumbled down and those
standing ready to fall, the parapet afforded but little cover for our
men. The bastions ill contrived of no service till made so by the hard
labour of our men who were constantly annoyed by the enemy's fire
from the houses, while we could not see so much as one of them. The
inhabitants gave us to understand the use of the water would be
entirely destructive to our men and the hopes of fresh supplies entirely
cut off, besides our quantity of ammunition far short of what would
be judged sufficient for our defence.

'The enemy entirely surrounded our walls, placing their men in the
houses upon the side of the ditch and kept a continual fire all round so
that our people could no sooner look over the parapet but they had a
whole volley of small shot fired at them from the houses not thirty
yards distant, by which we lost a good many men.'

Arcot stands in a stony plain; the sterile red rock does nothing to
temper the harshness of the sun. The fort is not raised up on a height
that might catch a breeze; the houses cluster thickly round the walls.
It was September, close, hot and moist; in red coats and tight stocks,
heavy felt hats, belts and pouches, the men must have poured with
sweat. Water was bad and short; food was short. There were nothing
like enough men to man the walls; they had to go short of sleep.
There was not much hard fighting but constant danger of death;
Clive went the rounds with a sergeant by his side; on three separate
occasions, the sergeant was killed and Clive saved.

This went on till October 7th, when the enemy brought up an
eighteen-pounder and some smaller guns and began to batter the
walls. The two English eighteen-pounders brought in from Madras
at such pains were soon dismounted and no effective reply could be
made to the bombardment but small arms fire against the gunners.
It is true that a platform of earth was made and a gigantic piece of
antique ordnance hauled on to it, pointed at the headquarters of
Chanda Sahib's son, and fired once a day for three days before it burst
but this was done mainly to display the energy and resource of the
besieged and it did not stop the enemy's battering. In two days a

breach was made, and now began the toil, heart-breaking at the best of times, doubly so in the heat, of improvising a trench and breastwork from the rubble and broken fragments of the breach, made up with fascines or faggots and earth, work constantly interrupted and destroyed.

On October 21st, the siege having now lasted a month, the President at Fort St. David laid before his Council a letter from Captain Clive, who never seems to have had any difficulty about sending messages. 'He thinks himself able to defend a breach should the enemy make one; his only apprehension, therefore, are his people's falling down through fatigue; that he thinks no less a force than 1000 Blacks and 200 Europeans can attempt to relieve him, as the enemy's situation is strong and their numbers increase daily. . . .'

Once again, Mr. Saunders found every man he could for Clive's relief and dispatched them under Lieutenant Innes. In Arcot, they turned anxious eyes towards Madras and the sea, from whence their help would come. The enemy began to batter a new breach to the South-West. 'Our parapet being pretty good in this place, we drove them several times from their guns by our small arms, killing several of their gunners. But they by degrees beat down that defence and breached without any other opposition than from a six-pounder . . . which they soon disabled and made a practicable breach of forty yards wide. . . .'

Here too the defenders dug a trench and threw up a breastwork, toiling in the steamy heat, dazed for want of sleep. There was less food now, and they were near exhaustion from toil, heat, thirst and anxiety. The siege had lasted forty days. There was still no sign of help from the East. 'Our people sickly,' writes the sergeant. 'Not above eighty military fit for duty.'

Now at last came news of Lieutenant Innes. He had met a strong force of French and Chanda Sahib's troops, fought a hard fight, lost many men and fallen back into a fortress. There was no more hope of relief from that side. Clive sent out another messenger, this time to a Maratha chief who had been hired to help Mohammad Ali, the English candidate for the Carnatic, but who had so far judged it futile to help those who did not help themselves. Answer came back: he would not delay a moment to send troops to the aid of 'such brave men as the defenders of Arcot, whose behaviour had now convinced him that the English could fight'.

The enemy must have heard that help was coming. There came a flag of truce and a call to surrender from Chanda Sahib's son — 'a

summons from young Chanda,' Clive called it, 'to whom he returned
an answer and let him know that neither threats nor bribery should
hinder him from doing his duty'.

The storm must come now. On the evening of November 13th a
spy brought the news that the assault would be at dawn next day; at
midnight the warning was confirmed by a second. 'But as our people
were night and day on their posts we made no alteration in our disposition.' There were now eighty English and a hundred and twenty
sepoys fit for duty.

Clive was awakened a little before dawn; it had begun. It was the
tenth day of Moharram, the climax of the fast and of the mourning for
Hasan and Husain. The attackers came on with a desperate enthusiasm, regardless of life, sure of a martyr's crown if they fell.

'The parties who attacked the gates drove before them several
elephants who, with large plates of iron fixed to their foreheads, were
intended to break them down; but the elephants, wounded by the
musketry, soon turned and trampled on those who escorted them.
The ditch before the breach to the north-west was fordable; and as
many as the breach would admit mounted it with a mad kind of
intrepidity . . . a number of muskets were loaded in readiness, which
those behind delivered to the first rank as fast as they could discharge
them. The two pieces of cannon from the top of the house fired likewise on the assailants, who in a few minutes abandoned the attack,
when another body, and then another succeeded, who were driven off
in the same manner; . . . there were 12,000 cartridges expended
during the action, which lasted not an hour, so it will be readily
allowed we were not idle,' writes the sergeant. It was only a little
after day-break when the enemy fell sullenly back, leaving the defenders to gaze at each other in the first garish brilliance of the
suddenly uprisen sun; leaving them to sweat and watch among the
baking red rocks and ruined parapets as the sun grew intolerably
higher; leaving them on this, the fiftieth day, to peer out with gritty
red-rimmed eyes, watching for help from the East, watching for
another assault. All day the enemy fired at the fort, and breaches, till
in the middle of the afternoon they asked for a truce to bury their
dead. At four in the afternoon they began to fire again and kept it up
till two in the morning. Then the fire died down and in the morning
they had gone 'to the inexpressable satisfaction of everybody'.

Soon after came more 'agreeable news, which gave us unbounded
joy when we heard Captain Kilpatrick was within a few hours' march
. . . Thus did providence disappoint our fears and relieve us from the

dread necessity of starving or submitting to the terms of merciless barbarians. And Captain Kilpatrick's command joined us in the afternoon. We fully and unmolested enjoyed the fruits of the earth so long denied us, tho every day in our sight, and solaced ourselves with the pleasing reflection of having maintained the character of Britons in a Clime so remote from our own.'

The siege was over. And not the siege only; other things too were over, though no one in Arcot can have guessed how many. It was not only the Marathas who had learnt that the English could fight; the tale of the siege spread east and west, south and north; there will be no more turns of the tide now; now steadily comes flooding in the main. There is much hard fighting still to be done, but in ten years it will be the French who are confined to a few trading-stations, the English who have rich provinces at their feet.

It was not Clive's genius alone that let in the waters. Nor, for all his splendid qualities, was it all the British infantryman; it was Clive and the soldier, but also the courage, foresight and wisdom of Thomas Saunders, the leadership of Stringer Lawrence, the gallantry of Captain Dalton, Captain Cope, Captain Kilpatrick, Lieutenant Bulkeley, Ensign Glass and many more of the Company's servants who with neither rank nor fame were content to maintain 'the character of Britons in a Clime so remote from their own'. Dupleix had been the most brilliant figure in the scene, but lonely brilliance was not enough; he was not served so well as Saunders. It was the British officer — whether he served first on the barrack-square or in a counting-house — who was better than the French.

The siege was over. The hour of the victory and the splendour of Dupleix was finished. It was goodbye as well to taffeties, ginghams, mull-mulls and muslins, indigo and saltpetre, vermilion, quicksilver and pepper. Not much longer would men aspire to be Warehousekeeper or Purser Marine; councillor to a Government, plenipotentiary at a Prince's Court — those would soon be the appointments on which their eyes were set. They would no longer seek profit in gold but govern rich provinces and rule the affairs of men. But no one yet knew that. The day after Arcot was relieved, the sun rose on a discomfort no less torrid than the day before; the soldiers had still to find food, to look to their ammunition, to take care of their feet. They had a long way to go and there was a great deal still to do. But the change had happened all the same.

II
THE REVOLUTION
1751-1798

CHAPTER I

THE REVOLUTION IN BENGAL

FOR a century and a half the English had been humble petitioners to the Mogul Emperors and their Viceroys. But within a few years of Arcot, all that was changed. When Mr. Vansittart, Governor of Fort William, arrived at Murshidabad one evening in 1761, it was the Nawab of Bengal, the Mogul Viceroy, who made haste to visit the English Governor at nine o'clock next morning. Already it was established etiquette that the Englishman should walk to the end of the hall to greet his visitor, should make him the offer of a ceremonial present, which would be refused as inappropriate from an equal, and should then lead him to a couch, where they would take care to be seated at exactly the same moment and side by side.

And Major Hector Munro, three years later, having just defeated in battle the Mogul Emperor and his ally, the ruler of Oudh, issues this order:

'Such of the officers as will be off duty tomorrow who choose to wait on the King and wish him joy of being put in possession of Oudh by the English, are desired to meet at headquarters at nine o'clock tomorrow morning; it is necessary to acquaint them that it is customary to make him a salaam. . . .'

In short, the rulers of these wide domains are puppets and the Great Mogul has become a raree-show.

The events which brought about this revolution are less confusing and more dramatic than those which in Madras had led to the undoing of Dupleix. To us now, reading the story two centuries later, the tiny companies of English soldiers move over the vast stretches of the rice-fields with the certainty of the King's youngest son in a fairy-tale. Whatever agonies they go through, we know they will win the Princess in the end. And there is no dull sameness about the last Mogul Viceroys of Bengal; they stand out clearly as people, the tales of their lives are worth telling. There is a flavour of the Arabian Nights in the sharp contrast between the magnificence of Suraj-ud-Daula's prospects when he was enthroned, the sumptuous folly of his brief reign and the wretchedness of his end; there is much to pity in the decline of Mir Jafar and his pathetic reinstatement; and there is tragedy in the picture of Mir Kasim fighting against the march of events and a people too strong for him, denied the right to rule with justice and economy, giving up hope and giving way to a frightened and despairing cruelty.

In the tracts and pamphlets published in England, bitter with party controversy, in the speeches in the Commons, no extravagance was spared to stress the completeness of this revolution. The Englishmen who had brought it about were impeached, assailed with the most shocking imputations, held up to public obloquy in the House of Commons, in the Press, on the stage and in the novel. Macaulay, master of every weapon of rhetoric but restraint, polished but did not exaggerate what had been said by the Whig pamphleteers seventy years before. 'The English government,' he wrote, 'resembled the government of evil Genii rather than the government of human tyrants . . .' and much more follows to the same effect. 'Even despair,' he continues, 'could not inspire the soft Bengalee with courage to confront men of English breed, the hereditary nobility of mankind, whose skill and valour had so often triumphed in spite of tenfold odds. The unhappy race never attempted resistance . . . ' The reader who remains undazed is left in the state of poised inquiry of a small boy listening to his form-master's guarded description of the orgies of a Roman Emperor. He wants to know what actually happened, how the hereditary nobility came to behave so badly to the soft Bengalee and what they did to him, and for that matter by what right the hereditary nobility came to be governing Bengal at all.

What the English did in that first, worst period of their rule is an essential part of this story. But their deeds cannot fully be understood without some account of the manner of the revolution and of the downfall of the Nawabs.

The last Viceroy of Bengal, Behar and Orissa who could truly be regarded as an independent Prince was Ali Vardi Khan, the Terror of War, Muhabat Jang. He was a usurper, but justified his usurpation by a reign of fourteen years during which he kept the Marathas out of Murshidabad, by eight years of fighting and six of blackmail. It is said that in the last years of his reign his advisers drew his attention to happenings in the South and urged him to expel both French and English before he shared the fate of the Nawab of the Carnatic. To which the wise old man is said to have replied that the Europeans were like bees; they would make him honey if left in peace but would sting an intruder to death. He was shrewd in most things but not in his choice of a successor.

Suraj-ud-Daula had been the favourite and the recognized successor of his great-uncle; when he took his seat on the throne of the three provinces, he had no need to fight an exhausting civil war, there were no external enemies threatening invasion, he had a full treasury. He has been painted as a monster of cruelty, but all Eastern despots of the eighteenth century were cruel by the standards of the modern West; if he was outstanding in anything it was in ignorance and indecision. He believed there were no more than ten thousand persons in all Europe — and the strength of European garrisons in the East certainly gave some grounds for the belief. He saw no reason why these aliens should live on any different terms from the rest of his subjects; they were merchants and moneylenders, no more, and like the rest of their kind ought to be subject to a capital levy whenever it suited their sovereign.

There is some evidence for believing that plunder was the main motive in what Suraj-ud-Daula did. The English Settlement had grown to a city of four hundred thousand inhabitants; it was a City of Refuge not only for men but for money from all over Bengal, Behar and Orissa. In Murshidabad, the capital, every man held his property as a tenant-at-will of the Viceroy and the richest banked in Calcutta as the only place where property was respected. It was not unnatural that a spoilt young man, suddenly elevated to supreme power, should cast his eyes on so rich and unplundered a store. It is alleged that fear was stronger with him than greed, that he was afraid the English would wrest whole provinces from him. But the Muslim historian gives the impression that contempt and dislike were Suraj-ud-Daula's feelings for these presumptuous merchants rather than fear. At any rate, whatever his motive, he seized the first occasion for a quarrel and in 1756 marched on Calcutta.

Calcutta was in no state to stand a siege. The fortifications were wretched, the garrison inadequate and the militia untrained. Even worse, there was no leader with the indomitable will to victory of Clive. It was soon decided that the best course was to take to the ships and leave the town and fort to Suraj-ud-Daula, a decision for which there was something to be said, though nothing can excuse the way it was carried out. There was a panic; most of the English, headed by the Governor, Roger Drake, fled incontinently to the boats without letting the garrison on the walls know what they were doing. Once they were in midstream they refused to come back for the companions they had deserted — less than two hundred English, of whom the senior was the same Mr. J. Z. Holwell who had been Zamindar of Calcutta and who referred with so little concern to the way murderers were executed. He was to know something of suffering himself.

Everyone knows what happened that evening of a Calcutta June, at the time when the torrid dark falls and the heat, sullenly rejected by walls and floors, seems to grow thicker and staler than by day. One hundred and forty-six English were confined in the punishment cell of the fort, a room 'about eighteen feet long by fourteen wide' with only one small window; twenty-three of them came out alive next morning. Holwell wrote later a detailed and most moving account of that night of horror; all that need be said here is that until they sank dying to the ground to be trodden underfoot his fellow-prisoners seem to have shown Holwell consideration and listened to his instructions.

Suraj-ud-Daula had given orders that the prisoners should be confined, no more than that; he cannot be held directly responsible for the way his instructions were carried out, but he showed no compunction when he heard what had happened and, being convinced that there was buried treasure he had not yet found, ordered Holwell and three others of the survivors to be fettered till they said where it was. They, and all the survivors of the Black Hole, were soon covered with boils; their fetters were heavy and so painful where they chafed the boils that it was easier to crawl than to walk; they were made to travel long distances and their diet was rice and muddy water. But it must be said in fairness that Suraj-ud-Daula showed no more persistence in trying to get information from Holwell than in anything else. After three weeks, he ordered the release of the prisoners with the words that they had suffered enough.

When this news reached Madras, an expedition previously intended for the Deccan was at once diverted to Calcutta. It does not seem to have been in a spirit of outraged vindictiveness that Clive and Admiral Watson led their forces back. They had no difficulty in recovering Calcutta; one night attack sent the Nawab scurrying northward and with no very serious fighting he was ready to sign a treaty. The main terms of the agreement were three; the English were permitted to fortify Calcutta and live there under their own laws and with their former privileges as regards customs; the Company were to be reimbursed for the goods and money lost in the looting of Calcutta, and Suraj-ud-Daula was to be the friend and ally of the English. The amount to be paid was left to the justice of the Nawab.

These terms are not vindictive. By no lesser standards than those of Nazareth can the English be blamed here. Clive was in fact blamed at the time, but for moderation not severity; more recent critics aim their shafts at what followed. In making any judgment, it is as well to remember that there were two clear points at issue between the English and the Viceroy.

From their beginning in Surat in 1608, the English in India had found, as the Portuguese had found before them, that they could not live and trade 'subject to the jurisdiction, the encroachments and the insults of the country government'. Indian rulers were accustomed to take a levy of what they needed from the bankers and merchants who were their subjects, as King John had done from the Jews. 'The Mahometan Governors', wrote Mr. Scrafton, 'look on the growing riches of a subject as boys look on a bird's nest. He eyes their progress with impatience, then comes with a spoiler's hand and ravishes the fruit of their labour.' Missionaries could live on these terms but not merchants who were responsible to directors in a country where property was respected and commerce encouraged. Such men must either go away altogether or make a Magna Charta of their own, have their own secure refuge and live under their own laws.

This was the first point at issue. It had been provided for in the treaty and if there had been nothing else, it may be that Suraj-ud-Daula could have been kept to this and Calcutta maintained as an island surrounded by land for the second half of the century, as it had been for the first. But there was at issue another point of the greatest consequence. Everyone knew that war was about to break out again with France, and that in fact in Europe it had probably broken out already; that was why there was an armament at Madras which could be dispatched so quickly to Bengal. The council at Madras had agreed to its going, but they wanted it back; it was needed badly in the South. The Deccan was under French influence, there were large French forces at Hyderabad and in war Madras would be threatened. Clive thought like a soldier; his first object must be to settle affairs in Bengal and get back to Madras. And it must be remembered that a European army wasted rapidly away; it would hardly be an army at all in two years. He had no time to lose.

But he could hardly leave Bengal without taking steps to mask or neutralize the French settlement at Chandarnagar, where there were both French soldiers and French-trained Indian sepoys. Suraj-ud-Daula was smarting from a set-back to his pride; he was as likely as not to join with the French as soon as Clive's back was turned. Clive offered the French in Chandarnagar an agreement to keep the peace in Bengal, but they delayed and temporized because they were not authorized to sign. News came at last that war had broken out in Europe; nothing remained but to take Chandarnagar.

It is easy enough, two hundred years later, to cut away the detail and present the situation in this clear light. But men in action are pushed and jostled by events, which hurry past in an eager stream like workers going home from a factory. Not every man can set his course across that compelling stream of day-to-day decisions. Clive could; when he was criticized for making a treaty with Suraj-ud-Daula too soon and in terms too moderate, he wrote of his critics:

'. . . surely those who are of this opinion never knew that a delay of a day or two might have ruined the Company's affairs, by the junction of the French with the Nabob . . . They never considered the situation of affairs on the Coast [of Madras] and the positive orders sent me by the Gentlemen there to return with the major part of the forces. . . .'

The English did not even now feel strong enough to meet the combined forces of the French and Suraj-ud-Daula. They must therefore obtain the latter's consent before they attacked the French. Mr. Watts, and later Mr. Luke Scrafton, civil servants of the Company, were sent to Murshidabad on this delicate and dangerous mission. It was dangerous, for although one day that 'giddy young man' Suraj-ud-Daula would embrace Mr. Watts and present him with a robe of honour, on the next he would swear to behead him and break with the English, only to change his mind within a few hours in an agony of fear. It was delicate, because the object of the mission was contrary to Suraj-ud-Daula's true interests; he was not stupid and he would much prefer, if he must have the English in his dominions to keep the French as a counterpoise. But an invasion was threatened from the direction of Delhi, and:

'Mr. Watts made so artful a use of his fears of the Afghans . . . that partly by these arguments and partly by a handsome present of money to his first secretary, he produced a letter from him to Mr. Watson . . .' which could be construed as a reluctant assent to the attack on Chandarnagar.

Chandarnagar was taken; Clive wrote to congratulate Suraj-ud-Daula on the victory achieved 'by the influence of your favour'. There were, however, other French factories; there were French fugitives from Chandarnagar; an extension of favour was required. Clive wrote to Watts:

'The Bent of our Politicks hitherto has been, by haughty and by submissive letters such as the occasion required, to persuade him to abandon the French to us. We must in pursuit of that system now endeavour to convince him that what we have done is best both for him and for us. . . .'

and in pursuit of that system he added to Suraj-ud-Daula:

'. . . circumstances make it absolutely necessary that your Excellency should deliver up to us the persons and effects of the French at Cossimbazar and their out settlements . . . We shall then be without rivals, and our whole force ready to obey your commands and assist you in punishing all those who dare to molest the peace of your kingdom'.

But Suraj-ud-Daula was far from sure that this was what he wanted. And now he came up against a principle which has usually been perfectly clear to the hereditary nobility of mankind, less obvious to other people. To the English it seems that when they are engaged in a life and death struggle with a continental despot, as for the last five hundred years they have been once a century, they are fighting to make the world a better place. Although other nations who will enjoy that better world may sometimes stay out of the fight, they must not get in the way. If they do come between mighty opposites, they must make up their minds one way or the other; they must be with us or against us. The Danes had to lose their fleet in 1807; Egypt and Iraq more recently had to be allies; there can be no compromise.

This was a principle Suraj-ud-Daula could hardly be expected to understand. He still wanted the French as a counterpoise; he took into his service the refugees from Chandarnagar and formed them into a military company; he wrote offering alliance to Bussy who commanded the French forces in the Deccan. It is true that he wavered about the French alliance as much as he did about the English, but Watts and Scrafton judged that he would waver no more when Clive's back was turned. Clive agreed with them, so did Admiral Watson, and there can be no doubt that their judgment was correct. Watson sent his famous letter telling the Nabob that if he continued to protect the King's enemies — that is the French — 'I will kindle such a flame in your country as all the water of the Ganges shall not be able to extinguish'; a few days later Clive wrote, enumerating the many respects in which Suraj-ud-Daula had failed to display the friendship promised in the Treaty: 'but these were trifles, compared to his open and avowed protection of the King's enemies, of which his letters to Mr. Bussey, wrote but a few days after his entering into solemn treaty with us, inviting him to his country, was a flagrant proof'.

For what followed in the Indian camp, the best evidence is the *Siyar-al-Muntakherin* of Sayyad Ghulam Husain Khan, a Mogul of noble family who for many years had held a place at court. He knows that the English resented Suraj-ud-Daula's intrigues with the French, but thinks Clive had been satisfied on this point. 'But now the dissensions between Suraj-ud-Daula and his two principal Generals rose to so great a height that these two Commanders confederated with . . . other disaffected Grandees; and all these joined together in the scheme of oversetting Suraj-ud-Daula, whose character of ferocity and thoughtlessness kept them in continual alarms and whose fickleness of temper made them tremble.'

It was the confederated grandees, he thinks, who by 'perpetually exciting the English to a rupture with Suraj-ud-Daula' caused the revolution; wherever it originated, the conspiracy came pat to Clive's hand when it was already clear both to him and Watson that there could be no relying on this wretched young man to keep the Treaty. There followed Plassey, surely the most miserable skirmish ever to be called a decisive battle; Clive with eight hundred Europeans and two thousand sepoys faced a force estimated at fifty thousand and far superior to him in artillery; Mir Jafar, the leader of the confederated grandees, confined himself to political warfare — but it was enough. Suraj-ud-Daula fled to his capital, escaped by night with a selection of his favourite jewels and women, was recognized by a private enemy and handed over to the agents of Mir Jafar, who led him back to Murshidabad.

'He was in so wretched a condition that the people of God who saw him in that wretchedness and remembered the delicacy, the glory, and the care and pomp in which he had been bred . . . forgot the ferocity of his temper and the shameful actions of his life and gave themselves up to every sentiment of pity and compassion.'

Suraj-ud-Daula was put down; Mir Jafar was put up. And there was nothing indefinite this time. The treaty stipulated the exact amount that must be paid to the English, in compensation for the losses of the Company and for the losses of the inhabitants of Calcutta, together with fifty lakhs as personal rewards for the army and navy; all French possessions in Bengal were made over to the English, who were also given the right to collect the King's share of the revenue in certain tracts of land. Clive had pursued his way with his usual dogged pertinacity; he had let nothing turn him aside, he had not shrunk from intrigue and deception. He had rid Bengal of the French and for the English had won security to trade. Those had been his two objects, but he had also won much more.

To an Indian brought up in the traditions of Sanskrit and Persian literature, who had never heard of the Greek city states, of Rome and Carthage, of the rights wrested in England from the Kings, to such a man nothing could have been more incomprehensible than the systems of checks to absolute power which in England already existed in various stages of growth, and in America were soon to be set up in all the radiance of conscious intention. To the Indian power was indivisible and lodged in the sovereign, whose will was absolute. But here was a power that could put down one King and enthrone another. It was clear now to every Indian where power lay and it was too late to pretend it lay anywhere else.

The point can best be seen from the angle of the Muslim historian. In his eyes, a recommendation from the English became from Plassey onwards the only sure way to office and it does not need much imagination to see that once the English had recommended a man they would inevitably become involved in the affairs of their nominee. One story is enough to show how this would come about.

In Behar, the deputy Viceroy or Governor was a Hindu, Ram Narain, a shrewd man and careful not to commit himself; the historian tells how, on some previous occasion, when two armies were approaching his capital, hostile to each other and of dubious intentions to himself, he had moved to a position on the flanks of either, opened secret negotiations with both and 'waited to see which of his two wives should first be brought to bed'.

Now, seeing Mir Jafar settled on the throne and moving towards him as though to inquire into his affairs, he arranged at once for a forged document to be presented to him by his secretary at that unwary moment when he was 'duly seasoned with his dose of bang'. Never a fluent reader, Mir Jafar was now particularly disinclined for business, but they were importunate; they pretended to read him the document. It was a guarantee to Ram Narain of life, property and honour; it confirmed him in his office without being called to any account. That of course was not exactly what the secretary read to Mir Jafar and at last in hemp-sodden irritation he agreed that his seal should be affixed. Clive was now asked to add his name; he supposed the document represented Mir Jafar's real intentions and since it was obviously desirable that the officials of the old regime should not be overthrown, tortured and despoiled at every change of

Nawab, he signed too. Mir Jafar could not remember what he had signed and grudgingly accepted the situation. But from now onwards the faith of the English was pledged that Ram Narain should not be called to account. Whether they liked it or not, they were responsible for his administration of Behar.

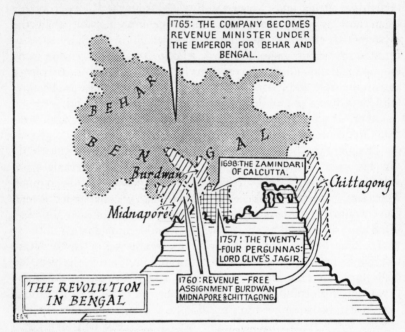

1765: THE COMPANY BECOMES REVENUE MINISTER UNDER THE EMPEROR FOR BEHAR AND BENGAL.

1698: THE ZAMINDARI OF CALCUTTA.

1757: THE TWENTY-FOUR PERGUNNAS: LORD CLIVE'S JAGIR.

1760: REVENUE—FREE ASSIGNMENT BURDWAN MIDNAPORE & CHITTAGONG.

THE REVOLUTION IN BENGAL

Here it will be convenient to set down the steps by which the English acquired Bengal. Calcutta and the villages immediately around it came in 1698 with the grant to Job Charnock of the right to collect the King's share of the revenue and all that went therewith. This was confirmed after Plassey. The Company were supposed to pass on to the Mogul authorities the King's share, keeping of course a commission; they were zamindars, like hundreds of other semi-feudal collectors of revenue. To Calcutta was added after Plassey the district called The Twenty-four Pergunnas, in which the Company were also zamindars, but they paid the King's share — with an ill grace — to Lord Clive. He was an assignee, like one of Akbar's commanders, but in perpetuity, and his interest passed eventually to the Company. The next accession came when Mir Kasim was enthroned in 1760; he rewarded the Company by the assignment, free of revenue, of the provinces of Midnapore, Burdwan and Chittagong. Here they collected the King's share and kept it; for the first ten years, it brought a profit of about half a million pounds a year.

Then in 1765 came a much bigger step. On the Company's behalf, Clive accepted from the Emperor the appointment of Revenue Minister for Bengal, Behar and Orissa. Thus the Company took their place in the line of succession of those representatives of the Emperor whom Akbar and Todar Mal had sent out into the provinces as checks on the Viceroys. It was an arrangement that suited the Emperor, for it was his only hope of getting any revenue, and he had indeed suggested it before. And it must have been more than acceptable to the Viceroy; Mir Kasim had throughout his reign feared that the Company would make themselves Viceroy instead of minister.

These were the first steps towards an Empire; now everything was ready for one of the worst chapters in English history. The English on the spot had, deliberately, and with the aid of force, both overt and diplomatic, of bribery and of intrigue, set out to attain two limited objects, to drive out the French and to make their own trade secure. They had been led further than they meant to go; they had wanted power but had not realized that it must bring responsibility. As for the Directors in England, they had been presented with an empire at which they looked with the incredulous elation, shot with sharp twinges of doubt, of a village grocer who has inherited a chain of department stores and is not quite sure whether they will pay him a profit beyond his dreams or drag him down to ruin.

CHAPTER II

ONE OF THE WORST

I F we are to understand what exactly it was that the English did
to the Bengali, it will be as well to shut down the telescope with
which we have been observing the fall of kings, lift into place the
microscope and look at something small and wriggling from a pond,
Mr. William Bolts, one of the worst of the Company's servants. One
of the worst, for he was an unprofitable servant to the Company, nor
can heaven have been pleased with what he did. It is a small drop of
water in which he lives, but to understand it is to understand the
pond.

The Company's cadre in Bengal was short in 1759, what with
fever and the Black Hole and the fighting round Calcutta. A special
entry of ten 'persons well experienced in business' was made accordingly; the ten were appointed direct as factors, skipping the first
grade as writers. William Bolts, the last of these ten on the list,
arrived in Bengal in the summer of 1760. He was not an Englishman
-- one is relieved to note — being the son of Dutch parents and born
in Holland, but he had come to England when he was fourteen and
had been an apprentice in London and later with an English firm in
Lisbon. He was twenty-five when he came to India, having been for
ten years 'regularly bred to business, almost from his childhood, in a
merchant's accompting-house'.

He set to work at once to learn Bengali, thus by un-English industry
gaining a start over his contemporaries, who had at the best a smattering of Persian or Hindustani. When to this was added his commercial
experience, it is not surprising that he was soon able to enter into
partnership with two members of Council, Mr. John Johnstone and
Mr. William Hay. It was a partnership covering all forms of private
trade. This at the time was authorized within India, between Indian
ports, and from India to the Far East. The firm traded in woollen
goods, saltpetre, opium, cotton and diamonds, and were soon in a
position to add a subsidiary investment, for they were bidding in
1761 for the right to collect the King's share of revenue from certain
lands and also undertaking the tenancy of certain other land which
they were to clear and cultivate, paying a nominal rent for seven years.

The first charge against them is that they gave advances for crops, usually of indigo, opium, sugar or jute. This sounds harmless enough but in the months before harvest the peasant needs cash; if he sells his crop before it is cut, he sells to meet his need and to a man far better placed than he to judge what future prices are likely to be. He sells low and at a discount; then he will be charged interest, which he will pay in kind. This is a cash crop — it is the rice, the millet and the pulses from which he will keep something back for himself — and when he has handed over the whole crop, there will still be something owed for interest. So he will promise to sell next year's crop and in the spring he will take another advance on worse terms than the first. He will be sucked dry, as a spider sucks a fly; and as the carcase of the fly hangs dry and empty, stirring a little in the wind, with so little life he will move listlessly about the fields, his bones barely covered by dry and withered skin.

They gave advances to the peasants; they bought from the merchants at low rates, terrifying them by threats of force; they sold at high prices to the village shopkeepers, and they paid no duty on their goods. Those are the four charges and all seem to be true.

The last needs some explanation. Customs had been a grievance of the English from their first coming. A shipping of indigo, saltpetre or vermilion, such as Peter Mundy had brought down from Agra to Surat in 1632, might pay blackmail, tribute, or customs to a hundred petty chiefs on the way. It might become so ruinously expensive that the trade was not worth while. Such a cargo was not in competition with the grain, salt, cooking-vessels and the like which the native merchants might be carrying fifty or a hundred miles; it was a trade which did benefit the grower of indigo; it was fair enough that it should be exempt. To get a firman granting this exemption had been an object of all the early embassies; it had been achieved in the end by Surman's mission of 1715.

But there was then no question of internal trade, of buying up a crop in one province and selling it in another, of trade in such articles as salt, betel-nut and opium which were consumed in the country. No such trade had been carried on in 1715 by the Company or its servants; no one then could claim that it should be free of duty. This, however, was the claim now noisily made by such as Bolts. Not only the Company, not only the Company's servants, but the servants of the Company's servants, anyone who could show a pass with an Englishman's signature, could buy, sell or transport without duty, whatever he liked, wherever he liked. No one who paid duty could compete with such traders as these; not only must the Nawab's

revenues dwindle at once but the native merchants who were his subjects could no longer grow rich. It was no use the Nawab putting
an impost on something else to compensate for the loss of customs,
because none of his merchants had any money; nor were his cultivators
any better off, for now they were squeezed by the English traders and
their agents as well as by the Viceroy's collectors of tribute.

Mir Kasim saw it very clearly; he was a man of ability, energetic and
outspoken. He had been made Nawab of Bengal by the English as
Mir Jafar sank lower and lower in drug-soaked indolence. This is
what Mir Kasim wrote to the Governor and his Council in May
1762:

'And this is the way your Gentlemen behave; they make a disturbance all over my country, plunder the people, injure and disgrace
my servants . . . Setting up the colours and showing the passes of
the Company, they use their utmost endeavours to oppress the
peasants, merchants, and other people of the country . . . In every
village and in every factory they buy and sell salt, betel-nut, rice,
straw, bamboos, fish, gunnies, ginger, sugar, tobacco, opium, and
many other things . . . They forcibly take away the goods and com-
modities of the peasants, merchants, etc., for a fourth part of their
value, and by ways of violence and oppressions they oblige the
peasants to give five rupees for goods which are worth but one rupee;
and for the sake of five rupees they bind and disgrace a man who pays
a hundred rupees in land-tax; and they allow not any authority to my
servants. . . .'

This is Mir Kasim; his evidence is supported by the better men
in the Company's service. Mr. Gray, Chief at Malda, writes that
'the country is torn to pieces by a set of rascals . . . who in Calcutta
walk about in rags but when they are sent out as agents lord it over
the country, imprisoning the peasants and merchants and talking in
the most insolent domineering manner to the police and revenue
officers'. Warren Hastings, still a junior, writes to Vansittart in the
same strain of oppressions committed 'under the sanction of the
English name'. 'This evil, I am well assured, is not confined to our
dependents alone but is practised all over the country by people
falsely assuming the habit of our sepoys or calling themselves our
agents.' He is probably right; for one act of oppression the English
knew of, there would be ten done in their name of which they never
heard. But there was plenty that they knew about.

In his first attempts to fight these evils Mir Kasim can only be
admired. He seems to have instructed his governors to prohibit any

trade with the English or their agents that was based on advances; to cash transactions there was no objection and indeed over these his officers would help. Hear now the indignant voice of Mr. Bolts and his partners, addressing the governor of Purnea:

'Our agent Ram Charan Das . . . meets with obstruction from you in whatever business he undertakes; moreover, you have published a prohibition that whoever shall have any dealing with the English, you will seize his house and lay a fine upon him . . . the Royal Firman, which the English nation is possessed of, is violated by this proceeding; but the English will by no means suffer with patience their Firman to be broke through. . . .'

The governor, in a courteous reply, explained that he was acting in accordance with Mir Kasim's orders; eventually, the whole correspondence came before the Governor and Council in Calcutta. Messrs. Hay and Johnstone as Members of Council do not seem to have been at all embarrassed; they took full responsibility with Bolts for the letter to the Mogul governor and retaliated with a fierce attack on Vansittart, the Governor of Fort William.

Vansittart was disliked in the first place because he was a Madras civilian. He had been brought in over the heads of the Bengal Council on Clive's recommendation as an honest man; the implication that there was no honest man in Bengal of the right seniority seems to have been justified. And he was disliked too, just because he was honest, within commercial limits, and did seek justice. He had, when this case came before the Council, recently been to visit the Nawab, and had negotiated an agreement about trade. The right to external trade free of duty was confirmed, but on internal trade, whether the merchant was English or Indian, there was laid a uniform duty of nine per cent, while English traders were forbidden to give advances and were made answerable to the Nawab's officers. This was a fair settlement; but in Council the Governor had only a casting vote, and there was no one but Warren Hastings to support him. His agreement was denounced; to be fair to Indians was in the eyes of the majority to be prejudiced against the English. The word went round that Vansittart was weak; he favoured the Nabob. The behaviour of Messrs. Johnstone, Hay and Bolts was upheld by a resolution of Council and it was many months before the orders of the Directors reached Bengal and reversed the decision of Council.

Since the English would not pay duty, Mir Kasim's next step was to restore the balance by freeing Indians as well. All trade became free; all customs were abolished. He lost revenue, but his merchants could at least now compete with the English and store up some eggs in the nests he eyed so jealously. But this was as shocking an infringement of the rights of Englishmen as the other. Vansittart and Hastings alone were of the opinion that:

'The Nawab has granted a boon to his subjects and there are no grounds for demanding that a sovereign prince should withdraw such a boon or for threatening him with war in the event of refusal.'

It was not an argument that appealed to Messrs. Hay and Johnstone, and they dispatched Mr. Amyatt to visit Mir Kasim and compel him to tax his subjects for the benefit of foreign trade. And at this Mir Kasim lost all patience and in something of Macbeth's last mood began to wade deep in blood. Mr. Amyatt was assassinated; Ram Narain, the former governor of Behar who had relied on Clive's guarantee, was tied to a stone and thrown in the Ganges; the grandees who had helped to overthrow Suraj-ud-Daula were executed, and at least one hundred and fifty English merchants and soldiers, unarmed prisoners at Patna, were slaughtered in cold blood.

'Those unfortunate men,' writes the author of the *Siyar-al-Muntakherin*, 'without losing courage, marched up to their murderers and with empty bottles and stones and brickbats, fought them to the last man until they were all killed.' It is said of Lushington, a survivor from the Black Hole, that although wounded in the first discharge of muskets he ran at the man who had shot him, wrenched the sabre from his hands and cut him down. When scavengers came next day to clear away the bodies, they found Gulston 'still breathing and in spirits and they talked of saving him; but the young man having given them much abusive language and threatened them with a severe revenge, they threw him in the pit and buried him with the rest'.

It is time to bend the eyes once more to the murky progress of Bolts. Exonerated by the Council, he was reprimanded by the Directors for his insolent letter; we next hear of him making a fraudulent attempt to avoid signing his covenant. Clive had brought back, on his third journey to India in 1765, strict orders that all the Company's servants were to sign covenants undertaking not to receive valuable presents from natives of India. This was one of the first; the last such covenant was signed in 1939. But it was, surely, with a good deal less than his usual astuteness that Bolts handed in a covenant on which his signature had been forged by someone else. Presumably his intention was that it should not be binding; but as it was only by exposing himself to a charge of forgery that he could make such a plea, it is difficult to see what use it could be to him.

Apparently he realized this; at any rate, he tried to get the document back. But the Assistant Secretary to the Board, Baber, was incorruptible and would not hand it over.

This was in 1766. In the same year, Bolts was examined by the Board about a quarrel with his senior, Marriott, the Chief at Benares. Marriott had taken the contract for the Mint at Benares. This was against the Company's orders forbidding their employees to take any post under a country government and he had made the offence more heinous by making too much profit. Bolts asked for a share; Marriott would see him further; Bolts reported his senior to the Council, and the whole affair branched off into a labyrinth of charges and counter-charges. The chief thing against Bolts was that he had shown disrespect to his Chief in arresting a merchant known as Sadallo. After a prolonged inquiry, the Council recorded a finding that Marriott had done wrong but should be excused on account of his good character, while Bolts was in several ways highly deserving of censure, a view in which the Directors concurred.

But soon after the quarrel, and before the Council's finding on that head, Bolts had been recalled from Benares, where Sage, his junior on the list, was appointed Chief. This began a new chain of events. Bolts came to Calcutta, obediently enough, early in 1766, some four months after the order for his transfer, because he had to give evidence in the dispute with Marriott. But as soon as his evidence was finished, he asked for leave to return to Benares, to join his family and to wind up his affairs. This was one of the indirect evils of private trade; a man always needed a few months to call in his agents and collect his debts; he always fought against his transfer. Bolts was given till the end of June, by which date he must positively report for duty in Calcutta. But at the end of July, he was still in Benares; he was still there in August, still making excuses, and the Council say, with some irritation, that they are 'well assured that instead of making it his business to settle his affairs, he has entered into new concerns . . .' He is suspended from the service with effect from August 28th, but if he is in Calcutta by October the 10th, his suspension will be taken off. And the Resident, Sage, is to send him off by force if he does not leave by October 1st.

On August 26th, however, Mr. Bolts is writing virtuously to report that Sage has eloped with Mrs. Bolts, making no arrangements at all for the care of the Company's money. Of this, Bolts has taken charge and dispatched it for safety to the Chief at Patna. Sage, being asked for his explanation in writing, replies that he had left Benares for a few days only, as he had to attend a court-martial at Patna; he denies absolutely the charge of eloping with Mrs. Bolts, and he is thankful the Company's affairs have suffered no loss through the officiousness of Bolts.

He would be a bold man who would attempt to pronounce with certainty on a matrimonial dispute two centuries old and the law of England requires strong evidence to prove that a man has winked at his wife's plurality. But the letter Anne Bolts wrote to her husband, asking for his forgiveness, is a very odd document. She makes every point against Sage which Bolts could have wished; she is afraid that to counter Sage's tale her husband will have to produce to the Board 'this letter of mine'. She was quite right; he sent it straight to them; but it does not sound a very feminine thought.

But let us have no more of Bolts. He left the Company's service after five years and in the end he and the £90,000 he had made were forcibly shipped to England, where he made the retirement of Verelst miserable by vexatious law suits. He was not a nice man and he has served his purpose. There are, however, still aspects of the evil done in Bengal in those first years after Plassey which hardly appear in his career. One is touched on in the matter of the covenant. Clive, as everyone knows, had been astonished at his own moderation in taking so little when he put Mir Jafar in Suraj-ud-Daula's place; it is possible to share his surprise when we compare his acts and their reward with those of Johnstone, Bolts's partner; he received presents for himself and his brother — a private trader — equivalent to £28,000 on the peaceful accession of Najm-ud-Daula, the son of the last Nawab. And when Mir Kasim's reign ended in the carnage of Patna and Buxar and the pathetic figure of Mir Jafar was brought out, shaken, dusted, and a second time enthroned, presents were promised amounting to £300,000 to the Company, £530,000 to the gentlemen of the Council, and £250,000 to the army and navy.

In the eight years that followed Plassey, there were four enthronements of Nawabs, each accompanied by presents. It would be difficult to be precise about the income of the last Nawabs of Bengal, but when the Company came to collect the revenue, they found that in the first five years, from 1765 to 1770, the sum available, after necessary payments had been made, was never more than two and a half million pounds in a year. As for the stored-up riches of the province, there can be no doubt they were greatly exaggerated, and there was certainly no such fund as could stand presents of over a million pounds to the Company every two years.

Presents on this scale stopped when Clive came back to India in 1765. But there continued for some years an even worse drain. One of the Company's greatest difficulties had always been the argument that they were impoverishing England by draining the country of bullion. They had to export silver to pay for the goods they brought back from the East, and permission to export was given as grudgingly as today for dollars. But when in 1765 they began to collect the revenues of Bengal and Behar, they found a fund of silver to their hands. With this not only could they pay for the annual investment — the purchase of goods in India for England — but they could export silver to the East for the investment in China and Japan. Verelst, who was governor for three years from 1767 to 1769, says that in the year 1771 the purchases of the Company amounted to £768,500, 'wholly purchased with the revenue of the country and without importing a single ounce of silver', while over the five years 1765-70, exports of silver to China were £1,284,000. From a total revenue of less than two and a half million pounds, Bengal was paying every year three-quarters of a million for goods sent to England and a quarter of a million for purchases in China. The remaining sum, of between a million and a million and a half, was spent on the civil and military establishments of the Company, the military taking about two-thirds.

A man who has lived in India becomes suspicious of evidence, particularly if he has been a district officer in the last thirty years. He knows the telegram to a member of the Legislative Assembly, cataloguing atrocities and the mounting list of slain. He has hurried to the village of the outrage, expecting — in his early days — to see the mud walls standing bare, each hut a ruined cell, the thatch burned to black feathery ash, the streets deserted, here and there a single contorted corpse. And he has found the village peaceful beneath the flat lines of blue evening smoke, the women busy with the evening cooking, the cattle coming back from the grazing-grounds in a haze of dust, the hubble-bubble gurgling placidly on the platform beneath the *pipal* tree. All the same, something has happened; the village has not been burned, someone is left alive, but he knows that some ancient right has been violated, someone is sullen and unhappy, some heart is fierce with anger.

If it was difficult to be sure what had happened even when one could go to the place, it is impossible to be dogmatic when peering through the dust of two centuries. One may doubt whether things were as bad as Macaulay thought but no one can study the evidence and deny that there were many and grievous wrongs. Fortunes were made by oppressive trade and sent home to England; corrupt and exorbitant presents drained the treasury; there was a drain of silver to China and Japan. The author of the *Siyar-al-Muntakherin* writes:

'Money had become scarce in Bengal; whether this was owing to the oppressions and exactions committed by the rulers, . . . to the vast exportations of coin which is carried every year to the country of England, it being common to see every year five or six Englishmen or even more who repair to their homes with large fortunes . . . Nor is the cheapness of grain to impose on the imagination. It arises from nothing else but the . . . non-existence of that famous Hindian cavalry which used to fill up the plains of Bengal and Behar. . . .'

And he writes again of the English:

'. . . They join the most resolute courage to the most cautious prudence, nor have they their equals in the art of ranging themselves in battle and fighting in order. If to so many military qualifications, they knew how to join the arts of government; if they . . . exerted as much ingenuity and solicitude in relieving and easing the people of God as they do in their military affairs, no nation in the world would be preferable to them or prove worthier of command. But such is . . . their apathy and indifference . . . that the people under their dominion groan everywhere and are reduced to poverty and distress. . . .'

Nor was it mere oratory when Burke cried out in the Commons against the servants of the Company:

'. . . animated with all the avarice of age and all the impetuosity of youth, they roll in one after another; wave after wave; and there is nothing before the eyes of the native but an endless hopeless prospect of new flights of birds of prey and passage, with appetites continually renewing for a food that is continually wasting. . . .'

There were many wrongs. But we are judging by high standards. These men were conquistadors; Genghiz Khan and Tamerlane, Cortes and Pisarro, would have joined Clive in opening their eyes at his moderation. It is hardly to be wondered at that merchants suddenly entrusted with an empire should have enriched themselves; it is comforting that though they displayed avarice, ignorance and indifference, they are not charged with deliberate cruelty or with malice. What is surprising is that along with such men as Johnstone, Hay and Bolts there should so soon have been such men as Vansittart and Hastings, Verelst, Shore, Grant and Duncan.

It was an age when in England, boroughs, votes and places were looked on as property, when political society was by nineteenth century standards corrupt. But in the short space of the twenty years after the Revolution of 1758 there developed in Bengal a body of true public servants, men who in ability, industry and sense of duty were ahead of those in Whitehall and who exercised from the earliest age a responsibility that never would and never could fall to any professional public servant in England. It is pleasing to turn from one of the worst to some of the best and to observe that from the start there was someone trying to clean the stables.

CHAPTER III

SOME OF THE BEST

I. VANSITTART

THEY came out young. Henry Vansittart was only thirteen when his father discovered that he was already a member of the Medmenham fraternity, the Hellfire Club, and shipped him off to reform or be rid of him. Perhaps there has been some mistake about the date of his birth; he had already been both at Reading Grammar School and Winchester and was a fair scholar, so that he had had to pack a lot into thirteen years. But sixteen was common. They were boys by our ideas when they came out as writers in the Honourable East India Company's Service and first wrote H.E.I.C.S. after their names. They were boys who had said goodbye to their parents, for five or ten years at the least, perhaps for much longer, perhaps for ever. Their chances of seeing home again were not so good as those of a young man leaving for the trenches in the First World War.

It was a long voyage. William Hickey took eighteen months when he came out with the lovely Charlotte, but that was in time of war and he had exceptionally bad luck; six months was more usual, but even six months is a long time at sixteen. John Shore, a serious young man of seventeen, travelled with 'a disorderly set of Cadets and Writers, about a dozen in number', and in his first letter to his mother describes how at first they 'used the great cabin promiscuously; but finding the Cadets were troublesome and quarrelsome we *brought a Bill into the House* for their ejectment'. He writes of the boon of privacy; an officer of the ship lent him a cabin in which he could sometimes be alone.

When at last they saw the surf of Madras and heard the gulls, it must have seemed to each that he had been a lifetime in that swaying, creaking wooden world, a small familiar world where he saw only the faces of his messmates and the officers and sailors of the ship. To all, the adventure of going through the surf in a catamaran or a masoola boat must have been exciting, for it really was dangerous and looked far worse; hardly any Englishman in the eighteenth century could swim. But once past the surf there came the beginning of a new life on shore and that was another affair, a question of temperament. To one it was the joyous prelude to success, to be faced with high hopes and keen spirits; to another, perhaps, a matter of shrinking apprehension, of distaste at the thought of new faces and a new life.

There was not much of interest in the work at first; the young man was a writer; he copied letters; when a ship was in, he checked cargoes. There would be perhaps many hours when he lay on the string cot in a corner of the bare high-ceilinged room, watching with aching eyes and a lonely heart the little gekko lizard with his round prehensile toes stalk a fly along the whitewashed ceiling. The relentless empty hours of the Indian afternoon would be over at last and he would go out in the warm of the evening to take the air, stale as though from a dying furnace, perhaps to wonder how his life had fallen into such arid days, into ways so pointless and idle. But perhaps in every dozen not more than one or two would think such thoughts. Perhaps one more would have the resolution to spend his leisure toiling over Persian texts. And eight or nine perhaps would sleep sound and pass their lives without a backward look.

But responsibility would come soon. Hastings at twenty was organizing a sub-factory for collecting and winding raw silk; at twenty-five he was conducting negotiations between the Nawab and Governor Roger Drake of shameful memory; at twenty-seven, he was Resident at Mir Jafar's Court, perhaps the second post in Bengal. To Shore's generation responsibility came earlier still. And looked at from the observatory of history, it was a staggering responsibility.

They were faced with a complex civilization, with thirty million or so of subtle and intelligent people, professing one or the other of two ancient religions whose sacred books the English could not read. Their law was strange to the English and in practice was seldom observed; their institutions were overlaid and obscured by the dust of invading cavalry and the mould of despotism in decay. To this vast, this almost infinite, mass of incomprehensible material a few of the English from the start bent themselves laboriously and set about the task of understanding, straightening and controlling — a task that seems as hopeless and unending as any devised by witch for the humiliation of transformed princess.

I have mentioned six names, Vansittart, Verelst, Hastings, Shore, Grant and Duncan. Many more could be added — Scrafton, Becher, Baber, Anderson, Croftes and Bogle; but these are enough, so long as it is remembered that these men of courage, industry and good conscience must be seen against a background of Messrs. Johnstone, Hay and Bolts.

Vansittart is usually described in the history books as a weak well-meaning man, a judgment that seems not only crude but untrue. Freed from the influence of his friends at Medmenham, he worked hard as a junior writer in Madras and acquired a good knowledge of Persian — though Raymond adds that no Indian could understand him when he spoke it. He worked hard and the going was good; after five years, at the reputed age of eighteen, he went home with a fortune. It was soon spent in gambling and riotous living, and he was back in Madras, much employed in delicate diplomatic missions to the French. He had become a close friend of Clive's and it was on Clive's recommendation that he was appointed President of the Council and Governor of Fort William, where he arrived in July 1760. He had fourteen years' service and was twenty-eight. It was not, so far, a colourless career.

In Bengal, he found the treasury empty, the income insufficient to meet the expenses and the troops unpaid; in short, Clive's rapid organization of the affairs of the province was not working. Vansittart came quickly to the conclusion that nothing would go right so long as Mir Jafar was on the throne. In this view he agreed with Holwell, who had been acting as governor, but ignored the advice of Verelst, who maintained that though Mir Jafar was idle, treacherous and drunken, he had been all that when he was enthroned by the English, who had made their bed and must lie on it. In October, within three months of his arrival, Vansittart went with a body of troops to see Mir Jafar at Murshidabad. His object was persuasion; the Nawab was to be induced to hand over power at once to Mir Kasim, his son-in-law, whom he would also nominate his successor. But he would not be induced. When this became clear to Vansittart he surrounded the palace with troops, deposed Mir Jafar and put Mir Kasim in his place.

This was not the act of a weak man, but it was an offence against the baron of Plassey, who had taken so much trouble to set Mir Jafar up. It was followed by worse, something which must surely have been the main reason for the dislike and hostility that Clive showed later. Vansittart reversed Clive's policy with regard to Ram Narain the governor of Behar, who had obtained Clive's guarantee by such dubious means. It was just such an act as would be classed as weakness and betrayal. Verelst says of it: 'From that hour, no person of rank would venture to correspond with the English and we no longer had a friend in the country.' Yet in the circumstances in which each man was placed at the time, Clive's support and Vansittart's repudiation seem equally intelligible.

The background to Clive's actions in 1757 and immediately after was a Bengal in which the Nawab had been all-powerful. What was needed was some guarantee against irresponsible tyranny and it was reasonable that the former officers of the state should be protected against their new master. But for Vansittart the whole situation was reversed. For three years no one had known who was ruler. Power lay with the English, but they would not govern. It seemed essential that someone should, and Mir Kasim had been chosen. His hand then must be strengthened and surely he could have only a semblance of power if his officers could defy him on the strength of a perpetual English guarantee. There is reason for believing that at the revolution of 1760 Ram Narain had set on foot trains of action which might lead to his own independence but which could up till the last possible minute be denied. Was he to be guaranteed for ever against all inquiry into such an allegation? And if so, what but chaos could result? Vansittart refused to continue the guarantee and left him to the mercy of Mir Kasim. The Council endorsed his action.

There were twelve members of Council. Council was supreme and the Governor had only a casting vote in the event of a tie. Between meetings, he was the executive officer of the Council but he did everything in their name. We have seen already how Vansittart was humiliated and his policy reversed by Council when he attempted to make a fair settlement of the customs with Mir Kasim. It was not by any means a solitary instance. Everything indeed was against him. Clive thought him weak because of Ram Narain; his colleagues called him weak because he stuck to his opinion that their views were unjust. But Vansittart's policy of supporting the Nawab was the only reasonable alternative to government by the Company, and that was a step for which no one was yet ready.

Everything was against him. The Directors, nine months away, dismissed three of his supporters in the Council and appointed his most bitter opponent, Ellis, to be Chief at Patna, now the nearest station to Mir Kasim's court. Ellis was violent, loud-mouthed and rude, the kind of man who makes himself offensive to his fellow-travellers in a railway carriage, the kind of man that young Indians in our own day too often pictured as the typical Englishman. He insulted and tried to bully Mir Kasim; finally, with no authority, he surprised the Nawab's garrison in Patna and by a *coup de main* took the town, only to lose it after a few hours and eventually to lose his own life in the massacre of Patna. There followed the battle of Buxar and the defeat of Mir Kasim.

Clumsy blustering little Ellis was the occasion only for what was inevitable. The tragedy of fate and character was played out; there was no alternative now but to rule and to this conclusion the Company and Parliament were gradually brought. Vansittart's policy had failed; he retired and became Member of Parliament for Reading. His reputation grew after his return to England, he became a Director of the Company in 1769 and in the same year was appointed one of the three Supervisors who were to reform the whole government in India. The three Supervisors sailed in September; the other two were Luke Scrafton, who had been with Watts at Kasimbazar before Plassey, and Colonel Forde, who had stormed Masulipatam and beaten the Dutch at Biderra. It was to Forde before Biderra that Clive had scribbled: 'Dear Forde, Fight them immediately' and with that had picked up the cards he had laid down and finished his rubber of whist. The three Supervisors sailed from the Cape on December 27th, 1769, and were never seen again.

If he was really only thirty-eight, as he is said to have been, Vansittart's life had been full enough. He had found time, all the same, to publish the inevitable book on Indian affairs and several oriental translations. He had been surely the youngest governor Bengal has ever had; it is true his policy had failed but it had never had a fair chance. One may wonder what would have happened if he had had his way over the customs dues, had been able to over-rule his council and to send Ellis home. He had formed a plan, possibly premature, for restoring Oudh to the direct rule of the Emperor and helping him to recover Delhi, so that there would be not only an English Nawab of Bengal but an English Emperor — and a powerful one. In such matters, he had something of Hastings's vision, but lacking his tenacity he left India too soon, a brilliant disappointed man, but none the less one of the first to be a public servant. He was the first Governor after Clive, the first after that reversal of roles by which the English became the dispensers of favours and the Moguls petitioners. And in that capacity he is by no means a man to be ashamed of; he had courage and ability and he did try to be fair.

Vansittart came of just the kind of upper middle class family who were to supply most of the entrants to the Company's service. His father and grandfather had been directors of the Russia Company; his father was for some time a director of the East India Company. The family supply the *Dictionary of National Biography* with an Admiral, a General, and a First Lord of the Treasury as well as the Governor. Harry Verelst's family were more recently Dutch and no less than six of them are mentioned in the Dictionary as painters of flowers. Willem Verelst, however, the uncle who brought up Harry, had turned from flowers to portraits and at one time had been employed by the East India Company; it was no doubt in connexion with a sitting that he obtained his nephew's nomination.

Verelst arrived in Bengal in 1750, being presumably 16 or 17 years old; his first post of any importance was charge of the factory at Lakhipur, where he arrived in February 1757, immediately after the recapture of Calcutta and the treaty with Suraj-ud-Daula. He was taken prisoner in April and only released after Plassey, a fact which he mentions in a footnote to his book without comment on the way he was treated, simply as an illustration of Suraj-ud-Daula's failure to keep the treaty. By 1760 he was a member of Council and very decided in his views. He believed it was a mistake to elevate Mir Kasim and a worse mistake to abandon the guarantee to Ram Narain. He does not seem to have looked far ahead or had any clear picture of how he thought the Company's policy should develop. He thought that from the moment of his accession Mir Kasim was determined to free himself from the English — and there can be no doubt that this was true from the time when the customs agreement was rejected. On the other hand, Verelst disliked the way the other members of Council conducted their difference with Vansittart; he says 'they urged a measure of national policy with the little peevish petulance of a personal quarrel' — which with them, of course, is just what it was.

But the great thing about Verelst is that he was a district officer before he was a governor, and indeed he may claim to be the first of district officers and the first of revenue officers. When Mir Kasim made a perpetual grant of the three provinces, Burdwan, Midnapore, and Chittagong, it was decided to appoint an Englishman to collect the revenue, and from 1761 to 1765 Verelst was in charge of the province of Chittagong. In 1765 he took charge of Burdwan and in 1766 of Midnapore. He had thus a unique experience of revenue work. He was a good business man; he collected more than had been collected before, but though this was his first object, it is clear that it was by no means all he thought of.

Akbar had known that the first task of any ruler in India was to collect the King's share of the revenue in a way that would combine a steady and dependable flow to the treasury with a steady and dependable peasantry. The Company of course did not know this at first; they were not even clear that they meant to be rulers. But their servants saw it very soon; Verelst understood it perfectly by 1770.

During his first years in Chittagong, it was only in the three provinces or districts with Calcutta and its surroundings that the English collected the King's share. Nor was there much change in 1765 when Clive decided to accept the post of revenue minister to the Emperor. He had no intention yet of really governing or collecting the revenue in the rest of Bengal; what he did was to appoint an Indian Naib Dewan or Deputy Minister on a salary of £90,000 a year to collect and account for the revenue, under the supervision of the Resident at Murshidabad. The administration of justice remained with the Nawab; the English took no responsibility whatever. This was Clive's dual system; he stated it clearly enough and with some complacency, writing to the Directors: 'We may . . . be regarded as the spring which concealed under the shadow of the Nabob's name, secretly gives motion to this vast machine of government without offering violence to the original constitution . . . The Nabob holds in his hands, as he always did, the whole civil administration. . . .'

Verelst signed that letter as well as Clive; he was Clive's right hand man at the time. But he did not stick to the Dual System long after Clive had left him as Governor; he was proud of his three 'provinces', the districts of which he had been himself in charge, and he wanted to extend the benefits they had received to the rest of Bengal and Behar.

'The condition of these provinces,' he wrote, 'formed so striking a contrast to the other parts of Bengal, where the oppression of the ancient government was universally felt, that foreigners as well as natives began earnestly to wish for a more extensive reformation.'

He and his committee therefore undertook in 1769 the 'very arduous task' of extending to the whole of Bengal and Behar the supervision by English officials which had now been tried for eight years in Burdwan, Midnapore and Chittagong. If there is any one point other than Elizabeth's charter to the Company at which the Indian Civil Service may be said to have begun, it is now. The members of the service were to become used to tasks more than human, but perhaps never were men asked to perform such feats as are set out in Verelst's instructions to his supervisors. They were drafted by Becher, but it was Verelst who presided over the Committee and who is responsible.

There was to be a Supervisor to each province or district — thirty-nine altogether. He was in the first place to collect and trace a summary history of the Province, including 'every transaction which . . . has produced any material changes in the affairs of the province'. Next, he was to prepare a rent-roll, with the areas in each district, and 'the method in which they are laid out and appropriated'. 'The next task is to fix the ancient boundaries and divisions . . .' — and so it goes on. All titles to land are to be investigated and the different kinds of land distinguished; the various amounts of revenue and cesses carefully set down, commerce regulated, justice administered. But to us now the most important part of the instructions is the attitude they impress on the Supervisor-to-be:

'Amongst the chief effects which are hoped for from your residence in that province . . . are to convince the Ryot [the peasant] that you will stand between him and the hand of oppression; that you will be his refuge and the redresser of his wrongs; . . . that honest and direct applications to you will never fail producing speedy and equitable decisions; that, after supplying the legal due of government, he may be secure in the enjoyment of the remainder; and finally to teach him a veneration and affection for the humane maxims of our government.'

And later he writes: 'Versed as you are in the language, depend on none where you yourself can possibly hear and determine. Let access to you be easy and be careful of the conduct of your dependents. . . .'

Verelst retired with a fortune that was small for a Nabob and it was soon spent in defending himself against law-suits brought by Bolts. He was forced to pass his last years at Boulogne and died in exile and poverty. His life may perhaps be written one of failure. Certainly, the tasks he so carefully enumerated were more than anyone could carry out at the time and it was many years before even part of what he envisaged was achieved. But by the intention of his instructions let him be judged.

CHAPTER IV

WARREN HASTINGS

WHETHER it was the surf of Madras or the long reaches of the Hooghly that he had to face when he left his ship, the young Writer was greeted at last by an Indian agent, a *banyan*, who undertook to find him servants and a house, to lend him money, to buy him a horse. The agent must have looked at his employer with a speculative eye; if he survived the first two years, he would provide a stipend for life, but if he went to the graveyard within six months — and the chances were that he would — then those over-drawals, those bills for punch, fodder and saddlery, insensibly mount-ing month by month, all were lost. It was perhaps with more dis-cernment than his English messmates that his agent that first morning cast an eye over the slight figure of Hastings. Those grave calcula-tions would not be deceived; already a good agent would know that those who were stout of build and ruddy of hue did not last the longest and perhaps he would detect the glint of an obstinate deter-mination not to die. But he could hardly have guessed that since Akbar no one of this stature had walked the Indian stage.

What Hastings did is written in many books, but the man himself does not easily stand out to the eye as a character. The sturdy violent figure of Clive is familiar; self-centred but unable to see himself, brilliant in sudden danger and adversity, profuse, moody, recklessly generous, unable to endure himself or to subsist in idleness, virile in action, emotionally feminine — he is a man you have met and would know again. Hastings is more elusive, a far subtler character. Perhaps no two men could superficially be less alike than Hastings and Marlborough, the little plain man in a snuff-coloured suit and the bland beautiful milord, darling of the courts and victor of the battle-fields of Europe, a Prince of the Empire, the favourite of Kings, glittering with success. Yet in some of the essentials of character they are alike.

Both men could love. In each a passionate absorption in his work was nourished by a deep, constant and unselfish love for one woman. Each was profoundly reserved to the world yet found complete release in letters to one person; to turn over the pages of Hastings's letters to his wife is to feel even now some shame at one's own indelicacy. Hear him on the poignancy of separation, when his wife was by his arrangement leaving for Europe to improve her health:

'. . . it seems to me the greatest of follies that I should have taken so much trouble to make myself miserable and you unhappy . . . The reflexion often occurred to me that we were wrong, but I instantly repressed it. I urged every thing that could fix the resolution beyond the power of recall and felt a conscious pride in the sacrifice I was making. It is now past. . . .'

And later:

'. . . I taxed myself with indifference to your happiness and my own and was stupefied with astonishment at the labour which I had with so persevering an industry taken to destroy both.'

It was a theme that was to be constant in the history of the English in India, a pain that coloured the most humdrum life. Hastings went on in his first letter after parting:

'I followed your ship with my eyes till I could no longer see it, and I passed a most wretched day with a heart swollen with affliction and a head raging with pain . . . of one thing I am certain that no time nor habits will remove the pressure of your image from my heart nor from my spirits, nor would I remove it if I could, though it prove a perpetual torment to me. . . .'

It is the voice of a man who loves deeply but is utterly alone; there is nothing in these letters of that rare approach to equality in marriage that appears in Marlborough's. Here the finer spirit is the suppliant. None the less, Hastings's love did not distract him but nourished his work as Marlborough's did; and he had two other qualities that are the cornerstone of Marlborough's greatness, an inexhaustible patience and a readiness to accept personal humiliation if by that means he could gain his ends.

As Marlborough watched a French army march out of the hand which he might have clenched upon it if the Dutch deputies had let him — as he sank his feelings and without a sign began again the long sequence of planning and manœuvre that might lead to victory if his allies would permit — so Hastings persevered in the face of a Council of which he was the nominal head, whose members outvoted him on every point, who undid every item of his work which they sufficiently understood, who heaped him with calumny. It was he who 'led and laboriously promoted the current business', combining 'the loose and incongruous opinions of the other members into a form which they might all approve, though foreign from my own'. This he did 'for the sake of despatch, from a conviction that even wrong movements are preferable to inaction, which is the death of public affairs'. One by one his enemies 'sickened died and fled'; he outlived and outstayed them all until power was his once more and he could start to build again. The patience was Marlborough's, the readiness to forgo a present personal triumph, and Marlborough's too was a readiness to use the first tool he picked up without considering whether the handle would come dainty to the fingers. But it is a parallel that could be carried too far.

Hastings was Governor for thirteen years, for eleven of which he was Governor-General, with a supervising authority over Madras and Bombay. For part of that time he was thwarted in everything he did by the majority on the Council, but for the whole of his thirteen years he had great influence, and for the greater part of the time he had control. Industrious, tenacious, quick in decision, rich above all in a sense of the practical — it was by those qualities that he achieved what he did but it was not by those qualities that his name lives, and indeed it is not easy to put his greatness down to any one quality of his varied personality.

He was remembered by Indians because he thought of Indians as human beings, because he usually liked them and treated them always with courtesy. Himself a good orientalist with a considerable knowledge of Persian, he laboured constantly to convince the Directors that the people of India were not savages, that they had laws of their own, that their customs should be respected. He thought of the rulers of India as men like himself who could be trusted if they were properly treated and who could be honestly disliked as equals if they opposed him. In the last part of his reign he was fiercely intolerant of opposition, but that is a quality in a ruler which is not usually resented in India. It is contempt and indifference that breed resentment.

When Lord Moira, later the Marquis of Hastings, was appointed Governor-General of India, Warren Hastings wrote to him:

'Among the natives of India, there are men of as strong intellect, as sound integrity, and as honourable feelings as any of this Kingdom ... by your example make it the fashion among our countrymen to treat them with courtesy and·as participators in the same equal rights of society with themselves. . . .'

And the same spirit is to be found in his views on the religion of the Hindus:

'They are gentle, benevolent, more susceptible of gratitude for kindness shewn them than prompt to vengeance for wrongs sustained,

abhorrent of bloodshed, faithful and affectionate in service and submission to legal authority. They are superstitious, but they do not
think ill of us for not behaving as they do . . . The least therefore that
can be expected of the most liberal and enlightened of all nations, that
which providence has appointed the guardian of their civil rights, is to
protect their persons from wrong and to leave their religious creed to
the Being who has so long endured it and who will in his own time
reform it.'

All this is very different from the picture presented by Macaulay
of the cold hard man swayed only by reasons of state. There is no
need to discuss here that piece of Whig pamphleteering; no one now
regards Macaulay's essay as a true picture. But two episodes must be
mentioned; the execution of Nuncomar and Hastings's treatment of
Chait Singh, the Rajah of Benares. The last was the one fact which
made Pitt change his mind and vote for impeachment, the charge on
which in the end most votes were recorded against acquittal, the
charge on which most modern historians are inclined to convict.

Nuncomar was a man who had been all his life an intriguer, an
arch-suborner of false witnesses; his name is constantly occurring in
the crowded tale of these successive revolutions and always with
discredit. He had long been an enemy; Hastings said afterwards: 'I
was never the personal enemy of any man but Nuncomar, whom from
my soul I detested . . .' And no doubt Nuncomar knew this, for it is
the kind of thing a man does know.

Everyone knows that a time came when Hastings was in a minority
in Council, outvoted daily, faced by Philip Francis, who added personal ambition to a fiercely priggish Whig rancour and who had strong
backing in England. It must have seemed to many in the bazars that
Hastings's days were numbered and it was now that Nuncomar
brought against him grave charges of bribery, which the majority
insisted on treating seriously. No one now doubts that they were false;
the Company's legal advisers in London later pronounced them
so manifestly untrue that they should be disregarded. But at the time
they were, to say the least, awkward. They included one element of
truth, an indiscretion about money, defensible only on the doubtful
ground that it was what everyone else did. This was misrepresented
and made doubly awkward by the majority's frame of mind. 'There
is no form of peculation,' they remarked once in an official minute,
'from which the Honourable Governor-General has thought it
reasonable to abstain.'

Into this atmosphere fell suddenly the news that Nuncomar had been arrested for forgery, committed for trial and sent to gaol. Within three months he had been tried, found guilty and hanged. His guilt is beyond serious dispute, nor does his trial seem to have been unfair. It is the execution that sticks in the gullet.

Mr. Moon has written admirably on the whole affair, pointing out that this sudden appearance of a serious charge is the kind of thing that does happen in India. Not a district officer but can remember some such tale. Someone is known to be an enemy of authority, a master of subtle intrigue. He will call on a new official; he will feel his way, he will try to make friends; he will mean to use the friendship to satisfy that Iago-like itch for power that drives him to scheme the downfall of others. If the new official learns the truth of past machinations and refuses friendship, then Iago will proceed by subtle webs to undo him. He will save up orders and quote phrases out of their context, he will appeal to higher authority against the monstrous tyranny displayed by his oppressor — as Nuncomar did of Hastings.

A shrewd district officer knows how to deal with all this. The technique is very simple; he rests confident in his own integrity; he takes no action; he waits. It is a situation on which he has given his juniors advice. 'Wait for him,' he has said; 'sit up for him in a tree; don't move or you'll frighten him; sooner or later your sights will be on him.'

That is what Hastings did with Nuncomar. Such a man would have in progress a dozen disputes and intrigues in none of which would his conduct bear examination; someone — no doubt a friend of Hastings but Hastings need have said no word to him — someone stirred up the embers of a dying quarrel and brought to light a bond Nuncomar had forged for unlawful gain. He was hanged for forgery according to the law of England, but the bazars of Calcutta — to whom forgery was just as serious as accepting a few ounces of meat beyond the ration — the bazars knew very well that Nuncomar was hanged for telling tales against the Governor-General.

And in the same way the affair of Chait Singh, Rajah of Benares, is hard to understand except in the light of what happens in a district. There is little evidence in the library or the study; it is surmise, but any district officer can guess why Hastings acted in what looks like plain contradiction of all his character and policy. The story is simple. Money was badly needed for a war; Chait Singh, richest of the Company's subjects, was asked for a supplementary subsidy of men and money, something beyond his fixed revenue. He wrote standing on the letter of his agreement — courteously enough by European standards, though with less than the grovelling humility that to a Persian letter-writer in the eighteenth century was common politeness. Hastings went to his capital with a few sepoys, refused to see him, put him under arrest, incidentally provoking a short-lived rising, and eventually deposed him. It looks from the library like a brutal exhibition of despotic power and that is what it is usually judged to be.

But though Hastings was always intolerant of opposition he was usually most scrupulous of existing rights, and it does not seem unreasonable to suppose that here too he was dealing with a familiar situation, and one similar to Nuncomar's. At first there is nothing tangible, only whispers, fragments of conversation reported doubtfully, moves meant to trap the unwary into an act that looks like tyranny. Then there is something open, perhaps a small but deliberate discourtesy; if this is ignored, there will be something worse and then sooner or later more liberties and perhaps in the end riots and bloodshed. If the rebel is spoken to, firmly and politely, as soon as he oversteps the limit, his opposition will fade back into obscurity. It will be there none the less, fed by the memory of rebuke; every chance will be taken, a sly word dropped here, a man sent to make trouble there, a bigot provoked to obstinacy in one village, a landlord encouraged to oppress his tenantry in another. With such a man, a resolute ruler will take the first chance that comes and show no mercy.

It is something more than a guess that Hastings was confronted with some such situation as this. Chait Singh had certainly tried to ingratiate himself with Francis and the majority in Council. When the tide turned, he made his submission and offered amends, but Hastings apparently judged that he did so without sincerity and that he was waiting only for another opportunity. He took his chance therefore and struck.

Even so, even if Hastings knew that Chait Singh was secretly stirring up trouble, his action was one of the most ill-considered of his life. A statesman — and even a district officer, who is a statesman in miniature — must be concerned with how his acts appear to an audience. Hastings of course was unfortunate; his acts fall to be judged by three audiences, the people of Bengal, whom he seldom forgot, his countrymen and contemporaries in England, whom he sometimes ignored, and the blurred critical faces in the vast auditorium which fills as posterity is admitted.

But in spite of that arrogant and over-masterful passage in his life, it is by his moral fervour and his imaginative range that Hastings lives.

It was not that he was always right about administration or that he foresaw the future accurately. It is not surprising that he was sometimes wrong, for to him, more than to most men, the future must have seemed utterly unpredictable. He found, when he came to Bengal, 'a confused heap of undigested materials, as wild as the chaos itself'. A vast empire had come into English hands 'by perilous and wonderful paths', but English power in India seemed to Hastings something alien and exotic, likely to be short-lived. He understood the profound difference between English and Indian institutions and he refused the blunt vigorous assumption that one culture was necessarily and in every way better than the other. Clive had hoped for power without any of the responsibility of government; Hastings was forced to go further; before his arrival as Governor the Company had decided to 'stand forth as Dewan', that is to say, themselves collect the revenue. But the manner of its collection was still undecided, nor was it clear who was to administer justice. It was left to Hastings to reform chaos as he wished and the ideal he had in mind is clear to the view. He would have liked something not far beyond the old dual system; he did not want Englishmen in the districts; he wanted to centralize all English influence in Calcutta and to keep there the persons of all Englishmen but traders.

'There is a fierceness,' he said, 'in the European manners, especially among the lower sort, which is incompatible with the gentle temper of the Bengalee and gives the former such an ascendant as is scarce supportable, even without the additional weight of authority.'

But when he came to Bengal as governor in 1772, already the supervisors to whom Verelst had addressed his instructions were settled in their provinces, or districts as they were to be called later. 'Will you believe,' wrote Hastings, 'that the boys of the service are sovereigns of the country under the unmeaning titles of supervisors, collectors of the revenue, administrators of justice, and rulers, heavy rulers, of the people?' His complaint was that the young man's agent, the banyan, was lord of every supervisorship, and that the name and the arms of England were being used as the instruments of oppression.

The real cure for this was to improve the training and prospects of the supervisors, to help them to gain experience and establish a real control. Verelst had been right when he told his supervisors to find out for themselves how things happened. It was a longer task than he thought; it was to be many years before the English had the information they needed for a fair collection of revenue, but to set about getting it at once was the right thing to do. Hastings preferred instead to recall them to Calcutta, to centralize control there, and to collect the revenue and administer justice through Indians.

He was wrong and he was fighting against the genius of the country. The way India wants to be governed, the way she feels to be naturally right, is not by centralized rules but by personal decisions, on the platform beneath the pipal tree in the village, on the threshing-floor of polished mud, on the balks between the rice-fields. The true master of India will put power in the hands of the chairman of a village committee, supervised by a ruler of two hundred villages, who again is supervised by the district officer, the supervisor of a province.

It was, strangely enough, corruption in England that prevented Hastings from doing the wrong thing. He could not abolish the district officers because to do so would interfere too sharply with the patronage of Leadenhall Street. Their names were changed from supervisors to collectors in 1772; their powers were reduced; they were forced to hand over most of their functions to an Indian deputy who was called a dewan or revenue minister; the number of provinces or districts was reduced from thirty-five to twenty-three; six boards of revenue were appointed to control the district officers; a touring board was instituted. It is a tale of experiment and confusion and to set down every detail of the changes that followed each other so rapidly would make only for bewilderment. It is enough here to say that the district officers survived Hastings's attempts at centralization and a modified form of indirect rule.

But for the moment it is Hastings himself we are concerned with. He was wrong about the administration of the districts and the collection of revenue, nor did he foresee the course of political events. 'I am morally certain,' he wrote in 1779, 'that the resources of this country in the hands of a military people and in the disposition of a consistent and undivided form of Government, are both capable of vast internal improvement and of raising that power which possesses them to the dominion of all India — an event which I may not mention without adding that it is what I never wish to see.' What he did want to see was a British power in Bengal so strong that its influence was felt in every corner of India. Bengal was to be a base from which by a series of treaties and alliances indirect rule through Indian chiefs would be exercised, peace maintained, and a strong moral influence permeate the whole.

The alliance with Oudh was the keystone of his arch; he would gradually have extended this system until it covered India. And Oudh is the perfect example of its weakness. The Kings of Oudh, once they could lean on British strength, had no more fears of insurrection and not much of external attack. They were encouraged in irresponsibility. Hickey tells a story of the King of Oudh entertaining an English officer of rank to whom he showed a new gun, just bought from Manton or Purdey in London. He was proud of the distance to which it would carry a single ball with accuracy, to display which he raised it to his shoulder and fired from the veranda where they stood. 'The officer, observing a man in that direction instantly to fall, exclaimed: "Good God, what have you done? I fear your Highness has shot an unfortunate man." "A man!" exclaimed the King with the utmost coolness, "it is only a washerman!" ' That story — and there are very many of the same kind — is really the condemnation of the indirect system.

That he did not perceive the dangers of supporting Princes in irresponsible rule is one side of a medal of which the other is his trust in Indians and his wish to employ them in the districts, a point in which he was a century and a half before his time. And no one, not even Macaulay, has ventured to impugn his skill as a diplomat. Consider for a moment the skill, the patience and above all the courage, with which this lonely man concluded the Treaty of Salbai.

The Treaty was made when France and Spain were in arms to help the seceding American colonies, when there was a real danger that the French might re-establish themselves in India, when England was alone and hard-pressed. These were considerations that Hastings never forgot. In a world so dangerous, the Governor and Council of Bombay had chosen to embroil themselves in a war with the Marathas on behalf of a pretender to the seat of the Peshwa who had little to be said for him as a man and little support among his own people. Of this war, it is enough to record the variety of opinions held. Hastings considered that, though unjustly and unwisely begun, the war should none the less be brought to a conclusion that would not diminish English credit; Philip Francis, in high moral indignation, wished to repudiate everything the Bombay Council had done; the Directors were piously opposed to all wars of conquest or aggression but reluctant to give up the fruits they yielded; the Bombay Council were obstinately determined to show Bengal that they could get along very well without a Governor-General and win a war on their own.

By the summer of 1780, the contradictions produced by these confused counsels had brought the English name very low. The Bombay army had been surrounded the previous year and forced to surrender, their commanders accepting ignominious peace terms for which they had no authority and which were immediately repudiated by Hastings. The memory of this disaster had not been wholly wiped out by the brilliant march across India on which Hastings had dispatched Colonel Goddard from Bengal; the treasury was low in each of the three Presidencies; the French had a squadron off the East Coast; Hyder Ali from Mysore had attacked the Madras Presidency and was in alliance with the Marathas, the Nizam of Hyderabad was on the point of joining them, and it even seemed as though the five Maratha states would once again act as one great confederacy. Mysore, the Nizam and the Marathas in arms against us — it was a prospect far more serious than any that had threatened the English since the days of Dupleix and Governor Sanderson.

Hastings, his hands at once on the strings of a hundred different sets of diverging circumstance, was faced not only by this impending onslaught of all the most formidable powers in India, not only by the usual dissension in his own Council but also by insubordination in Bombay and Madras. The gentlemen of Madras, who were responsible for turning the Nizam's eyes away from his English allies, actually suspended from duty their agent at the court of Hyderabad for the offence of having 'betrayed the secrets of his trust to the Governor-General and Council of Bengal'. And the attitude of Bombay, though they had been saved only by Goddard's march, was little better. But with coolness and patience Hastings set about his solitary task of gently prising apart from each other the enemies who opposed him. He was successful mainly because each of them felt a confidence in the power of Hastings to turn intention into action, while not one placed a similar reliance on the fidelity of his associates.

Hastings superseded the influence of Madras at Hyderabad and contrived to keep the Nizam neutral while he split the Maratha confederacy and brought its members one by one to terms. The Bhonsla and the Gaekwar of Baroda were first detached by diplomacy, bribery, and the presence in Baroda of Colonel Goddard. Next Scindia was brought in, influenced by Hastings's encouragement of jealous minor chiefs to resist him and by Captain Popham's success in storming by night the impregnable fortress of Gwalior. Scindia not only decided to treat but induced the two remaining Maratha princes, Holkar and the Peshwa, to do the same. The Treaty of Salbai was signed in May 1782; it was based on instructions given to David Anderson in the previous November when Hastings was at Benares in the thick of the Chait Singh affair, faced by a local rising and in danger of his life. At such a moment, he had been able to dictate the terms that were to be made with a combination of enemies still apparently far stronger than the English and at a time when the English wanted peace badly. 'By the influence of his good fortune,' as the Persian would say, but really because of the tenacity and fidelity of Hastings's character, the terms were accepted.

It can hardly be counted against Hastings that, in the eighteenth century, it seemed to him out of the question to transform India into a democracy, or that he failed to see that support of despotic princes would in the end lead to their corruption and moral downfall. It is surely to his credit that he wished to treat Indian princes as human beings. And though he was wrong about the administration of Bengal, he worked patiently and indomitably for the right things. He worked always to instil into the Company's servants habits of industry and a sense of responsibility to the people of India. 'It is on the virtue, not the ability, of their servants that the Company must rely for the permanence of their dominions.' And it is most significant that in his farewell message to the Company's servants he speaks of 'the gentleness and moderation with which they have generally, and almost individually, demeaned themselves towards the native inhabitant'. The final verdict on Warren Hastings must be that of the House of Commons, pronounced in 1813 when he was eighty-one, eighteen years after his formal acquittal of all the charges brought against him. He was called again to give evidence in the place where he had suffered so long and so deeply. When he ended, 'all the members by one simultaneous impulse, rose with their heads uncovered, and stood in silence till I had passed the door of their chamber'.

This was not because he had made the Company the paramount power in India, not even because he had achieved what he did in the teeth of factious opposition, because he had to the full in his own words 'explored the wilds of peril and reproach'. It was not because he had treated the people of India with consideration and endeavoured to make all the servants of the Company do the same. It was, I think, because the House recognized the fervour of his spirit, the flame of purpose that shines in everything he wrote or said, the glow of his indefinable imaginative greatness.

CHAPTER V

SIR JOHN SHORE AND THE LAND REVENUE

1. JOHN SHORE

IT was 1769 when John Shore landed in Bengal after that tedious voyage in which the Writers had found it necessary to eject the Cadets from the cabin. This was the year when Verelst gave the Supervisors of districts their excellent instructions; this year was perhaps the beginning of an end to the confusion and corruption that succeeded Clive's revolution. By the time Shore left India, thirty years later, something like order had been achieved in Bengal. A settlement of the Land Revenue had been made; the district officer was firmly established as the basis of the administration; the civil service of the Honourable East India Company had become a true service, its functions reasonably clear, its branches established, the salaries and prospects of its members settled. Shore's life in India covers that period of settling down; what is more, he was the last Governor-General till John Lawrence to be a covenanted member of the service.

But in spite of his importance to the story, he is not a character to arouse warmth of feeling; there is no strong love or hate, there is no passion in his life. He was fair, he was thorough, he was painstaking, he was temperate, he was honest. Though he is often right where Hastings was wrong, his words do not vibrate with force, he does not live in the imagination as Hastings does. His conscience drove him unremittingly to duties that he found mildly distasteful, in a climate which he regarded as unpleasant but less unhealthy than was generally supposed. He said judiciously of the people of India and of British rule in Bengal:

'Upon the whole, if we should confer happiness upon them, it will be in spite of themselves.' And again he wrote: 'Every hour I stay in this country, my situation becomes more irksome . . . The knowledge, such as it is, which I have acquired of the people, their customs and manners, does not make me like them the better. The disgust may possibly exist without reason and may arise from the languors of my constitution.'

The two strongest feelings of his life were a dutiful affection for his mother and the mild evangelical religion to which as President of the British and Foreign Bible Society he gave the later part of his life. But here too there was no fire in the man:

'The climate of Bengal (ridiculous as the assertion may seem) is not favourable to Religion. It produces a languor, after long residence in India, which renders the faculties of the soul inert — and I have always observed that indifference is a worse foe to Religion than Sin.'

This is honesty. He was always honest with the Company and with himself, and it was not always easy. When he first landed, his salary was ninety-six rupees a year, while he paid one hundred and twenty-five for 'a miserable, close and unwholesome dwelling'. He wrote however:

'Rest assured, my dear Mother, nothing shall allure me to part with my honesty . . . Poor I am and may remain so; but conscious rectitude shall never suffer me to blush at being so.'

His first appointment was as a Writer in the Secret and Political Department, but after a year of this drudgery, he was appointed in 1770, when he was still only nineteen, to be Assistant of the Revenue Council of Bengal, stationed at Murshidabad, the seat of the Nawab and still the nominal capital of the Province. The Chief was idle, the others were usually away on tour, and the burden of the Council's work fell on Shore. He tried revenue suits by his own authority and records how when work was heavy he would sometimes continue in court from breakfast one morning till supper-time the following day. He settled six hundred suits in a year and there were only two appeals from his decisions.

This needs explanation. The Company still held no more important position for Bengal as a whole than Revenue Minister, a post which entitled them to collect the revenue. Collectors of inland revenue in England do not settle disputes between contending parties, but in the East they do, because by accepting the revenue for a plot a collector automatically bestows a title; it is therefore much the most convenient arrangement that he should settle any dispute first. Gradually it comes about that the Collector of Land Revenue spends only a few minutes a week on seeing that collections are coming in to his subordinates, but many hours deciding disputes.

After two years of this kind of life, the great changes of 1772 brought Shore back to Calcutta. This was the year when the Company decided to stand forth as Dewan; no longer would they shelter behind an Indian who as Naib or Deputy Dewan collected the revenue and administered justice. It had been a situation fantastically unreal. An Emperor who dared not go to Delhi had made the Company his revenue minister at the Court of a Viceroy who already drew his breath and his monthly pay at the Company's will — but the Company had till now shrunk from accepting the responsibility of their post. Now they stood forth. Now they acknowledged that they were masters.

The Supervisors were re-named Collectors, only to be recalled from the districts in a few months' time. Hastings feared they would oppress the peasantry; the Directors were apprehensive that their servants would use their power to make money the Directors might have made themselves. Shore found himself Assistant to a new Board of Revenue and in some danger of being involved in the controversy of mighty opposites. For the Council had been reduced in number to five and Philip Francis and his two colleagues had arrived from England, a majority who knew that they were right and that the Governor-General and everyone else in India was wrong.

Nearly a hundred years earlier, Hedges had come to India in just that spirit, and Francis was not to be the last. It looks so easy from a distance; it is simple for a quick mind to decide in Whitehall that in India everyone is second-rate, steeped in luxury and idleness. Not that the recurrent scornful influx of the beautifully tailored has been a bad influence through the centuries; on the contrary, again and again it has forced the man who knows what he is talking about to reconsider his prejudices and defend and adjust them.

This is not the place to recount the controversies of those years. Enough to say that though on revenue matters Hastings knew more than Francis, he was at his weakest in this subject and Francis, briefed by younger men, was sometimes right. It will be seen that however much Shore wished to avoid controversy, he really had no chance. It was in the air; it was the question of the day. No one arranged places at dinner without considering who was a Hastingsite and who a majority man.

And in controversy about revenue, Shore, already an expert, had to be involved. He had to have views, because the English were trying to control a complicated and obsolescent machine which they must try to understand. It is much easier for us today; we are far enough away to see things in perspective and we have the advantage that we know much more than John Shore about the way Akbar ruled.

2. THE REVENUE CONTROVERSY

There were two questions to be answered; if those could be settled, everything else would fall into place. The first, the less important, the one that caused most rancour and discussion, concerned the zamindars. Everyone had different views, the most extreme at one end of the scale being that they were mere officials removable at will by the sovereign. At the other extreme was Francis, who, being unencumbered with information, thought it simple; the zamindars were proprietors. They owned the land just as the landlords did in England.

The truth of course was that the zamindars' rights had originated in several different ways. Some were the descendants of assignees, officials to whom in lieu of a salary the Emperor had given the right to collect and keep the King's share of the harvest. With the decay of the Empire, it cannot have been difficult for an unscrupulous assignee to rivet his hold so firmly that it would descend to his son. There were others to whom the assignment had been made not as salary but as pension; these rewards, known as *jagirs*, would still more easily become hereditary. There were also a few jagirs which were meant to be in perpetuity.

Then there were mere farmers of taxes, contractors who had bought from the Emperor permission to collect the King's share, or who had contracted to collect it in return for a commission. Some of these too had acquired a right of their own and their origin had been forgotten.

One class only really resembled English landlords. They were the descendants of chieftains who before the Moguls came had either been independent or had paid a shadowy allegiance to some greater Chief. They had submitted and paid the Emperor a tribute, perhaps half the share they were computed by the revenue office to collect.

These were the zamindars. But there were lesser zamindars with other names, there were subordinate holders of rights sub-infeudated by the zamindars, and below them too other grades until at last, below layer upon layer of sub-sub-infeudation, lay naked and despoiled the tiller of the soil.

Nor was his case uniform or simple. He and his fellows might be descended from those who once, long ago, constituted the old village brotherhood, each man with a holding he tilled himself, but all joint as shareholders in the waste land, the grazing, the woodland, and certain special rights. That ancient joint-stock brotherhood is still to be found in some parts of India, and where it no longer exists its outline can sometimes still be traced below a palimpsest of royal grants. Emperor or Viceroy would give a concubine's uncle or a favourite cook the right to collect the King's share from the brotherhood, who would gradually become tenants where once they had tilled in their own right.

The brotherhood whose rights had been extinguished thus made an aristocracy among the tenantry; at the other end of the scale was the village that had once been waste land, a sandy strip left desolate by the river's changing course, to which a zamindar had sent men to bring the land into good heart, lending them seed and bullocks and forgiving all rent for the first five years. Here the zamindar's capital, enterprise and energy had re-made the land, and he had a better right to be called the owner than his tenants.

The rights then were not simple. And in practice they were complicated beyond belief because it is seldom that one man holds one right. Here five brothers are joint heirs of the son-in-law of the original assignee, one of them being manager and payer of the tribute. Here seven families, each headed by one of the seven grandsons of one man, hold shares of varying size, because there were three sons and the right to collect rent was first split into three and then — but it is needless to go on. The shares sometimes go into thousands. And tenant rights too are split between families and a tenant's holding is made up from many scattered plots.

Who was the zamindar and who the tenant was not easily to be understood by a young man who had left Westminster or Harrow at sixteen to spend nine months on book-keeping at a commercial academy. But this first question was nothing like so difficult as the second; to decide what were the rights of the zamindars was a matter of historical research, but to find out what the tiller of the soil actually paid as rent was like a criminal investigation to which the answer was guarded by two powerful trade unions.

Akbar and Todar Mal had been at pains to fix a fair King's share and their assessment was still the basis of what the tiller of the soil was supposed to pay, though it had been enhanced again and again. But even in Akbar's day, it must have been easy for whoever collected the King's share to extort more than had been fixed and then take his bill and sit down quickly and write less. The peasant would not tell the truth; he feared the lord who lived in his own district more than the King in Delhi. As central control decayed, this deliberate ignoring of the true rates grew worse and the zamindars became united in a determination not to reveal to the new government how much in fact they collected.

There was one theoretical check, the *qanungo*. The word means 'speaker of the law'; he was originally an official, the King's watchdog on the zamindar. He was there to record the collections and the records were his own property, an arrangement that had perhaps been a useful safeguard in Akbar's day against the power of the zamindar, but which was now a grave obstacle to justice. The post had become hereditary and once that had happened it was inevitable that hereditary record-keepers who owned their own records should become the allies of the zamindars whose excesses they were supposed to check. It was the object of both to keep the government in the dark.

This then was the complex situation with which John Shore and his contemporaries had to deal. It was one which those below the first rank understood better than their seniors on the boards and councils in Calcutta, and far better than the Honourable Court in Leadenhall Street. It was a situation which cried out for understanding and swift action. The districts had been depopulated in the famine of 1770. Shore himself forty years later described that year in verse which does not seem to have exaggerated its horrors:

> In wild confusion, dead and dying lie; —
> Hark to the jackal's yell and vulture's cry,
> The dog's fell howl, as in the glare of day
> They riot unmolested on their prey!

There will be more to say of famines later; for the moment it is enough that various estimates put the losses at between one-third and one-fifth of all the people of Bengal, and that this famine was over long before Leadenhall Street were made aware of it by a falling off in revenue.

But even without the famine, the Directors would have been disappointed. The right to collect the revenue had been put up to auction; speculators had competed with zamindars for their own districts and when the zamindar had bid desperately to keep his land and maintain the glory of his ancestors the speculator scented hidden profit and frantically raised the bid. The revenue was inflated far above a reasonable level and was sharply punctured by the famine. At every council meeting in Calcutta was read over a melancholy list of defaulting revenue contractors, of imprisonments and mounting debts.

3. REPORTS FROM THE DISTRICTS

Shore as Assistant to the Board was at the centre of all this and it must have been he who first read and who presented to the Board the reports that came in from the districts or provinces. They are strangely interesting. In the first place, they all have a ring of honesty. In every case the writer seems to be giving genuine advice, seeking neither direct self-interest nor the favour of the Council. There is shrewdness and ability — that might have been expected — but it is unexpected to find so strong a consciousness of duty to the people governed. It is sometimes expressed in language slightly apologetic, with a suggestion that after all it is good business to feed the goose so that she may lay more eggs, but a sense of that duty is unmistakably there.

They are well-reasoned and carefully worded reports but lengthy; there is no room here to do more than pick a phrase or two, but hear Mr. George Vansittart, lately Chief at Burdwan. He recounts what has been done; the old bad system of passes free of customs signed by an Englishman has been abolished, duty is brought to a low and uniform level, new taxes on the tillers of the soil and 'the exertion of influence' have been prohibited, and all these measures are salutary, but slow in operation. He can think of no quick way of raising the revenue.

'The reduction of the ryots' rents . . . and the letting of the country on fixed and easy leases for life would probably be very useful,' he says wistfully, 'but instead of an immediate increase of the revenue would occasion a considerable reduction.'

George Vansittart was a friend of the author of the *Siyar-al-Muntakherin*, who always speaks of him in terms of great affection. He sounds a gentle and amiable man. Others were ready to state their views more forcibly — Samuel Middleton, for instance. He was brother of Nathaniel, known as 'Memory' Middleton, because at the impeachment of Hastings he was unable to remember anything against his old chief. He wrote of Murshidabad:

'If a remission be now afforded and care taken that this indulgence extend to the poor labourer and do not centre with the under-collectors, I do declare it as my opinion that most salutary effects will be derived therefrom. . . .'

Contractors, he goes on to say, can only fulfil their engagements 'by such an oppression of the ryots as must in the end prove destruction to the Company's revenues . . .' while the zamindar is 'the properest and only person to whom Government can, consistently with the welfare of the country, let the lands . . .', because he alone can be trusted to avoid 'every oppression which, as it will injure the country, must also lead in the end to the detriment of himself and family'.

There is something here to note; the welfare of the country is clearly regarded as a good in itself, though sensibly recognized as something which it is also good business to promote. And 'Government' means the Council in Calcutta; only five years ago, 'the government' meant the Nawab. Already the definite article has dropped; in countries where there is a periodical change of rulers we speak of *the* government, the government of the moment. But in India, from 1774 to 1947 it was Government, a fixed impersonal corporation.

P. R. Dacres too put down the poor returns to over-assessment and the famine; he writes of Jessore district:

'. . . the soil is very unfertile and the ryots from the same cause so very indigent that it is with difficulty that they are able to subsist upon their labour and pay their rents: from hence it is evident that they are taxed beyond what they can afford.'

His remedy is the most sweeping anyone has yet suggested: 'Grant the ryots a total remission of the taxes which have been accumulating on their payments for these last fifteen or twenty years past: let a settlement then be made with the zamindars, fixing the rent to perpetuity, and trust to a sale of their property as a security for their payments. . . .'

G. G. Ducarel, who had been Collector of Purnea, was also of the opinion that a permanent settlement 'upon an equitable valuation' would be most advantageous, but he suggested that while in some areas it should be made with the zamindars, in others it should be made 'with the ryots themselves, if possible upon a fixed and permanent rent'.

Hunt from Patna also thought the revenue too high; W. Harwood of Dinajpur wrote vividly of the oppressions of petty revenue officers, who 'by the artful contrivance of receiving and paying fallacious sums have blended together the different years' accounts and collections and have confused and perplexed the business almost beyond the possibility of remedy. . . .'

N. Bateman of Chittagong tells the same tale and adds the pregnant observation that 'the man who causes those oppressions governs the country with such absolute sway that the injured find it easier to suffer than to complain'.

SIR JOHN SHORE AND THE LAND REVENUE

There is enough here to show that the Company's servants did sometimes think of something besides claret. Shore was all his life at the centre of a society with urgent problems to settle; rightly or wrongly, one way or the other, many of them were settled by the time he left India, but they were not settled quickly. It was in 1789, the year of the taking of the Bastille, the year when, if you care for the butcher's work of cutting up history into sections, you might say the modern world began, that Cornwallis announced the permanent settlement of Bengal and answered the question of who was the zamindar. The influence in London of Francis and of Charles Grant, who had recently retired, played a part in this, but most of the district officers welcomed the settlement; almost to a man they were convinced that a long-term settlement was required. Shore himself believed that a settlement for ten, twenty or thirty years would have given as much confidence as the announcement of permanency and he was probably right as usual. Everyone except Mr. Ducarel was agreed that the settlement should be made with the zamindars, and that being so perhaps it was as well to cut through complexities and turn the zamindars by Act of Parliament into proprietors. At any rate, it was done; that point was settled.

But when Shore left India, the question of how much the tenant paid was still not known with accuracy. It was, however, on the way to being known. In 1774 the Board had reached the conclusion that they would continue the office of qanungo, although they took over his records, for the pleasantly English reasons that it had been instituted by Akbar, that otherwise the officials and their families would lose a hereditary employment, and that it was useful. But ten years later it was not useful and Cornwallis ended it on the ground that the rights of the zamindars were now known and recorded in papers that had now become the property of the government. The *patwari*, the village accountant, who eventually became the backbone of the British system, was still the servant either of the zamindar or of the villagers.

The position of the district officer was now assured. The keynote of the Directors' attitude to their officers in the districts had at first been suspicion, and the Council had not been far behind. The latter had been able, in 1773, to reach the extraordinary conclusion that the provincial council of Chittagong should make its headquarters in Calcutta, all collections being received hundreds of miles from the districts where they fell due. Touring had been forbidden except for specially selected officers in special circumstances, and from 1773 to 1781 there were really no district officers. But in 1781 they were restored, though these new Collectors had very limited powers. It was in 1786, after Pitt's India Bill of 1784, that the district officer really came into his own. The Collector now became responsible for the settlement in his district and for the collections; there was an end of the dewan or Indian deputy to whom each Collector had handed over in 1773.

The new district officer had the power of a magistrate to arrest and imprison, but not to try a criminal. He could settle what was later called a revenue dispute and he sat as a minor judge in civil suits under a European civil judge, but criminal jurisdiction was still in the hands of Mahommedan officials; it was the excellent intention of Parliament to combine European ideas of justice with Indian procedure.

This was one stage in the evolution of the judicial system, of which the details had changed constantly in the previous twenty years. The withdrawals and restorations of power, the new schemes, the returns to old schemes, would make a book in themselves, but when all are forgotten it would be well to remember the words of Mr. Thomas Pattle, writing from Lashkarpur in 1774, on the occasion of powers being withdrawn. He speaks of the 'great relief the country experiences from a regular, impartial and speedy administration of justice'. And he goes on:

'How far my ryots have availed themselves of the opportunity you were pleased to afford them of reaping these advantages the proceedings . . . forwarded monthly . . . will show, and I have every reason to think that they reckon an easy and uninterrupted access to justice as one of the greatest blessings they enjoy.' 'My ryots', he says. And he was speaking for many of his successors when he added that he found his judicial work 'not only by far the most laborious, but the most ungrateful and unsatisfactory part of my duty; ungrateful, because whatever pains I may take, I can seldom reconcile both parties to my award; and unsatisfactory because with the best intention, I am liable to error'. Every judge and magistrate since then has felt something like that. And since it is a dull dead eye that does not kindle as the brain calls up pictures of a man's first district, most would confess an affection similar to that Mr. Pattle admitted 'for the people of this province for whom I shall always feel a degree of partiality, and I trust that there is no impropriety in the avowal'.

4. SOME QUESTIONS ANSWERED

This was the age of the Encyclopaedists, of the American and French Revolutions; half the century had been spent under a Whig administration; Locke was still a prophet. There were many to complain that the system which was developing in India combined executive and judicial powers in one hand. It was the tradition of the country that one man should rule, uniting in himself the supreme power as maker of the law, as judge, tax-collector, soldier and policeman; it was the way India liked to be ruled, but it was repugnant to English ideas, to liberalism and the Whig view of the constitution. For a hundred and sixty years, from 1786 to 1947 liberal principles and the practical needs of administration made an uneasy bargain, sometimes inclining one way, sometimes the other. Already, in the eighteenth century, a distinction was made between frontier districts, often under military Collectors, and the more settled areas. Already in the settled areas there is a judge distinct from the district or revenue officer — a concession to liberalism — but the revenue officer has power of arrest — a concession to convenience which Shore defended:

'It is impossible to draw a distinction between the Revenue and Judicial Departments in such a manner as to prevent their clashing; in this case either the Revenue must suffer or the administration of Justice be suspended. . . .'

That question was answered only for the moment and was to be opened again and again. Another was settled before Shore left India and never became serious again. His salary when he landed was not enough to rent his quarters; inadequate salaries were a tradition dating from Elizabethan days and the Company's old difficulties over silver and foreign exchange. The obvious point that men must be decently paid if they are to be honest was made to the Directors again and again. 'If forbidden to trade, without some reparation for the loss and some assured means of livelihood and even the prospect of a competency, the feeble words of a public edict will not hold them . . .' wrote the Council in 1773, but the same thing had often been said before. Clive had tried to settle the question by founding a corporation with a monopoly of trade in salt and certain other goods, from the profits on which the Company's senior servants would be rewarded; this eminently reasonable plan the Directors rejected, perhaps mainly because it was not put before them with the submissive tact they would have liked.

Pay, like everything else in this period, was the subject of alternate advance and retreat, a confusing record of administrative experiment, a wash of waves crossing and re-crossing. But on the whole, a contemporary of Shore's who was reasonably honest would have had to live in penury and debt in the early years of his service, to be amply recompensed in his later years if he survived. Shore himself in the first five years of his service never earned £500 a year and at the end of ten years he had saved nothing. He was less than thirty years in India, he was Governor-General, he was — as he seldom fails to mention — scrupulously honest; he retired with a modest fortune of £25,000. Many were ruined in their early years by irretrievable debts; some retired with far larger fortunes.

The old idea that trade was the main means of livelihood died slowly. In 1772, inland trade was forbidden to revenue and judicial officers, but even they were permitted to buy goods in Calcutta for sale overseas, and to sell in Calcutta, but nowhere else, the cargoes that came back. The salaries which they might thus supplement were Rs.3000/- a month (or by the reckoning of the day about £3600 a year) for the Chief of one of the six provincial councils, with Rs.600/-, 500/- and 400/- for the members and Rs.100/- a month for the secretary. At the same time, an inspecting officer in the revenue department drew a salary of Rs.1500/- a month, but was not allowed to take his own clerks or servants with him on the touring that was his main occupation.

A few years later it was agreed that revenue officials might receive a commission of 1 per cent on their collections, in addition to salary; in a large district, the Collector drew a salary of Rs.1500/- a month and a commission of Rs.2000/-. This was not ungenerous, but the highest officers at this time were lavishly rewarded. The figures quoted in Parliament by Philip Francis in 1785 were never controverted, and he spoke of the chief of the Salt Board receiving £18,480 in a year, the five other members amounts varying between £13,000 and £6000 each. Members of the Board of Customs and the Board of Revenue were almost as well off. It was thus quite possible to bring home a fortune honestly earned that might be much larger than Shore's; but these very high salaries were reduced in Cornwallis's time.

It does not follow that because salaries were improved most of the Company's servants were yet honest in the sense in which they were to be honest a few years later. The older among them had been brought up under a system by which honesty was made almost impossible — and habits are not changed in a moment; Johnstone, Hay and Bolts died hard. It has also to be remembered that the society from which the servants of the Company came was one in which rotten boroughs were bought and sold and all appointments were by influence, for which consideration was often received. 'For one sinecure place in Bengal, there are ten in England,' Shore wrote, and again: 'People in England disdain patronage but expect their protégés should reap the benefit of it.'

Shore and the younger men of the new kind, men with a sense of responsibility to the people they ruled, would hardly have been human if they had not writhed beneath the sneers flung at the Nabobs by the very people who sent out their younger sons to profit by the corruption they denounced. Jobbery from England went on a long time; not only did politicians and directors nominate men to the service, they took a hand in appointments to actual posts. It was Lord Chancellor Thurlow who nominated Hickey's friend Bob Pott to be the next Resident at Murshidabad; the Prince Regent, none less, wrote to Cornwallis for a post at Benares — and was firmly turned down. A succession of Acts of Parliament put an end to this, and the Act of 1793 laid down that all offices, places and appointments in the civil line under the degree of Councillor should be filled up from the civil servants of the Company, a provision that with modifications continued till the end.

It was a bewildering world in which these new men worked, for while they were trying to understand what it was they had to cope with in India, in England there went on a parallel series of experiments to settle the relation between Parliament and the new Empire in the East. The question was fiercely argued. In the eighteenth century, the House of Commons did not empty when India was mentioned; members crowded in, they stood in hushed expectancy below the bar, they listened for hours on end to the oratory of Burke, to the broadsides of mighty rivals. Pitt stole the best of Fox's India Bill, re-dressed and passed it; North's coalition fell because of India; it was India that put Fox out for life. During the years of Shore's service, no one subject took up more of the time of Parliament than India.

It must have been with anxiety that senior men in the Company's service opened their letters and scanned the gazettes when the mail came up the Hooghly. The three great Acts of 1773, 1784 and 1793 made changes that were vital to them, changing all the conditions of their life and work; there were debates, proposals and abortive bills that promised or threatened changes even more far-reaching. Not till the nineteen-thirties did men again read their mail with that particular interest. But if the interest was partly selfish, the question in dispute was fundamental. Hastings put one side of the case when he described his charge as:

' . . . a dominion held by a delegated and fettered power over a region exceeding the dimensions of the parent state, and removed from it a distance equal in its circuit to two-thirds of the earth's circumference', from which he argued for a greater, an almost total, independence.

Burke put the other view:

'The East India Company,' he said, 'did not seem to be merely a Company formed for the extension of British commerce but in reality a delegation of the whole power and sovereignty of this kingdom sent into the East.'

And the body who delegates power must ultimately control it. Burke on this point and at that time was right and Hastings wrong, and Burke won. Parliament's supremacy was established.

The Acts of England's conscious will were therefore directed to establishing control, but they proceeded step by step, with an English respect for what was working, however imperfectly. Perhaps they were too cautious — and again there is a parallel with the last thirty years of the story. The Act of 1773 at any rate was too English; it did not go far enough. It established a Governor-General, but gave him so shadowy a control over the Governors of Madras and Bombay that he was little more than first among equals; we know from Hastings's bitter experience that the Act did not even give him control over his own council. In England, the Company was compelled to lay before officers of the Crown certain correspondence, but nothing was settled as to how the officers of the Crown should proceed if they disagreed with the Company's policy.

Pitt's Act of 1784, of which the structure was to last fifty years, cleared these opacities to some extent. The Governor-General had now a real control of Madras and Bengal; his councillors were reduced to three covenanted servants of the Company and he was given (two years later) power to override them; in England a Board of Control was set up of six persons answerable to Parliament, two of whom were to be Ministers of the Crown. The Board of Control did not as a rule initiate, but it had access to all the Company's papers and its approval was necessary to all the Company's dispatches. The custom grew up that the Chairman of the Directors first talked things over with the

President of the Board of Control; the Directors then sent an informal draft of their dispatch to the Board and the Board sent back their comments, which were now embodied in a formal draft. To this at last the Board gave formal approval. It was slow and clumsy dyarchy, but it worked; if a real disagreement ever arose, the Board could apply to the Court of King's Bench for a *mandamus* or, in the last resort, pass a new Act; the knowledge of this was usually enough.

Thus by the time Shore leaves India, Parliament is supreme, commerce in the background, livelihood is no longer dependent on the hazardous outcome of each speculative venture but pay is something to be drawn automatically at the end of the month And lesser things, the morning ride, the day in office, the competitive dinner-party, the ball at Government House, all begin to be established. Hours of work grew steadily longer; Shore wrote in 1787:

'I rise early, ride seven to ten miles and breakfast by eight o'clock; after that, business occupies my time until the hour of dinner, which is three. Our meals here are short: and in the evening when the weather permits I walk out. The remaining time between that and ten o'clock, which is my hour of rest, I spend with my friends; as I make it a rule not to attend to business of an evening.'

A reasonable and not an arduous régime; when, only a year later, he writes: 'The life of a man in Bengal who does his duty is really that of a galley-slave', he is thinking less of hours of work than of its conditions, for he goes on: 'he is in constant warfare with innumerable opponents and must submit to the common tax of censure and calumny'. He was always inclined to be conscious of calumny and ingratitude: 'Shall I ever be thanked for what I do?' he wrote in 1789 to Ducarel, the same who had advocated settlement direct with the peasant.

By 1795, however, the pace had grown hotter, and he writes to a friend in England: 'When you were in Bengal, the business was transacted between the hours of nine and two. At present, the interval of occupation in almost every department is between seven and four, and I doubt if there is more regularity in any Government in the world: and I will venture to say there is as little peculation or sinister emoluments.'

It is a temptation to make fun of Sir John Shore but one that ought not to be indulged. He was the first of a new age, born a Victorian long before Victoria. Nor was his life all duty. He was Harrovian enough to play cricket even in Bengal. He used his leisure to translate into English in three manuscript volumes a Persian form of the *Jog Bashust*, a Sanskrit exposition of the doctrines of *Vedanta*. He constantly slipped into his correspondence verse translations from the Arabic or imitations of Horace; his recreations were, in short, those of a scholar of the period. He found time all his life for letters to his friends and when he could forget his conscientiousness must have had many endearing qualities. He speaks of his 'love' for Cornwallis and there is real affection beneath the conventional language of his ode on the death of his cousin, Augustus Clevland, who in early days was perhaps his closest friend.

And since in his own right Clevland is the earliest example of that district officer who comes most near to the sealed pattern laid up in heaven, let us digress and read Bishop Heber's words written of Clevland forty years later. The Bishop is writing of the Sonthals, aboriginal hill tribes of Chota Nagpur:

'A deadly feud existed till within the last forty years between them and the cultivators of the neighbouring lowlands; they being untamed thieves and murderers, continually making forays, and the Mohammedan Zamindars killing them like mad dogs or tigers, whenever they got them within gunshot. An excellent young man of the name of Clevland, Judge and Magistrate of Boglipoor, undertook to remedy this state of things. He rigorously forbade and promptly punished all violence from the Zamindars, who were often the aggressors against the Mountaineers. He got some of these at last to enter his service and took pains to attach them to him and to learn their language. He made shooting-parties into the mountains, treating kindly all whom he could get to approach him; and established regular bazars at the villages nearest to them where he encouraged them to bring down for sale game, millet, wax, hides and honey, all which their hills produce in great abundance. He gave them wheat and barley for seed; he encouraged their cultivation by the assurance they should not be taxed and that nobody but their own Chiefs should be their Zamindars. And to please them still further . . . he raised a corps of Sepoys from among them. . . .'

All this Clevland had done by the time he was twenty-nine. The Governor-General and Council of Bengal raised a monument in honour of his character and for an example to others, recording how he had 'without bloodshed or the terrors of authority' inspired 'the lawless and savage inhabitants' with 'a taste for the arts of civilized life. And attached them to the British Government by a conquest over their minds, the most permanent as the most rational mode of dominion'.

This was the 'blurred inscription' which in Kipling's tale John Chinn the Younger found on the tomb of his ancestors: this was one source at least for the picture of 'Jan Chinn who made the Bhil a man'. On the other side of the tomb, the 'ancient verses, very worn', are quotations from John Shore's monody on Clevland:

> . . . the savage band
> Forsook their Haunts and bowed to his command·
> And where the warrior's arm in vain assail'd,
> His gentler skill o'er brutal force prevail'd . . .
> Now mended morals check the lust for spoil
> And rising Hamlets prove his generous toil . . .

Clevland died in 1784, and the legend inscribed on his monument is legible today. There was in 1947 many an English grave in India at which a lamp was still lighted to quiet the uneasy ghost, but though he was till the last remembered as something very close to a deity, Clevland's monument is no longer 'hung about with wild flowers and nuts, packets of wax and honey, bottles of native spirit and infamous cigars', as Jan Chinn's was. He died, Shore mourned him and turned again to his thankless labours. Clevland, one feels, had not expected thanks and had been loved.

Solemn, conscientious, a little heavy on the bridle-hand, Shore plods through his thirty years at the dogged stone-breaking trot of a battery wheeler. But he must not be mocked because he does stand for something good, for the new service and the end of Johnstone, Hay and Bolts. Hear him as Governor-General:

'When I consider myself the Ruler of twenty-five millions of people, . . . I tremble at the greatness of the charge . . . I consider every native of India, whatever his situation may be, as having a claim upon me; and that I have not a right to dedicate an hour to amusement further than as it is conducive to health and so far to the dispatch of business.' And he concludes:

'I look forward to the time when I must render an account of my commissions as well as omissions.'

He was not thinking of Parliament there. He was a man of faith, and of the faith of the new century. The Elizabethans had cast themselves fearlessly on the bosom of the ocean because they knew themselves in the hands of God; the Victorians — and Shore was essentially a Victorian — with as lively a faith felt they were God's trustees for every corner of the world where they could plant the flag. 'Has not Providence imposed upon you the care of millions?' Shore, as a reasoning being, asked of himself when depressed and ill. Again he writes:

'Our reputation for justice and good faith stands high in India; and if I were disposed to depart from them, I could form alliances that would shake the Maratha Empire to its very foundations. I will rather trust the permanency of our dominion to a perseverance in true principles. . . .'

He made many mistakes but no one could say that he ever departed from that standard. Let him, however, pronounce his own epitaph:

'. . . the Company's affairs in India will never thrive unless there be at the head of it men of ability, integrity and close application. You do not want extraordinary abilities: a sound judgment and application will do all that is required.'

CHAPTER VI

THE WORLD OF WILLIAM HICKEY

I F an Englishman in the reign of Queen Anne had been suddenly and miraculously transported from London to Calcutta, he would have had no real excuse for surprise at what he found. The society he came to would have seemed dull, provincial, pedestrian and behind the times; his fellow-countrymen would have seemed strangely oriental in habits of food, dress and speech, a company of merchants busy as a rule about cotton piece goods and sometimes tiresomely concerned with grievances against the government of the country where they lived. But all this he might have foreseen.

In the later part of the reign of George III, however, the passenger by magic carpet would have been aware of an independence that was more than provincial, of a city with life of its own. He would, it is true, have found Englishmen who were superficially more like himself in their habits than their grandfathers had been to his. Moormen's trousers and bunyan coats, the loose Indian clothes of cotton stuff which had been the usual undress in the seventeenth century, were becoming yearly rarer in Calcutta, though they lingered on in Madras. Clothes indeed followed the London fashions, usually panting some way behind a mode which was interpreted, in the case of men, more garishly than a London tailor would have permitted. Hickey's gay coats caused so much talk when he first went home that he had to discard them all, and it was a tradition that died slowly; even in the last years of Anglo-India an observant eye could detect an additional exuberance in the check tweed, a jauntier angle in the slanting pocket, of the cavalry subaltern on leave from India.

Indian food, too, was much less general; it would appear at the punch-houses and taverns as an alternative to plain roast and boiled, but at a private dinner-party there would be curry only for the eccentric; gone were the days when Peter Mundy had written: 'ordinarily we have dopeage and rice, kedgeree and pickled mangoes'. And the visitor would have been less surprised than we are to find men not always pedantically scrupulous about money, not always fastidiously temperate, men not always chaste and very seldom prudish. That is what he would have expected because men were like that in London too.

But from this similarity he would have found growing a new inde-

151

pendence of outlook, a consciousness that the rulers of this young empire were citizens of a metropolis of their own. We are made aware of the feeling in Warren Hastings's impatience with the hampering fetters of home authority; in the practice (a bad one, which Cornwallis stopped) of residents and secretaries writing privately to directors of the Company and Members of Parliament; in the tone of the district officers' reports, writing of the good of 'their ryots' and referring only in an apologetic after-thought to the interests of the Company. It was there, too, in the life of the capital, in its lavishness, its insolence, its improvident defiance of the climate and of common sense and of the hard economic facts of retirement in England.

No Englishman in the narrower sense can ever quite forget his place in the social structure. The visitor who was aware of this independence of outlook would also observe, and perhaps with some amusement, that in Calcutta social position in Europe was not forgotten but suspended and overlaid by a varnish of official rank through which it still gleamed darkly.

To him it would have seemed that the Company's servants were a very mixed bag. There were cadets of noble families, such as the Honourable Robert Lindsay, son of the Earl of Balcarres, who did extremely well out of various transactions in salt, lime and shipbuilding and crowned his career, when Collector at Sylhet, by regularly remitting the land revenue to headquarters in limestone, the principal article of his private trade. Another was the Honourable Frederick Fitzroy, a younger son of the Earl of Southampton, who came out a Writer at thirteen; Hickey at first supposed him 'what I had been myself in my early days, that is a complete pickle', but eventually records on him the sad verdict 'that there was more of sheer vice than boyish mischief in his pranks'. Since Hickey's boyish mischief included misappropriating cash from his father's office and sleeping with the nurse-maid, it is hard to guess what Fitzroy did.

These aristocrats were the exception, though if you look through the pages of the first civil list you will find a scattering of Honourables and Baronets, about one in every fifty names. They were to be found not only among the gentlemen of the H.E.I.C.S. but in the army and among the judges who came from England to the Supreme Court. Lady Russell, wife of the Sir Henry who was so good a friend to Hickey, was a sister of the Earl of Whitworth; her niece, Rose Aylmer of the poem, was one of the first of those young ladies of fashion who for a hundred and fifty years were to be sent out by their parents to seek the right husband or avoid the wrong one.

But the bulk of the Company's servants were uncompromisingly middle class. There are wide gradations, however, within that company; in the lower reaches, perhaps, was to be classed such a man as Sir George Barlow, at whom Hickey never loses the chance of a gibe. He was:

'the son of a silk mercer in King Street, Covent Garden and nature had certainly intended him for nothing more elevated in society than a measurer of lute-strings from behind a counter . . . His manner in society was cold, distant and formal. I do not believe he had a single friend in the world . . .' He was an able man all the same and honest; it was he, as assistant, who helped to turn Gya into a model district; it was he who drafted the resolutions embodying many of Cornwallis's reforms and he acted as Governor-General for nearly two years, not with much effect and badly hampered by his instructions. All the same, Hickey seems to have been right about his unpopularity. He quarrelled with everyone worth making a friend of.

There were many from Scotland, as mixed as the English. Dundas, for many years President of the Board of Control, was accused on all hands of making posts for his fellow-countrymen and with truth; but his nepotism put India in his debt. The Scots were always to form a core to the service, sons of the manse, younger sons of the big house, sons of doctors or crofters, more industrious than the English, less aloof, hardheaded but emotional, more romantic at heart, but to the Indian indistinguishable.

Of the English in the narrower sense, the most numerous were men of the social position of John Shore, although of him too Hickey remarks that he was 'of low origin', while Wellesley from Olympian heights said the same. Hickey was not to be expected to like Shore, for no two men could be more different, and Hickey seems to have disliked all the new generation of the sober and industrious. But from him the sneer was unwarranted as well as ungracious; the Shores had been small landed gentry for two centuries at least and one had been knighted by Charles I. Public school snobbery as yet was hardly born, and in any case Hickey from Westminster could not have looked down on Shore from Harrow. The objection seems to have been less to origin than to tastes; Hickey loved company and claret and always had the best of both, while Shore did not care much for either; perversely virtuous, obstinately middle-class, he spent his leisure mugging up Persian — and did not even pretend to be idler than he was.

Another who, though indistinguishable to a statistician, is traceable by a snobbish English nose to a slightly more upper middle class is Thomas Lewin, of Madras, the father of Harriet Grote, the biographer and wife of the historian. Hickey would certainly have liked Lewin better than he did Shore. He was appointed a writer in 1770 and retired in 1800 after a dispute with the authorities about the furlough due to him; he was left a substantial income and a house by his father, was a member of the Beefsteak Club and is described as having been a fine musician, playing well on the violin and violoncello, a chess player far above the average, and familiar with some modern languages and with French literature — though not apparently with any Indian tongue. It was he more than anyone else who educated his daughter, a woman of wide intelligence and culture. He sounds a man very different from Foote's Nabob or Jos Sedley; two portraits show him as a handsome diffident youth and in late middle age with the charming mellow smile of a man who has tasted and enjoyed life without excess and looks back on it without regret. He is notable, really, for one fact only; he was the only man who paid for her life a pension to the Princess Talleyrand. Grand, her first husband, sponged on that lovely creature when she became a Princess; Philip Francis, the occasion for her leaving Grand, seems to have felt his obligations discharged when he paid her passage from Calcutta to France; Lewin, whom she met on the voyage, settled on her an annuity which his daughter believed she was still drawing when she received all Europe in her salon at the Congress of Vienna.

The traveller just from London then would look round on a Calcutta of social differences which were not forgotten but ignored. Faced by the gulf in manners and thought that lay between themselves and their Indian subjects, between themselves and the rank and file of the British Regiments, the middle and upper classes in India closed together. Everyone called at Government house, everyone was asked to the Governor's Ball, everyone belonged to the Club; that was to be the rule and already in Hickey's day it was becoming accepted. Mr. Prendergast, for instance, when he refused to give Mr. Paull satisfaction on the ground that he was the son of a tailor, was generally held to be wrong; Mr. Paull, 'no matter in what line of life his father was, had been received and treated everywhere as upon a footing of equality with the rest of the society in Lucknow. . . .'

With this levelling up went a fashionable raffishness that imitated London not quite successfully. A man who in England would have lived soberly and respectably, as a lawyer or civil servant should, acquired in Calcutta the vices of the aristocracy; he learnt to keep a mistress, to give large parties, to sit up with Hickey, 'continuing our orgies until a brilliant sun shone into the room, whereupon we staggered to our palankeens . . .' What gave offence to the visitor from England was not so much that his fellow-mortals should behave like this — he was tolerant enough about Mohawks in Covent Garden — but that the middle classes should. And it would have angered any heart alive to see the extravagance and improvidence of a world in which men got through fortunes as fast as they made them. More Nabobs ended bankrupt at Boulogne than with seats in Parliament.

All this, with a spice of plain envy, colours the pages of Mr. William Mackintosh's travels. He was in India for a few months at about the time when Mrs. Grand was under Philip Francis's protection. He describes a day in the life of a Bengal Nabob:

'About the hour of seven in the morning, his durwan (door-keeper) opens the gate and the viranda (gallery) is free to his circars, peons (footmen) hurcarrahs (messengers or spies), chubdars (a kind of constable), houccaburdars and consumahs (stewards and butlers), writers and solicitors. The head bearer and jemmadar enter the hall and his bedroom at eight o'clock. A lady quits his side and is conducted by a private staircase, or out of the yard. The moment the master throws his legs out of bed, the whole force is waiting to rush into his room, each making three salaams, by bending the body and head very low, and touching the forehead with the inside of the fingers and the floor with the back part. He condescends, perhaps, to nod or cast an eye towards the solicitors of his favour and protection . . .' He is dressed 'without any greater exertion on his own part than if he was a statue'. Tea and toast are taken in the breakfasting parlour; 'while the hairdresser is doing his duty, the gentleman is eating, sipping and smoking in turns'. He talks to his agent and various visitors. 'If any of the solicitors are of eminence, they are honoured with chairs. These ceremonies are continued perhaps till 10 o'clock; when attended by his cavalcade he is conducted to his palanquin, and preceded by eight to twelve chubdars, hurcarrahs and peons . . . they move off at a quick amble.' He dines at two; 'and the moment the glasses are introduced regardless of the company of ladies, the houccaburdars enter, each with a houcca, and presents the tube to his master watching behind and blowing the fire the whole time'. At four, dinner being over, he goes to his bedroom, 'when he is instantly undressed to his shirt . . . and he lies down in his bed where he sleeps until about seven or eight o'clock, when the former ceremony is repeated and clean linen of every kind as in the morning is administered; . . . After tea he puts on a handsome coat, and pays visits of ceremony to the ladies, returns a little before ten o'clock; supper being served at ten. The company keep together till between twelve and one in the morning, preserving great sobriety and decency; and when they depart our hero is conducted to his bedroom, where he finds a female companion to amuse him until the hour of seven or eight the next morning. With no greater exertions than these do the Company's servants amass the most splendid fortunes.'

There is some observation in this, coloured a little by malice; it bears perhaps the same relation to life as a Rowlandson sketch. There is no exaggeration in the number of servants; when a man dined at the house of a friend he took with him two men to wait at table, the hookah-burdar who prepared his hubble-bubble, and all the running retinue — the mace-bearers, the palanquin-bearers, and a light screen of messengers and scouts. Hickey, who at that time was a bachelor, listed sixty-three when he left India — excluding Tippee and Gulab who are described as female servants and provided for more generously than the others. Many households would have employed a hundred.

Certainly, there was no need for anyone of the new ruling caste to do much for himself. But it was not true that two or three hours a day of attention to business were enough to amass the most splendid fortunes and it was definitely misleading to suggest that eight o'clock was a usual time for getting up. Already the morning ride was not unusual; already there were men who worked before breakfast; Shore talks of offices opening at seven.

In the world Hickey knew, it was possible already to distinguish the three main divisions of Anglo-India, the Company's civil servant, the military officer, and the independent merchant whom a later generation was to know as a box-wallah. There was perhaps more intermingling then than later; the civilian became inclined to withdraw from general society in Calcutta as his work grew heavier and as he came to spend an increasing amount of his service in the districts. Also, it became increasingly difficult for a civilian to stay the pace; from now on he has enough to be comfortable but not lavish.

That, however, was not true of everyone. There was no sign of withdrawal about Hickey's friend Bob Pott, the handsome, spoilt young man whose image is flashed so clearly across the centuries. He took to Hickey when he first saw him and won from him a real affection, but he did not always take the trouble to win hearts. He was far from polite to people he did not find amusing, and his impertinence must have made more enemies than his good looks and laughter won him friends. He was the son of rich parents, ship-owners, and had 'uncommon taste in everything to do with houses and grounds, a qualification which cost him dear wherever he went'. He had, for example, spent thirty thousand rupees, then more than three thousand pounds, on improving the house at Burdwan where he knew he was to stay only a few months.

To these gifts he added influence. He had secured through Lord Chancellor Thurlow the nomination to the next vacancy as Resident at Murshidabad, the most coveted appointment in the service. But he could not wait till it fell vacant, and paid Sir John D'Oyly three lakhs of rupees, or about thirty thousand pounds, to retire at once, not to mention a sum of about nine thousand pounds which he gave for 'a parcel of trumpery old furniture . . . the greater part of which he ordered to be thrown away as soon as it became his property'.

He spent a good deal more 'on his palace at Moorshedabad', where some thirty guests sat down daily at two o'clock to a most sumptuous dinner and from which he drove abroad with a party of sixty light horse, 'dressed in rich uniforms and mounted upon beautiful Arabian horses', and where in short 'everything was in a style of princely magnificence'. He is on one occasion described as inspecting some barracks, but there is otherwise no suggestion in all Hickey's memoirs that Bob Pott had any duties to perform. But we, who know Bob Pott and 'his disposition at all times to laugh', may suspect that like one or two of his successors he did a little more work than he pretended. At least he must have understood the language well, for he knew that the beggar to whom he laughingly threw a rupee was not thanking but cursing him with a torrent of gross abuse. Hickey, it will be noted, did not understand this. Hickey was concerned with the English courts of law, which had jurisdiction only in Calcutta and whose proceedings were in English. Neither Jemdanee nor Kiraun, Gulab nor Tippee, taught Hickey so much of the language as the graceless Pott had learnt in court.

Poor Bob Pott lost his lovely Emily, who died of a drink of cold milk-and-water when suffering from prickly heat and whom he buried 'among herds of tigers' at Culpee, and he lost his job because he quarrelled with his head assistant. He was unemployed till the day of his death and he had not saved a guinea but, though he passes out of Hickey's story when he marries the charming and respectable Miss

Cruttenden, one can be sure that he did not starve and never wanted a bottle of claret for a friend. He was the kind of man who is always short of money but always able to spend it.

Pott perhaps is sharp enough contrast to Shore but another figure from that world must stand by his side. She was courted by at least four members of the covenanted service and married a fifth, so she earns a place here in her own right, and apart from that she is a figure that appears again and again in Anglo-India. Kipling knew her; everyone met her somewhere, in Peshawar or Madras, in Lucknow or Delhi. Here is Hickey writing of her eighteenth-century incarnation:

'. . . a fine dashing girl, not by any means a regular beauty but an uncommonly elegant figure and person; remarkably clever and highly intelligent. Her natural flow of spirits frequently led her into extravagances and follies . . . ; instead of seating herself like other women on horseback she rode like a man astride, and would leap over any hedge or ditch that even the most zealous sportsmen were dubious of attempting. She rode several matches and succeeded against the best and most experienced jockeys. She was likewise an excellent shot, rarely missing her bird; understood the present fashionable science of pugilism and would without hesitation knock a man down if he presumed to offer her the slightest insult; in short, she stopped at nothing that met her fancy, executing whatever she attempted with a *naiveté* and ease and elegance that was irresistible.'

This was Miss Emma Wrangham, who kept the gossips busy for ten years at least and enjoyed their malice as much as everything else. Francis, leaving India, mentions four possibles in a letter to a friend, Livius: 'If you have literally married the Wrangham, or if Mackenzie should have married her, or Collings, or Archdekin . . .', he wrote. And her name was coupled with several more in the *Bengal Gazette*, the witty scurrilous paper for which William Hickey's much-imprisoned namesake Augustus Hicky was so often in trouble. Miss Wrangham was a godsend to this paper, in whose columns all the notables of Calcutta appeared by nicknames; she was the Chinsura belle, or Turban Conquest, or Hookah Turban — she must have smoked a hookah for a bet — and she is mentioned with great regularity in such items as:

'Public Notice: Lost on the Course, last Monday evening, Buxey Clumsy's heart, whilst he stood simpering at the footstep of Hookah Turban's carriage. . . .'

Several of her beaux are identifiable under various offensive aliases. Durzee being a tailor, as everyone knows from Rikki-Tikki-Tavi, John Taylor must have been Pigdanny Durgee, who is adjured to:

> Sit cross-legged on thy Board of Trade . . .
> Drive Emma W——m from thy head. . . .

But the poor fellow could not, for in a later number he is credited in an imaginary concert programme with the song: 'That girl runs in my head strangely', while an elderly suitor, with a more offensive implication, sings: ' 'Tis impossible for me, as I hope to be saved, Madam', and the entire company join in: 'Our Emma is a sad slut, nor heeds not what we taught her . . .' Hicky was generous with his scurrilities, for in the same programme the Chief Justice, Sir Elijah Impey, is linked with a contract for a bridge that had just gone to his cousin, and is billed for the song: 'Gold from Law can take the Sting', while Hastings, who appears as Sir F. Wronghead, the Great Mogul, the Grand Turk, and quite simply as the Dictator, is down for such songs as: 'Know then War's my pleasure. . . .'

In the end, Emma Wrangham married John Bristow, a dark horse, unless it is he who occasionally appears among the suitors as 'Pomposo'. It was he who had been sent as Resident to the Court of Oudh by Francis's majority, their object of course being to replace Hastings's nominee Middleton — 'Memory' Middleton, who married the sister of Hickey's friend Morse and held strong views on the settlement. Bristow was an able man, and although Hastings turned him out of Lucknow as soon as he got the chance, he bore no personal malice and Bristow did well. He was re-appointed to Lucknow in 1782, the year of his marriage, but soon came back to Calcutta — perhaps at his wife's wish. He was thirty-two when he married and was able to settle forty thousand pounds on Emma; he was a member of the Board of Trade by the time he was thirty-eight. She continued to be the talk of the town and in the intervals of presenting him with 'four lovely children' was a brilliant success as an amateur actress. They seem to have been very happy and it was all very suitable.

Miss Wrangham, one feels, would have enjoyed the society of Miss Sanderson, her predecessor as reigning belle, who before one Government House ball confided to each of her beaux that she would look with special favour on a man who came to the ball in a livery she had devised. Sixteen of them turned up, each in pea-green 'trimmed with pink silk and chained lace with spangles'. Each had the pleasure of a cotillon, reel or country-dance with Miss Sanderson, and 'we gravely attended her home, marching by the side of her palankeen, regularly marshalled in procession of two and two'. She married Richard Barwell, the Councillor who supported Hastings against Francis and retired with a colossal fortune; but she lived only two years after her marriage.

It was a small world, linked closer by marriage, almost weekly contracted by death, a world in which one of the principal recreations already was gossip about everyone else. If you put on a handsome coat and one evening went visiting at the house of that famous Calcutta figure the Begum Johnson, as like as not you would know everyone there and everything about them. You would certainly know that your hostess was the daughter of a Madras civilian, that she had been twice widowed in four years, had taken as third husband Watts, the diplomatic hero of Clive's revolution, and had been imprisoned by Suraj-ud-Daula when he attacked Calcutta. Her fourth husband had been the Reverend William Johnson, usually referred to in the *Bengal Gazette* as the Reverend Tally-ho — but he would not be mentioned at the Begum's house. He had sailed for England in 1788 'with a comfortable fortune' — 'an event for which no friend of Mrs. Johnson can be sorry'. She was to stay on in Calcutta for twenty-four years, keeping open house every night, a garrulous dark-featured old lady — for both her father and grandfather had married in India and her mother had an ominously Portuguese name. She did not die till the year of her triumph, when her grandson Lord Liverpool became Prime Minister.

You would not meet many Indians at the Begum Johnson's though. There were formal entertainments; Raja Nobkissen gave a dance in commemoration of Miss Wrangham's birthday in 1781 and thanked her as he said goodbye for having 'illuminated his house with her bright appearance'. But there is no trace of informal friendliness or equality. Hastings spoke of Beni Ram Pundit as 'one whom you know I reckon among my first friends', but Hastings was exceptional in every way and even Hastings could not ask the Pundit to dinner. Hickey's 'lovely Jemdanee' used to mingle with the company, but that again was regarded as unusual. The barriers of religious custom were probably stronger then than they were ever to be again; there were as yet no Indians who had accepted European ways. It was defilement for a Hindu to eat with an Englishman or even to touch him, while hardly any Muslim would drink wine in public or take the risk of eating meat which might not have been killed ceremonially by a Muslim. On the English side, there was not, I think, more than a slight consciousness of colour as a bar — and that mainly on the part of the newcomer; the constant use of the word 'black' was not, as a rule, derogatory but followed the model of Hindustani and of Elizabethan English. But it was much less trouble to stick to people of one's own kind and in any case how could you entertain people who would neither eat nor drink nor smoke with you?

A trivial world enough no doubt, perhaps almost as silly and vulgar as Lord Wellesley haughtily pronounced it, and certainly one in which it must have been difficult for a woman to employ herself rationally. There was little or nothing she could do about the house or for her children; for long hours she was forbidden to stir abroad because of the heat; if she had no resources such as translation, sketching or music, she was lost indeed. But while this Calcutta life was something the free merchant or the solicitor such as Hickey seldom left, it was already something to which the soldier and the civilian came back from long spells of loneliness. After three years at Burdwan or Chittagong, a man might well feel inclined for a little silliness and he was surely to be excused if it seemed for the moment that no pleasure in the world compared with sitting down to table with twenty-four of his fellows and the prospect of talk and wine far into the night.

There were others, though, with no recent experience of solitude, who turned in the evening to what Hickey called hard living simply because they had spent a day of uncomfortable steamy heat in exasperating work, much of it conducted in a foreign tongue and based on habits of mind that were elusive and only partly understood. What is more, death was never far away. The funeral bells toll through Hickey's pages as steady as the hours in a cathedral close. And death was utterly unaccountable. No one knew that water had anything to do with cholera or mosquitoes with malaria. Much of the drinking water of Calcutta was drawn from the Lall Diggee, a large open pond in what later became Dalhousie Square, where one day (wrote a correspondent to the *Bengal Gazette*) 'I saw a string of parria dogs without an ounce of hair on some of them and in the last stage of the mange plunge in and refresh themselves very comfortably . . .' The ignorance of the doctors was as ludicrous as tragic. 'After Sir John Royds had laid twelve days suffering under a cruel disorder and wholly insensible, the doctors gave up all hope of saving their patient.' Dr. Hare went so far as to say: 'It is impossible he can survive two hours more,' whereupon all evening parties were cancelled and a Field Officer's party ordered to hold themselves in readiness to attend the funeral. But Sir John disappointed them all. He was 'indebted to claret for his very unexpected recovery; during the last week of the disease they poured down his throat from three to four bottles of that generous beverage every twenty-four hours and with extraordinary effect'.

With doctors like that and death so close, it is not hard to understand that relaxation from the land revenue system of Bengal might often be frivolous. What is surprising is that in that improbable soil there should have flourished such leisure occupations as the concern of Sir William Jones, Halhed, Wilkins and half a dozen others with Sanskrit and Persian, with Hindu chess, music and chronology: that men tormented by heat, mosquitoes, ill-health and the frustration of their daily work, should have laid the foundations of the noble work of scholarship continued in the next century by the Germans.

> So, with the throttling hands of death at strife,
> Ground they at grammar;
> Still, through the rattle, parts of speech were rife . . . .

Hastings was the first President of the Asiatic Society, and not only because of his official position; Shore succeeded Sir William Jones, becoming the Third President, and he too earned his place. It is true the Orientalists lived a life apart in many ways from their fellows — but that would have been true of them in any age or climate.

CHAPTER VII

A COUNTRY STATION

HICKEY'S Calcutta was mainly a place to which the servants of the Company came back from spells of loneliness in a district and from now onwards life in the district is the foundation of Anglo-India. One young officer in the judicial service, Mr. Henry Roberdeau, has left a sketch of life in Mymensingh that will stand by itself for every other district in Bengal and needs little change to fit any district in the North-West for some time to come. Roberdeau came to India in 1799 and was posted to Mymensingh in 1801; he died there in 1808; his sketch was probably written about 1805.

'All retired stations in this Country are alike in general,' he explains, Mymensingh being different only in being a little more retired and not on the way to any other district. It is about the size of an English county and the population is estimated at rather under two million. The Land Revenue is not so much as £90,000 sterling annually, so that each inhabitant may be supposed to pay less than a shilling a year, which Roberdeau thinks too little; 'the settlement was made without sufficient consideration but as it was made for *ever* it cannot now be altered'. It is twenty-five years since all the Company's servants thought the assessment too high. Twenty-five years of peace have made a difference.

'I get up between five and six,' writes Roberdeau, 'mount my Horse for a Ride, return about seven, bathe and dress for breakfast, to which I sit down about nine o'clock. This meal is soon despatched and then comes my Hookah, I smoke and read or write until eleven when the "Nazir" of the Court informs me that business is ready.'

He does not say so, but it was probably now that Roberdeau saw visitors; his successors did so at least. He stayed in court from eleven till 'four, five or six according to the season of the year. On leaving Court I take a Ride or drive or walk or lounge until the light begins to fade, when I dress for Dinner. I get into my Tonjon [a kind of palanquin] and go wherever Dinner may be and get to Bed again by eleven o'clock. This is literally my life, with exception to changes made by little sporting excursions'.

He goes on to explain that there ought to be a society of six officials, but at present there is no doctor and Roberdeau himself has no Assistant, as he should have. There are therefore four men, the Judge, who is also Magistrate and head of the district, the Registrar — Roberdeau — and the Collector and his Assistant. 'You will wonder how we can find conversation, considering the smallness of our Party, but our Evenings are, I assure you, very cheerful.' For the hot weather and rains — about eight months of the year — they have nothing to do but talk to each other. 'We are for two-thirds of the year in a kind of vacuum . . . A Billiard Table affords occasional relaxation and beyond that I have nothing further to mention save Books and the Pen. This dearth of Recreation is not however much felt because all Civil Servants in the country have business to perform and that business must be done . . . However to speak generally, a Country life in India is dull gloomy spiritless and solitary, and a Man doomed to it is much to be pitied if he has not lasting amusements and resources within himself.'

Just such a conclusion, nearly a hundred years later, set a cavalry subaltern in the long leisure hours of South Indian cantonment life to read Gibbon and forge a rhetoric that changed the history of the world.

In the cold weather, however, Roberdeau explains, there is some diversion; the country abounds in game, and expeditions of all kinds are made. Hog-hunting is the first sport, 'and is thought very fine, in as much as the animal is fleet wild, savage and resolute to the last extremity'. 'There is something grand in first rousing a Boar, for the grass being as high as your Horse's Belly, you cannot see the game until you are close upon it. When he perceives his danger, he gives a loud grunt and sets off as hard as he can go. Tally ho! You ride after him at a strong gallop and by keeping this pace you soon blow him . . . It is not until he gets tired that . . . the Boar turns and charges and this is the moment to deliver the Spear. . . .'

Next to hog-hunting came shooting, all of which 'with the exception of snipe and quail', was done from the backs of elephants, surging slowly through the waving grass like ships in line. The small game seems to have been mainly partridge, jungle-fowl and the bustard or floriken; there is no mention of duck. You might, with a long line of elephants, put up anything, tiger, panther, bear, deer, partridge, peafowl and jungle-fowl. A servant sat behind you — a hundred and thirty years later; Roberdeau says nothing about it — holding a rifle which he exchanged for your shot-gun if big game appeared.

It will be noticed that dinner is now much later, between half past six and eight. Those who have leisure have a light meal called tiffin or lunch in the middle of the day and may take a nap afterwards, but that is chiefly in Calcutta; except on Sundays and holidays lunch makes too much of a break in business to become general. Water is 'the universal drink', though milk and water is sometimes taken; Roberdeau has milk and water instead of tea for breakfast. The wine is always claret; 'a pint of port would throw a man into a fever and Madeira is too strong to be drank freely'. There is a great deal of meat on the tables — in Calcutta sometimes venison, beef, mutton, pork, veal and poultry at one table — and since it will not keep and the servants will not eat what has been on a European's table, a great deal is thrown away. In the country, waste is unavoidable; you cannot kill part of a sheep nor eat a whole one at a sitting.

There is no market in the country to supply eatables; you buy and fatten your own 'deer, oxen, sheep, calves, kids, ducks, geese, rabbits etc.' Middling-sized roasting fowls are twenty to the rupee — about a penny each — a sheep can be had for a rupee, and an old ox for three or four, but they all have to be fattened before they come to the table. Bread is made at home and so is butter from your own cow; the cream 'is poured into very large open-mouthed Bottles, which are closely stopped and then gently thumped up and down on the ground until the liquid becomes consistent'. And that 'gently' is well-chosen; the butter man is very clear to the eyes, squatting there with infinite patience, hour after hour if need be, oblivious of all the world, content with his gentle thumping.

There are no brick houses in the district except the jail and those of the half-dozen officials. Thatch and dried mud does for the rest. Even the Englishmen live in what are really stationary tents, tents which have run aground on low brick platforms. They are 'Bungalows, a word I know not how to render unless by a Cottage. These are always thatched with straw on the roof and the walls are sometimes of Bricks and often of matts. Some have glass windows besides the Venetians but this is not very common . . . To hide the sloping Roofs we put up a kind of artificial ceiling made of white cloth . . .' There are 'curtains over the doorways to keep out the wind and . . . I have two Bungalows near to each other, in one of which I sleep and dress and in the other sit and eat'.

'Bed in the hot weather is dreadful, sometimes not a breath of air and we are obliged by the musquitoes, to sleep behind curtains.' 'Another plague is a small Red Ant, which bites very sharp'; they are dealt with by standing the bedposts in pans of water.

Roberdeau expresses in just the way that four men out of five would have put it the attitude of his station and of his day to Indians.

'The natives of every cast,' he says, 'are in their manners and customs so totally different from us that beyond what duty and business compells we can have no association. I believe they privately look on us with a great deal of contempt and generally believe us to be wanting in Religion, merely I suppose because we have not the idle and superstitious outward forms of worship which they so much pride themselves in. In the *arts*, tho', they look on us as Gods. . . .'

And again he says:

'You are aware that the Natives will not eat or drink with us nor partake of anything from our Tables; do not therefore imagine any black faces at our Dinners. . . .'

The Judge, it will be noticed, is also the magistrate; it is he who is district officer and head of the district and not the Collector. Judge-Magistrate and Collector now stand side by side, and it is the Judge-Magistrate who is senior. This was Cornwallis's dispensation, confirmed under the Act of 1793, the third of the three great acts. Later — from 1831 — it was the Collector who was also the Magistrate and who became the executive head of the district. In Roberdeau's day, the head of the district had two functions; he was a civil judge and also a magistrate. In his civil capacity, the Judge administered Hindu or Mohammedan law; he had a Pundit and a Qazi to expound the law and assist him, but his was the decision, both as to fact and law, and it was he too who adjudged and pronounced the award. He was concerned with all disputes about property and for the present there is no such thing as a revenue dispute; the pendulum has swung towards liberalism and the Collector of revenue now collects revenue and nothing else.

The Judge is helped by a Registrar, or Register — who in Mymensingh is Roberdeau — 'whose mode of proceeding are precisely the same as that of the Judge' except that he cannot deal with a dispute involving more than five hundred rupees. Then in outlying parts of the district there are Qazis, or subordinate native judges, from whose decisions there lies an appeal to the Judge. Nor are the Judge's decisions final; there are six Provincial Courts of Appeal.

So much for disputes about property. For the purposes of Criminal Law, the judges of the Courts of Appeal from time to time resolve themselves into separate criminal courts, called Courts of Circuit, which visit each district twice a year and there deal with the criminal cases committed to them. The Circuit Judge is helped by a Muslim

Law Officer, who gives a written opinion, both as to guilt and punishment; if the Judge of Circuit agrees with his Law Officer he gives orders for the sentence to be carried out; if he disagrees he refers the whole case to a superior Court in Calcutta.

These are the more serious cases. For lesser crimes the District Magistrate — who, we must never forget, is the District Judge as well — can himself punish with up to six months' imprisonment, a fine of five hundred rupees or thirty strokes on the back with a cane — much of the powers of a second-class magistrate, which a young man in the twentieth century would be granted after about one year in India. Liberalism is strong here; no officer resident in the district can give more than six months' imprisonment and there is not much room for tyranny.

But there is one proviso — and one may guess that an energetic District Magistrate made use of it. 'He may confine any Person, however, of a notorious bad Character for any period of time until such person can give good security for his future good behaviour.' Here was the origin of that provision of the law that was always to be so strange to eyes fresh from England, the backbone of the police administration of the district, the point beyond which liberalism never advanced in its struggle with orientalism. A notorious bad Character! It was a good thing for many an English poacher that liberalism never admitted to the English statute-book that superb opportunity for the practical administrator. The Magistrate is the arbiter who decides what is good security; and in a district where the police are efficient in the oriental sense no really respectable person will offer security for someone the Magistrate considers a notorious bad character.

Cornwallis at this stage of his reforms was trying to provide safeguards: 'No system will ever be carried into effect,' he wrote, 'so long as the personal qualifications of the individuals that may be appointed to superintend it form the only security for the due exercise of it.'

Or in other words, it is no use trusting the district officer too far. Exactly the reverse would be at least as true; no system of counter-checks will ever be effective without the right men and on the whole the nineteenth century proved that to choose the right men and trust them was the way to administer India. But it was in the contrary belief that Cornwallis framed his code and one may suspect that he did not realize the full implications of this power of demanding security. Did Sir George Barlow — Hickey's bête noire — lay the draft before him with demure face and let him put his name to it in ignorance? Or did he persuade him of its necessity? There it was, at any rate, and it went on into the Code of Criminal Procedure and laid many an habitual burglar by the heels.

Roberdeau's District Judge and Magistrate was Mr. James Rattray, who previously had been Collector of Tirhoot; now he was promoted Judge and Magistrate and in that capacity went on five years later to Jessore. That was the general rule now, but fifteen years ago there had been one confusing morning when the District Officer changed his title and function. He had gone to bed the Collector; he woke up as Judge and Magistrate and his assistant became the Collector.

Before that sloughing of the old man, the head of the district had combined all powers in himself. In addition to all he now did as Judge and Magistrate he had collected the revenue and, if anyone would not pay up, attached his estate or confined his person. But the new Collector had no power to settle disputes or to detain the persons of defaulters. What is more, he was personally answerable in law for any act done as Collector; here was a new idea for India, as revolutionary as the theories of Copernicus.

The new district officer, like the old, had to keep order in his district. Twenty years were still to run before Peelers appeared in the streets of London, and a district magistrate in Bengal could hardly be expected to have a regular police force. He had, however, a force of two hundred and fifty armed irregulars who performed the duties later given to armed police and jailers; that is to say, they guarded convicts, jails, treasuries, record offices and the like. 'They are', wrote Roberdeau, 'in general a worthless undisciplined set of Scoundrels very different from the Regular Troops which are brave, honourable and obedient.'

Armed police, stationed at headquarters, do not catch criminals, and Roberdeau, who had nothing to do with the Magistrate's side of Mr. Rattray's work, says nothing about the arrangements for police administration proper. Such as they were, these were based on the village watchman, who for thousands of years had been the servant of the village community. The brotherhood allowed him some grain but it cannot have been often that he received any cash payment. He usually came from one of the lower castes; he was always poor. His real power depended on the character of the man he reported to. This had been the Mogul official, either the assignee of the revenue or an official called the *faujdar* who in areas directly administered was the King's representative. As the Mogul system broke down, the faujdars disappeared and the watchman's allegiance usually reverted to the zamindar. Cornwallis abolished the feudal powers of the zamindars and made the watchman responsible to police officers who were called *daroghas*. Each was in charge of a part of a district called a *thana*, but they seem to have had no trained regular constables. They answered to the Judge and District Magistrate, to whom they must deliver a criminal within twenty-four hours of arrest. This was the system in Mymensingh.

Roberdeau has a good deal to say about salaries, which are those fixed in Cornwallis's time. The Head of the District gets between two thousand and three thousand rupees a month, the Collectors a salary of fifteen hundred, with a percentage on collections which brings him up to nearly as much as the Judge and Magistrate. A rupee a month was then rather more than a pound a year and they paid no income tax. Commercial Residents, the third main branch of the service, get five hundred only as salary, but have a percentage on the 'investment' they provide for the Company, and are also allowed the privilege of private trade. There are, Roberdeau adds, some appointments of Collector of Customs, and four Secretaries to Government and Secretaries to various Boards, 'all of them capital appointments'.

'In the *outward* forms of religion,' Roberdeau writes, 'Englishmen are rather lax, indeed except in Calcutta all devotion must be private, and which is surely as acceptable.' Everyone seems to be agreed on this point; indeed in Madras, the church was used for storing bags of rice, which had to be cleared away for the funeral of Eyre Coote. In Calcutta, there were two churches and it was long a convention that any gentleman — that is, an official of the Company, or someone accepted by the officials as an equal — might hand any lady from her palanquin to the church door without introduction. It must have needed a lightning appraisal, a swift decision, to be the first to spring forward from the crowd of ardent bachelors at the church door when a new ship was in and when Miss Wrangham, Miss Aylmer or Miss Sanderson might emerge from the panelled chair-palanquin. Not always, perhaps, a very decorous scene; eighteenth-century paganism lingered on in India and only slowly gave way to the absorption in religion of Shore and his Victorian successors.

Roberdeau's sketch of a country district ends with a character of the Englishman in the East, as misleading as all generalizations are apt to be, but no doubt true of many in Bengal. 'An Englishman in India,' he writes, 'is proud and tenacious, he feels himself a Conqueror amongst a vanquished people and looks down with some degree of superiority on all below him. Indolence, the disease of the climate, affects him with its torpid influence . . . A cool apathy, a listless inattention and an improvident carelessness generally accompanies most of his actions; secure of today, he thinks not of tomorrow. Ambitious of splendour, he expends freely . . . Generosity is a feature in the Character too prominent to be overlooked, but as it sometimes borders on extravagance it loses some of its virtue. Bring distress before his eyes and he bestows with a liberality that is nowhere surpassed . . . In the public Character, whatever Calumny and Detraction may say to the Contrary, he is minutely just, inflexibly upright and I believe no public Service in the whole world can evince more integrity. . . .'

That was the claim. Of course, there were exceptions. Middleton in 1806 was removed from his post as Judge and Magistrate of Jessore because he had held interest in several indigo works in his own district; Le Gros at Mymensingh misappropriated public money in 1808; the Collector of Birbhum was removed from his office about the same time for personal violence and for confining Hindus in the house of a Muslim official, where on account of caste rules they could not eat. But the claim was made and these were now exceptions.

Not much need be added to its outward life to turn Roberdeau's Mymensingh into a classical small station of Kipling's day. A separate Judge was still to come and the Magistrate would once more be Collector as well; the Superintendent of Police, a Canal Engineer and another for Roads and Bridges; a railwayman, perhaps a Forest Officer, would complete the familiar little circle. In the kind of life the civil servants of the Company lived there would be only one big change before the opening of the Suez Canal brought more English women and more frequent leave. Minor changes there would be; oil lamps would take over the duties of candles, there would be more ice, there would be soda-water and topis would replace top hats. And opinion would follow the English model; an earnest evangelical religion would take the place of Roberdeau's mild rationalism; as Arnold's teaching spread outwards from Rugby, the Englishman's day would come to be governed by exercise and it would become essential to health to add to the morning ride an evening game of polo, tennis or rackets, followed if possible by a swim. But none of these changes made to the district anything like so much difference as the reunion of all executive power in the hands of the Collector and the general introduction of camping.

Until that happened, the administration was dead. No one at headquarters knew what was happening in the villages. There was much crime of which no one ever heard and the people were afraid to come to headquarters and report it. The Judge-Magistrate sat at headquarters 'in a kind of vacuum' and dealt with the cases that came to him. But the system would spring to life when he had to go out into the fields and decide who had paid his rent and who had not, whether Lokhe Nath had ploughed this field himself or let it to Gangu Chamar. That would happen when the Magistrate became Collector again and men began to camp.

The same thing happened to almost everyone. The first sniff of wet straw from the floor of the canvas bathroom behind the tent; the first sip of smoky tea; the kiss of the pillow on your cheek, cooler than in a bungalow and perhaps slightly moist with dew; above all, the first morning ride from camp with the scent of sugar-cane cooking at the corner of the field, the tops of the tall feathery grass still silver with dew — one by one each remembered scent and sound peeled away one layer of sweaty saline incrustation, the deposit of eight months of irritated wrangling and intrigue. Within three or four days, you were a different man. The people of your district were no longer cases to be got through, no longer tiresome creatures always making work by their absurd inability to agree. They turned suddenly into human beings who would squat on the ground and tell you their troubles, people childish no doubt, cunning but simple, laughable, stubborn, affectionate people, callous and gentle, cruel and compassionate, people for whom you too felt a real affection as you sat on a string cot in the village street and drank buffalo milk in which sugar had been stirred by a dirty finger. It was an affection that would survive the next hot weather, though it might lie dormant, aestivating beneath the parched and dusty surface of the sun-baked soil. It was from camp, not from Indian mistresses, that some of the English learnt what India was like.

But this was not yet. Minutely just, inflexibly upright, that was all Roberdeau claimed to be so far.

CHAPTER VIII

THE INDIA SHORE LEFT

I T is time to stand back from the detail of lives such as Roberdeau's and Hickey's, to rise high enough in the air to see all India at once and compare it, on the day in 1798 when Wellesley arrived, with the India Clive had left.

It is a picture very confusing indeed until a height is reached from which the tiny human figures, fighting and struggling and marching, have dwindled smaller than ants, so that only a consciousness of masses and movements remains. The surface of the dusty brown map so far below heaves and stirs a little here, shrinks and writhes backwards, twitches like a horse's skin, but no fly can be seen to settle; the reason for these contortions lies in the minds and personalities of men and can only be understood by what we remember as we peer down.

From such a height, the Great Mogul is lost to view; we remember that he is there in Delhi, an old man, blinded, listlessly holding a tarnished sceptre in trembling wrinkled fingers. The Afghans have swept down to Delhi more than once and each time have washed back in a contemptuous undertow, esteeming the throne not worth the keeping or distracted by trouble at home; they still threaten from the north, a terror to all peaceful folk. The Sikhs are as yet hardly stirring. To the east of Delhi are the ill-governed dominions of the Nawab-Vizier of Oudh, a fantastic figure, lavishing his affections on an English dray-horse, preparing sumptuous entertainments for English gentlemen at breakfast, immersed in wild-beast shows and the most trivial amusements of despotism, but contriving always to find the annual subsidy for the English Company. In the south, Tippoo Sultan in Mysore, with all his father's ferocity but none of his wisdom, alternating between sadistic foppery and bouts of Muslim fanaticism, contributing immense energy to a dozen ill-judged enthusiasms, is constant only in his wish to be rid of the English, while the Nizam of Hyderabad, prince of a country larger than Spain, wonders uneasily whether it is more to his interest to be the ally of the English or of the Marathas.

It is these two powers, the English and the Marathas, who when Shore hands India to Wellesley, fill in the chinks and gaps and hold together those fragments of Mogul masonry which survive in the composite rubble of India. And both are composite and complex organisms in themselves. The Marathas still pay a nominal allegiance to their old king, the Raja of Satara, but he has now become a ceremonial figurehead. Power passed long ago from the Raja to his five principal officers, each now the head of a state; first among these five was once the Peshwa, originally the Brahman Prime Minister, but in the shifting play of their politics it is at the moment Scindia of Gwalior who is the most powerful of the five, while in the Peshwa's own kingdom it is not the Peshwa but a minister who is most to be reckoned with. It is Scindia who holds the person of the blinded Mogul Emperor, but tradition still demands that he shall instruct his captive to appoint as Imperial Commander-in-Chief not Scindia himself, not the Raja of Satara in whose name each of the five still rules, but the Peshwa — the last Mayor of the Palace but one.

Pretence is thus piled upon pretence but the reality remains that the Maratha strength coils and twines round all the northern part of the Nizam's territory, reaches across India to threaten Madras and hold Orissa, sends long tenacious tendrils north to grip Delhi, Agra and Bundelkhand, surrounds and encysts the proud states of Rajputana. Compared with this strong growth, the English dominions are not impressive and Scindia once dared to send them orders to pay him the tribute due to the Mogul for their fief of Bengal and Behar. That fief is all they hold that makes a show on the map; Madras itself is almost too small to be seen from this dizzy height and the British hold is not strong on the Northern Circars, taken from Dupleix, nor on the new districts taken from Mysore; Bombay is quite invisible. But the English are stronger than they seem on the map. Oudh is really the Company's for the taking; Rohilkand, beyond Oudh, will be theirs within five years; the Carnatic they can have when they want it. And even the Marathas reckon that the numbers of every one of the Company's battalions should be multiplied at least by ten before an account is cast up and the decision taken to fight.

Looking down then on India at the turn of the century, forgetting for the moment what is to come, one might picture the Afghans, the Marathas, or the English gaining dominion over the land. But the Afghans had never made any attempt to administer their conquests and surely in the end victory is likely to be with the power that pays its soldiers and keeps its peasants on the land. If that is the right measure to judge by, a wise man would have no doubt who is to get the mastery.

The Maratha state was in its essence predatory; outside the Maratha homeland, there was no administration but simply tribute. The ruler had to pay the Marathas a fourth of what he collected. So long as there were fresh conquests every few years, the confederation hung together, but as soon as expansion ended, it was in danger and could barely hope to survive even if the administration of the homeland was sound.

Within Maharashtra, the home country of the Maratha people, the system of administration was one that suited the people and originally, with a vigorous ruler, it had worked well. As in the north, the village community or brotherhood was the foundation; there was a headman, a village clerk and other officials who were the servants of the brotherhood. The names are different but the society is the one we know. Villages were grouped together into units which might as well be called districts; there was a district officer responsible to a secretariat in Poona. The district officer — the *mamlatdar* — was responsible for everything; he settled with the headman what figure should represent the King's share of the harvest, he collected it; he was responsible for order. Crime was to some extent regulated by the payment of blackmail or insurance to certain recognized criminal tribes, hereditary trade unions, who undertook to provide village watchmen and to warn off unauthorized wrongdoers. Criminal justice was mainly a matter of the district officer's whim, the punishments being death, mutilation, flogging or fine. Civil justice was a matter of arranging arbitration; the headman in the village might arbitrate himself, appoint an arbitrator, or refer to a board of arbitrators. There might be an appeal to the district officer, or he might himself initiate arbitration. Law was a matter of custom and tradition, interpreted according to the circumstances of the case and the taste of the arbitrators.

It was a loose but not a bad system, provided there was a strong ruler, a strong revenue minister at the head of the secretariat and a good supply of honest, energetic and able district officers. But by the end of the eighteenth century, none of these was forthcoming and the administration was hardly distinguishable from that anywhere else in India. The district officer, like the contractor or feudal chief elsewhere, screwed as much as he could from his district and remitted as little as he dared to the secretariat; lawlessness was endemic and there was no remedy; what for the Marathas was worst of all, warfare, the normal condition of their state, had ceased to pay. They were fighting against each other as often as against any prince outside the confederacy, while in the homeland there was no tough administrative framework to hold society together and enable it to survive political disunion.

Whether you judged that such a net bound the English dominions into a stronger whole would depend on where you began to look at them. Of Madras, certainly, it was possible to be doubtful. In the new districts there was life, new-stirring and exciting, but in Madras itself, in the Secretariat, hardly anyone was yet aware of what was happening. Madras had stood still. She had made none of Bengal's progress because she had stayed in the stage of the dual system and her Governor and Council, which in the seventeenth century had seemed so far ahead of the others, had not till thirty years later than Bengal been forced to administer provinces and learn by experience how to do it.

The English advance to power had begun in Madras and in the form of a race with Dupleix, but once the French were beaten in India and the English candidate on the throne of the Carnatic, things had begun to go wrong. It was perhaps partly due to the character of Mohammed Ali, the successful candidate. A man of an impressive and indeed imposing appearance, he united great charm of manner with extreme pliancy and a cynical readiness to accept any arrangement that suited him for the moment. He took up his residence in Madras instead of his own capital of Arcot because Madras was a better place for arranging things; here he lived like a prince, entertaining royally, spending with lavish folly, denying himself nothing. At least as often as the annual payment fell due which he had to make to the Company for his defence, he needed hard cash — and when he was in need he borrowed. There would have been nothing original in this had he not hit on the brilliant device of borrowing personally from individual servants of the Company — and often at 36 per cent interest, but he really did not trouble himself how much. He would mortgage as security a district or part of a district, of which he made over possession to the creditor, who now collected the revenue of the district and repaid himself as he chose. No doubt the Nawab could have got the money from an Indian moneylender and perhaps at a lower interest; indeed, at least three parts of the money lent to the Nawab probably did come from the moneylenders, merely passing through an English official's hands. But by enmeshing the Company's servants in each transaction the Nawab was able to ensure that he had a crowd of eager backers whenever his affairs were discussed. As long as he had a district to mortgage he need never want.

This is no place to follow the tortuous and unsavoury ramifications of the Nawab of Arcot's debts. It is enough to say that he kept the game on foot till his death, that is for nearly fifty years, surviving three inquiries by the Court of Directors and one in Parliament, continuing his course unperturbed after the settlement imposed by Parliament and incurring by the time of his death a fresh debt that stood nominally at thirty million pounds, though much of it was fictitious. Nothing can be said in extenuation; almost every servant of the Company in Madras was involved in the scandal, the worst being the notorious Paul Benfield. He had come out as an engineer in the Company's service and surely holds a record that will never be beaten, having been dismissed the service after six years, reinstated, suspended, reinstated a second time, suspended and sent to London to answer charges, reinstated a third time, and finally dismissed, just eighteen years after he joined, with a fortune of half a million.

The shameful part of the whole business is that the sufferers were the people of the districts pledged by the Nawab as security. It was not a dispute between Benfield and the Nawab. 'If the hoards of oppression,' said Burke, 'were the fund for satisfying the claims of bribery and peculation, who would wish to interfere between such litigants? But . . . the Nabob of Arcot and his creditors are not adversaries but collusive parties.' The true litigation, he goes on, is 'between these two, combining and confederating on one side . . . and the miserable inhabitants of a ruined country on the other'.

So for the present Madras was damned and lost, engulfed in corruption. But there was new life already in the districts and she was soon to take the lead again, going ahead just because she had been backward when Bengal made the permanent settlement. For the moment, however, to sail to Madras is to go back to the middle of the eighteenth century, and not only in administration but in manners. Indian clothes and food linger on here among the English; perhaps the gulf between the races is less wide because it is bridged to some extent by those Portuguese who with their dusky wives had taken shelter in Fort St. George from the raids of marauders.

The old college mess at which all the servants of the Company ate together lasted longer here and survives right through the century in the form of the Governor's dinner, at which the junior ensign present takes the foot of the table. Trade is far more general for far longer; a soldier or civilian till the end of the century will buy up a consignment of field-glasses or escritoires and try to dispose of them at a profit. There is less luxury than in Bengal, partly because money is not come by so easily and partly because good living is more difficult to arrange. Turkeys, ducks, sheep, geese, all have to come from Bengal, though the two Presidencies are on a level as regards the three great luxuries of Anglo-India, wine, cheese and ham, which must always be imported. But there is a different attitude to luxury too; when Lord Macartney came to Calcutta from Madras in 1785 he was 'greatly prejudiced against the European inhabitants for indulging themselves too much in what he considered extreme indolence and luxury' as compared with the 'less assuming residents of Fort St. George'.

The curious Madras custom of arresting and imprisoning the Governor also survived very late, successors of Sir Edward Winter, who did the same thing a hundred years earlier, confining Lord Pigot and even allowing him to die in captivity. The members of his Council had some grounds for irritation, as Lord Pigot had made a very reasonable fortune out of his first governorship in Clive's day, but came out a second time with the specific and declared purpose of ending the scandal of the Nawab of Arcot's debts. In Bengal, too, there had been irritation when Clive, the arch-Nabob, came back to purge the country and live clean, but it never took a more violent form than boycott.

If Madras was provincial, still more so was Bombay. Cornwallis could not see why a Governor with a Council was needed at all to load one ship a year; a small mercantile station with a commercial resident was all, he thought, that was needed. Certainly, Bombay's incursions into war and politics had been amateurish and unsuccessful, though they would have had a better chance of success if every treaty, every expedition, had not been countermanded from Calcutta. Certainly the impression of bad faith and divided counsels was almost inevitable when it took the Governor weeks to hear from the Governor-General. But it was as well Cornwallis did not pursue the matter and make an end of Bombay as a Presidency; a Governor would be needed soon and Jonathan Duncan was to come from Benares and to rule for fourteen years, building up the jumbled congeries of the Bombay Presidency as the Maratha power crumbled.

We are, however, still trying to decide whether in the light of what has already happened by the turn of the century the English power or the Maratha is the sturdier growth. And if, looking at Madras, there is not a great deal in it, Bengal is another story altogether. Progress has not only been rapid; it has been irresistible. The chief actors themselves have been swept along by its force. Clive wrote in 1765:

'. . . it is scarcely hyperbole to say that the whole Mogul Empire is in our hands. The inhabitants of the country have no attachment to any Nabob whatever, their troops are neither disciplined nor commanded nor paid as ours are. . . .'

But he received no encouragement in London for his dream of an India governed by the Crown; he had fallen back on the 'dual system' that is, government by Indian puppet rulers; this he thought the only alternative so long as the Crown would not accept the responsibility and the Company was in charge. The Directors liked the dual system too and hankered for it long after it was outdated, though Hastings told them with his usual vigour and clarity:

'All the arts of policy cannot conceal the power by which these provinces are ruled, . . . it is as visible as the light of the sun that they originate from our own government, that the Nabob is a mere pageant without so much as the shadow of authority. . . .'

But even Hastings tried to rule the country by Indian subordinates, controlling them by a centralized authority in Calcutta. That too was abandoned and at last direct rule by British officers had become general.

And now, in 1798, two quick-breeding generations have lived in Bengal and begotten sons without seeing an invading foe; the famine of 1770 is far away and already it begins to look as though the Government had been too easy with the zamindars when they made a settlement with them for ever. Grain is cheap; the cultivator is less wretched than he was thirty years ago and he has become aware of a new idea, that men are ruled by law, not by the whim of a ruler. Indeed, already a danger can be seen here; the quick-witted Bengali has perceived that here is a weapon that can sometimes be twisted to achieve injustice as well as justice.

Although there is still a great deal of crime, the rule of law has been introduced, and a service has been created to administer it. There is something like a civil list and the appointments are familiar to the ears of to-day; Secretary to the Board of Revenue, Collector of Midnapore, Deputy Secretary to Government, Assistant to the Accountant-General, Officiating Collector, Acting Judge and Magistrate — they are all posts we understand. The men who hold them do not trade and are paid a salary on which they can live and save money if they take the trouble — but not all do save and in any case the odds are still against their retiring to enjoy their savings in England. The

Company still carries on trade but the Commercial Department is the least important and men go to it for life and have nothing to do with the revenue and justice of the country.

These first civil servants were chosen on the nomination of one director, a system theoretically indefensible but in practice by no means a bad one. The only training they received was a year or more of employment as copyists, which did little but give them time to settle down, after which they were appointed to a post and learnt its duties as they carried them out. That first year might well have been extended and used for general education; but there is only one way to learn the duties of an appointment and the Company had hit on that already.

The Company's servants already consider that no public service in the world can evince more integrity; they pride themselves that they are minutely just, inflexibly upright. They have already included in their number men such as Clevland who made the aboriginal a man; Tilman Henckel, Collector from 1781 to 1789 of the district of Jessore, whose inhabitants were so grateful for his fatherly care that they made an image of him and worshipped it; or Jonathan Duncan, sent to Benares to end corruption among the English but adding to that a private war of his own to stamp out the practice of killing unwanted daughters. They have included Charles Grant, of the commercial branch, who periodically submitted his private accounts to the Government, a man scrupulously honest and deeply religious, an evangelical like his friend Shore; he was Cornwallis's adviser in all matters of trade and later a leading adviser of the Government in England; his son, Lord Glenelg, was President of the Board of Control, Macaulay's first official chief. They have included James Grant, Shore's rival as a revenue expert, who took charge of the revenue records when the qanungos first made them over to the Government and kept his charge for many years, an accurate scholarly unpractical man.

There are others, no doubt as flippant though not always as decorative as Bob Pott and young Fitzroy; there are still men in the Bolts tradition who are merely gross, selfish and greedy. But Roberdeau stands for the majority and for him it was enough to do his duty and no more; the idea is not yet general, as it is soon to be, that the English are in India for God's purpose. Pride in the service is born but in its infancy and it is still rare for men to camp in their districts and get to know the peasants; it is still rare for the peasants to speak of an Englishman as their father.

But the time is coming. The period of corruption is over; the period of experiments is coming to an end and will be done with when all executive power is back in the Collector's hands. Then comes the flowering, the highest peak perhaps in the lofty range of what the English have done, when a handful of our countrymen, by the integrity of their character and with not much else to help them, gave to many millions for the first time for some centuries the idea that a ruler might be concerned with their well-being.

III

THE GOLDEN AGE

1798-1858

CHAPTER I

MUNRO AND THE PEASANT SETTLEMENT

YOU must fly over India if you want to see how it is put together. From a train, there is not enough in the eye at one glance and it is gone too soon; by bullock-cart the journey takes too long; you have forgotten what you saw last week before you are in the next district.

Fly from West to East, along the broad band of flat country that lies below the Himalayas. Come down from time to time and skim low over the tree-tops, climb again till a cow is the size of an ant, come to the ground every three or four hundred miles and talk to the people, see what they eat and look at their fields.

You begin over windy plains of wheat, where the men might be Italian except that they are much bigger than Italians, where people eat wheat and milk and butter, and meat when they can get it. Fly on towards the East, a faint jagged arabesque of snowy dome and icy peak on your left, and now the rivers run the other way, towards the rising sun, and you are still over plains, very flat, sprinkled here and there with plump square pincushions of glossy green which are groves of mangoes. There are more little squares of brown now among the young wheat, where in a few months' time there will be the vivid, emerald green of rice. Fly on all day till you come down in the evening in a country where wheat is unknown, where rice and fish are what the people eat, where there are boats instead of bullock-carts.

You have flown all day, from the Salt Range to the mouths of the Ganges and all day the land has been a flat chess-board with tracks and waterways wriggling among the squares of cultivation; the only change has been in the people and in what they grow. At each halt, you met men a little darker and squatter than at the last, but beneath a different colouring, the shape of their features did not seem so very foreign, and the languages they spoke were all dialects of one tongue that was a cousin to Latin.

But if you had turned to the South, the Deccan, the country of the right hand, there would have been a change at once and you would have flown over a tangle of hills and forests, rocky rivers and gorges, ruined forts on red sandstone crags, temples with bloated spires and little lakes, a country of red rocks, red gravel and dark green foliage, sharp and garish after the almond-green and almond-buff plains of the North. And you would have come down among a strange people, among Brahmins with the arched nostril, the sharp-bridged nose, of the temple carvings, among labourers with the heavier features and darker skin of the aboriginal, among people whose many tongues were as incomprehensible as the clucking of hens or the conversation of squirrels.

It is strange today after the North and a century and a half ago it would have seemed at first sight just as strange. Beneath the strangeness, though, there is a unity. If you understand the India Akbar ruled it is not hard to understand the South, because the foundation is the same, the village brotherhood, in a dozen different forms, hidden here by the obliterating cruelty of conquest, there by natural disaster and re-settlement, but surviving somehow, reappearing in one dress or another, Tamil, Telegu, Kanarese or Maratha.

The tradition was much stronger in some areas than in others. In one district, the peasants believed their common ancestor had occupied the village and that they jointly owned the land, though each man had a share of his own which he could pass to his son or even sell if the shareholders agreed. They would hold the waste land in common and pay the King his share in one lump sum from the whole village. Two hundred miles away, there would be a headman who leased lands annually to the peasants on behalf of the King; here the waste land would be the King's. In a third district, a man would claim his right to cultivate a plot because he or his father had first broken the soil and would pay the King's share direct.

It was very confused, but there is a similarity behind the confusion. Almost everywhere there was a headman and a village committee, there were village servants; there was usually an accountant and a watchman. On the whole, the stronger the memory of a corporate village society, the better was the peasant's position. In the worst case, all corporate life was forgotten in an extreme of misery and each man, by hiding half his crop or by bribery, put off the moment of payment until either torture exacted the last ounce of grain, or in despair he fled to a land where his face was unknown.

In one way, the state of the villager was worse in the South than in the North. What traces there were of a systematic assessment were centuries old; there had been no attempt for half a millennium to set on every field a fair yearly price. In a few districts only, memories survived of an ancient settlement. In most, it was simply a matter of what could be wrung from the peasant; rents were collected with whips and pincers and apart from the remedy of flight, all that enabled a man to live was the hope that amidst the confusion of warring states his village might sometimes be overlooked.

For centuries, five main kingdoms had fought each other over the peninsular part of India and there was no peace yet. For the peasant, the sight of strangers was always matter for dread and it made little difference to him whose horses ate his fodder, whose men burnt his thatch, whether what they took was loot from an enemy or taxes from a subject.

'The ten years of Mogul Government in Cuddapore has been almost as destructive as so many years of war,' wrote Munro of a district ceded by the Nizam in 1801, 'and this last year a mutinous unpaid army was turned loose during the sowing season to collect their pay from the villages. They drove off and sold the cattle, extorted money by torture from every man who fell into their hands, and plundered the houses and shops of those who fled.'

Because there had been no secure rule within human memory, there was no network of collectors of the King's share, as in Bengal. Here and there, notably in the Northern Circars, feudal chiefs were found, but these *poligars* were not as a rule officials become hereditary as in Bengal. They were more often condottiere, who had for the moment been able to establish independence against an overlord, to whom when it seemed expedient they made an annual present and to whose standard in war they would send, if they thought he was likely to win, a specified number of lances. He in his turn watched them with a jealous eye and when he felt strong enough would make an end of them.

In this South India, the Presidency of Fort St. George was responsible until nearly the end of the century for a small area round Madras itself and for the Northern Circars and for no more. Absorbed in making what they could from the Nawab of Arcot and in wars with Mysore, the Governor and Council made no serious attempt to administer their possessions. Even the Jagir, the grant the Nawab had made them of land immediately round Madras, they leased back to him officially — and then as individuals lent him money in return for the right to collect the rents. Even as late as 1801, when the Northern Circars had been British Territory for forty years, Brown, the Collector, wrote that his province was in complete distraction, that refractory poligars were plundering the country and burning villages were to be seen on all sides, that it was unsafe for English travellers without a hired escort.

But the tide had already turned before this. A moment came for a step forward towards a sound way of ruling men in India, comparable to one of those steps forward in the evolution of a species, when suddenly a variant begins to occur and to drive out the unimproved pattern. The giraffe with a longer neck, the kangaroo with a deeper pouch, soon ousts the old type; in Bengal, Johnstone, Hay and Bolts were already giving place to Verelst, Shore and Duncan; in the South, the leap forward produced something better than Shore, a group of men of whom even a people who have had their share of great men may still be proud.

When Cornwallis's Mysore War — the Second — came to an end in 1792, certain districts were taken over from Mysore. They lie inland from Madras, to the West and a little South; one of them was called the Baramahal; it is now Salem. This district had to be settled; Cornwallis, a man of sturdy common sense and unusual honesty of character found that the civilians available from Madras knew the languages or the customs of South India hardly at all. Though they may have included some amiable and accomplished men such as Lewin, those who could be spared were useless for the task of pacifying a newly ceded district, stabilizing the revenue and settling the peasantry on the land. But men of the first quality were available from the Madras army and Cornwallis chose soldiers, putting Captain Alexander Read at the head of the district, with Thomas Munro, a lieutenant, as one of his assistants. He thus strengthened the civil administration in two ways, adding at the same time new blood and the stimulus of a competitive spirit.

Read was a most unusual man. Munro wrote of his chief:

' . . . I shall get no pickings under a master whose conduct is invariably regulated by private honour and the public interest. These, and an unwearied zeal in whatever he undertakes, constitute the great features of his character . . .' He goes on to speak of Read's 'intimate knowledge of the language and manners of the people and happy talent for the investigation of everything connected with the revenue'. Every word might have applied just as well to Munro himself. And for the next thirty years the story of Munro's doings tells in itself how the service and its work developed.

Munro, who in 1791 was thirty years old, had already some experience of work which had brought him into close touch with the people of South India. He had been an intelligence officer under

Read. He now began a life which was to last not only for the seven years he stayed in Baramahal but for nine years thereafter. Indeed, the life of a settlement officer at the end as at the beginning was one of the busiest, the most tedious and the most satisfactory ways of spending his hours on earth that man has devised; not many other duties will send him to bed with so thorough a sense of having stretched limbs and brain, legs and spirit, and spent his strength to good purpose. Hear Munro:

'I go from village to village with my tent, settling the rents of the inhabitants; and this is so tedious and teazing a business that it leaves room for nothing else — for I have no hour in the day that I can call my own. At this moment while I am writing, there are a dozen of people talking around me: it is now twelve o'clock and they have been coming and going in parties ever since seven in the morning . . . One man has a long story of a debt of thirty years' standing contracted by his father. Another tells me that his brother made away with his property when he was absent during the war; and a third tells me that he cannot afford to pay his usual rent because his wife is dead, who used to do more work than his best bullock.'

This was written in 1795, three years after the districts had been ceded; already the people were crowding round a ruler who would listen to them, just as they would still crowd a hundred and fifty years later.

Later in the same letter, Munro tells how rain came suddenly while he was out and he came back to his tent to find that it had been pitched in the dry bed of a swamp, which was now almost knee-deep. 'After two hours work in cutting trenches to carry off the water and in throwing baskets of sand on the floor of the tent to make it firm, I have at last got a spot to bear my table and chair . . .' and before his letter was finished his tent was 'blown away one afternoon by a hurricane of dust'. That kind of thing too did not change much.

In the Baramahal, there was not much corporate feeling in the villages and Munro speaks of the 'farmers' leasing land from the Government. The term 'farmer' is misleading, for:

'Whenever a farmer's servant saves a few rupees he buys a pair of bullocks. His plough does not cost him a rupee: he rents a few acres from Government and commences farming himself. . . .'

And again, there are not ten men in the district who pay a rent of sixty pounds. It was a land of small cultivators; there was no one between the peasant and the Collector. Munro all his life remembered this district; to him it was the archetype, and his memory of it changed the administration of South India. He wrote to his father in 1795, setting out at length in his usual sensible and temperate language his views on the way the country should be managed. In the first place, Collectors must know the language of the people — 'and Government have at last been convinced of the necessity of such a regulation . . .' Next, they must be well paid, and by that he means at least four thousand pounds a year. At present he believes that under the Company, just as under Tippoo, some Collectors of the revenue still send in false returns and pocket the difference. When these first elementary steps have been taken, a reduction in the revenue and a long settlement will, with the natural fertility of the soil, greatly increase the prosperity of the people — who will then be able to buy English goods.

To the reduction of taxation he came back again and again all his life. He wrote to his father three years later:

'The Baramahal has now been completely surveyed and the rents of it fixed. They are on an average nearly what they were under Tippoo.' But although they are fixed at a slightly lower level, greater exactness in accounting and less corruption means that just as much is collected as before and more of it reaches the Treasury. 'The rents here, as I believe in every other part of India, are too high . . . Government have desired it to be made so as to sit light on the inhabitants, but they were not aware that in order to effect this they must relinquish twenty or twenty-five per cent of the present revenue. This reduction will be recommended to them with every argument that can be thought of, but. . . .'

He goes on to explain the present system, which he hopes may long be continued of 'letting every farmer please himself; he may take as much or as little land as he pleases every year; he may reject his old fields and take new; . . . and as every field has a rate of assessment which never varies, he knows perfectly what he can trust to. . . .'

Such a system of course could only last so long as there was more land than the inhabitants needed; that margin was soon to be exhausted. But Munro was perfectly right when he said that the King's share was fixed too high all over India. This was because the English began with the idea that the books of the King from whom they took the district showed a true revenue. And having acquired a district reputed to be worth a certain yearly sum, a governor and council would be disappointed if they did not get it.

But Tippoo had never expected so much as his books showed against the district. For centuries there had been no assessment of what the land could fairly pay; all that was fixed was what in the jargon of today would be called a target — and, what with corrupt and idle officials, what with perennial war, insurrection and civil commotion, what with plague, drought and famine, a target that was not often hit. But the English expected to hit it every year. It took them a long time to learn that if the King's share was to be collected regularly and efficiently it ought to be less.

From the Baramahal, Munro went as joint secretary to the Commissioners who were to draw up the treaty that followed the Third Mysore War. This was in 1799; here he made two lifelong friends, Arthur Wellesley and John Malcolm. Next, to his disgust, he went as Settlement Officer and Collector to another new district, Kanara, on the West Coast. He was in charge here, while in the Baramahal he had been assistant to Read, but he did not take kindly to Kanara. His way of getting a transfer was to work so hard that the back of the task was broken in two years. 'I am anxious to get Kanara into such a state that it may be managed by anybody; and I am convinced that the people of this country, by my spending all my time among them under the fly of a marquee, are already better British subjects than they would have been in twenty years had I lived in a house on the sea-shore. . . .'

In the Baramahal, the peasantry had been a docile and amenable folk, but Kanara had to be pacified by force. Munro had no troops at his disposal; he had instead a number of 'peons' — a word which literally means a footman, the pawn of chess. The total cost of paying, clothing and arming a peon was reckoned by Munro as no more than seven pounds a year, but they were just what was needed. 'My peons in the neighbourhood of Jumlabad have defeated a party of the enemy and taken some prisoners,' Munro says casually in the course of a letter. But he had no high opinion of the enemy; 'a desperate rebellion' being started by one Fateh Hyder, he writes: 'I imagine I shall have less trouble with Fateh Hyder than with Cecil Smith' — the Accountant-General.

The insurrections were the overflow of the war; parties of Tippoo's disbanded soldiers were the people who took to brigandage and had to be dealt with. They did not stop the work of settling the revenue which went forward at a prodigious pace:

'From daybreak till eleven or twelve at night,' Munro wrote to his sister, 'I am never alone except at meals and these *altogether* do not take up an hour. I am pressed on one hand by the settlements of the revenue and on the other by the investigation of murders, robberies and all the evils which have arisen from a long course of profligate and tyrannical government. Living in a tent, there is no escaping for a few hours from the crowd; there is no locking oneself up on pretence of more important business, as a man might do in a house ... I have no refuge but in going to bed, and that is generally so late that the sleep I have is scarcely sufficient to refresh me. I am still, however of Sancho's opinion, that if a governor is only well fed, he may govern any island, however large. . . .'

Kanara was a very large district; 'I cannot go the rounds, by any road, under six hundred and fifty miles,' and since his camp cannot move more than ten miles a day, that is sixty-five days of the year. On the other hand, 'it is on marching days that I have most leisure; for by starting early I get to my ground several hours before the inhabitants come up ... but if I stop near a village I am instantly surrounded by the inhabitants with all their stories of grievances ...' And it is difficult country to get about in; 'no wheel-carriage can be used, not even a buffalo-bandy; in many of the inland cross-roads bullocks cannot travel loaded and tents must be carried by coolies. . . .'

In the intervals of marching, hearing petitions and fixing the King's share on every field, he found time to collect notes of 'all old accounts that throw any light on the former state of the revenue'; but though he could finish the settlement by April of 1800 — six months after his appointment, for a district a hundred and twenty miles long — his notes on the old revenue would not be ready so soon, 'for I must first settle with three troublesome fellows of Rajas who are interrupting the collections'.

As a boy of sixteen, Munro had learnt Spanish, by lamplight and long before dawn, in order to read Cervantes in his own language, but he was not, like Elphinstone, a voracious reader. Nor was he a lover of field sports like Malcolm. Fives was his chief recreation when in a cantonment, but there was no time for recreation at all in Kanara. He was working partly to get away from the place, but mainly from an incorrigible inability to leave a thing half done or badly done. That with a sturdy common-sense and an invincible fairness of mind are his first qualities; he possessed these three prosaic virtues in such good measure that they make his character heroic. There was indeed more than a slight resemblance between Munro and his friend and correspondent Arthur Wellesley. Neither stopped to ask why a thing should be done; each saw what he had to do and went straight at it by the simplest way. Neither had the least doubt that his work was good.

'As for the wishes of the people, I put them out of the question;

they are the only philosophers about their governors that ever I met with, if indifference constitutes that character.'

That is Arthur Wellesley; on the same subject Munro wrote:

'The people are but one people; for whoever be their rulers they are still all Hindoos: it is indifferent to them whether they are under Europeans, Mussulmans or their own Rajas . . . they consider defeat and victory as no concern of their own but merely as the good or bad fortune of their masters; and they only prefer one to another as he respects their religious prejudices or spares taxation.'

Munro brought Kanara 'into such a state that it may be managed by anybody' and handed it over to two assistants, civilians he had trained. It was split into two now, as being more than any one man could manage. He went on to the districts ceded by the Nizam in 1801. Here he stayed seven years, with four civilian assistants; the area was 27,000 square miles and later became four districts. It was in part the same tale again: as he had said of settlement in the Baramahal 'there is no difficulty in it; nothing is required but constant attention'. It was his custom when he was not in camp, which was seldom, to stop work at half past four in the afternoon to dress for dinner, while an assistant read to him. He would dine at five and sharp at eight he would be again receiving petitions and his night court would be open as a rule till midnight. Next morning as soon as it was light he would be out of doors, pacing to and fro in discussion with whoever had come to see him.

It was the same tale in part, but in the first years there was added a much sharper conflict with poligars who under the Nizam had made themselves almost independent. If they were wise enough to submit, they were permitted to retain estates in which they collected rent, part of which they passed on to the Government as Land Revenue, but they must give up their feudal powers of justice, their armed retainers, all the tattered shreds of sovereignty they had pulled round themselves. It was the work Henry VII of England did; Munro had sometimes to use artillery and dragoons, but in the main, he did it with three thousand peons, and in the intervals of his main work of settling the Land Revenue.

In 1807, he went on leave; he had landed at Madras in 1780 and may be allowed to have earned it. The first part of his life was over; he was not again to have charge of a district. The period of high office and controversy comes next, but in the new period as in the old Munro saw every problem from the point of view of the district officer.

The air was full of controversy. In 1798, the Governor-General, Wellesley the elder, with his usual imperious certainty, had ordered the Government of Madras to adopt the Bengal system as codified by Cornwallis. He was determined to waste no time seeking the perfect solution or arguing with those whose interest it was to obstruct. They were to swallow a permanent settlement with zamindars as well as the separation of the Collector's powers from the Magistrate's — the whole glassful at a gulp. He had some justification; Madras was to all appearance hopelessly behind Calcutta, and the work done by Read and Munro, by Lionel Place in the Jagir round Madras, was not yet visible.

The argument for the permanent settlement in Bengal had been that there could be no improvement unless the King's share was fixed in perpetuity. Everyone had agreed that a long settlement was needed, but it was now beginning to be felt that Shore had been nearer right when he spoke of ten years than Cornwallis who decided for eternity. As to who should be the parties, only Ducarel, to whom nobody paid any attention, had ever suggested that the settlement should be with anyone except the zamindars.

In Madras the arguments for and against perpetuity were not very different from those in Bengal, but in a great deal of the country there was no one at all like a zamindar to settle with. In some areas, of course, the poligar, though in his nature a different beast, could be tamed and made to pass as a zamindar. In the rest of the country, there was nothing for it but to create zamindars.

It is hard to understand how any sensible man could have agreed to anything so inept and iniquitous as to start, where it was not established, the practice of farming out the revenue to contractors who would bid by auction for the right to screw what they could from the peasant. But it was a godsend to the idle collector because it was much less trouble than Munro's way; it had worked in Bengal and everyone was under the spell of Cornwallis's achievements. The one saving grace was that the Directors cautioned the Government of Madras to go slowly.

The best argument for the Bengal system was that it worked. But in Madras it did not even work. By 1806, the system had been started in less than half the districts; the bad harvest of 1806-7 convinced even the system's supporters that it was not a success. It was agreed to go no further and now the debate began between two systems which had at least the merit of being native to South India.

Munro's we know already; the Collector assessed the King's share which every field could reasonably pay and every year let out to each cultivator as many fields as he wanted. The alternative may be called Hodgson's. John Hodgson took rank from August 1st, 1792, being at least ten years younger than Munro. As early as 1794, he was Assistant under the Secretary in the Revenue Department and went on to the same kind of post under the Board of Revenue; his first district appointment, in 1796, was in the Jagir — the district round Madras — where he was Assistant to Lionel Place, who had begun a serious attempt to administer that district two years after Read went to the Baramahal. Hodgson succeeded Place as Collector in the Jagir in 1799 and next year — 1800 — came back to the Secretariat, which he never again left. He was Secretary in the Revenue Department and in 1803 became the Junior Member of the Board of Revenue. He became successively Second Member, Senior Member and President of the Board, went on leave in 1821 and in 1823 left the service. He was a Headquarters man if ever there was one; he had been only four years in a district, three as Assistant and one as Collector, and all in one area, the Jagir. He had been on a Commission to Tanjore as well, but that is second-hand knowledge.

Place had found in the Jagir a strong corporate village life, something that hardly existed in the Baramahal. Hodgson believed, rightly, that this was something of value in the life of the country which ought to be encouraged; he proposed therefore that the settlement should not be with individuals but with the village as a whole. The committee of shareholders or the village headman would enter into an agreement, for three years, or ten years, or preferably for ever and they would decide what each man should pay. Not every Collector, Hodgson argued, was a Munro; there would be idle men among them who would leave everything to their subordinates. And the villager would rather deal with men he knew, with the shareholders of the village, than with underlings of the Revenue Department. Besides, it had been decided that in future the Collector was to be what he was in Bengal, a collector of the revenue and nothing more, and Munro's system could hardly work unless he had the full authority of the sole district officer.

It sounded convincing enough and the Board of Revenue was convinced; the Government too agreed with Hodgson and the scheme was introduced, but for a three-year period only and not throughout the Presidency. It did not work well. The assessment was in any case too high; that was an evil in itself but where each cultivator every year made a personal agreement with the Collector it was not insuperable. It was quite another thing to make promises for three years ahead and on behalf of other people. Headmen and committees of co-sharers were frightened of the new agreements. The less personal touch there was and the longer the term for which the promise was made, the more need there was to reduce the revenue.

Now came one of Parliament's periodical reviews; the Fifth Report of the Select Committee of the House of Commons was published in 1812, and it came down uncompromisingly in favour of Munro. The Committee believed that the Collector could and should be the best safeguard of the interests of the peasant, that when he dealt direct with the peasant he would get to know what was happening and what a man could fairly pay, that any intermediary would keep the Collector in ignorance and oppress the tiller of the soil. And as for the argument that Munro's system would not work when the Bengal judge-magistrates had superseded the collectors, that was to make one evil shelter behind another, for the Committee were inclined to agree with the Collector of South Arcot, who had written of the peasants' troubles:

'I have no power to grant redress; I can only refer them to a Court; and the Court, if it did nothing else would not have time to redress such grievances, even if they came before it; but the road to justice is so clogged with forms that nine out of ten of such grievances never can come before it.'

On the peasant settlement, Munro had won; the Committee's report settled that question and Munro was sent back to Madras to introduce his system everywhere. From now onward, the settlement in Madras was made direct with the peasant. There remained the judge-magistrate and the road clogged with forms; but on that too Munro won in the end and the Madras Collector kept his powers. Munro had had the backing of most of the district officers, many of whom had been trained under himself and Read, and his victory was the triumph of the district officer. It was more; it precipitated, it crystallized, the idea of a district officer; henceforward he was not to be a distant guide, but in close contact with the peasant, the father and mother of his people, controlling everything that happened so completely that a time came when the child felt the control irksome and wanted his own way.

It must not be supposed, however, that Munro was one of those who believed nothing would go right unless controlled by British officers. All his life he protested against this idea:

' . . . more European agency', he wrote, 'is recommended as a cure

for every evil. Such agency is too expensive; and even if it were not
. . . it is in many cases much less efficient than the natives . . . I have
never seen any European whom I thought competent from his knowledge of the language and the people to ascertain the value of the
evidence given before him'. He goes on to rebut the idea that 'the
natives are too corrupt to be trusted', arguing that if they are trusted
and properly paid they will respond just as the English did when their
allowances were raised — 'though not perhaps to a similar degree,
for we cannot expect to find in a nation fallen under a foreign yoke
the same pride and high principle as among a free people . . . Foreign
conquerors have treated the natives with violence and often with
great cruelty, but none has treated them with so much scorn as we,
none has stigmatized the whole people as unworthy of trust. . . .'

And now, though he had insisted that power should be with the
district officer, he wanted Indian judges, he wanted to recognize
village *panchayats*, village committees to which he would give the
powers of petty courts to try small offences, just in fact the kind of
powers that these village courts were to be given more than a century
later in the last phase. He met just the difficulties his successors were
to know — but there is a great deal about Munro for which there is
no room here.

The Third Maratha War came and he begged to be allowed to
revert from civil employment; at last his request was granted and he
became a soldier again after a quarter of a century away from the
parade-ground. He was given the rank of Brigadier-General but
very few troops; with these he advanced into an enemy district, and
settled with his left hand the land revenue while with his right he
raised troops with which to complete his brigade and continue his
advance. He emerged from his new districts after several skirmishes
and sieges in perfect step with the main operations, but distinguished
from other column commanders in that he left behind him a civil
administration already established and proceeding smoothly. He
became Governor of Madras; he was Governor for five years and he
regarded his province as a larger district. He had been father of his
district; he would be father in just the same way of this much larger
area.

There is no room here for the moving restraint with which he
writes of his separation from the elder son whom he left at three
weeks old and never saw again, from the younger son whom he had
known till he was two; nor for his farewell visit to the district he had
held as Collector for seven years, made against all advice and in

defiance of the epidemic of cholera which killed him. But room must be found for his friendly relations with the Madras civilians of the new school. To Cockburn, of the Board of Revenue, he wrote habitually in slippers and shirt-sleeves, saying just what he thought; Webbe, the Chief Secretary, wrote to Munro in 1800, giving him advance information of his move and of other formal orders that would follow:

'Remember, you will be required to move at short notice . . . know by these presents you are authorized to grant the whole extent of the remission of land-rent recommended by yourself . . . provided you shall be able to make it appear that you do not go snacks with the innocent Gentoos . . .' Dishonesty is now something about which it is possible to make a joke; ten years ago it had been too serious.

And his views on young civilians must be remembered. To them, when he was Governor of Madras, he said:

'The junior civil servants of the Company have a noble field before them. No men in the world have more powerful motives for studying with diligence, for there are none who have a prospect of a greater reward and whose success depends so entirely on themselves . . . language is but the means, the good government of the people is the great end . . .' And again:

'The advantage of knowing the country languages is not merely that it will enable you to carry on the public business . . . but that by rendering you more intimately acquainted with the people, it will dispose you to think more favourably of them. . . .'

To the Court of Directors he wrote on the same subject:

'We can never be qualified to govern men against whom we are prejudiced . . . If a young man be sent at once from the training college to the revenue line, the usual effect will be to render him attached to the natives . . .' and he argued that every man should begin by at least two years in the business of revenue and general administration. No one should start in the Secretariat and spend his life on an office stool.

And beside this must be set his view of the future, which he expressed with his usual conciseness and directness:

'Our sovereignty should be prolonged to the remotest possible period . . . Whenever we are obliged to resign it, we should leave the natives so far improved from their connection with us, as to be capable of maintaining a free, or at least a regular, government amongst themselves.'

Munro had carried South India forward from the eighteenth

century into the nineteenth; he had come to a world of sloth and corruption, he left when he died a body of young men whom he had trained himself, Read the younger and Ravenshaw, Cochran, Thackeray, and Stodart, men in whom any administration in the world might feel pride. But the last word on Munro shall be left to a contemporary, another Scot, Mountstuart Elphinstone; who after a first meeting wrote of his

'. . . strong practical good sense, his simplicity and frankness, his perfect good nature and good humour, his real benevolence . . . his activity and his truthfulness of mind, easily pleased with anything and delighted with those things that in general have no effect but on a youthful imagination. The effect of these last qualities is heightened by their contrast with his stern countenance and searching eye'.

There it is, a picture of the new ruler of India; a stern countenance, a searching eye, a real benevolence, a youthful imagination — and a constant attention to business.

CHAPTER II

MALCOLM AND CENTRAL INDIA

MUNRO had seen a new age before he died. The red of British districts, the pink of British allies, had spread over the map; the Company was now unquestionably the first power in India and did not hesitate to say so. It was recognized now that the Company's servants must rule the districts the Company had taken over and it was a common subject for speculation how long it would be before the whole country was in their hands.

A great part of the change had taken place during the seven years of the Marquis Wellesley's administration. What he achieved, merely in terms of size on the map, can be compared with the conquests of Napoleon and lasted much longer. Like Hastings before him, he held in his hands the strings that controlled a hundred chains of circumstance and policy, each carried on by his agent on the spot, a man who must be trusted to do the best he could to advance his lordship's views. He had immense energy and immense capacity for detail; everything was centred in himself. All the same, he could have done nothing without the Company's servants, a team of trusted agents, brilliant young men, of whom some had started as soldiers and some as civilians.

To make what Wellesley did intelligible — and we must understand what he did to understand his agents — it is enough to instance four main acts. To speak of an act is again to simplify, because each act in its final form was the culmination of months, sometimes years, of negotiation; but it is not misleading to simplify so long as you know what you are doing. It is in fact possible to simplify still further and reduce those four acts that were typical of Wellesley to two pairs of acts, what he did to his two main allies and what he did to his two main enemies.

His two principal allies were the King of Oudh and the Nizam of Hyderabad. Each of these paid an annual sum to the Company for the upkeep of certain troops which were to be maintained for his protection. In each case Wellesley demanded the cession of territory which would provide for ever for the upkeep of those troops. The pound of flesh was to be taken where the Marquis chose; it completed the encirclement of Oudh, it shut off the Nizam from the sea and

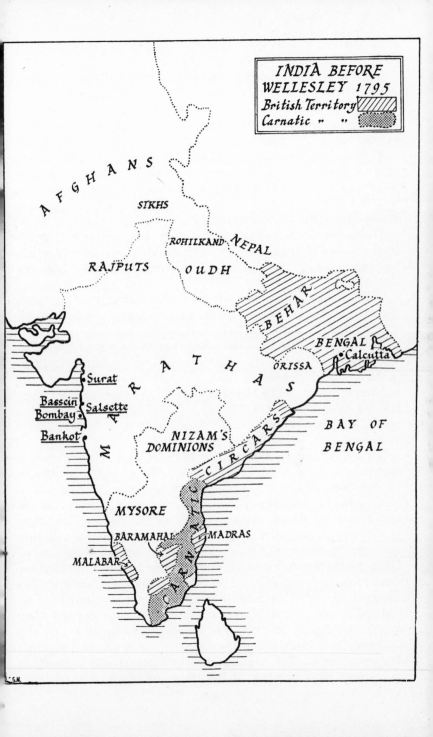

INDIA BEFORE
WELLESLEY 1795
British Territory
Carnatic „ „

AFGHANS

SIKHS

ROHILKAND   NEPAL

RAJPUTS   OUDH

BEHAR

BENGAL
Calcutta

ORISSA

M A R A T H A S

Surat

Bassein   Salsette
Bombay

Bankot

NIZAM'S
DOMINIONS

CIRCARS

BAY OF
BENGAL

MYSORE

BARAMAHAL   MADRAS

MALABAR

CARNATIC

G.M.

from Mysore. The King of Oudh was not only to cede territory but to disband all his own troops as well.

The two principal enemies were Tippoo Sultan of Mysore and the Marathas. It is difficult to see how war could have been avoided with either. Tippoo Sultan hated the English and to them he was an ogre more hateful even than Bonaparte. Wellesley ensured, by careful preparation, sound planning, and choosing the right men, that the force brought against him should be overwhelming, that the inevitable war should be ruthless, quick and therefore merciful. Tippoo was crushed and killed, his dominions reduced to half their previous size, and on the throne was placed a ruler of the Hindu dynasty from whom Tippoo's father had usurped it.

The Maratha states were essentially predatory; Warren Hastings by the Treaty of Salbai had kept them in check for twenty years but war had to come. The Nizam's Chief Minister told John Malcolm in 1802:

'If they mean to keep their lawless bands together, they must lead them to plunder . . . These Maratha gentlemen need a lesson and we shall have no peace till they receive it. . . . '

Their lesson began at Assaye, administered by Arthur Wellesley, it continued at Laswari, the culmination of Lake's brilliant campaign in the north, which wrote 'Lake and Victory' on the colours of half-a-dozen regiments. The Marathas were at the Company's feet when the Directors decided to recall Lord Wellesley and reverse his policy, sending Cornwallis out a second time to undo as much as possible of what he had done.

But the withdrawal was a slight one; the face of the map was changed and it had been changed by Wellesley's will. 'I can declare my conscientious conviction,' Lord Wellesley wrote, 'that no greater blessing can be conferred on the native inhabitants of India than the extension of the British authority, influence and power.' That conviction was his motive in all he did and it is arguable that with that conviction he might even have gone further. To read of the state of Oudh thirty years later is to feel that he would have been justified, on those grounds openly declared, in annexing the whole country. But unfortunately while he acted on his conscientious conviction, he justified his acts by arguments which were really untenable and when argument failed he fell back on turkey-cock indignation and the language (as Edward Thompson says) of the headmaster's study. Pompous, humourless and arrogant, he stormed and lectured; it might hurt him more than it hurt those he chastised but he was

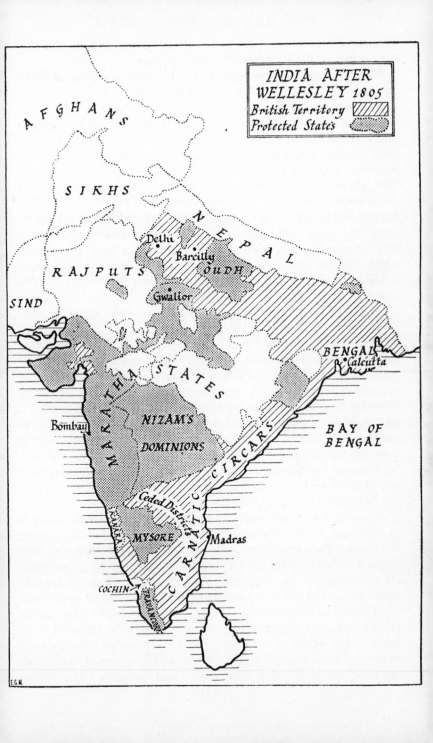

INDIA AFTER
WELLESLEY 1805
British Territory
Protected States

AFGHANS

SIKHS

NEPAL

RAJPUTS

Delhi

Barcilly

OUDH

Gwalior

SIND

MARATHA STATES

BENGAL

Calcutta

Bombay

NIZAM'S

DOMINIONS

CIRCARS

BAY OF
BENGAL

KANARI

Ceded Districts

MYSORE

Madras

COCHIN

TRAVANCORE

CARNATIC

E.G.M.

resolute in his indignation. Moral obliquity and nothing else was responsible for the least flinching from the cane.

When the pressure upon him grew intolerable, the King of Oudh decided to abdicate, meaning to leave to his minor son the humiliation of ceding half his dominions without striking a blow. The Governor-General welcomed his abdication and blandly assumed that there would be no heir and the whole territory would lapse to the Company; when he learnt of this assumption the King not unnaturally withdrew his abdication. 'My duty,' wrote his lordship, 'compels me to communicate to you in the most unqualified terms the astonishment, regret and indignation which your recent conduct has excited in my mind.' And on the King continuing the correspondence by a really unanswerable reference to past treaties, he received a scolding for not sealing his letter in due form, an omission which 'besides indicating a levity totally unsuitable to the occasion is highly deficient in the respect due to the first British Authority in India'.

Bullying is never pleasant to watch and it is with distaste that one must regard the manner of Wellesley's diplomacy. All the same, it was the very fact that he could see no one else's point of view that gave him the cutting edge to get things done, it was his tremendous certainty of the respect due to him that gave him complete control of everything in India. 'His great mind pervaded the whole,' wrote Malcolm, '. . . his spirit was infused into every agent he employed; . . . all sought his praise, all dreaded his censure.' He did what he set out to do and however much one may wish that he had used different language there can be no doubt that his swiftness was merciful, that for instance much human misery in Central India would have been prevented if he had himself been allowed to conclude the war with the Marathas that began with Assaye.

As it was, Wellesley's work was left to be completed by the Marquis of Hastings. Cornwallis came out in 1805 to undo Wellesley's work; the Rajputs were abandoned to the Marathas and for the moment the English withdrew from Central India. The patched-up peace lasted for ten years, but they were years of unimaginable chaos and lawlessness. Each year, as the rains came to an end, the Rajput or Maratha chief looked to his harness and sharpened his sword; he called up his vassals, mounted his horse and rode off to see what he could bring back on his saddle-bow. Those who by old age or infirmity were prevented from taking the field themselves kept gangs of marauders, 'as poachers in England keep dogs', said Sleeman. The Pathan

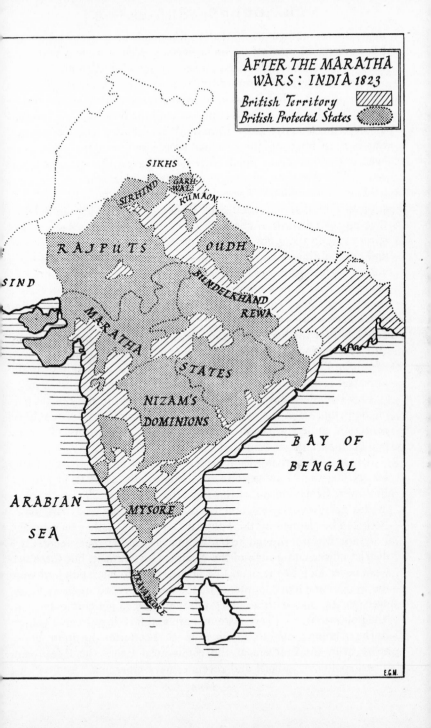

AFTER THE MARATHA
WARS: INDIA 1823
British Territory
British Protected States

SIKHS
SIRHIND
GARH-WAL
KUMAON
RAJPUTS
OUDH
SIND
BUNDELKHAND
REWA
MARATHA
STATES
NIZAM'S
DOMINIONS
BAY OF
BENGAL
ARABIAN
SEA
MYSORE
TRAVANCORE

E.G.M.

mercenaries, known as Pindaris, who had been attached to the Maratha states, now set up on their own, each as a chief without a state, dependent on plunder as a sole means of livelihood.

In the Pindari War from 1817 to 1819 Lord Hastings set out to end these gangs. But it was seen from the start that it would not be easy to kill the dogs without a quarrel with the poachers. So the Pindari War became the Third Maratha War; it ended with the annexation of great tracts of land in which there was now to be peace, while even in the dominions which were to remain with the princes it was established that there was to be no more moss-trooping.

'The native chiefs', wrote Sleeman some years later, 'feel like squires forbidden to chase foxes.' Bishop Heber, in 1825, found men digging their irrigation channels or hoeing their crops each with a spear stuck in the ground by his side. All was peace now, they said, and the bad times had gone — but they would come again; the habit stuck. 'A few years ago,' a peasant told Sleeman in the 'twenties, 'I could not have gone a hundred yards from my village without having the clothes ripped from my back.' And to Tod another said: 'Who durst have passed this spot eighteen months ago? They would have killed you for the bread you had about you; now you may carry gold . . .' And he found that the universal greeting to an Englishman was: '*Atul Raj!* May your rule last for ever!' 'This,' he added, 'is the universal language of men who have never known peaceful days.'

This is the evidence of the men who travelled in the central part of the peninsula in the years after Lord Hastings's war. It could be continued endlessly; a country the size of Spain, France and Germany had been pacified, and men felt a deep relief.

It is to Malcolm and Elphinstone that most of the credit must go for settling the Maratha country, though both learnt from Munro. Both were Scots; indeed, of this great four only Metcalfe was English in the narrower sense — and he was part French and part Irish. Both can be claimed by the Political Department rather than by any Province; Munro, though he had begun as a soldier, was essentially a district officer and a man of the Madras Government, but these two were never long in the main line of district administration and were the Governor-General's men. In the surge forward of those years, every young man with a noble ambition tried to get employment in 'the political line'. There were no hard and fast departments yet, no rules confining a man to 'the line' he had been brought up in, but — apart from the outcasts of the commercial line — the three main 'lines', political, judicial and revenue, were emerging. And so long as in the settled districts — the 'regulation provinces' — the judge-magistrate was still rooted in his court chair, there could be no question that the political was much the most attractive.

Malcolm was older in service than Elphinstone by some ten years. He was a grandson of the manse, his father being a small farmer of Eskdale. He was one of seventeen children and when his father fell suddenly into financial trouble it became necessary to settle as many sons as possible. The Directors of the East India Company were doubtful whether they could stretch things so far as to commission a boy of thirteen. 'Why, my little man,' said one of them playfully, 'what would you do if you met Hyder Ali?' he being the father of Tippoo and the ogre of the moment. 'I would draw ma sworrd and cut off his heid,' replied the candidate, and was commissioned at once with acclamation.

There is a glimpse of him at fifteen, described as 'a bright-faced English boy', in independent command of two companies of infantry, but it is the glimpse of a moment only. Till he was past twenty, he enjoyed himself unreservedly; he got into debt, as a young man should, he became a fine horseman and rubbed off the awkwardness he had brought from Eskdale. He remembered those days with a twinkle when he re-visited Hyderabad eighteen years later and was sent several trays of fruit and her portrait, 'meant, she said, to revive pleasing recollections', by 'his old friend, Chandah, the celebrated dancing-girl'. But soon after he was twenty he began to feel the urge of ambition; he began to spend his leisure with a Persian grammar, he began to hope for staff appointments. Years later, he wrote to a young officer that he would never rise without:

'that noble resolution of the mind which no labour or danger daunts in the pursuit of its object, which fixes the subaltern for years to studies that are to enable him to excel when he is a field-officer, which leads him to inure himself to privations in the time of plenty that he may not heed them where they are unavoidable. . . .'
and he wrote on another occasion to Tod:
'I have been all my life an aspirant. . . .'

Certainly ambition was always a part of his character in a sense it never was in Munro's or Elphinstone's. He did in his own words 'court every kind of service that can increase his chance of notice and distinction' as the other two did not. But it was a frank open ambition; he courted service and he admired power, but he would not flatter a power he did not admire. His ambition was that of the boy who wants to be captain of the eleven and head of the school; indeed, it was not only because he was commissioned so young that he was known for many years as Boy Malcolm. Nor was it only because of his high spirits, his animal vigour, his delight in games and practical jokes. There is something of the jovial head prefect about him always, the big able boy who is good at everything, but who is not quite grown up because everyone has always liked him, because everything has come easily to him and because he does not yet know how unpredictable men can be.

Malcolm's political career began when he received a letter from the elder Wellesley appointing him Assistant to the Resident at Hyderabad. 'I wish to see you . . .' wrote the Governor-General, '. . . it will be advantageous to the public service that you should thoroughly understand my opinions on various points . . .' and Malcolm accordingly reported at Government House in Calcutta. Here he was at once in a congenial atmosphere. Wellesley found able men and attached them closely to himself; if to disagree with him was wicked, to accept his leadership loyally was well on the road to being always right. Edmonstone was there, officially the Persian translator, soon to be Private Secretary to the Governor-General, the first of five Edmonstones to be Writers in the Bengal service; Henry Wellesley, brother of the Lord and of Arthur; the elder Kirkpatrick, who had just resigned the Residency at Hyderabad — Malcolm knew them all and they all liked him; he became one of the Government House set.

The Governor-General's ideas about the Indian states were exactly those which Malcolm had hoped to find. It was with a genuine delight that he recognized a vigour and forthrightness that matched his own, and though there was always an element of awe in his regard for 'the Lord', or 'the glorious little man', as the set called him among themselves, there was undoubtedly affection too. There was something in Malcolm's boyishness that welcomed a hero he could give his devotion to; this was the first he had found, and it was devotion of a quality that cannot be given twice.

Employment came soon; in the Mysore War, Malcolm was the Governor-General's agent with a force which by the end of the campaign was commanded by Arthur Wellesley. Soon after this came his Persian Embassy; he was thirty-one when he set out on this mission, with a train of five hundred assistants and servants and the expensive presents which the Governor-General — but not the Directors — thought suitable for Lord Wellesley's representative at the court of a foreign power.

The mission achieved its most lasting result in a treaty of friendship with the Imam of Oman, then reckoned the principal State in the Persian Gulf, and in permission to establish an English resident at Muscat. In Persia itself Malcolm was an immediate success; he had a fine imposing appearance and a good seat on a horse, a ready laugh and a tongue that was quick to that kind of humorous fooling flattery in which at a Persian court it was a fashionable game to compete — and above all he had presents. While little was achieved but friendliness and a good impression, a formal treaty would not perhaps have been worth much more.

There followed a series of confidential and delicate missions; 'send Malcolm' became a catch-word among the set, and he was sent to persuade Lord Clive to stay another year as governor of Madras, to Bombay to smoothe ruffled plumes after the murder of the Persian ambassador — and he smoothed them with such Wellesleyan magnificence that the Persians said among themselves that at this price the English were welcome to kill ten ambassadors. He was Private Secretary to the Governor-General; at thirty-four he was Resident at the Court of Mysore.

He had very definite ideas of what a Resident should do; he should, he wrote, 'stimulate the first minister to improve the state of the country and of its inhabitants and to impress him strongly with the idea that his favour with the English Government is in proportion to the activity of his exertions in this pursuit'. But he did not have much time for this task; he was almost at once deputed as political adviser to Arthur Wellesley in Lord Wellesley's Maratha War, and he was engaged in negotiations with the Maratha chiefs till Lord Wellesley left India.

Malcolm's diplomacy had a high-spirited schoolboy flavour to it that was not quite so simple-minded as it appeared. When he broke off the discussion of a treaty with a cry of 'Tiger! Tiger!' and carried the plenipotentiaries off to shoot the beast before he would treat any further, he was acting in the spirit of the chairman who adjourns a committee for lunch when tempers begin to rise. Once during a sharp shower of rain the water which had collected on the flat part of a tent suddenly descended in one engulfing souse on the head of Mr. Pepper, an officer of the escort, and 'the gravity and dignity of the Durbar degenerated into a *Malcolm Riot*', as Arthur Wellesley wrote, using what must have been another phrase well known to the set. The riot, you can be sure, was a chance Malcolm had seized as something likely to promote good temper and friendliness; it was policy, but that is not to say that he did not enjoy both the tiger-hunt and the riot; indeed, it was his obvious enjoyment that made them effective. Who could suspect or dislike this great laughing boy?

But the sky was obscured by a cloud, nothing less than a difference of opinion with the Lord. Scindia had been defeated and negotiations were in progress for a peace, Scindia's representative being a Maratha Brahman known to our ancestors at first as Wattel Punt. Malcolm, however, remarked that he never saw a man with such a face for a game of Brag, or as we should say Poker, and Wattel Punt was ever afterwards referred to as Old Brag. In Paris after Waterloo, Malcolm asked the great Duke what kind of a man Talleyrand might be. After a moment's thought, short and sharp — 'you know his way', as Elphinstone wrote — the Duke replied: 'Very like Old Brag, but not so clever.' With this man, Malcolm was negotiating a treaty; the treaty was drafted in vague terms but both Old Brag and Malcolm understood that the fortress of Gwalior would be restored to Scindia. Malcolm believed that this was in accordance with the Lord's views.

But the Lord had quite different ideas. When Malcolm learnt this, he explained that he had misunderstood his instructions and apologized suitably. If he had stopped there all would have been well, but he ventured to go on. He ventured to urge that what he had supposed were the Lord's views would actually be the wisest to adopt — whereupon the storm broke. 'Although Lord Wellesley is excessively angry at your conduct, every animadversion which he has found it necessary to make upon it has cost him pain . . . Your having shown a great disposition to admit the justice of Scindia's claim to Gwalior . . . is likely, Lord Wellesley thinks, to give his enemies in Leadenhall Street room to found an accusation against Lord Wellesley of injustice and rapacity. . . .'

Malcolm wrote: '. . . I am perfectly heart-broken by these communications . . .' and he was not thinking only of his career. There was real affection on both sides between the Lord and his ambassador and there was real pain on both sides over this difference. Nothing could reveal more clearly the strength and integrity of Malcolm's character than his refusal to give up his point. 'There is one evil in this world which I dread more than the Marquis's displeasure — the loss of my own esteem, which I must have incurred had I acted contrary to what I have done on this occasion. . . .'

However, the Marquis wrote, with his own hand, a fifteen-hundred-word letter praising Malcolm for all he had done except with regard to Gwalior, and stating his sentiments clearly on that question.

Malcolm ought to have refused even to discuss it with Scindia; he should have baldly asserted our right and if he felt any personal doubt referred the matter to Calcutta for instructions. 'But my principal objection to your conduct arose from observing an appearance of a more zealous desire to reduce my judgment to your opinion than to examine carefully the real objects and foundation of my instructions . . .' However, 'the vexation and distress which I have suffered (and never have I suffered more) have been entirely removed . . . and . . . I have dismissed all trace of my suffering from my mind'.

It is difficult to understand how anyone could feel affection for such a man, but the key must have lain in a sudden unbending, the revelation of a real warmth that glowed behind the pompous mask; as Malcolm's biographer points out, the most important part, perhaps, of this long letter may well have been the postscript, a few lines of friendly gossip about a horse sent to brother Arthur. Malcolm seems to have felt this; in his reply, after acknowledging 'the extraordinary kindness with which your Lordship has condescended to explain the causes which led to your displeasure', he goes on to talk about the horse, and the episode was ended. And as to Gwalior, it all made very little difference in the end for Cornwallis and Barlow restored the fortress to Scindia.

But it is this intimate, this curiously emotional, relationship with Wellesley which explains the disappointments of Malcolm's later career. He was identified, in the eyes of the Directors and the Ministers, with the magnificence of his master, with his extravagance, his disregard for his employers, his large ideas of empire. That was why, when Lord Minto, alarmed by Napoleon's alliance with Russia at Tilsit, sent Malcolm again to Persia, those at home hastily appointed an ambassador from the Court of St. James. Obviously a King's ambassador trumped a Governor-General's and though there was no doubt in anyone's mind that Malcolm was twice the man Sir Harford Jones was, and much better liked by the Shah, he had to come back. All he achieved was some consolidation of British interests in the Persian Gulf and the order of the Lion and the Sun, created solely in order that the Shah might give Malcolm some mark of his personal liking.

Leave in England — a trifle of five years — and long talks with the Duke in Paris; back to India — and a letter from the Governor-General who was to become Lord Hastings hinting at the coming of the Third Maratha War, but holding out no hope of any suitable employment for some four or five months. 'Perhaps in that interval you may be tempted to pay a visit to Bengal . . .' But actually it was within two months that Malcolm was employed, and in an appointment the best he could have hoped for — Agent to the Governor-General in the Deccan and Brigadier in the Force advancing against the Pindaris. Those were days in which it was still possible to enjoy the best of two worlds, to be a diplomat in peace and a soldier in war, and very often to draw the pay of both. Malcolm won a battle — and by no means an easy battle — waving his sword at the head of his troops and charging home, resumed his diplomatic status and parleyed with the enemy, threatening, if negotiations became too slow, to turn soldier again.

But we are concerned with his settlement after the peace. He took over Malwa, a network, an archipelago, a Milky Way, of small states and estates, each claiming some ill-defined shreds of sovereignty. It is roughly what later became the Central India Agency. Here was indescribable confusion; it was a land of Rajput chiefs who had been overrun and ground up piecemeal by the Maratha conquests. During the last century a boundary that had lasted ten years without change was unusual and such a country was of course the ideal breeding-ground for Pindari gangs. As for the peasants, if their condition was to be pitied in other parts of the peninsula, it was worse here.

The first part of Malcolm's task was a hunting party. He must hunt down and catch the leaders of the Pindari gangs who were still at large. Next he must make a settlement with the various chiefs. Here what he did was very simple; the principles he followed were:

'a resolution to alter nothing that can be tolerated, to distrust as little as possible, to attend to usage more than reason, to study feelings and prejudices and to make no changes but such as I am compelled to do . . .' They might indeed from now on be taken as the principles of the first years of British administration everywhere in India. In practice, they meant that he found out as well as he could what each chief owed to his overlord in dues and what support he might expect in return; the result was embodied in an agreement between the parties which was counter-signed by John Malcolm on behalf of the British Government.

Here was no brilliant reform, no rationalization of a political map on to which the little states seemed to have been 'shaken as if from a pepper-pot'. But it worked. 'The fellows that I was hunting like wild beasts are all now tame and combine in declaring I am their only friend . . . ,' he wrote, and again: 'The peasants . . . actually have reappeared in thousands, like people come out of the earth to claim and re-cultivate lands that have been fallow for twenty years. . . .'

They came because Malcolm restored order, because of his name and fame and because he was ready to see them. He had the knack of putting a point in the vivid phrase that a peasant understands. To a Bhil tribesman who, after a long tale of woe, begged him for justice at once, here and now, on an oppressor who had not been heard in answer, Malcolm asked:

'Why do you suppose God gave me two ears?'

That would be enough; it would carry instant conviction where half an hour's explanation would have produced only a sullen bewilderment. It was an answer which ought to have been taught to every young man entering the Company's service.

'I often wish you were here,' Malcolm wrote to his wife, 'to enjoy the blessings I obtain from the poor inhabitants, who all continue to refer their happiness to me; and it joys my heart to find myself . . . restoring great provinces to a prosperity they have not known for years.' And a robber chief to whom he threatened to show his power replied that he was well aware of it, adding that to struggle would be useless for 'such is your reputation . . . that the sword that is drawn against you will be weighed to the earth by curses'.

This was Malcolm's great task; these were his greatest days. Meanwhile, Elphinstone was performing a similar task in the country round Poona.

CHAPTER III

ELPHINSTONE AND THE MARATHAS

WHILE Elphinstone's methods and opinions were not very different from Malcolm's, their characters were poles apart. Admiration is the feeling with which one looks on Munro and Malcolm, but it is a dull creature who can read or write of Mountstuart Elphinstone without affection. It would be with some trepidation that the young officer on first joining sat down to breakfast opposite the stern countenance and searching eye of Munro; it might be with a sigh for the boisterous health and robust high spirits of his companion that an older officer sat down with Malcolm; but breakfast with Elphinstone would have been all pleasure. A companionable silence would be possible; there is wit in his face and in all he wrote or said, but there is no cynicism or spite or self-seeking in the salt; he can be detached, humorous, resigned to the inevitable, and yet enthusiastic as a boy.

He was born in 1779, just ten years after Malcolm; he had been intended for a cadetship, but when influence secured him more profitable employment as a Writer he wrote cheerfully: 'All the cockades in the world are never to be compared with Bengal.' He landed at Calcutta in 1796 and was first employed at Mirzapur and Benares, where he spent most of his time rather gloomily reading Latin and Persian. But he made friends. There was a Sanskrit scholar, Mr. Samuel Davis, as Chief at Benares, while near by at Ghazipur, his brother James was under H. T. Colebrooke, the father of Elphinstone's future biographer.

Colebrooke invites a digression. The son of a banker who became Chairman of the Company, he was a mathematician and astronomer by taste and at first acquaintance found the metaphor and hyperbole of Eastern literature repellent. But he was disturbed by the uncertainty of Hindu law; the opinions obtained from Brahmans were vague or contradictory and repelled his exact mind. He set to work to learn Sanskrit in order to read the ancient texts himself and became in a sense the first great European scholar in that tongue, for he went much deeper than the pioneer, Sir William Jones. He was a judge-magistrate, and may be thought to have been a conscientious one, for he had 'to hear from 300 to 500 causes a month, record his proceedings at large, with all the pleadings, evidence, etc., in writing, furnish monthly reports of every cause decided, monthly accounts of all moneys passing through the court and correspond on the business of the police, etc., with the native magistrates under him, with the magistrates of other districts and with government'. But in spite of these labours he found time to leave a formidable list of learned works, mostly on the Sanskrit law with excursions into ancient Hindu astronomy, a masterly survey of Indian husbandry, and accounts of the religious beliefs of the Jains as well as of the ancient Hindus. All his reading was of course from manuscript sources; it must be added that he took on the whole more pride in his skill with a shot-gun than in his Sanskrit.

At Benares, Elphinstone made another lifelong friend in Edward Strachey, who before long was to be one of 'the set' who ruled India under Wellesley. He was in Benares in 1799 when Mr. Cherry was murdered by a pretender to the throne of Oudh; Elphinstone escaped by hard galloping — but that exciting tale is one that must go back in the cupboard.

Training at the college of Fort William — appointment with Strachey to the Residency at Poona — a leisurely march from Calcutta to Poona by way of Hyderabad, taking nearly a year on the way, learning a good deal of the country through which they travelled and reading voraciously — reading Persian, Greek, Latin and Italian poets, Indian history and politics, English philosophy, the English poets of the seventeenth and eighteenth centuries — always reading — that was the next year. They stayed three months at Hyderabad, where the young Kirkpatrick was Resident; he had a Persian wife and dyed his fingers with henna; at a visit to the Nizam, 'Kirkpatrick behaved like a native, and with great propriety'. But at last they joined their station, where they were to serve under a great man, Barry Close, one of those founders of the Political Service who is not remembered only because he is overshadowed by his pupils. Elphinstone wrote of him when he died:

'I doubt whether such an assemblage of manly virtues remains behind him . . . A strong and hardy frame, a clear head and vigorous understanding, fixed principles, unshaken courage, contempt for pomp and pleasure, entire devotion to the public service, joined to the utmost modesty and simplicity, formed the character of Sir Barry Close. . . .'

Here Elphinstone learnt his work. But there was not much time for routine; almost at once the complications of Maratha politics swelled and burst in a war between Holkar and the Peshwa, which forced the Peshwa away from Poona and led in the end to the Second Maratha War. Malcolm was to be political adviser to Arthur Wellesley, but Malcolm to his life-long regret went sick; Elphinstone took his place and was present at Assaye, riding by the General's side throughout the battle.

'The General galloped forward to a line which was before us and we were getting near it very fast when it fired a gun our way: we were barely out of musket-shot. Somebody said: "Sir! That is the enemy's line." The General said: "Is it? Ha! Damme, so it is!" (you know his manner) and turned.'

This is from a letter to Strachey; in another he describes a day of the camp-life that followed as they pursued the beaten enemy. 'The tent-pins rattle and I dress while they are striking my tent . . .' There is breakfast before the general's tent; 'it is bitter cold and we have our great-coats on. At half after six . . . we mount and ride . . .' They reach their ground later in the morning; 'the General lies on the ground and we all talk till breakfast is ready. Then we breakfast off fried mutton, mutton-chops, curries, etc.' The middle of the day is spent by Elphinstone in arranging his 'harkaras' — a word which can mean either messenger or spy — 'and sometimes I talk politics and other privitie with the General.' Later, he dresses and goes to dinner, 'and we all talk about the march, and they about their former wars and this war and Indian courts and politics . . .' — sad stories of the deaths of kings. And he adds, most characteristically: 'I have enjoyed — I mean relished — society and study and business and action and adventure, all according to their several natures.'

A little later in the campaign, at the siege of a fort, he writes:

'Breakfasted with Kennedy and talked about Hafiz, Sa'adi, Horace and Anacreon. At nine I left him and went to the trenches . . . I went up to Colonel Kenny, said I heard he was to lead the storming party and that if he would allow me I would be of his party. He bowed and agreed . . . We drew our swords, stuck pistols in our belts or handkerchiefs tied round our middle and . . . marched on to the breach . . .' There is a long and spirited description of the storm; the party going to the storm reminded him of the eighth and ninth verses of the third book of the *Iliad*. 'And after one gets over the breach one is too busy and animated to think of anything but how to get on.'

Resident at Nagpur, at the noble age of twenty-four, the Lord's representative at the court of the Bhonsla; but instead of Malcolm's eager adulation for the glorious little man, Elphinstone displays an amused, a critical, disrespect that was not without admiration. 'Old Villainy', he calls him in his intimate letters; there is a clean, dry sparkle to Elphinstone, like the best champagne, *goût anglais*. He owed this of course partly to social background; he was the younger son of an old Scottish barony and he could look with detachment at Anglo-Irish pomp. For the next importation, Lord Minto, he felt the familiarity of a Border neighbour, and wrote home with amusement of the doings of Gibby Elliott.

He went on leave to Calcutta in 1807, after six years spent 'where people speak what they don't think in Moors — ' that is Urdu. Here there were 'such lots of women and laughing and philandering that I was in heaven'. Then came Gibby Elliott's diplomatic move to counter the Treaty of Tilsit; Malcolm left for Persia, Elphinstone for Afghanistan, and Metcalfe for Lahore, each commissioned to get as much and give as little as he could in the way of a defensive alliance that would bolster India against the sinister pact of Alexander and Napoleon.

It was a mission of which Elphinstone always said that it cured him of ambition; certainly not much in the way of diplomatic triumph came of it. Calcutta had not yet learnt that diplomacy is only a kind of bargaining and that not much trade is likely to take place if the side which starts the discussion has nothing for sale. The mission was thus doomed to failure even if it had not been accredited to a king on the point of losing his throne. All the same, it was probably worth undertaking if only for Elphinstone's history of the Kingdom of Cabul, which was long the standard work. He had been encouraged by the example of Malcolm, who in the course of a crowded life found time to write a history of Persia and a history of Central India as well as a collection of Persian fairy tales, the life of Clive which occasioned Macaulay's essay, and other works.

Elphinstone came back to be Resident at Poona and now had leisure both to read and to write. He rode ten or twenty miles every morning and did a bodily exercise known as the *kasrat*, spent the morning on public business, lunched at two on 'a few sandwiches and figs and a glass of water' and about three 'began to read or examine people about the Afghans'. He then did the kasrat a second time, dined 'on a few potatoes and one or two glasses of claret and water', read some more and went to sleep at eleven. He was a man who revelled in the stress of circumstance when it came his way but who never courted it; when at last the Peshwa's evil genius, Trimbakji, was imprisoned and Elphinstone was freed from his intrigues, his comment was: 'Now I have time to read Cicero in the mornings.'

Of Baji Rao, the Peshwa, to whose court he was accredited, he wrote, with Tacitean insight and conciseness:

'He is eager for power, though he wants the boldness necessary to acquire it, and tenacious of authority though too indolent to exercise it. Though capricious and changeable in his humours, he is steady in his serious designs . . .' Much more follows that is wholly to the purpose and markedly fair; he adds, what many a Resident has thought of many a Prince; 'His superstition imposes no restraint upon his pleasures and the greater part of his time that is not occupied by religion is devoted to vicious indulgences.'

And of Malcolm he wrote in his diary:

'Never was anybody so frank and good-humoured . . . his activity of body and mind, his inexhaustible spirits and imperturbable temper are truly admirable; and all these qualities are accompanied with a sound judgment and a great store of knowledge. . . .'

Years later, saying goodbye to Malcolm, he wrote: 'We shall doubtless often miss his spirits and good humour, while we forget his noise and egotism. I have all along reproached myself for my want of tolerance for the single defect of one of the first and best men I know.' Even now, at one of their earlier meetings, he could qualify his rapture and write: 'Malcolm certainly has wise and enlarged views of policy, and, among them, the kind and indulgent manner in which he regards the natives (though perhaps originating in his heart as much as in his head) is by no means the least.'

It was this indulgence of Malcolm's that led to the most dramatic episode in Elphinstone's life. Malcolm was the chief political officer in all that led up to the Pindari and Third Maratha Wars. He could thus override Elphinstone's opinion; he went to see the Peshwa Baji Rao, who — sparing a moment from either religion or vicious indulgence — gave the new arrival all the benefit of manners which, as Elphinstone had said, were 'at once courteous and dignified'. He persuaded Malcolm that he was a loyal friend who could be trusted to be neutral in the trouble that was coming. Elphinstone knew better, but he was overruled; troops were taken away from Poona.

Elphinstone, left with a handful of Indian troops at the heart of the Maratha confederacy, knew how hard it would be to win if the five Maratha powers combined. He had seen Assaye; he knew how easily that field might have been lost by any other general. And in that war only two of the five Maratha powers had been engaged. Now the five must be kept apart; the Peshwa must be neutral so long as possible. He must not show his hand until Scindia has signed an agreement, or Scindia will join him against us.

The Peshwa Baji Rao was as a matter of fact in an unenviable frame of mind. He was tortured by fear and indecision, urged by hatred to attack the English but confused by the fumes of indolence and debauchery and bewildered by the conflicting counsel of sooth-sayers and astrologers. To be near him was to be in the presence of a tiger cornered in a ravine with no way of escape; a step forward or backward would mean a charge.

Elphinstone kept perfectly still; a British battalion was on the way, news might come from the north that the treaty with Scindia was signed; meanwhile he would not move hand or foot. He would not order his few Indian troops to stand to; he would not move them or the Residency staff to a more defensible position. Baji Rao continued to collect and arm troops; the inhabitants began to leave Poona before the coming massacre of the British. Elphinstone wrote:

'October 27th. After all kinds of warnings of plots against my life and the public peace, I have at last obtained clear and distinct information of intrigues carried on by the Peshwa with our troops, to support which he has almost surrounded our cantonment with his camps. The necessity of seeming friendly here while negotiating with Scindia prevented my resisting these dispositions . . . This is certainly the most embarrassing situation I have ever been placed in and is of course accompanied with much anxiety; yet I never wish I were anywhere else. . . .'

News came to the handful of English in the Residency that the Peshwa and his advisers knew that a British battalion was coming, that they were deciding whether to attack before it arrived. A little before midnight on October 28th came the fresh intelligence that 'their guns were yoked, their horses saddled, and their infantry in readiness', and the Peshwa and his councillors, now, in the dark of night, hot in debate whether to march at once. It was a question whether to send orders to the troops to stand to, or even to attack the enemy in self-defence. 'As Mr. Elphinstone now stood listening on the terrace, . . . the British cantonment and the Residency were per-fectly still, but in the Peshwa's camp, south of the town, all was noise and uproar.' The night at that time of year would be warm and so soon after the rains there would be a scent of flowers on the breeze; one can see him stand listening, straining to detect a change of note in the confused clamour from the town, thinking of the lives in his care and the Governor-General's plans. Everyone would know if he sent a message to the troops; it might be just the spark that would touch off the mine. In the end:

'the motive which had hitherto prevented preparation determined Mr. Elphinstone to defer it some hours longer'.

The noise died down; whether prudence or the word of an astrologer prevailed, the attack was not made that night. Next day, Elphinstone directed that the troops should be put under orders that made surprise impossible; the day after, the British battalion marched in. Baji Rao had missed his chance; it was a week later that he burnt his boats and made his attack.

'We had only time to leave the Residency with the clothes on our backs, . . . marching off with a little firing but no real fighting. The Residency, with all my books, journals, letters, manuscripts, was soon in a blaze . . . We went to observe the enemy. The sight was magnificent as the tide rolled out of Poona . . . Everything was hushed except the trampling and neighing of horses and the whole valley was filled with them like a river in flood . . . I now . . . sent an order to move down at once and attack . . . Soon after his whole mass of cavalry came on at speed in the most splendid style. The rush of horse, the sound of the earth, the waving of flags, the brandishing of spears, were grand beyond description but perfectly ineffectual . . .' At one stage, 'I own I thought there was a good chance of our losing the battle . . .' but in the end 'we found ourselves alone on the field and the sun long set'.

The British force had consisted of less than three thousand men, of which perhaps a fifth or a sixth were European born, while the Peshwa is said to have had eighteen thousand cavalry and eight thousand infantry, but it was not a hard-fought fight like Assaye or the battle Malcolm won against Holkar. There cannot, however, have been many battles that have been personally directed by a man with no military rank, nor many in which the leader of so small a force has recorded so much aesthetic pleasure at the onslaught of his assailants. 'Grand beyond description but perfectly ineffectual . . .'; it is a particularly Elphinstonian combination of romantic pleasure with calm intellectual appraisement.

When this war was finished, there came the settlement of the Peshwa's country, now annexed. 'Officers will be forthwith appointed,' ran Elphinstone's proclamation, 'to collect a regular and moderate revenue on the part of the British Government, to administer justice, and to encourage the cultivation of the soil.' 'My employment', wrote Elphinstone to a friend who sent him a work of

Jeremy Bentham's on legislation, 'is very humble. It is to learn which system is in force and to preserve it unimpaired . . . I shall think I have done a great service to this country if I can prevent people making laws for it until they see whether it wants them'.

The truth, he believed, was that the old Maratha system worked well enough when there were good officers and integrity at the top. The essence of the Maratha system of civil justice, if it can be called a system, was reference to a panchayat, which is to say a committee of arbitration. What had actually happened was usually known to the arbitrators, it was not easy to bribe them all and in any case public opinion acted upon them strongly; they would sink in the esteem of the village and no more cases would be referred to them if their judgments were outrageous.

Criminal justice was erratic but it was what the people expected. On one occasion, when two men had been convicted by the same judge of highway robbery, with no noticeable difference in the circumstances, one was ordered to be thrown from a height on to an arrangement of steel spikes and the other fined a few rupees; in the second case the property stolen had been accidentally recovered. This, however, was not felt to be strange. An indifference to abstract ideas such as justice, an unquestioning acceptance of the inevitable, these were features of the Indian peasant's outlook which the English were never to understand.

Malcolm, travelling in this country before it was annexed, came on a party of soldiers escorting a bound prisoner, a fine-looking young man, and, being Malcolm, fell into talk with them. There had been a highway robbery at a spot a little further along the road; they were taking the young man there to cut off his head. 'And how did they know he was the culprit?' Oh, there was no question of that; he probably knew nothing at all about it. But they had orders whenever there was a robbery on this stretch of road to catch a young man from the district and execute him on the scene of the crime; it worked very well, there had been far less robbery on the road since these orders had been passed.

They reached the spot. All dismounted and they sat down to smoke. Escort and prisoner sat together in the shade by the side of the road; the prisoner's hands were freed so that he could draw the smoke through his palms without touching the mouthpiece with his lips. They smoked in friendly silence, sitting in the thick dust of the wayside, till the pipe was finished. It was time to be getting along; one by one they rose to their feet, and made ready to go. Some of the troop led out the horses. Someone told the young man to kneel. Another told him to bend his head; he obeyed and it was struck from his body with one blow of a two-handed sword. The body was slung by the heels to the bough of a tree and they rode back the way they had come. What they left hung swaying from the bough; the blood would soon cease to drip and soon it would be covered with a white film of dust.

Strange justice, but perversely preferred to the English courts, to the stamps, the petitions, the lawyers, the judge-magistrates and the courts of circuit. Everywhere, in Central India and the Deccan where the English became rulers, there seems at first to have been relief. There was peace now and good order, no more troops of horse on forays for what they could get. But there was also a fear, which Elphinstone was anxious to allay, that the English courts would come with all the apparatus of the Cornwallis Code of 1793, the same Bengal system of regulations from which Munro had only just managed to save Madras. To keep out the regulations, Elphinstone made his own simple rules.

All power — except of capital punishment — was vested in the Collector, who was also Magistrate, Judge and head of the police; under him were the old Maratha officials known as mamlatdars, who were magistrates and collectors of the revenue. Their salaries were increased and as much as was convenient done to raise their consequence. The *patel* or village headman was retained and encouraged; the panchayats were reformed and regularized. Before the magistrates, the laws of evidence and procedure were made as simple as was consistent with a thorough sifting; the trial was arranged with a view to publicity, known principles, and speed, retaining, however, one main principle of English law — acquittal when there was any doubt of guilt. There were local modifications; in Khandesh 'a regular jury is generally assembled'; 'in Satara, the Political Agent calls in several respectable persons . . . and benefits by their opinion . . . .'

But whatever the variations, punishment was clear and rigorous. 'Punishments,' wrote Elphinstone, 'I think, might be made more intense but shorter: severe flogging, solitary confinement in dungeons for short periods . . .' When a plot was detected among the Brahmans of Poona to murder all the Europeans, Elphinstone did not hesitate to order the ringleaders to be blown from guns, observing that this method of execution 'contains two valuable elements of capital punishment; it is painless to the criminal and terrible to the beholder'.

And he was in favour of confining suspected persons under surveillance in conditions more like a workhouse than a prison.

Method and system, in short — but not too much of either — were introduced where they had never been known before. The whole was kept flexible and personal; all rested on the Collector, who must be a philosopher king. And wherever possible respect was shown for old institutions. Elphinstone had a high 'sense of the importance of preserving the privileges of chiefs whose friendships we have acknowledged . . .' He had planned — but this was not carried out — to add to their order by giving to retired mamlatdars not a pension but lands, creating thus 'a source from which to draw respectable and well-educated men to fill our public offices' and a class of society attached to the Government.

During this time he wrote to Sir James Mackintosh, the Recorder of Bombay, of the future of 'our Indian Empire'. He did not think it would be long-lived, and adds: 'The most desirable death for us to die of should be, the improvement of the natives reaching such a pitch as would render it impossible for a foreign nation to retain the government; but this seems at an immeasurable distance.'

The news came that he was to be Governor of Bombay. He was by no means elated; he had been cured of ambition long ago, his brain was too fine, his temper too philosophic, his humour too astringent, to take pleasure in power or success or adulation for their own sake, nor would he believe that his Governorship would bring many benefits that Malcolm's would not have done. Malcolm, a spirit not so fine, was bitterly disappointed; he had at first hoped that Central India would be made a lieutenant-governorship and the Governor-General had agreed with him. But the Directors would have none of it. To such a province they could not possibly appoint anyone but Malcolm, who was still tainted with the magnificence of Wellesley. His hopes turned to Bombay, but Bombay was to include the districts Elphinstone had reclaimed and Elphinstone was the obvious man. Malcolm might be ten years senior but he was not really a civilian at all.

Malcolm had some grounds for bitterness that this reason should be given for passing him over; his appointments, he pointed out to his friends, had been civil for the last twenty years. He would have had even stronger grounds if he had not been at the moment enjoying the pay of a brigadier in addition to that of Agent to the Governor-General and had not reverted to the army to fight his battle. But he was right in thinking the argument a poor one and it became ridiculous when his old friend Tom Munro, no more a civilian than himself, became Governor of Madras. Munro had never been Wellesley's man. Malcolm had to wait for Bombay till Elphinstone had done with it, but there was no bitterness towards Elphinstone; they wrote to each other of what had happened with true friendship, a true greatness of soul.

It was with almost unmixed sadness that Elphinstone left the Deccan for the splendours of Bombay. '. . . I sighed for my tent and its compact equipment and the fine climate we have left. Perhaps I have taken my leave of tents . . .' 'The period which approaches has neither the literary leisure of my first years at Poona, nor the exertion and variety of the last . . .' 'Still, I go to Bombay in good spirits. . . ,' he reassures himself, but adds: '. . . I feel a sort of respect as well as attachment for this fine picturesque country . . . and I cannot but think with affectionate regret of the romantic scenes and manly sports of the Deccan.'

He had to move on and he went feeling as every man feels when he leaves his first district. 'Wolves,' he wrote, quoting from Theocritus, 'O foxes, O bears hiding in the mountains, oh farewell! I, Daphnis the herdsman, no more will climb in wood and grove and glade. Farewell, O Arethusa and the Rivers.'

CHAPTER IV

ACROSS INDIA

1. WITH HEBER

THERE are the biographies by Gleig and Kaye, the kind of books Macaulay reviewed, three volumes octavo, with rather narrow margins, the pages turning a little yellow at the edges; there are the sumptuous leather quartos of Heber and Tod; there are Jacquemont's French folios in six volumes, and a host more from which in a phrase or a paragraph a man may spring to life. There are the memorials compiled by careful research in retirement, privately printed for circulation in the family: — Notes from the Cash-Book of H—— C——, H.E.I.C.S., — 'for my son Robert's board and tuition at Westminster School for six months, due Christmas 1801, £41.0.0.'—; there are the private journals, which begin: 'My dear Children, As it may be both pleasing and instructive for you to have a short sketch of my life . . .'; there are the records of family service which lie 'in a worn old ledger on the Chinese lacquer table behind the piano in the Devonshire home, and the children are allowed to look at it on Sundays'. The pages turn and one wraith after another sidles into view for inspection; from a hint here or there you can guess something of what he was like, and what more can you do than guess, even for living people? There they are, a gallery of pictures in the mind. But to generalize, to say in broad terms what kind of men went to rule India for the Company, that is something much more difficult and apt to be dangerous. The effort, however, must be made and the risk taken; we must generalize, and at the first attempt two composite portraits build themselves up which are not easy to reconcile.

We may discard the 'savage old Nabob with an immense fortune, a tawny complexion, a bad liver, and a worse heart'; he really belongs to the last century, though as late as 1854 Mr. Jorrocks was induced to take the mastership of the Handley Cross hounds by the news that 'a Nabob with a bad liver' was being canvassed for the distinction. But there is a portrait, perhaps rather a caricature, that everyone knows, and drawn by someone with knowledge of the subject. William Makepeace Thackeray's grandfather had been a Bengal civilian but his father and his father's three brothers were in the

223

Company's service in Madras, and there may be the faintest touch of provincial malice in the picture of Jos Sedley whose 'name appeared in the Bengal division of the East India Register'. Jos, of course, was not intended to be a type; he was a character in a novel and the main reason for his first appearance was to show Becky Sharp's green eyes at work on a man. The novel, too, is one of which the author himself wrote: 'Don't you see how odious all the people are?' All the same, there is no denying that a great deal about Jos was apt to be true. Even in our own day there have been men — but that would be to digress.

'Like most fat men, he would have his clothes made too tight and took care they should be of the most brilliant colour and youthful cut' — and William Hickey had made the same mistake. 'He was as lonely in London as in his jungle at Boggley Wollah' — and there have been others whose eye brightened when it fell on someone who would listen to conversation about India. 'There was a girl at Dumdum, a daughter of Cutler of the Artillery, and afterwards married to Lance, the surgeon . . .'; that was the opening with which Jos sent his father to sleep after dinner, and although it is malicious, it is malice with a point. That is how we do talk and always have talked.

Jos, it must be remembered, had lived for eight years of his life quite alone at Boggley Wollah, 'scarcely seeing a Christian face except twice a year, when the detachment arrived to carry off the revenues which he had collected, to Calcutta'. Roberdeau was luckier at Mymensingh, where he had three companions; he died there, poor fellow, in 1808, but if he had not, he too, when he went on furlough, might have found it a little difficult at first to enter into general conversation. To talk about the things from your own small world that have interested you so long is to be a bore, so perhaps you try not to be a bore and keep quiet and then you are dull.

Men rather stolid and mediocre, then, their lightness of touch and gaiety deadened by solitude, perhaps a little over-concerned about food and drink and their consequence in the eyes of the world — that is one kind of picture for which there is support. By its side may be placed some words of Malcolm's about the Secretariat officer, the sedentary civilian; 'I do not think there is a human being . . . I dread . . . half so much as an able Calcutta civilian, whose travels are limited to two or three hundred miles, with a hookah in his mouth, some good but abstract maxims in his head, the Regulations in his right hand, the Company's charter in his left, and a quire of wirewove foolscap before him.

That is one side of the coin; on the other are Malcolm and Elphinstone and the assistants who nobly supported them — 'Norris in Cutch, Barnwall in Kattewar, Miles on the North-West Frontier, Grant at Sattara, etc, etc, would have zeal enough for this,' wrote Elphinstone — men always ready to listen to a peasant and to right a wrong, men half the day in the saddle, spending what leisure they found in writing histories, as Mark Wilks did of South India and Henry Pottinger of Sind, men witty, generous, and hospitable, a band of brothers nobly emulous. Malcolm wrote of the tomb of Munro's old friend Webbe, once Secretary at Madras and later Resident at Nagpur:

'the remains . . . of the most virtuous and ablest man I had ever known were interred amid a wild waste from which human beings had been driven by the leopard and the tiger and their precursor and ally the merciless Pindarree . . .' Sir Barry Close however had erected a tomb and paid 'a Mohammedan priest' a small salary to guard it; a lamp is kept burning and Webbe's monument is 'a shrine which no one can pass without hearing the story of his life, one which cannot be heard without stimulating the coldest to exertions in the cause of humanity and his country'. Read of Malcolm's delight when he asks where he is and is told by a villager: 'In Munro Sahib's kingdom'; note the pleasure of Mark Wilks when he records a tale of how peasants threatened with injustice retort that they will complain 'to their father' — meaning Munro; hear Mark Wilks again, dedicating his learned work on South India to Barry Close, 'the friend whose instruction and affectionate attachment have been the pride and delight of the best years of his life . . .'; read of Malcolm's young men in Central India, of the assistants trained by Sleeman to hunt the Thugs, read the letters written to and by Henry Ellis, Edward and Richard Strachey, John Adam, the generation who came next after the great quartet; and from all this comes a picture of men above the common stature of mankind, striving with chaos in a spirit which Malcolm's words again express most clearly:

'. . . we shall have much work and I am to have (for which I thank God) more than a common share . . . I am delighted with the work I have, the object of which is, beyond all wars, to give peace and prosperity to a miserable people and a wasted country. . . .'

There seem to be two races, then, the Malcolms and the Sedleys. But whether they were really Sedleys, those who were not the giants, just what in fact was the general level, that is the question on which further evidence is needed. And the best witnesses are newcomers and foreigners and the best of these are Heber and Jacquemont.

Bishop Heber travelled across India, from Calcutta to Bombay, with a loop into the hills to Almora, in the years 1824-25. It was an adventurous journey; for a good deal of the way he was out of British territory and an escort was needed. He left Mrs. Heber in Calcutta and he missed her, particularly in the evening, as he sketched in the last sunlight, or when the lamps were lighted and he fitted his emotions neatly into placid verse:

> I miss thy kind approving eye
> Thy meek attentive ear,

he wrote, and he sent her very full accounts of the people he met. It was he who found the memory of Clevland so green forty years after his death, there being every year a meeting at his monument and 'a religious spectacle in honour of his memory'; the school he had founded was full and his work was being carried on. The Bishop is amiable and acutely intelligent, a strange figure in a land still fierce and turbulent, through which he moves with unruffled courage and an invincible determination to keep his engagements. He made ceremonial gifts of lavender-water to his more exalted callers and moved into the wildest country with the observant tolerance he would have shown to 'Scenes from Cranford' in the village hall.

He called on the Nawab Shams-ud-Daulah of Dacca and was 'gratified by seeing the humane (for it was even more than good-natured) respect, deference and kindness which in every word and action Mr. Master showed to this poor humbled potentate'. Gilbert Master was second Judge of the Provincial Court of Appeal at Dacca; the Bishop's next host was Mr. Warner, then Judge-Magistrate of Dacca Jelalpore, a man of sixteen years' service. He had 'a very well-furnished library', including a dialogue from an ancient Arabic manuscript containing a dispute between a Christian monk and certain learned Mussulmans, and in the evening the Bishop notes: 'between the books I found, the things I saw, and the people I met with, I passed a pleasant and I trust not an unprofitable Sunday'.

Mr. Warner had as a rule no European society, not even a medical man; he told the Bishop how things happen in an Indian court, how a man who has been knocked down and beaten by two others will spin a tale he almost comes to believe of a hundred men in buckram who left him for dead. He told the Bishop a great deal about gang robbery, about the increase in it due, he believed, to the spread of spirit shops, and about the protection often given by a large landowner to a gang who pass as peaceful citizens. 'He had learned from different circumstances more of the internal economy of the humble Hindoo families than many Europeans do and had formed a favourable opinion of their domestic habits and happiness.' Altogether Mr. Warner sounds as though he was amiable, industrious, intelligent and interested in his profession.

At Dinapore, the Bishop's host was Sir Charles D'Oyly, then opium agent for Behar, successor to the baronetcy of Sir John, who had done so well out of Bob Pott over the Residency at Murshidabad; he was, wrote the Bishop, 'the best gentleman artist I ever met with'. His drawings of the contemporary scene are certainly pleasing and his 'Tom Raw the Griffin' is still amusing, though the plates, rather in the manner of Rowlandson, are on the whole better than the verses. He did not rise high in his profession and sounds a witty, idle, agreeable fellow, not at all the kind of man whose conversation would send one to sleep.

At Benares, the Bishop was the guest of Mr. Brooke, who 'has been fifty-six years in India, being the oldest of the Company's resident servants, a very fine healthy old man, his manners singularly courteous and benevolent, and his tone, in speaking Hindostanee or Persian, such as marks a man who has been in the habit of conversing much with natives of high rank'. At dinner, he met Mr. Macleod the Judge and Magistrate of the City Court — this would be Norman Macleod not Hugh, Duncan or Donald — whom he had known by sight at Oxford and now found 'a very agreeable and well-informed man, less altered I think than most of my college contemporaries'. Here he was told of an incident that was to become sadly familiar: 'the two religious processions of the Mohurrum and the Janam Asthami encountering each other, the Muslim mob killed a cow and poured her blood into the sacred water. The Hindoos retaliated by throwing rashers of bacon into the windows of as many mosques as they could reach . . . ; both parties took to arms, several lives were lost, and Benares was in a state of uproar for many hours till the British Government came in with its authority and quelled the disturbance'.

When the disturbance was over, it remained to purify the holy river. 'All the Brahmins in the city amounting to many thousands, went down in melancholy procession, with ashes on their heads, naked and fasting, . . . to the river and sate there, their hands folded and their heads hanging down, to all appearance inconsolable. . .' But after two or three days of fasting, a hint was given that if the magistrates would go down and beg them to eat once more perhaps they might relent '. . . Accordingly all the British functionaries went to the principal bathing-place, expressed their sorrow for the distress in which they saw them, but reasoned with them . . .' and at last after much bitter weeping it was resolved that Ganges was Ganges still. 'Mr. Bird, who was one of the ambassadors, told me that the scene was very impressive and even awful . . .' But an observer unused to India might perhaps have found that a smile mingled with his awe at the spectacle of haughty foreign rulers pleading with their subjects to spare themselves further mortification.

Up to Benares, the Bishop had travelled by river; now he takes to the land, he must have an escort and his servants are armed with spears. He finds a tent much more comfortable than he had expected; as he moves on through Oudh and into Rohilkand, as the cold weather advances, he finds a new delight and pleasure in camp life:

'The morning was positively cold and the whole scene, with the exercise of the march, the picturesque groups of men and animals round me — the bracing air, the singing of birds, the light mist hanging on the trees, and the glistening dew . . .' was such that '. . . I have seldom found anything better adapted to raise a man's animal spirits and put him in a good temper with himself and all the world . . .' He was pleased too by a conversation overhead by the Archdeacon between two villagers, 'and not intended for his ear': 'A good rain this for the wheat', said one; 'And a good government under which a man may eat bread in safety,' came the answer.

Rohilkand — which had been sold to Oudh and taken back again by Lord Wellesley — was ruled by Mr. Hawkins, who had been forty-two years in India without ever going home. He 'holds to all intents and purposes the situation of civil governor'; he seems to have been in Bareilly from 1811 to 1829, being for many years Senior Judge and in the end Agent to the Governor-General. 'I have not for a long time met anyone so interesting,' wrote the Bishop, to whom Mr. Hawkins gave a very vivid impression of the great curse of the country, the hordes of landless Rohillas who had been soldiers and whose occupation was now gone.

The Bishop left Bareilly and made for the hills. At Shahi, the first stage out, he found Mr. Boulderson, the Collector of the district, 'encamped, in the discharge of his annual duty of surveying the country, inspecting and forwarding the work of irrigation and settling with the Zamindars for their taxes'. Mr. Boulderson had 'good-naturedly waited two days at Shahi' and went with the Bishop six days on his way. He was his own master and could arrange his camping as he liked.

The comfort of Mr. Boulderson's tent 'or rather his establishment of tents' impressed the Bishop. His living tent had 'glass doors, a stove, and a canvas enclosure at one end which in Calcutta would have passed for a small compound'. The Bishop felt that such luxury would be very cumbrous for himself but recognized that Boulderson was differently placed as he 'spent so much of his time in the fields' that some comfort was not unreasonable. The joint caravans moved slowly northwards; the Bishop took part rather doubtfully in a 'tyger-hunt' and felt 'intense delight and awe' at the sight of the Himalayas. At last Mr. Boulderson turned back; 'and I believe we parted with mutual regret; his pursuits and amusements were certainly very different from mine' — for he was an enthusiastic sportsman — 'but I found in him a keen temper and an active mind, full of information respecting the country, animals, and people, among whom he had passed several years'.

In Kumaon, the Bishop found that 'the British Government was most popular' and that 'we are still really regarded as the deliverers of the people from an intolerable tyranny'. He had the foresight to note that: 'Unless some precautions are taken, the inhabited parts of Kumaon will soon be wretchedly bare of wood, and the country, already too arid, will not only lose its beauty, but its small space of fertility.' Indeed, in his short stay, the Bishop perceived a great deal. He was able to understand something of the affection the English who have served there have usually felt for the land between the jungle and the glaciers, for the people who live there and for the country itself, a people so honest that a man would go away for months to fetch salt from the plains without troubling to fasten the door of his house, a people brave and humorous as soldiers, faithful as friends and servants; a land of swift thunderous rivers and clear brooks on stony beds, of mighty gorge and precipice, of ridge on broken ridge shaggy with dark forest, of bare stony pasture scorched by sun, of snow pastures knee-deep in the scented flowers of Alpine spring. Something Bishop Heber saw, something he guessed and something he learnt from Mr. Traill.

Mr. Traill first went to the hill districts of Kumaon in 1815, when the Gurkha tyranny of which the people still talk came to an end. He had become Commissioner for the affairs of Kumaon and Garhwal in 1817, and with one brief absence, stayed there till 1836. He it was who carried out the first survey; sketchy indeed it was, and sometimes the records he left were a sad puzzle to his successors a century and a quarter later, but he was right to get it done quickly. He wanted to know how many villages there were in his kingdom, what the fields could reasonably pay, where the peasants thought the boundaries ran between one village and the next. In a few years more, peace and freedom from Gurkha oppression would make them wax fat and kick and begin to quarrel; but in those first few years, they did not think of quarrelling and they had not learnt to tell anything but the truth.

Mr. Traill's men went from village to village and wrote down where the boundaries lay. 'North, the white rock where the vultures sit; West, the tall pine by Gopalu's cowshed; South, Bhim Sen's Ridge; East, Thorn-bush Burn' — that was the kind of thing. It was sketchy, but anyone who invented a different tale later had to take account of it.

Mr. Traill's authority was absolute. He was judge, magistrate and policeman and had power of life and death — but there was so little crime that these functions were less important than others; he was assessor and collector of the revenue and director of the corvée, the feudal service due from the tiller of the soil to his ruler. If Mr. Traill sent orders to a village community that a road was to be made to the next village, the shareholders of the village would turn out and make a track passable for mules and loaded men. When Mr. Traill said he would visit Marora village, the trail from Bhainswara to Marora would be cleared of undergrowth, steps would be hacked in the steepest banks and the streams would be lightly bridged or made fordable. Till the next rains, there would be a passable track. That was how the first roads were made.

In the course of his wanderings, he discovered Traill's Pass, at a height of eighteen thousand feet, by which it is possible in the summer to go north of Nanda Devi from the old Kingdom of Kumaon to the old Kingdom of Garhwal. Nanda Devi is over twenty-five thousand feet and was then believed to be the highest mountain in the world. In the early history of Himalayan mountaineering, the discovery of Traill's Pass is something to be remembered; there were no goggles, crampons or alpenstocks, no knowledge of mountaineering craft, only a 'measuring of our lean humanity against yonder sublime and infinite'. It was done by the way, a game with the left hand, as the Indian says. Years later Ruttledge in the same district learnt the mountain science that took him to Everest as leader.

Bishop Heber, of course, did not know everything about Mr.

Traill and he could not guess that more than a hundred years later
the people of the hills would set finality on discussion with the words:
'It was so in Traill Sahib's day.' What he does say of him is this:

'It is pleasing to see on how apparent good terms Mr. Traill is
with all these people. Their manner in talking to him is erect, open
and cheerful, like persons who are addressing a superior whom they
love, and with whom they are in habits of easy, though respectful
intercourse. He says he loves the country and people . . . and he has
declined . . . several situations of much greater emolument for the sake
of remaining with them . . . it was a mere chance which gave me the
advantage of meeting him. . . .'

Bishop Heber left Kumaon and went south through the plains
towards Agra. His picture is not all rose-coloured; young Mr. Lushington has 'memory, application, good sense, excellent principles
both religious and moral, and, what I have seldom seen in young
Indian civilians, a strong desire to conciliate the minds and improve
the condition of the inhabitants of the country'. Again, in Agra,
inquiring how the French officers had behaved who served there
with Perron under Scindia, he heard that though often 'oppressive
and avaricious', they were of more 'conciliating and popular manners
than the English Sahibs'. He speaks of the 'exclusive and intolerant
spirit' of the English, their 'foolish surly national pride'; 'we are
not', he goes on, 'guilty of injustice or wilful oppression, but we shut
out the natives from our society and a bullying insolent manner is
continually assumed in speaking to them'.

Sir David Ochterlony, the victor in the Nepal War, now Agent
to the Governor-General in Rajputana, was an almost legendary
figure whom the Bishop had the good fortune to meet in the course
of a day's journey; he was said to maintain kingly state, his income
being about fifteen thousand pounds a year, almost all of which he
spent. His train included 'a very considerable number of led horses,
elephants, palanqueens, and covered carriages, . . . an escort of two
companies of infantry, a troop of regular cavalry, . . . forty or fifty
irregulars . . . a very long string of camels . . . and the whole procession
what might pass in Europe for that of an Eastern Prince travelling'.
Sir David had been fifty-four years away from England; though himself 'uniformly spoken of as a kind honourable and worthy man . . .
the venality and corruption of the people by whom he was surrounded
was a matter of exceeding scandal'.

Mention must be made too of Captain Tod, not yet the author of
the *Annals and Antiquities*, 'whose name appears to be held in a

degree of affection and respect . . . highly honourable to him and sufficient to rescue these poor people from the often repeated charge of ingratitude'. And at Baroda there was Major Walker, who like many before and after waged a war against the murder of unwanted daughters, and was rewarded by 'the most affecting compliment which a good man could receive, being welcomed at the gate of the palace on some public occasion by a procession of girls of high rank who owed their lives to him, and who came to kiss his clothes and throw wreaths of flowers over him as their deliverer and second father'.

When it comes to summing up, the Bishop has done it himself in a long letter to Charles Williams Wynn, President of the Board of Control. 'Neither civil nor military have much intercourse with the natives . . . society is less formal up the country than in Calcutta, and this plainness and cordiality of manners increases as we approach the northern and western frontier, where everything still remains, as they themselves call it, "Camp Fashion" . . .' 'A life in Hindostan proper,' he goes on, writing of the civilians, 'is far happier than on the banks of the Hooghly. Of course, . . . there is an abundant difference of character and talent, but the impression made on my mind is favourable on the whole to their diligence and good intentions; nor can there be more useful and amiable characters than some of the elder servants of the Company, who, eschewing Calcutta altogether, have devoted themselves for many years to the advantage of the land in which their lot is thrown and are looked up to, throughout considerable districts, with a degree of respectful attachment which it is not easy to believe counterfeited . . .' and he mentions Hawkins, Brooke and Traill as examples of what he means.

With this must be read the Bishop's words to a father, whose boys 'throughout the course of this long journey have been very frequently in my mind. Great wealth is no longer to be looked for, but, though the dangers of the climate are rather underrated than otherwise in Europe, the service is still one of the best within an Englishman's reach, affording to every young man of talent, industry, and good character, a field of honourable and useful exertion . . .' While as to moral and religious dangers, he considers that though still many and great, they are much less than they were. 'Drunkenness is almost unknown in good society' and is 'regarded with much disgust and dislike by the majority'; 'connection with native women, though sadly common among the elder officers of the army, is among the younger servants by no means a fashionable vice . . .' In short, the dangers of India seem to be 'in Calcutta ostentatious expence and continued dissipation, and in remoter stations a forgetfulness or disuse of the external means of grace and godliness'.

2. WITH JACQUEMONT

It would be hard to think of a traveller whose character makes a sharper contrast with Bishop Heber's than that of Victor Jacquemont. The Frenchman was travelling in search of botanical and geological information; he too went from Calcutta to Bombay, seven years after the Bishop; like the Bishop, he travelled light; like the Bishop, he kept a journal and wrote many letters. But there the resemblance ends. A rationalist and an agnostic, Jacquemont is gay and pointed where the Bishop is mild and amiable; a liberal in French politics and a supporter of Louis Philippe, his liberalism does not survive salt water and he is a critic of English liberalism in India. His wit plays over the English with admiration, affection, envy, contempt — but with laughter when he most admires and liking when he most despises.

'The English,' he wrote, 'who inspire so much respect in the natives of India by their power, strength, wealth and morality (always true to their word, upright and just ninety-nine times out of a hundred) who ... receive from them so many Asiatically servile demonstrations of respect and submission, the English are the only European people that do not take a pleasure in these marks of respect. They esteem themselves too highly, they despise the coloured races too much, to be flattered by their homage ...' Where the Frenchman would think himself the first, the Englishman, he goes on, would regard himself as alone — hardly counting as fellow men the millions who surrounded him.

That is a verdict that no one can controvert; common speech bore testimony to its truth till the end — 'a district where I was quite alone' — except for a million or so who do not count; everyone has said it. But the implication that the French would manage better Jacquemont constantly denies, writing to French friends in Pondicherry that the English system was better than the French, whereby the salaries of the eight Englishmen he found in Burdwan would be divided between fifty or a hundred Frenchmen. The English, he always considered, had an *habileté gubernatrice* in which the French were lacking; and he never wavered in his opinion that English government was a great benefit to the people of the country. From that opinion, however, he drew a conclusion that was French, logical and illiberal.

'Some officials,' he wrote, 'desire the Government to apply itself to the task of elevating a polished, literate educated class, enriched by the exercise of its talents, above the level of the people as a whole . . . They say openly that English supremacy in Asia cannot be eternal, and that it is a duty to humanity to prepare India to govern herself by raising the moral and intellectual capacity of its inhabitants thro' a liberal education . . . one often hears this language even on the lips of officials of the English government . . . If I thought that the foundation of English schools . . . would hasten the fall of English power . . . I would certainly close those schools, for I have a deep-rooted conviction that no national government would secure them the benefits which they owe to the English government: peace both external and internal and equal justice for all. . . .'

This is positive enough for anyone, but Jacquemont wrote, one feels, at top speed and a few months later he seems to think it would be a good thing to adopt English as the official language. He is inconsistent, too, about the Englishmen he meets, sharply sarcastic about their way of life and their large salaries, indignant that they should run into debt, constantly shrugging his shoulders in humorous despair at their neglect of the emotions. 'Even when Englishmen have really kind hearts, they are strangers to that tenderness, that sweet abandonment, to which we continentals owe so many pleasures or consolations . . . They purchase this outward semblance at the cost of many of the pleasures of the heart . . .' And 'Les femmes anglaises sont exactement comme si elles n'existaient pas . . .' while a large dinner-party is a vacuum 'plat des idées, mais pleins des requêtes de passer la bouteille.' As for the people of Poona, he can hardly contain himself: 'The stupid creatures! The idiots!' he cries again and again: 'What stupid creatures! What nonentities!'

That is the outcry of impatience; at Benares, he writes: 'These are no vulgar Nabobs . . . the conversation during the evening will be both solid and elegant . . .' 'English hospitality is splendid as a rule. Men overwhelmed with work acted as my guides round the stations at which I halted; not only did they lend me their elephants, horses and carriages but they always accompanied me when I visited the ruins. . . .'

He was charmed by Simla, finding it added an extra flavour to a truffled *pâté* of hare from Perigord to eat it in the middle of the

Himalayas. 'Isn't it strange to dine in silk stockings in such a place, to drink a bottle of Rhine wine and another of champagne every evening, to have delicious Mocha coffee and receive the Calcutta papers every morning?' He stayed with an ex-gunner, a political officer, Captain Kennedy, who has ' a hundred thousand francs pay,' commands a regiment of mountain chasseurs, the best corps in the whole army, and 'discharges the functions of a collector, acting as judge over his own subjects, and, what is more, those of the neighbouring rajas, Hindu, Tartar, and Tibetan, sending them to prison, fining them, and even hanging them when he thinks fit.'

Kennedy and his guest go every morning for 'a gallop of an hour or two along the magnificent roads he has made'; at sunset, fresh horses are at the door and 'we ride round again, picking up the pleasantest and gayest of the rich leisured people whom we meet . . . We sit down at half-past seven to a magnificent dinner and rise at eleven o'clock. I drink Rhine wine or claret or nothing but champagne . . . I do not remember drinking any water for a week. There is never any excess, however, but great gaiety every evening.'

'The men I like most,' he writes, 'are the soldiers detached from regular service who have spent a long time in political work or more often in discharging functions which are political, civil, judicial, financial and military all at the same time. It is from them that I learn most about the affairs of the land. I am like one of themselves . . .' Not altogether, perhaps, for before long, and in this same company but when confessedly suffering from indigestion, he writes: 'The English have no conversation; they sit at table for hours after dinner in company with quantities of bottles . . .' But the occasional irritation would melt as he remembered individuals; in Delhi, he dined habitually with the Resident, Martin, 'a man with a subtle and well-stocked mind and retiring habits, who talks better than most Englishmen', but at ten every night Jacquemont would say goodnight to his host and 'with Maddock and Bell — the gay and witty assistant I mentioned — retire to the latter's apartments, where sitting close together round a good fire, we talk till midnight. There is no inducement to go to bed . . .' Andrew Bell was a writer of about three years' standing; to him perhaps Jacquemont came as a breath from Europe, a memory of a world he had renounced.

Jacquemont went on into the Punjab when few Englishmen had been there and into Kashmir, where, he says, no European had been but Moorcroft, 'whose principal occupation was making love'. 'One has to have travelled in the Punjab to realize what an immense benefit the domination of the English in India is to humanity. What misery eighty million people are spared by it!' He ardently desired to see the English carry their frontier to the Indus, but adds that they lose through negligence many potent sources of influence; 'in nine years, M. Allard' — Ranjit Singh's French general — 'has gallicized the people of Lahore, where he is not even master, more than you have anglicized your Indians during the last hundred years. . . .'

It is a pleasure to quote from Jacquemont because there are no half measures about him; he is all noble scorn or generous praise. In Mhairwara, a part of Malcolm's Malwa, he found 'a people of murderers, now changed into a quiet industrious happy people of shepherds and cultivators'. 'A single man has worked this wonderful miracle of civilization, Major Henry Hall . . . and he has accomplished this wonderful social experiment without taking a single life.'

But the mood changes sharply: 'I am an English gentleman,' he writes, 'that is to say, one of the most brilliant animals in all creation. I have left the joys of Europe, the charms of family life, behind me; I have said farewell to my friends to come and live in this dog of a country. *Ergo* by way of compensation, I have the right to excellent food, drink, clothes, lodging, carriages, etc. And if my pay is insufficient, I shall run into debt in order to cope with this necessity.'

But Jacquemont forgets satire when he writes of his parting from William Fraser, one of the commissioners for part of the Delhi territory. Fraser had been with Elphinstone to Kabul and had been reckoned one of Metcalfe's right-hand men in Delhi. He must have been nearly twenty years older than Jacquemont, but they felt an attraction for each other at their first meeting in Simla and travelled together for some time. Fraser is indeed a character to be remembered. To him the most keenly enjoyed of all emotions is the excitement of danger and he has a mania for fighting but because of his humanity will never kill a man; 'whenever there is a war anywhere, he throws up his judicial functions and goes off to it'. He is always the leader in an attack and has 'two fine sabre-cuts on the arms, a wound in the back from a pike, and an arrow in the neck which almost killed him'. 'His mode of life,' wrote Jacquemont, 'has made him more familiar, perhaps, than any other European with the customs and ideas of the native inhabitants. He has, I think, a real and profound understanding of their inner life . . . Hindustani and Persian are like his own mother-tongue . . . .' And incidentally Metcalfe told Lord William Bentinck that Fraser knew more of revenue matters in that part of India than any other man.

'He is an original, who really ought to be exhibited for a fee, but a very good fellow, whom I love as I do no others of his fellow-countrymen . . .', Jacquemont wrote. 'He has killed eighty-four lions, mostly on foot and on horseback and has had quite a lot of his hunters eaten. He has six or seven legitimate wives, but they all live together, some fifty leagues from Delhi and do as they like. He must have as many children as the King of Persia, but they are all Moslems or Hindus according to the religion and caste of their mammas. . . .'

The time came for parting with Fraser, and a long-drawn and emotional business it was. When it was over and he was a little calmer Jacquemont wrote: 'What good fellows and pleasant people there are among these Englishmen in the North of India! In Bengal, I do not know why, it is not quite the same thing. There is less cordiality and less wit. . . .'

And here, it may be, is the reason for the diversity of those two portraits; the Sedleys, perhaps, come from Bengal, the regulation provinces, where the judge-magistrates sit in their office-chairs; the Malcolms are the frontier men from the North-West and from the provinces where the regulations have not yet taken hold, where the district officer is everything. This is a theory worth considering; there is more in it than in that other thought that it was the men who started as soldiers who provided all the heroes. That occurs only to be rejected when such names as Elphinstone, Traill and Fraser are remembered. There is more in this one.

But it is not a theory to be applied too rigidly; writers were sent to their first appointments more or less at random, and though it was true that more than a due proportion of the more energetic and adventurous tried to push on to the frontier, many stayed where their lot fell. It was true no doubt, as well, that from those who stayed behind the climate of Bengal usually took off the finer edge of zeal. But make allowance for Heber's kindliness, his reluctance to think evil; take Jacquemont at his most critical, when his host's rich dinners are taking toll of a stomach that has grown used to griddle cakes and milk — and you will still be left with a feeling that many of the Company's servants were not quite like Sedley.

CHAPTER V

BOMBAY

I. JONATHAN DUNCAN

THE story of the English in India begins at Surat; circling counter-clockwise the focus of interest, a little ring of golden light, shifts to Bombay, swings round the coast to Madras, darts with Clive from Madras to Calcutta, and there dwells, spreading in a more and more widely diffused pool over newly acquired lands as new problems arise behind new frontiers. Then again there is a concentration on Madras as Munro fights his battle against the dead hand of the permanent settlement and the regulations; now the beam dances on to Central India and the Maratha country, where Malcolm and Elphinstone are at work, taming those to whose company the peasant had so recently preferred 'the milder neighbourhood of the hyaena and the tiger'. And the loop is completed at Bombay.

Cornwallis, it will be remembered, had thought Bombay did not need a governor; he did, however, send a good one, and just when he was needed. Fort William and Fort St. George had grown into vast provinces as the Mogul power crumbled before them; Bombay meanwhile added to the original island only a few insignificant territories, won with difficulty from the virile and predatory Marathas. But expansion began during the long governorship of Jonathan Duncan. During his first years there was no large increase in territory, but an almost annual increase in the importance of the decisions he had to make. Bombay took the lead in Western India; the governor was the first to know what was happening in the Persian Gulf and the Red Sea and became also the suzerain of many small princelings as the Maratha supremacy washed back and left them strewed along the coast-line.

Jonathan Duncan had come to India two years after John Shore in 1772 (see p. 133); he was a man of Shore's new school, an administrator not a merchant, a solid creature, upright and incorruptible, righteous and just, not at all like the brilliant young men of the set who ruled India under the glorious little man. He was Cornwallis's man, and Cornwallis did not like anything flashy or pretentious. Good honest worth was what he looked for and in this case found.

Cornwallis had listened to Duncan in revenue matters almost as much as to Shore; in 1788 he sent him to Benares as resident to clean up the corruption which was probably worse there than anywhere in India at the time. Seven years he stayed at Benares, fighting the scandal of illegal gain, struggling with the practice of killing unwanted daughters and incidentally finding time to found and encourage the Sanskrit college. Thirty years later, Bishop Heber found his name still alive in Benares and recorded that the highest praise that could be given by an Indian to an upright and considerate Englishman was to call him 'Duncan Sahib's younger brother'.

In 1795, Duncan went to Bombay as governor. He died there in 1811, having stayed sixteen years, during which the Bombay army fought in Wellesley's Mysore and Maratha wars. For much of his time, his first duty was to find the draught-bullocks, the oxen and goats for slaughter, the grain, the carts, the powder, all that Arthur Wellesley's army needed. Then there would be a ship to send to Bushire and negotiations with the Persian court; then there was new territory to settle, Salsette and Broach, Surat and Gujerat. He was faced, as Malcolm had been in Malwa, with many small chiefs, but there was the difference that they had no longer any feudal superior. Duncan might have reduced them to the status of landowners but he preferred to recognize them as sovereign princelings — and it was no doubt an exaggeration to say that one of them was sovereign of no more than a well. They became princelings, not princes; they did, on the whole and within tolerant limits, what they were told. Here before anywhere else the principle of paramountcy was demonstrated.

In Kathiawar Duncan found that the custom of killing daughters was as general among certain castes as it had been on the borders of Oudh. The reason was the same; women of a high caste — it was almost always one of the higher Rajput castes — cannot marry into a lower sub-caste nor within their own; there are few marriages they can make and for these a substantial dowry is needed, while to be single is to be unchaste and a disgrace. Disgrace or expense, one or the other is on the way when a daughter is born and so she is destroyed soon after birth. A pill of opium is given, or the mother's nipples are rubbed with opium or the baby is simply denied all nourishment.

It was not an easy problem. An even earlier Bombay civilian has told of three Muslim travellers who chanced to look through a window and see an old woman of a Rajput clan eating her midday meal. She was so deeply dishonoured that she begged her grandson to kill her.

He was not man enough to carry out what he recognized as his duty; he left her and she proceeded to batter out her life by dashing her head against a stone wall. He came back to find her dying and then at last he did as he knew he should have done before and stabbed her to the heart. He was hanged by the English, and went proudly to his death, happy to atone for the weakness that had led him to delay the execution.

It was difficult to know how to deal with such people as this. Any surveillance would be an invasion of female privacy and might lead to horrors worse than those it was meant to check. As well, perhaps, instruct a fish of the sea to make a monthly return of his offspring as a Rajput chief. But first in Benares and later in Kathiawar, Duncan induced the leading chiefs to sign a solemn covenant with the English Company, denouncing a practice not authorized by Hindu scriptures and promising to give it up. The covenant was broken more often than kept but it must have had some influence and gradually, year by year, the custom became less general and less fashionable.

Jonathan Duncan was 'a simple-minded man of enlarged benevolence,' wrote Kaye; he was 'Brahmanized by long residence in India,' said the learned Recorder of Bombay, Sir James Mackintosh. Malcolm too wrote of 'the worthy Jonathan' with the good-natured contempt of a young and brilliant man, the favourite of fortune, for a senior he feels to have had his day. But he was not so Brahmanized as to be indifferent to the wickedness of practices sanctioned by the Brahman's religion and if to Malcolm he seemed old-fashioned, there had been nothing old-fashioned about the stand he made against dishonesty in Benares.

2. MOUNTSTUART ELPHINSTONE

Duncan died in 1811. It was not till 1819 that Elphinstone became Governor, and he too remained a long time, handing over to Malcolm only in 1827. We know Elphinstone and there is no need to dwell on his character. He continued to astonish everyone who met him by his official industry, yet there was always leisure for talk, for incredibly wide reading, in Greek, Latin, Persian, English and Italian, for a daily gallop, and from time to time 'he would proclaim a holiday and for one or two days' he would take his whole staff hog-hunting.

His two main achievements in Bombay were the codification of the laws and his encouragement of education; of the first it is enough to say that a code was prepared under his direction, a long dusty thankless toil of which the results lasted forty years. But education was more controversial. There were two questions constantly discussed in India among intelligent Englishmen when it became clear that the empire of India for better or worse was ours. They were colonization and the education of the natives. Should we import large numbers of Englishmen to settle in the waste lands? Or should we continue the old policy of warning off as interlopers all Europeans not employed by the Company? And were we to educate the natives and if so, to what degree, in what languages, and with what object?

It is the last question with which Elphinstone was concerned all the time he was at Bombay, and it is hard to see it with the eyes of our ancestors. They did not look at it as we should.

In the first place, it was the general belief that sound government meant leaving everyone alone unless they hurt each other. In England, it was only slowly and reluctantly agreed that the state had a duty to see that its citizens could read and write. Voluntary associations, such as the Society for Promoting Christian Knowledge; charitable bequests; old centres of learning; above all, the Church—it was from these that education spread, not from the state. It was not till 1833 that the reformed Parliament doubtfully voted £20,000 as a grant from national funds for teaching the people, and until 1856 no attempt was made by the state to control the way the money was spent. It was with this background that Elphinstone and his councillors approached the problem.

There was another difference from our own approach, one on which it would be easy to be too dogmatic. We know now that we of the West are over-concerned with the material, bogged deep in the lusts of the flesh, lost in the miasma of sex and the cinema, eaters of beef, drinkers of strong waters, impure and unclean because we use paper in the toilet and clean our teeth twice with the same toothbrush. That, we are told, is how we seem to Indians, and there can be no doubt that in certain moods many of them do think of us in that way. And most intelligent people from the West are full of doubts, far from convinced of Western perfection, ready to believe that we might learn much from the East. Even the least inquiring knows that Hinduism in its higher reaches has a philosophy that can satisfy the most intelligent and a spiritual message that can lead to saintly lives.

But our ancestors knew little of this. They do not seem to have thought the East less material or more saintly than the West. They speak with almost unanimous abhorrence of a religion which sanctioned and indeed sanctified burning women alive, throwing young children to crocodiles, suffocating sick old people with mud and marrying little girls to old men. They saw people who kept women like hens, penned together for life in dark and crowded quarters; they saw people who believed it was more offensive to Heaven to kill a cow than a fellow man; it seemed to them obvious that a religion which countenanced such practices degraded and misguided its followers. They did not inquire into philosophy; they judged by what they saw.

If then they went slowly, it was not because they had any doubt that their own learning and religion were infinitely superior to those of the Hindus; it was because they believed that impatience would defeat its own ends by breeding suspicion and that Portuguese intolerance was not truly Christian. This at least was true of the more serious-minded, while in other cases, no doubt it was idleness, indifference or cynicism that pleaded for doing as little as possible. Almost everyone, however, believed that as education spread the obvious superiority of Christianity would be recognized and there would be wholesale conversions.

It is in the light of these opinions that Elphinstone's ideas must be considered. He had been cautious enough at first. 'I do not perceive anything that we can do to improve the morals of the people except by improving their education,' he wrote while he was still in the Deccan, but went on: 'I am not sure that our establishment of free schools would alter this state of things and it might create a suspicion of some concealed designs on our part . . .' But soon after he reached Bombay he became President of a voluntary society which had the education of Indians as its main object; within a year he was making grants to that society from public funds — thirteen years ahead of England — and within three years he could write in his private diary of some 'extensive plans for the education of the natives'; 'I must take care to support them against the opposition and neglect of the executive officers, who in general are too much taken up with details to have time to consider new plans . . .' But by this time — 1823 — the Governor-General was interested in the question too.

'I am perfectly convinced,' Elphinstone wrote, 'that without great assistance from Government, no progress can be made . . .' And he went on to outline 'the principal measures required'. Better teaching and more schools; more books; encouragement to 'the lower order of natives' to use the schools made available to them; and much more, fourth, fifth, sixth and seventh. There were to be prizes, standard examinations, offers of employment. 'It is difficult', he wrote, 'to imagine an undertaking in which our duty, our interest and our honour are more concerned.' Early marriage, debt, apathy to all improvement — 'there is but one remedy for all this, which is education'.

'To the mixture of religion . . . with our plans . . .' however, 'I must strongly object.' He was convinced that the 'conversion of the natives must infallibly result from the diffusion of knowledge among them', but to introduce Christianity into the schools would sound the alarm; it would warn the Brahmans of what was coming and they would oppose all improvement.

There was opposition and lethargy but Elphinstone contended with both, seizing on the practical argument that Indian officers were needed as subordinate judges and for a hundred other posts for which they must be educated. He was always in favour of the greater employment of Indians, he was always against colonization, which would mean that 'the people of India would sink to a debased and servile condition . . . resembling that of the Indians in Spanish America'. So he would now educate Indians to a stage when they might 'superintend a portion of the district, as European assistants do now', rising perhaps even to be collectors and judges, 'and it may not be too visionary to suppose a period at which they might bear to the English nearly the relation which the Chinese do to the Tartars, the Europeans retaining the government and the military power, while the natives filled a large portion of the civil stations and many of the subordinate employments in the army'.

The new rulers of India were still a little awed by the vastness of their empire; it was still difficult to believe that the future was so completely in their hands as it seemed. But there it lay, a lump of clay for them to mould, and as they consider what they are to do with it they pause and try to think what will come of this great Indian adventure a hundred, two hundred years hence — and they let the mind range over Mexican conquistadors, Roman proconsuls, Athenian island colonies. They have still leisure to think historically, but not many can have foreseen the future with such strange accuracy as Elphinstone, who guessed exactly how we should govern India just a hundred years after he wrote.

The time came when Elphinstone began to count the Wednesdays that remained until his resignation should take effect. Wednesday was Council Day and so the black day of his week. He had been thirty-one years away from England and so perhaps had earned the right; he had wanted to go eight years before but had mastered the feeling as selfishness; now he was like a boy at the thought of travel in Greece and seeing Europe. Malcolm arrived to take over the governorship and Elphinstone left in a cloud of valedictory speeches and testimonials. He had already refused a baronetcy and he was to refuse everything else, even the Governor-Generalship; 'the courtier's, soldier's, scholar's, eye, tongue, sword,' were now to be given to friends and books. He lived for thirty years, one of the most selfless and lovable men who have ever achieved a name in the world of action.

But I cannot say goodbye to Elphinstone without one last look at his journal, at an entry written very near his death. During his time an increasing number of the Company's servants in India were men of deep religious convictions, often of the evangelical school, orthodox believers in the Word, not much troubled by doubt. Elphinstone's keen intellect belonged more truly to the inquiring rational atmosphere of the eighteenth century and he was thought by some to be godless. Nothing could be further from the truth; his attitude to the universe was one of a delicate and considerate reverence; he seemed almost to respect the privacy of the Almighty. He wrote of 'a doubt whether it is not presumptuous to pray at all, whether you can instruct omniscience even as to your wishes, and whether you can increase the bounty of perfect benevolence. But prayer is useful for its influence not on the Deity but on the suppliant'. There is something here of the Stoic, something of the Deist, but it is peculiarly his own. Perhaps as he wrote those words of trust in God's sufficiency he remembered the importunity with which he, and every civil servant of the Company, had so often been assailed in India.

3 . BOY MALCOLM

Elphinstone went, Boy Malcolm came; he was a generous open creature and it was unthinkable that he should give way to that petty form of self-assertion that changes everything a predecessor has done. 'The only difference', he wrote, 'between Mountstuart and me is that I have mulligatawny at tiffin, which comes of my experiences at Madras.' And as far as externals were concerned, he was quite right. The morning ride as soon as the sun was up, mostly at a hard gallop, the public breakfast at which anyone — but I think this means any English official — could talk to the Governor, the rest of the day till dinner secluded in business, the monthly ball — all this was continued, but not the wit, the learning or the selflessness.

Malcolm's Bombay had become rather more of a capital city but it cannot have changed much since Maria Graham described its society in 1812. She found the manners of the foreign colony 'so well represented by those of a country town at home that it is hopeless to attempt making a description of them very interesting'. Her 'fair companions' were 'like the ladies of all the country-towns I know, under-bred and over-dressed, and with the exception of one or two, very ignorant and grossière'. 'The men are, in general, what a Hindoo would call of a higher caste than the women . . .' but 'the civil servants, being for the most part young men, are so taken up with their own imaginary importance that they disdain to learn and have nothing to teach'. That, of course, was always to be a complaint. The society even of country towns, however, is not intolerable to everyone and her condemnations are certainly sweeping; 'the passive submission, the apathy and the degrading superstition of the Hindus; the more active fanaticism of the Mussulmans; the avarice, the prodigality, the ignorance and the vulgarity of most of the white people' were equally unpleasing to her acute but acid intelligence.

When she reached Calcutta, she 'grieved that the distance kept up between the Europeans and natives, both here and at Madras, is such that I have not been able to get acquainted with any native families, as I did at Bombay'. She had been in Bombay to the female quarters of a Muslim friend and had had long talks with a Brahman. Perhaps it was the influence of the Parsees, who have no scruples about food and drink, which had made for greater freedom on the West coast; perhaps Bombay's dependence on a hostile mainland forbade the English to assume the overweening airs of Calcutta; perhaps it was the greater virility of the Marathas. Certainly outside the island, in the newly won country, Elphinstone notes that every Maratha above the rank of messenger sat in his presence, while in Bengal there was hardly a native of the country permitted to sit before an Englishman. But the Maratha country was still a frontier province where things were done camp fashion.

Malcolm's time in Bombay was largely taken up by a quarrel with the Supreme Court. This Court consisted of three English judges; it administered English law, undiluted, in all its tangle of historical anomalies, and it was meant to apply within Bombay island and to the European Servants of the Company. That at least was the plain intention as Elphinstone and Malcolm saw it — for the first rumblings had been heard before Elphinstone left. In Calcutta fifty years before, Elijah Impey's Supreme Court had argued that everyone in any way connected with collecting the revenue was a servant of the Company and therefore subject to their jurisdiction. That meant that every zamindar, every village headman, every sub-proprietor — really, there was hardly anyone likely to want to go to law who was not in some way connected with the Land Revenue. That old Bengal dispute has been discussed often enough to be left out of this book; the Bombay case is less well known. The Supreme Court of Bombay went further even than Impey and by an argument not very convincing to a layman claimed jurisdiction over anyone who appealed to them.

The thing came to a head over an appeal which would have induced a tolerant smile in any young officer who had been a year in charge of a sub-division. A rich minor, one of the Maratha chiefs, lived with his father-in-law, as his father had wished him to; his uncle sought possession of the young man's person and purse; he spun a tale of violence and abduction that would deceive no one but a Supreme Court. It would clearly be right on such a complaint to make an inquiry as to who ought to be the guardian; it could only be wrong to assume that it was true and issue a writ of *habeas corpus*. But that is what the Supreme Court did, action plainly unwise even if the Court had jurisdiction.

The Court appealed to liberal principles and uttered stern declarations that all were equal before the law. But liberal principles can lead to gross tyranny and interference with personal liberty; in this case, the boy and his guardian, living peacefully and inoffensively as the boy's father had wished, were torn from their homes, dragged to Bombay and subjected to months of inconvenience and misery — in the name of liberal principles but in reality to satisfy a malignant rival.

Malcolm saw it all with soldierly plainness. It was to him simply a question of 'who shall henceforward be deemed superior in the Deccan' — and the Maratha Brahmans thought the same. They looked at each other and smiled, remembering the first quarrels that raised the Peshwa above his master. To them it was the beginning of the dissolution that comes to every kingdom in the East. Malcolm, however, was well equipped for such a contest. He saw things plainly and was determined to win.

'I shall not remain a week to have the government over which I preside trampled upon nor the empire to the prosperity of which the efforts of my life have been devoted beaten down, not by honest fellows with glittering sabres, but quibbling quill-driving lawyers. . . .'

He was vindicated, upheld by the Court of Directors on every single point and three years later when he left India, he too was ready to go at last. Even Boy Malcolm had had enough. Roads and telegraphs had been his special interests towards the end but he had shown in pursuing his hobbies far more financial moderation than his early days under the glorious little man would have led one to expect. All the same it was as true of him as Elphinstone that he never took a merely fiscal view of any proposal; he looked always far ahead, to the kind of society that would result.

He was Boy Malcolm to the last. 'We had glorious hunting and shooting — thirty-one hogs slain in the last two days by the spears of our party. I have had the opportunity of showing the boys that His Honour's dart is as sure and deadly as the best of them . . .' And so it was. He was a great man in a different way from the others of the great quartet; he had the same qualities, and in the same proportion, as a hundred other English officers of the empire-building days — energy, high spirits, good humour, justice, honesty, quick wits, the power to command men and be obeyed — but he had more of each. That was all.

CHAPTER VI

SOME EVILS ENDED

I. HUMAN SACRIFICE

To murder an unwanted daughter, to burn a widow alive, to push a child into the river among crocodiles or sharks — these were things that to the servants of the Company seemed cruel and wicked, while many other practices of the people among whom their lot was cast seemed to them only one degree less sickening. It was not, all the same, very easy to be sure what should be done. Even Adam Smith and the professors of political science were agreed that the State should interfere to prevent its subjects hurting each other, but they did not take into consideration the case of cruel deaths habitually inflicted in the name of a religion in which the subjects passionately believed while the rulers thought it a mischievous superstition.

Everyone was agreed that the English should be most chary of using their position as rulers to interfere with the religion of the people. This was not due to mere indifference. It was already said that English government was founded on the tacit consent of the people and there was a good deal in it. The sovereignty of a particular tract might have been wrested from its Brahman or Rajput ruler by naked violence but within a few months the English magistrate who took the Rajah's place could go anywhere in the district unattended, alone among a million of his subjects. And they would not put up with him, he argued, unless on the whole most of the people preferred him to any other possibility. The reason for that, surely, must be that he did not interfere with their religion. For such a man as Thomason of the North-Western Provinces, this meant a continual effort of forbearance; he was a devout Christian, the son of a missionary and the pupil and ward of the evangelical preacher Simeon, and to live among the heathen without attempting to convert them was a challenge to his conscience. He distinguished between his official and private capacities; as an official he must be strictly impartial, as a private citizen he could help missionaries by prayer and charity, but by no more. And this restraint was possible because he, and for that matter everyone, even the least devout, believed that as the Hindus learned to exercise their intelligence freely, light would prevail and more reasonable doctrines be accepted. To try to take short cuts and hasten that day would only delay it in the end.

Everyone agreed that this should be the general attitude to religion. But what about acts done in the name of religion which to a Christian seemed neither more nor less than murder? Were they to be tolerated, or must we challenge the religion of the people and stop such things?

It is easiest to begin with a case in miniature, something of extreme cruelty but limited extent, which will go neatly into a glass case in a showroom. It was less of a problem than some because the religion involved was on the extreme outer fringes of Hinduism. The tribesmen concerned gave allegiance to. Hindu chiefs but they would not have been admitted to a temple. This particular evil was confined to an area the size of Wales, the mountainous country in Orissa which lies about midway between Madras and Calcutta, near the point where the coast-line turns sharply east. Here the plains were inhabited by Hindus, but in the mountains were an older race, people darker and squatter of feature, who had been driven up into the hills when the invaders came, people still primarily hunters, turning only reluctantly to a half-hearted agriculture, much given to drunkenness and to the worship of strange and usually evil godlings. Not all but many of these tribes made a habit of particularly cruel human sacrifice.

The victims of these Khond sacrifices were kept in comfort by the villagers, as men keep and fatten pigs, but with the difference that the pigs do not know what death they are going to die. The Meriah, which in most of the tribes was the name of the victim, had to be bought with a price. The price must be paid in kind; thirty, forty, fifty or sixty *things* must be given for him, the *things* being pigs, goats, chickens, measures of grain, cooking-pots, spears or anklets. It was the village community who bought; the seller might be a parent driven by famine to part with one child for what would feed the rest, but more often he was a professional kidnapper who stole children from the plains. Once bought, the Meriah might be kept for years a servant of the village, well treated; but sooner or later, to end a drought, to banish caterpillars or locusts, to bring back game which had wandered away, or simply as a precaution to ensure fertility and happiness, as grass is limed every three years — sooner or later the day of sacrifice would come.

The rites would last two or three days. The victim, mercifully drunk, was tied to a post; there were dances, there were anointings of his head and strange prayers; he would be carried round the village bounds; at last on the second or third day the climax would be reached. They killed in different ways in different tribes; in one the victim — man, woman, boy or girl — was fastened to a pole by his hair and held horizontally above a grave; in another, he was held rigid by the neck in a cleft bamboo. In one tribe he was beaten to death with metal bangles, in another he was tied to a block of wood representing an elephant; this was spun round on an axle and the villagers hacked bits from the living victim as he passed. In all forms of the sacrifice, strips of flesh must be torn from the victim to be buried in the fields or slung on a pole above the stream that watered the crops; in all forms the victim was made drunk; in one he was suffocated in pig's blood before the dismemberment began.

One other feature was common to all tribes, a strange one; before he was killed, a representative of the villagers addressed the victim, explaining what they were going to do and insisting that he had been bought with a price for this purpose; no sin therefore lay on the villagers but on the seller. Here lay hope for a reformer, in this uneasy awareness of some undefined moral law, of something higher than the will of the devil godling.

Of these habits the English did not become aware till after 1830, when one by one the Orissa rajas became feudatory or forfeited their sovereignty. Then in 1836 the first report was sent in by Russell of the Madras Civil Service; he wrote ably and at length, reciting the facts. When he came to recommendations, he said:

'We must not allow the cruelty of the practice to blind us to the consequences of too rash a zeal in our endeavour to suppress it ... Are the government prepared to engage in an undertaking which ... must lead to the permanent occupation of an immense territory and involve us in a war with a people with whom we have now no connection and no cause for quarrel, in a climate so inimical to strangers and at an expense which no human foresight can foresee?'

He concluded that we must use moral influence rather than power to end the evil, and his view was not based only on expediency. 'Regarding the question as one of humanity only,' he wrote, 'would it be consistent with that principle to pursue a course towards a wild race, ignorant of our manners and character, and unable to appreciate our motives, which would leave them no choice but the immediate abandonment of ceremonies interwoven with their religion or an appeal to arms against our authority?' The Government of Madras perused Russell's report 'with feelings of intense and painful interest', and asked for more, instructing their officers at the same time to follow Augustus Clevland's policy of opening communications with the hill folk by weekly markets and enlisting them as peons. They agreed with Russell and were against the use of force and when they authorized Captain Campbell, the Assistant Collector of Ganjam, to go up into the hills, they made it very clear that his escort was to be used 'exclusively for the protection of his person', and not 'for any purposes whatever of compulsion or violence'.

Captain Campbell, however, was a man prepared to take risks. He began by summoning the chiefs and leaders of one part of the country. They knew him well, for he had commanded the troops in the war against their late raja and at the end of the war they had received 'the turban of investiture' from his hands.

Captain Campbell reasoned with them. He spoke of the horror in which the Great Government held human sacrifice; it was a rule of the Great Government — and one they themselves could well understand — to demand a life for a life. That was what the Government would demand if they persisted; and what was the use of it? Were their crops better or their men stronger than among the tribes who did not sacrifice human beings?

The chiefs and leaders retired to talk it over among themselves. Campbell remembered years later the anxiety in which he waited for their reply. He had already rejected a compromise; he would not permit one annual sacrifice on behalf of the whole group of tribes. He had gone too far now for anything but the use of force if they were obdurate — and then would come all the dreary consequences Russell had foreseen — long guerrilla campaigns in fever-haunted mountains, burning villages, arrows at dusk, men hanged on trees. Campbell had, incidentally, exceeded his instructions, but that does not seem to have occurred to him.

At last they came back and their spokesman gave the answer. It was their practice; it was what they had always done. They had thought it was right; the Rajas had never forbidden it. But now they were subjects of the Great Government and they must do as they were told. If the earth refused its natural increase — 'it is not our fault. It is on the head of the Government'. We will give up the sacrifice of men and kill animals instead; to the goddess we shall say: 'Do not be angry with us: vent your wrath upon this gentleman, who is well able to bear it.'

It was done; in that area at least the back of the thing was broken. There were set-backs of course, but only once did Campbell have to fire and on the whole progress was steady. The Khonds brought in the Meriahs they had bought and handed them over, for, as they said, if they kept them in the village, the temptation might be too much for them. John Campbell was employed in these hills intermittently over a period of sixteen years, much interrupted by fever, during which time he rescued one thousand five hundred and six Meriah prospective victims. These had been bought before his coming; they represented stock in hand only, so that obviously many times that number would have been killed if the sacrifices had gone on.

The Khond country stretched into Bengal as well as Madras. There, too, were some who believed in conciliation and persuasion, others who thought it must be force in the end. A year after Russell wrote to the Madras Government, Rickets made his report to Calcutta, where 'His Lordship perused the detail . . . with feelings no less of horror than surprise', but agreed that it would be a mistake to take too drastic action at once. Mills, of the Bengal Civil Service, was also against a broadcast prohibition or the wholesale use of force, but would not advocate 'a mere argumentary interference which would permit the agent to become a passive spectator of sacrifices committed all round him. He must on some occasions act with firmness. . . .'

That is what Campbell had done, what Bannerman, Magistrate of Ganjam, had done. 'It seemed to me,' wrote Bannerman, 'that interfering at the very moment, to prevent the consummation of the horrid ceremony, would have the effect of promulgating in the most unequivocal and public manner, the determination of the British Government to put a stop to the barbarous custom.' And Bannerman did interfere, arriving in the nick of time, when the victim was bound and the whole village drunk. He was lucky to get away without loss of life. As much was done too, by Miller, Hicks, Macpherson and many others.

It is an example in miniature of what was happening all over India. Everywhere, but particularly in the South and the Centre, there were odd little pockets of old evil animistic religion, customs of sacrifice to the forces of destruction. And since a sacrifice has the more value if the victim is valuable and since no animal is so valuable as man, in times of drought or pestilence a human victim would sometimes be found. There was the rope sacrifice in the Central Himalayas, in which the victim had it is true a sporting chance of escape; there were human sacrifices in a dozen forms of varying horror among the pre-Aryan tribes and lower castes; both the Todas of the Nilgiris and the Banjaras who carried loads all over India drove herds of cattle over

SOME EVILS ENDED

children half buried in the sand; in one Burmese district a living child was taken round the village and a finger cut off at each house before the victim was at last killed by repeated stabs, the blood from each stab being caught in a hollow bamboo. These were outside Hinduism or on its fringes; but at Tanjore a male child was sacrificed in the Saiva temple every Friday evening until British rule forbade it; in Bastar in 1830 the Raja sacrificed twenty-five men together at one time. 'While the gateways of the temples are drenched with the gore of sheep and oxen at the feasts of Doorga, who can tell whether some drops of more precious blood may not be spilt within?' said a Brahman evasively to Captain Macpherson while he was trying to save Meriahs. Brahmans of the Deccan sacrificed a young man at Poona every year and an old woman was slain every time the Raja of Satara went to Partabghar; as late as 1854, a writer on Medical Jurisprudence believed that there was scarcely a district in India where human sacrifice was not still practised occasionally as a religious rite.

Probably at least once every year in the first half of the century someone had to face Russell's problem; someone had to wait anxiously like Campbell to see whether persuasion and bluff would win or whether he would have to fight. Often there was caution and hesitation, a timorous shrinking from the worse evils that might follow, but in the end someone in authority was usually found to harden his heart, refuse all compromise and face the consequences, while there was never any lack of men on the spot to carry out the policy — and sometimes to hurry it on by a little healthy disregard of instructions.

2. BURNING WIDOWS

Burning widows alive was a worse problem. It was widespread, it belonged to the higher castes of Hinduism, it was believed passionately to be a road to Heavenly beatitude. It arose with some logic from the Hindu belief that for a married woman her husband is her god on earth; it was preserved by the general opinion that no one can live alone and chaste; it was fed by the natural jealousy of a man who does not wish to leave behind a young and beautiful woman as a plaything for someone else; it was spread by economic interest, for who wants to support a useless mouth? At its best, it implied a deeply dishonourable view of a woman's part in life, and no apologist has been able to suggest why, even if the widow must die, she should die painfully.

It is as well to be clear from the start on one point. The oldest Hindu scriptures, the *Vedas*, do not command the practice and though undoubtedly very ancient it was not general in Vedic times. One text only, and that one which seems to have been deliberately corrupted, may be taken to refer to it as praiseworthy. It is the *Shasters*, which are much later, which glorify it and promise that a woman who burns alive with her husband shall enjoy his company in the highest Paradise for as many years as there are hairs on the human body, which is three and a half crores or thirty-five million. But even the *Shasters* say that the act must be voluntary.

No one who is not a Hindu can view the rite with anything but horror. All the same, there is a savage nobility in some tales of Rajput suttees. Sleeman, with no authority but his own and simply because he thought it right, forbade the practice in his own district. A Rajput noble died; his widow sent word to Sleeman that, though her husband's body had been burnt without her own living body by his side, she considered herself dead. She had built a second pyre by the side of the first and would burn herself on this with a piece of her husband's clothing as soon as the English magistrate gave permission to her spirit to depart. Meanwhile she would sit by the side of the river and neither eat nor drink.

Sleeman went to see her. He told her the practice was not only unreasonable in itself but not explicitly enjoined by the Hindu scriptures. She smiled and pointed to the sky, where she could clearly see her husband's spirit and her own side by side. She was dead already and her body could feel no pain. She held out her arm and called for fire; if it was burned before her eyes she would feel nothing. She waited only for the Englishman's permission to go and was sure that he would not long refuse it.

He resisted till the seventh day and then gave in to her. The pyre was built in a pit; it was lighted and she walked once round, then stepped in and sank down among the flames without a cry as though reclining on a luxurious bed.

That is the noble side; there are many examples of it in Tod. There was the Rajput warrior who in the midst of his marriage ceremony received the call of his feudal overlord. He went at once to war and next day was killed in battle with the wedding garland still fresh on his breast. She, virgin, bride and widow, her flowers as fresh as his, without a tear or cry caused the pyre to be built, lighted it and died.

Such women expected of their men a courage as indomitable as their own. Tod has another tale of a chief who, after fighting all day against hopeless odds, towards evening cut his way through a circle of foes and rode for his castle with half-a-dozen survivors, blood-stained and weary. He reached his home; the gate of the fortress was barred; he beat on the heavy doors and called to the men on the walls above. At last a message came from his wife. Her husband would never leave the field of battle defeated and alive; the man outside the gate must be his ghost or perhaps some enemy in disguise. Her husband was dead and she had ordered her pyre to be prepared and lighted. He heard her message and there was nothing left for him to do but go back to meet his pursuing enemies. He mounted and forced the unwilling horse to turn; in the evening light, the wind towzled the flames above the dark ramparts as he rode away.

To defy pain and death so completely for so barren a cause cannot be regarded as reasonable, but must all the same be admired, though admired with pity and regret. But in most of its forms, and particularly in Bengal, there was nothing in the least admirable about suttee. It was sordid and cruel — doubly so because this was a country where the men did not risk their lives in battle. All the evidence goes to show that in nine cases out of ten, the woman in Bengal went to the flames in fear and horror. Everything had been against her. As her husband lay dying she had known what she would have to face and fear was added to the sense of loss; still sleepless from watching, exhausted by hysteria, the moment he passed she had to face persuasive relatives, anxious priests. Her death would bring honour to all her family; her husband would earn aeons of blessedness with her in a heaven of their own, he being released by her pain from the burden even of such sins as killing a cow or a Brahman. Flaccid with grief, she had only to raise her hand, to loosen her hair, to break a bangle; the tired gesture was enough, she had consented. It became the duty of a Hindu to see that she died.

In Bengal, she was usually tied to the corpse, often already putrid; men stood by with poles to push her back in case the bonds should burn through and the victim, scorched and maimed, should struggle free. She could hope for no pity from her own people. There is a case reported when a woman did succeed, in the dark of a rainy night, in escaping from the pyre and hiding herself among some brushwood. But they found her. Her son dragged her out and in spite of her pleading tied her hand and foot and threw her back into the flames.

This was the evil that faced the Company's servants. Sleeman has a tale of one of his colleagues in a predicament which in some degree everyone had to face, the choice between acquiescing in a cruel injustice and starting a riot, a choice as old as Pilate.

'Charles Harding, of the Bengal Civil Service, as magistrate of Benares, in 1806 prevented the widow of a Brahman from being burned. Twelve months after her husband's death she had been goaded by her family into the expression of a wish to burn with some relic of her husband. The pile was raised to her two miles above Benares, on the opposite side of the river Ganges. She was not well secured upon the pile, and as soon as she felt the fire she jumped off and plunged into the river. The people all ran after her along the bank, but the current drove her towards Benares, whence a police boat put off and took her in.

'She was almost dead with the fright and the water, in which she had been kept afloat by her clothes. She was taken to Harding; but the whole city of Benares was in an uproar, at the rescue of a Brahman's widow from the funeral pile. Thousands surrounded his house, and his court was filled with the principal men of the city, imploring him to surrender the woman; and among the rest was the poor woman's father, who declared he could not support his daughter; and that she had, therefore, better be burned, as her husband's family would no longer receive her. The uproar was quite alarming to a young man, who felt all the responsibility upon himself in such a city as Benares, with a population of three hundred thousand people, so prone to popular insurrections. He long argued the point of the time that had elapsed, and the unwillingness of the woman, but in vain; until at last the thought struck him suddenly, and he said that "The sacrifice was manifestly unacceptable to their God — that the sacred river, as such, had rejected her; she had, without being able to swim, floated down two miles upon its bosom, in the face of an immense multitude; and it was clear that she had been rejected. Had she been an acceptable sacrifice, after the fire had touched her, the river would have received her." This satisfied the whole crowd. The father said that, after this unanswerable argument, he would receive his daughter; and the whole crowd dispersed satisfied.'

Where the area was small, it was easy; Madras had forbidden the practice a century and a half ago, but there was no interference with religion there, for there were then no extensive dominions and all that need be done was to take the wretched woman a few miles over the border. The Danes at Serampur, the Dutch at Chinsura, the French at Chandranagar could all forbid suttee for the same reason; it was a very different matter for the English when their realm grew. But

SOME EVILS ENDED

Brooke (see p. 227) — he who was later at Benares — prevented a
suttee in 1789 by force; James Elphinstone rescued a widow of twelve
in 1805; Sleeman could forbid it in his own district, Charles Metcalfe
throughout the territory of Delhi.

In the Delhi area, Mogul influence had been strong and the Moguls
had discouraged suttee without actually forbidding it. 'It is a strange
commentary on the magnanimity of men that they should seek
their deliverance through the self-sacrifice of their wives,' Akbar
had said two centuries ago; in disliking suttee if in nothing else he
agreed with his fellow-Muslims, and his actions made it easier for
Metcalfe to go further. But even Metcalfe, when back in Calcutta
on the Governor-General's council, was for long doubtful about
total prohibition.

Wellesley had wished to forbid it but had been advised that prohibition would cause a mutiny in the native army. He let it drop for
the moment and then the events leading to his resignation crowded
upon him. Between 1805 and 1812, the Governor-General and his
Council were busy about other things and they permitted the question
to be discussed with languid inattention. They referred it for an
opinion to the Supreme Court, as fatuous an excuse for delay as
could well be conceived. There was no legal point involved; it was a
question of morality versus expediency. There could be no two
opinions among Christians about the morality, while on the expediency almost anyone in India was better qualified than the Supreme
Court to judge. The Court asked certain Hindu pundits what they
thought; eventually, in 1813, orders were issued which were meant to
check but in fact encouraged suttee. A widow must not be burned
without permission; an Indian police officer must be present and
must certify that she was not drugged, that she was not a minor or
pregnant, that she went willingly. The result was to set the stamp of
acquiescence on something previously done with a consciousness of
official disapproval; officially recorded burnings for Bengal, which
were 378 in 1815, rose steadily to 839 in 1818. It was not till 1829
that widow-burning was prohibited in the Bengal territories, Madras
and Bombay following six months later. That was because Lord
William Bentinck was the first Governor-General who was prepared
to take the risk of provoking a general cry of religion in danger.

The advice given by the Company's servants in the long-settled
districts had in the main been for abolition: 'I am decidedly of the
opinion', wrote Edmund Molony, Acting Magistrate of Burdwan,
'that the abolition of the practice by law would not be attended by

257

any evil consequences; on the contrary, I think the enactment of such a law is dictated by every principle of humanity. . . .'

Walter Ewer, a civil servant who became in 1817 Superintendent of Police for Bengal, Behar and Orissa, wrote a most clear and convincing account of the compulsion brought to bear on the widow and was most urgent that the practice should be forbidden. Henry Oakley, Cudbert Sealy the elder, Courtney Smith, held the same views; from Trichinopoly, C. M. Lushington wrote more emphatically than anyone:

'I look upon this inhuman practice as one tolerated to the disgrace of the British Government; it is even abominated by the better sort of natives themselves and nowhere is it enjoined by Hindu law. . . .'

That was in 1819; one must agree with him that it should not have been another ten years before the step was taken. When at last suttee was forbidden, a committee of Bengalis was formed and a petition, signed by over eight hundred persons, sent to the Privy Council appealing against this gross invasion of private liberty; it was largely owing to the advice given to the Privy Council by Ram Mohun Roy, who had believed the prohibition premature though he hated suttee, that the petition failed and the agitation died down.

The hateful business was forbidden in British territory and there was no flaring up of popular feeling. For the historian it is finished, except in the states. But though it was finished as an institution, it was never quite done with; you may decide to treat a plant as a weed, but it crops up again and for the servants of the Company and their successors suttee was something always to be watched against. Edward Thompson mentions a case in 1911; I have had two letters from living officers who were concerned in cases of suttee in the 'thirties of this century. It is still there, deep in the sub-conscious mind of a continent.

This was in British India; in the States, there was no general prohibition but the pressure brought to bear by the Paramount Power steadily increased until, by the time the Queen was pronounced Empress in 1877, it became out of the question for the wives of a ruling prince to die on his pyre. It was partly pressure, it was partly opinion, the one following the other. But the change came slowly. The number of women burned alive at his funeral had in many states been the criterion of a prince's success in life; the number of empty guns fired when he visited the Governor-General was felt to be a tame substitute. Eighty-four women died with Raja Budh Singh of Bundi; sixty-four with Ajit Singh of Jodhpur, and numbers in the neighbourhood of twenty were usual. It was not because there was anything unusual about it, but simply because prohibition in British India was recent, that British opinion was so shocked in 1833 by the funeral arrangements of the Raja of Idar, whose body was followed to the pyre by seven queens, two concubines, four female slaves, and a personal man-servant.

When Erskine, who was Resident both for Idar and Ahmadnagar, heard soon afterwards that the Raja of Ahmadnagar had died, he made up his mind to prevent another such slaughter and moved on the town with every man he could collect, some three hundred in all, mostly no doubt the same kind of half-disciplined peons that Munro had found so useful. The Raja's sons were determined to burn their father's wives; they too brought up every man they could raise. There was some fighting; Erskine had to fall back and send for artillery; during the night the five widows were 'dragged to the river-bed and burnt'. But the price of this contumely was that the new ruler was compelled to renounce suttee for himself, his children and his posterity for ever.

From this time on, the opportunity was usually taken when a state required any favour or indulgence of including in the treaty or covenant some such clause about suttee. 'When suttee has occurred in an independent state', wrote Dalhousie, 'no opportunity of remonstrating has been lost. When it has occurred in any [state] within our control, no indulgence has been shown to the culprits.' Beneath that bare statement lie a hundred stories of acts like Erskine's, risks taken of stirring up riots and losing life, risks of incurring rebuke for exceeding authority. All of them will never be told, but the thing came at last to an end. Only an odd case now and then survived, and of the numb misery with which each helpless creature went to the slaughter there remains for visible sign only perhaps the figure of a stone woman crouching at the feet of a husband of stone, or perhaps the more moving testimony of a red handprint on the frame of a door. For as she left her home, the woman on her way to death dipped her hand in red pigment and laid it flat on the doorpost or the lintel. The print of that small lonely hand remains but nothing else.

3. STRANGLING TRAVELLERS

Suttee was part of Hinduism; though not enjoined directly in the oldest scriptures it was extolled in the apocryphal writings. This could not be said of the practice of sacrificing children in the river.

A wife without children would vow her first child to destruction, trusting that thus appeased the gods would grant more. The child would often be kept till it was seven or nine years old; then it would go to the crocodiles of the Ganges or the sharks at Sagar Point. It was Hindu practice, encouraged by the Brahmans; it was forbidden absolutely by Lord Wellesley.

More difficult to control was the treatment of the old and sick. It is accounted virtuous to die on the banks of the Ganges — and all rivers partake in some degree of the sacredness of Ganges. Therefore when an old woman seemed likely to die, she was hurried to the water's edge. But there is no coming back from that journey; those who recover are beyond hope of blessing. There was a village not far from Calcutta for those who had refused to die and it was better not to live there, easier for all to aid the spirit in its passing by ladling Ganges water into the sick mouth and if that failed by stuffing nose and mouth with Ganges mud. And lepers, too; it was simplest to bury them alive.

All these things were forbidden but people do not change their ways because a man hundreds of miles away has signed a paper; news comes to them that there is an order and they talk it over in the village; they obey if it is a simple order that they can understand and if the village headman and his friends advise them to obey. That advice depends on the way the district is run. One case punished at the beginning, perhaps even one witty saying, and the thing is finished in that district; in the next, the nettle is not grasped and torn out by the roots but mangled a little by a timorous hand so that it soon grows again.

One more evil must be added. The facts about it came to light very slowly at first; it was a secret well kept. There had always been stories of travellers who were strangled by Thugs, but the mysteries of that murderous society were closely guarded and they left no survivors. It was the disappearance of parties of young sepoys going on leave that made the English take the tales seriously. Again, it was Lord William Bentinck who gave the orders which ended the Thugs. Sleeman was for most of the time in charge of the operations; he had a dozen young men working under him, mostly soldiers turned political with a few civilians.

The first step was the most difficult. But once a member of a gang had confessed, implicating the others in order to save his own life, providing corroborative evidence by pointing out the hidden graves, then others of the gang would usually hurry forward to gain a pardon and gradually the doings of that group would be cleared up. But it was slow laborious work. A gang would set out in the autumn, as soon as the rains were over; they would come back in the spring, having murdered anything up to a thousand travellers. They would not have been single murders; a whole party would be killed together, but there would have been fifteen or twenty such incidents in the course of the winter and it would not be easy to remember which was which. Was it at Payagpur, the fat moneylender with gold earrings and two fine sons? No, that was in the grove at Shahabad. At Payagpur it was the old man on his way back from a pilgrimage and the son with the pretty wife whose bangles had those unusual markings. But that surely was the year before, the year when Bhimu was involved in the affair of the Kotwal's slave-girl? That was the kind of uncertainty the inquirers were up against when they came to collect evidence and make things ready for a trial.

The circumstances were usually much the same in every incident. The gang would camp near a town or a large village; one or two chosen men of respectable appearance would go to the shops and wander about the streets. They might not find any suitable prey for a day or two but as soon as they saw a small party of travellers of the right kind they would move nearer and after a little seize on some chance of getting into conversation. And then the talk would slide round to the dangers of the road and heads would be shaken at the folly of travelling without a sufficient escort. Sooner or later the travellers would speak cautiously of joining parties for safety; the respectable stranger would be most reluctant but at last would suffer himself to be won over and would take the travellers to his camp. The leader of the gang would again require much persuasion, but in the end all would be settled and for two or three days the two parties would ride on together. There would be much laughter round the camp-fires at night and many stories would be told. Never, the travellers would think, had they met such good company, and they would congratulate themselves on their good fortune in being safe from the dangers of travel.

But a night would come when the company would seem even better than usual, the tales told with more gusto, the jokes more ready and the laughter more uproarious. They would not be likely to notice a little man who would sidle up from the shadows beyond the firelight to the jovial leader's side; they would not hear when the jovial leader leaned back and whispered to him in the thieves' slang that no one else could understand:

'Is it ready?'

'Yes, it is dug, deep and wide.'

The little man would slide away into the shadows, the leader would become even more jovial than before, and there would be a movement or two among the party round the fire. If he had happened to notice it, each of the smaller party would have found that now one or two of the others was at his elbow or just behind him. And he might perhaps have become aware of an expectancy in the air, as though the best joke of all was still to come. Then suddenly the leader would cry in a loud voice:

'Bring the tobacco!'

and clap his hands as though to summon a servant. And that clap would be the last thing the travellers heard on earth. In a few more minutes their bodies would be stripped naked and tumbled higgledy-piggledy into the grave; a few more and the grave would be filled and the senior gravedigger would be dragging a thorny bush over the sandy soil to hide all traces.

The killing was done by a handkerchief, a square of cloth, in one corner of which was knotted a silver coin consecrated to the goddess Kali. The knotted coin made a grip for the left hand; the free end went round the victim's neck, then a quick twist, the knuckles turned in, and in skilful hands the victim would be dead before he reached the ground.

All this Sleeman and his assistants soon found out; they knew too that at the end of the season the gang would scatter to their villages where they would become cultivators or merchants. Often a petty raja or a big zamindar was their protector; no word had been exchanged but after every season he took a present and no doubt he guessed it was not the result of honest trade. He would hold back at first but once he saw the way the stream was running, he too would anxiously show his zeal to suppress the Thugs.

It was not just plain crime for gain. Destruction of life was the first object; the booty was the devotee's earthly reward, granted him by the goddess. The Thugs told how the first god had taken to himself two colleagues, one to create and one to destroy, hoping thus to maintain a balance in the population of the world. This, though crudely put, is orthodox Hinduism. But finding that the forces of destruction were losing, the goddess Kali — who is also Bhawani, who is also Durga, who is also Parvati, the wife of Siva — came down to earth and taught the Thugs their craft, promising them her special protection. They believed then that they were carrying out a divine mission and that as a reward a heaven of their own would be reserved for them. To tell secrets of their craft was the greatest infamy a Thug could commit; to travel with a family of happy people as their friend, to sit with them laughing and telling stories, at last to kill them treacherously, this was a virtue, an act at which a Thug felt less compunction than even a quite unimaginative person does at killing a chicken. One Thug told Meadows Taylor that he had personally murdered seven hundred and nineteen people and that he would no doubt have reached a thousand if the government had not caught him. He felt no remorse at all and his only regret was that he had not killed more.

There was excitement and adventure in rounding up the Thugs. There would be a word whispered at a tent-door, a dark figure crouching in the shadows, a ride through the night to find perhaps that the caravan had got the alarm and fled. There was one young officer who came up with a big gang of Thugs when he had only a dozen orderlies with him. He dared not accuse them of being Thugs; they would fight rather than surrender on that charge to men they outnumbered. He dared not let them go or he might never see them again. He ordered them to come with him to the nearest headquarters to answer a trumped-up charge they could easily disprove. Loudly protesting, they did as they were told; not till they were surrounded and outnumbered was any mention made of strangling, graves, or Bhawani.

There were many such tales as this: there was excitement and adventure — but there was far more plain slogging hard work. It was the task of Sleeman's young men to build up a list of the members of each gang and a narrative of the incidents in which that gang had been involved in each hunting season for the last ten or fifteen years. No one in the world could be expected to remember exactly who had been in what gang in which year nor where each murder had taken place. But in court a discrepancy in the evidence would be taken as a sign of innocence. It must all be pieced together.

In court, the cases would be tried by judges in the Company's Service who had begun as Writers, who had perhaps been magistrates and police officers. But now they were judges, minutely just, inflexibly upright. It was no use telling them that everyone knew Feringia was a leading Thug and had taken part in a hundred murders. That was not evidence. They must have clear, corroborated, uncontradicted testimony. And they were quite right, because they stood for the rule of law as against the individual whim that had ruled before.

There were in the years 1831 to 1837 more than three thousand Thugs convicted, of whom about five hundred obtained life as a reward for betraying the others. More than four hundred were hanged, more than a thousand were transported for life, another thousand were in 1837 still waiting trial, two thousand known Thugs were still at large. That is six thousand; it would be a fair guess that there had been at least ten thousand operating before Sleeman's net drew tight, for many would give up their craft and go back to cultivation when they saw how things were going. Forty or fifty gangs; perhaps twenty or thirty thousand travellers killed every year. It is all guess-work, but that is the kind of figure.

The thing was ended. This evil was completely stamped out and the craft forgotten; it was done by long monotonous hours of questioning, by the laborious comparison of a hundred reports. The narratives that result make very dull reading; the horror wears off after a little; as the long record of treachery and murder goes on, you become yourself as callous as a Thug. But the work was done; that evil was finished.

Those were some of the things the Company's servants contended with. Writing about them is like sitting all day in court; a man is inclined to become cynical when he does not often hear the truth unvarnished. It is a wonder that so often a generous gullibility did survive that court training, a gullibility that because it was warm and human was worth far more to the state than any sharp-edged little cunning. It did often survive because men did not always stay in court but went into villages and saw there that the peasant could still be simple if he was left to himself. It was a matter of remembering that most people get through life without going to court at all.

A breath of that same air is needed to remind one at the end of such a chapter as this that there were many Indians who did not burn widows alive nor strangle travellers. The peasants were, a hundred years ago, what they always have been, what they are today, a people as a rule gentle and hospitable, feckless it is true and unconvinced of the need for doing anything properly, but not usually malicious and by nature kindly unless they are frightened or excited. But they are easily frightened and then of course they are capable of hideous acts, because in the long habit that religion has given them there is no ingrained discipline to restrain them from violence and cruelty.

The Hindus have not, after all, been converted to Christianity one by one as our great-grandfathers thought they would be. But the state, which in Europe is usually some way behind religion in its ethics, is in India now ahead of religion. That is because the state has been more willing than Hinduism to absorb Christian ethics. Even Hinduism has now come to pay reluctant lip service to an ethic it did not possess of itself; few Brahmans would now speak out loud in favour of burning widows. So that perhaps after all there has been conversion of a kind.

But of course it is open to anyone today to argue that the servants of the Company were on the wrong side, that they should have thrown in their lot with Kali and Siva and the devil-godlings of the Khonds and kept down the population, which is now certainly far too large.

CHAPTER VII

METCALFE AND THE SUPREME POST

CHARLES METCALFE is the last and probably the greatest of the great quartet. He is, as it happens, the last in time, having landed at Calcutta, not yet sixteen, on the first day of the new century, January 1st, 1801. And while Elphinstone and Malcolm are connected with the downfall of the Marathas and the reconstruction of their empire in the early 'twenties, Metcalfe's part in the story leads on to the great surge forward which followed the collapse of the Sikh Kingdom in the North and to the two crowded decades which ended in the Queen's proclamation of 1858. He is also the most difficult to understand and can best be seen against the background the others provide.

Munro and Malcolm have the simplicity of characters in Thackeray; they are as clear-cut as Dobbin or Pendennis. Elphinstone, with his Renaissance zest for scholarship, action, society and war, though more complex, is still easy enough to understand — but it would be a bold man who claimed fully to understand the majestic pessimism, the liberal realism, the magnanimity of Metcalfe.

He was in the first place English in the narrower sense. He was an Etonian of the Etonians, and thus from the start one degree more encysted than the three Scots, armoured, as the product of an English public school usually is, by an isolating crust of convention and social ritual. His mother, too, must have had something to do with his loneliness; Kaye, writing Metcalfe's biography in the middle of the century, when Oedipus was still safe in Greek mythology, says mildly that 'her affection for her children seldom displayed itself in any maternal weaknesses'. A later biographer says simply and repeatedly that she was 'grim'; she was undeniably beautiful by pictorial standards and 'a woman of strong understanding'. She made no secret of her preference for Theophilus, the elder brother, who was gay, thoughtless and charming; it is hard to believe that Charles as a small boy did not sometimes long for a little maternal weakness directed to himself.

He was from the first a rare phenomenon. A half holiday at Eton was to him an opportunity for translating Rousseau, for reading Gibbon, Ariosto, Lucan, Homer and Juvenal. Not often is there a hint of boyish mischief, but once 'I heard the boys shouting,' wrote Dr. Goodall, his tutor, 'and went out and saw young Metcalfe riding a camel; so you see he was always orientally inclined . . .' Dr. Goodall was probably right; it was not likely to be any pleasure in the exercise that led to this display, for Metcalfe never took any delight in horses or swift motion or the use of his body. He was, however, left to do as he liked at Eton, and that with him was a great thing. He was not without friends and seems to have been more truly happy there than he was to be again for many years.

He came to Calcutta, not quite sixteen, with introductions to everyone; his father was a Director, he shared Lord Wellesley's love of Eton and he was soon an intimate at Government House. He complained himself of the disadvantage of 'an ugly phiz', but it was the only disadvantage and it was outweighed by an attractive manner; 'the ugliest and most agreeable clever person — except Lady Glenbervie — in Europe or Asia,' wrote Lord Minto a few years later. He made friends; he was recognized almost from the beginning to be one of the inner set, one of the true rulers of India. All the same, he was lonely and unhappy; he wrote to his father for permission to give up his career and come home and in the same strain to his godfather, Jacob Rider, a friend of Hickey's, now Collector at Benares. From Rider, he received the advice:

'Your dislike to the country can't be greater than mine was for the first twelvemonth; it will wear off, I am convinced . . . Keep as long out of the judicial line and the line of collections as you can — altogether, I hope, or till some great reform takes place in those lines. . . .'

Rider showed understanding when he perceived that the line to recommend to generous and aspiring youth was the diplomatic or political; Metcalfe made a start as Assistant to 'King' Collins, Colonel Collins of Agra, Resident at this time at the court of Scindia. Collins was a famous eccentric, 'looking . . . not unlike a monkey dressed up for Bartholomew Fair . . . There was, however, a fire in his small black eye, shooting out from beneath a large shaggy pent-house brow, which more than counterbalanced the ridicule that his first appearance naturally excited'. He was not called 'King' Collins for nothing; he did not like being argued with and he was the last man in the world to understand Charles Metcalfe.

A situation developed that was to be common in India; it might happen in 1930 as often as in 1810. The young man new from England had been trained to express his opinions; instructors of youth had deferred to him with encouraging interest, he had perhaps distinguished himself in philosophy, his aunts had attended nervously to what he said. The Colonel, on the other hand, knew nothing of philosophy but had seen men killed, had ordered men to death, had handled fierce men of warring creeds; he was not much disposed to listen to academic lectures.

As a rule, it settled itself. Usually, one or the other, old man or young, had the good manners to smile inwardly at the other and let him have his say. But it was not so with Metcalfe and Collins; in their case, the older man was so much an autocrat that he never knew he had hurt the other's feelings and continued all his life to write him friendly patronizing letters. But Metcalfe, deeply sensitive, wrote to his friend Sherer: 'his conduct towards me has been such that I have not words to express my contempt of it', and he seems always to have felt it a humiliation.

The incident was not regarded as a blot. He became Political Assistant to Lake, whose views on 'frocks' may be guessed from his well-known saying: 'Damn your writing; mind your fighting.' It was not an easy assignment, but Metcalfe won the general's confidence by volunteering for a storming-party at Dig. He was known in after-dinner speeches for the rest of his career as 'the little stormer', but there is no indication that he enjoyed the experience, as Elphinstone had his.

Assistant at Delhi, he at first complained that Seton, his chief, did not give him enough to do. Seton again is a figure who was to become familiar; he was conscientious, kind, modest and unassuming, but no deputer of authority. 'He seldom comes either to breakfast or dinner. He rises before the day and labours until the middle of the night. He does not move out; he takes no exercise and apparently no food.' Self-immolation may be a private virtue but in a public man it is a vice and Seton's administration was mildly inefficient. He was too gentle with the Mogul Emperor, he did not collect all his revenue and his attitude to his Assistant was one of affectionate but slightly awed deference. It was certainly a relief to the latter when in 1808 at the age of twenty-three he was sent as Envoy to Ranjit Singh in the Punjab.

His mission was part of Gibby Elliott's triple diplomatic move against the Corsican bogey. Malcolm in Persia, Elphinstone in Kabul, Metcalfe in Lahore, each had a difficult task, each having been instructed to get something for nothing. But Metcalfe had the most difficult task of all, because Ranjit Singh was a great man, a man who can be spoken of in the same breath with Akbar. Although every night he inflamed and stupefied his nerves with a mixture of raw corn-spirit, opium, musk and the juices of raw meat — 'liquid fire, of which no European can touch a drop', wrote Miss Eden who burnt her lip with it — although he was treacherous and ungrateful in the highest degree, few men have equalled his courage, his perseverance or his political vision. His two great pieces of wisdom were his refusal to quarrel with the English and a tolerance for Muslims that enabled Muslim vassals to fight for him. Against this hard-riding, hard-drinking, lustful, shrewd barbarian was pitted young Charles from Eton, a complex, introspective creature who kept a diary and noted in it thoughts on self-love and duty, sin and suffering for others; it was a situation, said Edmonstone, just moving from Private Secretary to Chief Secretary, 'perhaps as delicate, difficult, and responsible as any public agent was ever placed in'.

Charles came out of it with great credit to himself. He did not get the alliance against Napoleon, but perhaps the news of Vimiera made that seem less important, and he had given away nothing, maintained a firm front, and made it perfectly clear that Ranjit Singh's empire was not to spread to the east bank of the Sutlej. What is surprising, he had won from 'the wily and unscrupulous Sikh' a kind of ironical and affectionate regard. That, however, was a thing that did again and again happen between Englishmen and Indian, even when interests were wholly opposed. It came of recognizing the situation and perceiving that it was not without humour; it could not live long in the air of moral indignation. In the case of Metcalfe and Ranjit Singh, it was perhaps the Sikh who had the greater need for a sense of humour; Metcalfe came to ask a favour, but changed his ground and stayed to enforce unwelcome conditions. There were moments, it is true, when Ranjit seems to have found the constraint intolerable; there were certainly some when Metcalfe gave way to indignation at the Sikh's tactical device of retiring to debauchery when diplomacy became awkward. But an awareness of reality never deserted either of them long and made the one thing they had in common.

Edward Thompson believes that there was more than this. Metcalfe's Victorian biographer does not mention his three Eurasian sons, of whom the eldest was born in 1809, the year in which this mission ended. That Metcalfe had for seven or eight years an Indian wife or mistress seems beyond doubt; that she was a Sikh of good family, perhaps even a connection of Ranjit Singh's, as Thompson suggests, is admittedly conjecture and to me seems improbable because such a match would have been impossible to keep dark. He was accredited to Ranjit Singh's court; there would surely have been anonymous letters to Calcutta and to the Directors if he had married into Ranjit's family. But there is not a word, not a syllable, of the whole affair extant, nothing but the sad tale of the three boys.

Seton went to Penang as Governor; Metcalfe at twenty-seven became Resident at Delhi. The Resident was in theory a diplomat at the court of the Mogul Emperor but in fact the Emperor ruled nowhere but in the Red Fort and Metcalfe was Governor and administrator of an area about the size of the six northern counties of England. At the same time he was political agent in charge of relations that were rather more than diplomatic with a network of states that were rather less than independent.

His administrative achievement was remarkable; Edward Thompson says 'the greatest single administrative work ever put through by a British ruler', a characteristic exaggeration. Metcalfe did what a number of other people were doing on a scale not very different and did it better than most; it was only in one respect — his attitude to punishment — that his achievement differed in kind from Elphinstone's or Malcolm's, and it was only in scale that it differed from Alexander Read's in the Baramahal or two dozen more. It is, however, possible to say that in some ways the Delhi administration was the most enlightened in the world. In England men could be hanged for a forty-shilling theft; the United States were still to permit slavery for another fifty years. But there was no hanging in Delhi and no selling of slaves.

Capital punishment began to fall into disuse during the mild rule of Seton, mainly because sentences of death had to be confirmed by the Emperor. But what had begun as a convenience became with Metcalfe a matter of principle; he was convinced of the fallibility of all human judgment and in particular of verdicts in Indian courts. And since sentence of death once carried out cannot be revoked he preferred not to inflict it.

He forbade the slave trade and the burning of widows; he collected swords and spears, beat them literally into ploughshares and returned them to the owners. He first discouraged and then stopped flogging, for he rejected the vindictive aspect of punishment and was sceptical about reformation. The great thing was to put the criminal where he would not be able to disturb society again; his sentences of imprisonment were therefore severe when guilt seemed tolerably certain.

Instead of whipping boys from criminal tribes caught picking pockets or pilfering from the market, he sent them to a camp where they were taught a trade. But it is really shorter to say simply that in most of his penal theory he was nearly a century ahead of his times.

As to how his government worked, the test is severely practical. Revenue rose from four lakhs, or about forty thousand pounds, in 1807 to fifteen, or about one hundred and fifty thousand, in 1813. That could happen only where peace was felt to be secure. The King's share which Metcalfe took was always light, and in the course of his revenue settlement he reached conclusions which made him sharply critical of the permanent settlement in Bengal. Like everyone who has ever had anything to do with land revenue, he was always inclined to think that what he had known as a young man was to be found with modifications all over India; he believed that the cultivator should be regarded as the proprietor and that the zamindar was really a representative of the government, falsely made a proprietor by Cornwallis. In the country round Delhi, this was usually not far from right, but in Bengal fifty years earlier it would have been much less like the truth.

He governed Delhi his own way, using a code of his own, just as Elphinstone had in the Maratha country and as Lawrence was to in the Punjab. One feature of his 'non-regulation' system became general over the whole of India; he would have none of Cornwallis's division of judicial from executive, he would have no one glued to his chair in court or office. The man who collected the revenue was also responsible for order, he was policeman, magistrate and judge. Metcalfe was thinking no doubt of the Delhi system years later when he was the Governor-General's adviser and wrote:

'. . . I should recommend, as . . . best suited to the character of our native subjects and best calculated to promote their happiness, the division of the country into small districts, in each of which an European officer should be superintendent, uniting all authorities in his own person and having under him native officers for the administration of the district in all its branches. . . .'

This was the view that prevailed and from the Act of 1833 onwards the Collector was also the Magistrate; the judge-magistrate who never left his court became a creature of the past and every year the head of the district went into camp and saw things for himself.

Metcalfe was King of Delhi from 1811 till 1819. He left for two appointments in Calcutta; he was to be both Private Secretary to the Governor-General and Secretary in the Secret, Foreign and Political

Departments, with the salaries of both posts — just under ten thousand pounds a year, with no income-tax and at a time when a pound would buy a good deal that was worth having. He was thirty-four; he was succeeded at Delhi by a man of sixty — Ochterlony, who was to be Resident, but with a separate officer to look after the judicial and financial work. 'It is not to be expected . . . of any other man, that he should go through the Herculean labours you have sustained,' wrote Adam, now to be Member of Council and later to be Governor-General for six months.

From Private Secretary Metcalfe went to Hyderabad as Resident, not without a wistful glance at Delhi; every man keeps a tenderness for his first independent charge and there was something that appealed to his lonely melancholy in the vastness of the dusty plains that lie round Delhi, in the brightness of its pale windy skies, in the sense of fallen greatness that it must bring to the least sensitive. 'The ruins of grandeur', he wrote, 'that extend for miles on every side fill the mind with serious reflection. The palaces crumbling into dust . . . , the vast mausoleums, every one of which was intended to convey to futurity the deathless fame of its cold inhabitant, and all of which are passed by, unknown and unnoticed, . . . these things cannot be looked at with indifference.' But he went all the same to Hyderabad, where he found things not much better than they had been near Calcutta in the days of William Bolts.

The Nizam's revenue was a feeble trickle at the end of a long and leaky pipe. He borrowed money to pay the troops from the house of William Palmer; in the end, the house of William Palmer — 'a gentleman not of pure European blood', says Kaye delicately — paid the troops and recovered what they had spent — plus twenty-five per cent — from the villages mortgaged to them. The peasants sank deeper in misery; they were shorn more evenly and more closely than ever before, but the officers got their pay and did not trouble their heads how it came. Europeans paid from Hyderabad revenues expected a house at the expense of the state, and not only a house but a long train of free servants in addition to their pay. Worst of all, Residency officials, even Russell the Resident himself, were said to have secretly ventured to take shares in William Palmer & Company. It was almost as bad as the old scandal of the Nawab of Arcot's debts.

Russell, Metcalfe's predecessor, seems to have been very wide awake, a man of acute intellect, but certainly not the man to carry through in the face of opposition and intrigue the reforms of which he saw the need — not even the man to stand aloof when he saw money crying out to be made. It was left to Metcalfe to fight a lonely fight against the house of William Palmer, to tour the country and find out what was happening, and to set about the steady and systematic cleansing of the administration from its worst faults.

He met with no support from the Governor-General. He was in fact censured by Lord Hastings, not only for hostility to the firm of William Palmer but for taking it upon himself to interfere in the revenue settlements, a course which though 'equally beneficial to the Nizam and his people' would 'estrange and irritate the better classes'. It is a long story, told in detail by Kaye and with relish by Thompson, too long to be told here, but one passage from one of Metcalfe's letters must stand for many and express his compassion, his honesty and his sense of what was practical. Charged by Lord Hastings with hostility to Chandu Lal, the Nizam's chief minister, he replied: 'It is very true that I think ill, in the highest degree, of the spirit of his internal administration; that I groan for the devastation inflicted on the country by his merciless extortions; and that I cannot love his heartless recklessness of the miseries of the people confided to his charge. I mourn also for the reproach attached by public opinion to the British Government as if it countenanced the criminalities which its support alone has given him the strength to practice; but it has never yet occurred to me as desirable . . . that he should be removed.'

And in his letter to Martin — Jacquemont's host at Delhi — who succeeded him, he wrote:

'I do not see cause to retract one word that I have ever said or written against the abominable corruption which prevailed at Hydera-bad . . . it tainted the whole atmosphere . . . the smell of it was sickening.'

Lord Hastings does not come out of the story well but Metcalfe had the support of the Council, in particular of 'honest John Adam', who acted as Governor-General when Hastings went home and of Butterworth Bayley, only two years his senior at Eton. In the end the Directors were clearly on his side, but the man who notices a sickening smell and mentions it is not often wholeheartedly forgiven.

He went again to Delhi; he came back to Calcutta as Member of Council; he was nominated successor to the Governor-General and deputy in his absence; he was provisional Governor of the Presidency of Agra, a still-born Presidency for which was substituted a changeling Lieutenant-Governorship of the North-West Provinces. But though he did not go back to England for thirty-seven years he never lost himself in the Indian scene. To his aunt, who resigned for her son an appointment in India, he wrote: 'So far am I from condemning you . . . , that I decidedly think you have done that which is best calculated to promote his happiness and your own . . . Why doom him to transportation from everything dear to him? What is there in India to recompense [him] for such sufferings?'

His private note-books tell how he tried to acquire the character of 'a good fellow' and though he does not seem to have taken much pleasure in the process, he did meet with some success. All speak of his gracious and sweet disposition; he seemed happier now than in his younger days. But it was not that he liked society any better; dinners, balls, the whole round of meeting people was to him always a tedious loss of time. And in his second reign at Delhi, he would not go out but took the air on the roof of his house to avoid importunity. It was not because he had become less sensitive that he seemed more at home in the world. 'If I am really the happy man you suppose me to be,' he wrote to a friend, 'I will tell you . . . the secret . . . I live in a state of fervent and incessant gratitude to God for the favours and mercies which I have experienced . . . The feeling is so strong that it often overflows in tears and is so rooted that I do not think any misfortunes could shake it.'

Metcalfe's life is too rich, too complex, for this small-scale map, but some mention of his magnanimity must go into an inset. When the Court of Directors singled out this most faithful of their servants for admonition and ordered him — alone among Residents — to pay Rupees 48,119 Annas 6 Pies 5 — nearly £5000 — for the furniture of the Delhi residency, his reaction was to vow, not that now he would make what he could, but that he would never, so long as he lived, make any application to them on his personal account. He pensioned for life the man who had taught him Hindustani for a few months in Calcutta when he first arrived and also the master of his preparatory school for Eton. Not that he was indifferent to money; he prized it, but he was magnanimous, a man of large soul.

And some of his opinions must go in. On the question of whether the Government was bound to continue to his descendants a grant of land made to an individual, there occurs this superb widening of the whole discussion:

'Our dominion in India is by conquest; it is naturally disgusting to the inhabitants and can only be maintained by military force.

'It is our positive duty to render them justice, to respect and protect their rights, and to study their happiness. By the performance of this duty, we may allay and keep dormant their innate disaffection; but the expectation of purchasing their cordial attachment by gratuitous alienations of public revenue would be a vain delusion. . . .'

This is realism; it is not contradictory of another opinion, expressed years earlier; 'It is impossible to live in this part of India and to see the scenes which pass before our eyes,' and not long that the Company should take these regions under its protection. The two are complementary; a benefit was conferred by the Company's rule but it was folly to expect gratitude when memories of anarchy had faded.

On another controversy of the day, he begins, as is usual in his minutes, by a statement of the essence of the situation: 'The English language seems to be the channel through which we are most likely to convey improvement to the natives of India. I should therefore be disposed to promote the use of it as much as possible in our courts of justice. . . .'

And on the question of interfering in the affairs of native states: '. . . we may thereby prevent evil . . . but on the contrary we are just as likely to create it. I should say, indeed, infinitely more so. And the evil created by interference is generally irremediable. It continually, if not ostensibly, destroys the state to which it is applied and leaves it only a nominal, if any, existence . . . Interference is so likely to do evil . . . and so little certain of doing good that it ought, I conceive, to be avoided as much as possible. . . .'

These words have a melancholy interest when they are placed by the side of his final views on the policy that ought to be adopted to Persia and Afghanistan: 'to maintain our relations on the most friendly terms that will not involve us in stipulations likely to lead to an unnecessary war with Russia'. And again: 'You may depend upon it that the surest way to draw Russia upon us will be by our meddling with any of the states beyond the Indus.'

Those were always Metcalfe's views. If they had prevailed, the worst chapter in Indian history need not have been written. It is the worst because it records actions the most unrighteous as well as the most disastrous. But Metcalfe was not Governor-General at the time. He had been adviser and deputy to Lord William Bentinck, with whom on most subjects he had agreed; he succeeded Lord William provisionally as Governor-General, he was strongly recommended for permanent appointment by Lord William and by the Court of Directors. But the Cabinet clung to the convention that the highest post in India should go to a noble lord from England. It was not a bad convention as a rule. When Cornwallis, the first

noble lord, set out, the President of the Board of Control exclaimed:
'Here there was no broken fortune to be mended! here there was
no avarice to be gratified! here there was no beggarly mushroom
kindred to be provided for! no crew of hungry followers gaping to
be gorged!'

That applied just as truly to such men as John Adam or Charles
Metcalfe; it had been true too of Sir John Shore or Sir George Barlow, but they had both been accused of being too subservient to
authority in England. A fresh mind — if a sufficiently powerful mind
— will come to Indian problems free from clogging detail, free from
long-established prejudices as to what can be done and what is
impossible, while a man who has held cabinet rank in England can
get his way in London far better than an obscure exile, however able.
Such a man will perhaps also know how currents of thought run in
England — or at least, how they were running when he set sail —
whereas the Company's servant had as a rule only a boy's idea of
what men thought thirty years ago.

Though not good enough for overlooking Metcalfe, these were
good general reasons for the convention. But more cogent was a
simple reluctance to forgo patronage. A Tory ministry overrode the
Court of Directors and made a Tory appointment. Lord Melbourne
came, cancelled the Tory, and changed to a Whig. George Eden,
Lord Auckland, was appointed. Metcalfe, who had been two years
Governor-General gave way to him with a good grace, and took up
the lieutenant-governorship of the North-Western Provinces. But
he had by now fallen from favour with the Court of Directors. He
had, while acting as Governor-General, passed a measure freeing
from the censorship the English-written press. It was a measure to
which Lord William had already expressed himself favourable. It
was not, said Macaulay, really a question of whether the Press should
be free but of whether, being free, it should be called free. Metcalfe
saw no virtue in a censorship that no one dared to use; his liberalism
and his realism were at one. Bentinck, Metcalfe and Macaulay were
agreed but Metcalfe was Governor-General when the Act was passed
and it was at Metcalfe that the Court's anger was directed. The
governorship of Madras fell vacant; they did not appoint Metcalfe
and he ascertained that the reason was the Press Act. He would not,
he said, serve on in disgrace; he resigned, going on to be Governor
of Jamaica and Governor-General of Canada.

Lord Auckland remained. He had a reputation in England for
ability, he had a mild preference for justice, a mild and amiable good

nature. In India, however, he was bored. Invested with the empire of Tamerlane and Akbar, made suddenly heir-at-law to Kubla Khan and Prester John, he was bored. Charged with the destiny of millions, moving in magnificence at which he mildly chafed through a country-side stricken by famine, among children dying of starvation, he was bored. 'G. detests his tent, and his march and the whole business so actively that he will not perceive how well he is', wrote his sister. She took him one evening for a walk to see an interesting ruin, but poor G. was more wretchedly bored than ever. Nothing seemed really to relieve the condition; it was chronic.

Lord Auckland was a humane man. It may be that he was appalled by the horrors of the famine and dismayed at his ignorance, his impotence to take any effective steps. It may be that he concealed his wretchedness behind an emotion that seemed more appropriate to his birth. That is an interpretation more charitable to the man and more in keeping with his character than to take his boredom at its face value; it does not, however, raise his reputation as a Governor-General. Either Metcalfe or Elphinstone would have known what could be done and having done it would have slept sound at night.

The famine was at least the result of the weather and cannot be attributed directly to Lord Auckland. Not so the Afghan war. Miss Eden has a pleasantry of a flying squirrel that sat on G.'s shoulder, apparently whispering to him, 'and though G. said the squirrel was only pulling his ear I am convinced he had more to do with public affairs than people generally supposed'. Some such explanation of public affairs was certainly needed. Lord Auckland — without oral discussion with his Council, who were in Calcutta — refused the friendship of the strong and able Ruler of Afghanistan — offered, it is true, on stiff and perhaps unacceptable terms — and invaded his country, with the object of putting on the throne a pretender who had been three times turned out by his people. There were many widows and orphans, Indian, Afghan and English, as a result of this policy; while with no shadow of justice, we plunged Afghanistan into four years of misery, saddled India with a bill for fifteen million pounds, and involved our armies in the most complete Asiatic disaster they were to suffer until exactly a hundred years later in 1942.

It must be acknowledged that Lord Auckland was misled by false intelligence and encouraged by the Cabinet to attach too much importance to the idea of a Russian advance to Kabul. But the two relevant dispatches left him a wide discretion and he always spoke of the decision as his own. Kaye believes he was manœuvred into it by his Secretaries but the theory does not seem to me tenable; in any case, no Secretary would have manœuvred Metcalfe. The verdict must be that here was a man morally and intellectually out of his depth, carried along helplessly by events too strong for him.

It was in January 1842 that Dr. Brydon reached Jalalabad, fainting from wounds, hunger and exhaustion. He was the sole survivor of the force that had accepted terms at Kabul. Another army had to be raised, another expedition had to go to Kabul, another war be fought, to put right the results of that cruel wrong. There were more widows, more orphans, but the widows were mostly Afghans this time. 'I cannot understand,' said Dost Mohammad, whom we had driven from his throne and maintained in exile, whom we now restored, 'I cannot understand why the rulers of so great an empire should have gone across the Indus to deprive me of my poor and barren country.' It is not easy to understand. Perhaps it was the squirrel. It would certainly not have happened if Metcalfe had been Governor-General instead of the wretchedly bored G.

CHAPTER VIII

FORT WILLIAM AND HAILEYBURY

ELPHINSTONE and Metcalfe were the kind of men who would educate themselves however they were placed and there were many others. 'I have found', wrote Lord Wellesley in 1800, 'the officers of the Secretariat to possess the industry of clerks with the talents of statesmen', but their merits 'are to be ascribed to their own characters, talents and exertions'. Their education was usually cut short at the age when it began to be most valuable; sometimes they had been sent for a few months to a commercial office but there they learnt only what would fit them for the 'menial, laborious, unwholesome and unprofitable duty of mere copying clerks'. It was hardly fair to expect that Providence would continue to supply the Company with men who would overcome these disadvantages by their own efforts. 'The empire', he went on, 'must be considered as a sacred trust and a permanent possession. Duty, policy, and honour require that it should not be administered as a temporary and precarious acquisition. . . .'

Wellesley was indeed a great man in his grasp of the whole and his vision of the future but he was not so gifted in the lesser art of getting what he wanted. His case for educating the Company's servants was unanswerable, but there was room for opinion as to how it should be done. Perhaps he was aware of this and afraid that discussion would go on and nothing happen until long after he had left India. At any rate, he made his decision and set the measure in hand, blandly informing the Court of Directors that their 'early support . . . will tend to give animation and spirit to the new Institution'.

This was the College of Fort William, in its first short-lived incarnation. It was a college in Calcutta in which every young man appointed to the Company's service was to spend three years. Newcomers, Lord Wellesley pointed out, were anyhow little use to the administration for the first three years; they would not be missed while they were at the College, and there would be a contribution from the salary of every member of the service towards the cost. The young men would learn Indian history, law and Oriental languages, but their general education would not be forgotten and the course would include ethics, international law and general history. The discipline and administration were to be on the lines of a college at Oxford and Cambridge and the staff included orientalists of considerable distinction. It was all in working order, the young men in residence and the teachers hard at work, by the time the Directors heard of the project.

The Directors can hardly be blamed for irritation at being confronted with so well-grown an addition to their responsibilities and this was probably the main reason for their refusal to approve. But there were sound arguments on their side. It might well be that England was the place to give a wider general education, while Calcutta had no advantages for teaching Tamil or Marathi. Wellesley had argued that his college would build up corporate spirit and pride in the service and would help to end jealousy between the Presidencies. But that might again be done just as well in England.

It is a complicated story because Castlereagh, who was President of the Board of Control and a friend of Wellesley's, was inclined to agree with the Governor-General, while the Court of Directors were determined not to be bullied by the first of their servants. That glorious little man found it necessary to record his 'unqualified contempt and abhorrence of the proceedings and propensities of the Court of Directors'. But the upshot of it all was that the Directors had their way; the College of Fort William was whittled down to a school of oriental languages for Bengal alone. For many years the young men who came to the Bengal service lived in Writers' Buildings until they had passed examinations in these languages; this was all that remained of the College of Fort William.

But although Wellesley's College did not last very long, it did produce indirect results. In the course of demolishing the Governor-General's arguments, the Court of Directors committed themselves to a college in England. 'The East India College, Herts', opened in 1806 at Hertford Castle and moved to Haileybury in 1809; it lasted just fifty years.

There was a good deal at Haileybury that was borrowed from Fort William. The subjects taught were divided into 'Orientals' and 'Europeans'. The Orientals were mainly languages; it was a two-year course divided into four terms and in the first term a beginning was made with Sanskrit, to which Persian was added in the second term and a third language, usually Hindustani, in the third term. That was the compulsory minimum; some students even tried to learn five oriental languages in the course of their two years.

'Europeans' included the classical languages and mathematics, and there was law, both general and Indian; what was less to be expected, there was great emphasis on political economy and general history, then hardly taught in the older universities. Malthus was the first professor in these subjects and held the chair till he died thirty years later; he was succeeded by Mr. Richard Jones, whose book on 'Rent' expressed considerable differences from Adam Smith, Malthus and Ricardo. He was apparently a brilliant lecturer, to whose lectures on political economy his pupils listened with breathless attention. He never hesitated to express his differences from the orthodox economists, so that the young men were brought up in an atmosphere of controversy by leading men in a subject in which England led the world, and which was certainly one in which administrators ought to take some interest.

Jones was an eccentric whose lectures were remembered long after those of his successor, Sir James Stephen, who lectured 'as though casting pearls before swine'. Jones was fond of his port and 'carried a vintage in his countenance'. He refused, apparently, to be bothered with subjects that did not interest him; among these, it is to be feared, were his sermons, but the standard of sermons at Haileybury was high. Mr. Melvill, the last principal, was one of the most famous preachers of his day and could hold a packed city church for two hours without — so it was said — his hearers being aware of the passage of time. At Haileybury, however, they did not think he was quite so good as his predecessor, or for that matter as the Dean, Mr. Jeremie.

Standing back from Haileybury to get the effect of distance, something between a public-school and a college at Oxford or Cambridge is visible. The students lived in small bed-sitting-rooms, a combination of cubicle and study which was shocking to a student fresh from Oxford, luxurious if you came from a public school. The day began about seven, when 'an aged bedmaker came in, lit the fire and disappeared. Then came the scout who filled the bath with cold water, laid the table for breakfast, cleaned the boots and made as much noise as he could in order to awaken the sleeping student. Gradually we got up, dressed, put on cap and gown and hurried off to chapel at 8'. There were long overcoats that buttoned up to the neck over pyjamas just as there were at Oxford a hundred years later. Back to breakfast, 'ingeniously balanced on the tongs before the fire', curried soles being a great favourite; the morning was packed with lectures and the more conscientious spent the early hours of the afternoon writing up their notes, but there seems to have been no 'tutorial' in the Oxford sense. There was no regular lunch — that meal being still mainly a feminine flippancy — but beer and bread and cheese were to be had at the 'trap', that is, the buttery — and served by two very pretty girls. They were the daughter and niece of old Coleman, the caterer, who weighed thirty stone when he died.

Games in those days were still played for enjoyment and exercise, not yet having become the business of life; there was fives and cricket and rowing and some managed to hunt. In the afternoon some went off to play games, 'the fast men on dogcarts to play billiards at Hertford or Ware, or perhaps to slip up to town by train for the afternoon, and the steady men to take a solemn constitutional along the roads'.

Dinner was in Hall at six and evening chapel at eight, after which 'the steady men went to their rooms and read far into the night'. A bell rang at eleven, but 'I do not remember that any attention was ever paid to it'. The writer, John Beames, describes himself and his friends as 'among the quieter and steadier, though not the very quietest and steadiest sets'. He read hard enough to get prizes for classics and the gold medal for Persian and was often disturbed towards two in the morning by 'faint sounds of distant voices singing very much out of tune', and 'presently one dogcart after another drew up at the back entrance and discharged its load of more or less intoxicated youths. . . .'

It would be easy to be tedious about Haileybury because in most respects it was like any other college of the time; it is a mixture of *Verdant Green* and *Tom Brown*. Discipline was lax, but so it was at Oxford and Eton; there was much talk of 'immorality', but this seems mainly to have meant swearing and bawdy jokes, which were bad form at Oxford but still the thing at Haileybury. These, after all, were not the only young men who simultaneously rolled their coal-scuttles down the stairs at midnight to draw the Dean, who paid snobs in the village a shilling a hundred for Latin lines and half-a-crown for Greek, who applied for exeats to visit their chiropodists in London.

But it should be said that the staff of distinguished men who taught at Haileybury — and they really were distinguished — had to contend with difficulties from which their colleagues elsewhere were free. The course lasted two years, but the age-limit for admission was from fifteen to twenty-two; they had to face boys who should have been still at school sitting side by side with young men who might have taken a university degree. Monier-Williams, for instance, who became the last Professor of Sanskrit, had been at Balliol in the first flush of intellectual primacy under Jenkyns before he was nominated to Haileybury. He found that he had to work hard, much harder than at Oxford, if he was going to keep in the first flight, but there was obviously a long tail to the hunt, and with such age-limits, there was bound to be. The lower limit was raised to seventeen in 1833 but even then there was too great a gap between the eldest and the youngest. But some attempt, however, was made to keep men up to the collar. There was an examination in every subject every term and every student was graded, the top grade being a G or Great, which stood for Great Proficiency. There were many prizes to be won and some of them were valuable; the Directors came down in a body twice a year, headed by the Chairman — 'Di's Day' it was called — and there were speeches and prizes and pats on the back. It was very much a family affair, since every young man must know at least one Director well enough to have been nominated and many had fathers, uncles, or godparents in the Court.

At Addiscombe there was a parallel institution, a kind of joint Woolwich and Sandhurst for the Company's army. A boy nominated cadet went here for his education and according to the results of the final examination went to the Engineers, the Artillery or the Infantry, in that order. But nothing so vulgar as training was required for the Company's cavalry; to a cavalry commission a Director could nominate direct. It became a convention then that if they found at Haileybury that a young man was 'too idle or too stupid' for the civil service, the Director whose turn it was to nominate to the cavalry postponed his choice and the vacancy went to the idler. This was a comfortable way out of a difficulty. The bad young man need not be ruined and the professors could be appeased. In this way or some other, about one-fifth of the Haileybury students are said to have fallen by the wayside; four-fifths entered the Company's Civil Service.

But of course the best way to keep up the standard was not to get rid of bad students but to find good ones. There was always a good deal of discussion about this. The orthodox view was that the question could safely be left to the conscience of the individual Directors; they were men of whom most had some experience of India and all had experience of Indian affairs; everyone knew the importance of choosing a young man who was able, industrious, had reasonably good manners, and would do credit to his nominator. But not everyone took the trouble he might have done to make sure the young man was all he was reported and sometimes even a Director might make an error of judgment.

Macaulay, who was not fond of anomalies, hit on a device which he thought would save the Directors' patronage and yet introduce the competitive principle he preferred. There were to be four young men nominated for each vacancy and a competitive examination to decide which of them was the best. This became law in 1833, but it only lasted a year. There remained, however, a qualifying examination to ensure a reasonable standard and if that let in one or two of not quite the right kind there was always the cavalry.

Macaulay's argument for competition was that if a selection is to be made from Choctaw Indians who have been trained to take scalps, you would choose the young braves who had distinguished themselves in that art. English boys had been trained in Latin, Greek and mathematics; the one who was best at the tasks that had so far confronted him was likely to be best at disentangling a rent-roll or seeing through a Raja's foreign policy.

The answer to this of course was that what most English boys had been trying to acquire at school was not so much Latin and Greek as the esteem of other boys. Like Charles Metcalfe, they had been trying to be good fellows. Of their success, a Director who knows them at home is at least as well able to judge as an impartial and impersonal examiner. Much stress was laid on the importance of sending to India officials who were gentlemen; it was perfectly justified, if it is remembered that the point to which Indians attached importance in Englishmen was consideration and good manners rather than pedigree.

The controversy continued; though conducted with bitterness, it was, when all is said, a dispute about emphasis. Those on the side of competition would still allow an interview in which pleasant manners and social background would count for something; the most entrenched Director would agree that some intellectual standard was needed. There were even cases of Directors offering a nomination to be competed for. Butterworth Bayley, Metcalfe's friend, once a member of Council and by now a Director, decided in 1841 to nominate the Eton boy who should succeed in a competition. Buckland won the competition from Thring, who was to be Thring of Uppingham; he won prizes in Classics and Sanskrit at Haileybury but does not seem to have gone further than the Board of Revenue in Calcutta. Buckland was known as the first competition-wallah, but

Sir Charles Watkin Williams Wynn had given a nomination for competition among boys at Westminster in 1826 and again in 1829. Again, John Beames, whose studies were so often disturbed at two in the morning, had had no connection with a Director, but a nomination was placed at the disposal of the headmaster of the Merchant Taylors' School, who thought Beames the best boy for it. This, however, was when the shadow had already fallen; in their last year the Directors decided to provide an entry who would show they could beat the competition-wallahs.

The controversy had at last been decided in favour of open competition in 1853, by the last Government of India Act which concerned the Company. This was seventeen years before the home Civil Service was opened to competition. A Committee, which included Macaulay and Jowett, was then appointed to consider what should follow. They came down against the whole existing system, although they might perfectly well have opened Haileybury to competitive examination without abolishing the college. The best argument in favour of Haileybury was that it fostered a close family spirit, a unity of interest; because of Haileybury, the Indian empire was administered by men who knew each other and strove together in the friendly spirit of the cock-house football match. They trusted each other and worked for the Company, the Queen, the team, what you will, but not exclusively for themselves and that was why they overran India.

That was the best argument for Haileybury; it was more doubtful whether there was a great deal to be said for teaching so many Indian subjects in England. It was true they would hardly find place in an ordinary university curriculum but even Monier-Williams, whose nickname of 'the solemn moneo' — the official Haileybury reprimand — was not entirely a pun, thought the smattering of Sanskrit learnt at Haileybury hardly worth the time and pains. It would have been possible to argue with force that only 'Europeans' should be taught at Haileybury, or that only a beginning should be made with 'Orientals'. But Macaulay's Committee was not likely to be in favour of half-measures. They believed wholeheartedly in general education rather than special training and recommended that Haileybury should end, which in that incarnation it did in December 1857. It was pure coincidence that this was the year of the Mutiny.

There were to be many more changes; choice by competitive examination had come to stay but some believed it should be made at the school leaving age, after which two years should be spent on probation at a university, while others thought selection should be after the normal university education when a degree had been taken. This view won in the end but both experiments were tried. As between Haileybury and a general education elsewhere, the final verdict might well be that the close ties that Haileybury knit were needed while the empire was expanding, but that the work of the college was done by the middle of the century and that in the second part of the century a less exclusive, a more open-minded, ruling caste was needed.

As to how Haileybury did its task, it seems obvious today that the course should have been longer, three years at least. Far too much was crowded into two years. And certainly the professors might have done much more to interest the students in the life they were to lead and the work they were to do; it was bad form to talk about India at Haileybury in the 'forties and 'fifties. Certainly it was a scrambling, illogical, English sort of way of teaching statesmen, but with a good deal of help from Providence it did work. The best men always spoke with respect of the mental training they had had at Haileybury, far wider, most of them believed, than they would have been given anywhere else, while to an observer it seems that Haileybury men, in spite of their clannishness, had a remarkably detached point of view when they arrived in India.

Coming from comfortable homes, most of them connected with the Directors of the Company, at a time when the wealthy were inclined to regard the misfortunes of the poor with some complacency, there are no signs of an outlook bounded by turtle soup. Most of them were found to be on the side of the tiller of the soil, surprisingly few believed in supporting an enlightened aristocracy who were supposed to look after the peasant and whose interests would coincide with those of the Government. Whether because of the sermons of Le Bas and Jeremie or the political economy of Malthus and Jones, they were most of them when they reached India on the side of the yeoman rather than the noble. And it is by the outlook in India of Haileybury men that Haileybury must be judged.

CHAPTER IX

THOMASON AND THE SETTLEMENT
OF THE NORTH-WEST

I. AN OUTSPOKEN SERVICE

IT is by the outlook of Haileybury men in India that Haileybury must be judged. It would be easy, however, to attribute too much to Haileybury's influence. In the words of those first district officers under Hastings who thought the settlement too heavy, in all that Metcalfe and Elphinstone wrote on the employment of Indians, there is a note that can be recognized in the sayings of the new Haileybury men. In their reports to the Government and their letters home to their parents, there is a thread of similarity. It was not only that they were writing about the same subjects; there was something there before Haileybury began which was to survive till the end.

What those men had in common is not easy to define. It is never easy to put in words the stamp that marks one profession, school, college or regiment from another; it is doubly difficult with men whose profession encouraged idiosyncracies because it put them where they were alone among men of an alien race, isolated by religion, food, custom and above all by responsibility. There were men among them who were industrious, men who were idle, men devout and indifferent, bent scholars in Sanskrit and cheerful sunburnt men with good livers whose leisure was spent shooting tigers and spearing hogs. But there was a stamp on them all, a combination of two qualities usually antagonistic.

There is in nearly all of them a consciousness that they have a great task and that they belong to a service. There is, so to speak, an official doctrine in which they all believe in varying degrees. But there is also another and distinctive under-note, an independence of outlook, a readiness to criticize and to state an opinion, however unfavourable to the administration. There are always one or two members of the service who are permanently in opposition, sharply critical in a land where as yet public opinion is not very vocal; but apart from that the staidest pillars of the régime are sometimes in disagreement and usually say what they think.

The official doctrine was put clearly by W. S. Seton-Kerr, speaking in 1864 about the new men, the competition-wallahs, who were replacing the Haileybury men. He was a successful member of the service, who had won prizes in Classics, Hindustani and Bengali when he was at Haileybury in 1841; he was a member of the Legislative Council before he had twenty years' service and was soon to be a judge of the High Court and Foreign Secretary to the Government of India. 'We shall welcome', he said, 'the new men. We shall be content to be far surpassed in talent if we are only equalled in integrity and honour. I trust . . . that from the first they will act steadily on the sure and simple maxim that we are bound to govern India in trust for the natives and for India itself. . . .'

F. J. Halliday, who was lieutenant-governor of Bengal in 1855, had put it even more clearly in his evidence before a Committee of the House of Commons in 1853: 'I believe', he said, 'that our mission in India is to qualify them for governing themselves. I say also that the measures of the Governments, for a number of years past, have been advisedly directed to so qualifying them. . . .'

That, then, had become the official doctrine; it had been implicit for a long time and no one had hesitated to say very clearly when he thought injustice was being done.

Charles Edward Trevelyan, for instance, went his own way all his life. He too won prizes at Haileybury; in India, he began by discovering that his immediate chief was corrupt. He exposed him; he stuck to his guns through the long dreary inquiries that followed; the man was at last removed from the service. Trevelyan became Metcalfe's favourite assistant, he was Secretary to the Board of Revenue; later he became Assistant Secretary to the Treasury in London and came back to India, after many years' absence, as Governor of Madras. He married Macaulay's beloved sister Hannah and was the father of George Otto Trevelyan, whose life of Macaulay is a model for biographers, and the grandfather of George Macaulay Trevelyan.

Charles was not exactly an ordinary man, but he was an Indian civilian through and through. He adopted very early certain pet reforms as his own and worked until his views were heard. He was the father of free trade within India, being more than any man responsible for the abolition of the transit dues, which had been levied in every state and city on goods travelling across the country; his report on this subject, said Macaulay, was 'a perfect masterpiece of its kind . . . I never read an abler State paper'. He worked all his life for the education of Indians, though in this he was not alone. Not

288

being able to persuade the authorities to do as he wanted about an improvement in the street planning of Delhi, he paid for it himself and the area became Trevelyanpur.

He was 'a great master in the most exciting and perilous of field sports, the spearing of wild boars . . . During the important years of his life, from twenty to twenty-five,' wrote Macaulay, telling another sister of the engagement, 'Trevelyan was in a remote province of India where his whole time was divided between public business and field sports and where he seldom saw a European gentleman and never a European lady. He has no small talk. His mind is full of schemes of moral and political improvement and his zeal boils over in his talk. His topics, even in courtship, are steam navigation, the education of the natives, the equalization of the sugar duties, the substitution of the Roman for the Arabic alphabet in the Oriental languages.'

To talk shop, 'even in courtship', was always to be a caste mark, one that Kipling knew well — though most men were more fortunate in their audience than Wressley of the Foreign Office, whose howwid Wajahs were such a bore to Miss Venner.

Trevelyan, however, carried his independence too far when he was Governor of Madras; he not only disapproved of the financial reforms which the Government of India were about to introduce but let the world know that he disapproved, so that it became necessary to recall him. And no doubt this became another argument for appointing amateurs to the Presidency governorships.

Nor was the spirit new. As far back as 1808, Cox and Tucker, appointed to report on the extension of the Permanent Settlement to the Upper Provinces, had recommended against what they knew to be the policy of the Governor-General and Council and resigned from the commission when the Governor-General persisted in his own view. Fortunately for India as well as themselves, the Directors agreed with Cox and Tucker.

There is intellectual detachment, too, though of quite a different kind, in the attitude of a far more typical man, Samuel Wauchope, who was at Haileybury in 1839 and became the special commissioner in Bengal for the suppression of dacoity — that is, robbery by gangs. On a man being brought before him who was accused of dacoity, Mr. Wauchope 'heard him out and then laughingly replied that the story was doubtless a very good one but that it was not good enough for him'. He went on to mention that this same man had been arrested under another name in such a district, under a third name in a third district, that his real name was yet a fourth and the nickname used in the gang to distinguish him from another dacoit was a fifth — 'and by that nickname Mr. Wauchope called him'. At this the man confessed all: what he found most frightening and surprising was perhaps less the knowledge than the laughing detachment with which it was displayed. Here was neither the indifference nor the ferocity which were the moods in which the Indian criminal had usually known authority, but a close undeviating interest, not unfriendly, quite without indignation, showing even a touch of rather grim affection — something, in fact, very like the attitude of a London policeman.

Independence and detachment of outlook were then the distinguishing qualities of the Company's civil servants. Independence of outlook does not usually occur without some material security; by now the Company's civil servants were reasonably well provided for, the young civilian being already, as mammas told their daughters, a match worth 'three hundred a year alive or dead'. An annuity scheme had been introduced; each man contributed 4 per cent of his salary and when he retired, with twenty-five years' service, the Company would buy him an annuity of £1000 a year. As to widows and children, they were covered by another scheme, by which the widow was entitled at least to the celebrated three hundred a year, while there was an allowance for each child.

Both schemes were the subject of a good deal of discussion; there were, as there always will be, those who calculated that so many civilians would die young that the Government could hardly lose much on the annuity scheme; some of the senior ladies on the other hand felt it was hard that in his old age, when he was enjoying the fruits of his early toil and the juiciest plums, dear George, who had never been dry-nursed when *he* was young, should have to pay for the improvident marriages of his juniors. But these were the grumblings of security; everyone was comfortably provided for, no one would be turned out of the service except for grave misconduct, incontrovertibly proved; men could afford to speak their minds.

Such men as Wauchope were not uncommon; much rarer were the rebels. There seems as a rule to have been in almost every generation at least one who expressed opinions critical of the régime. F. J. Shore, the son of Lord Teignmouth, better known as Sir John Shore, was such a rebel. He was older, when he began to publish his opinions, than when Bishop Heber first heard his name, leading the assault on a fort full of dacoits near Saharanpur and getting two sabre-cuts on the chest. He had twenty years' service when his papers were printed in book form in London in 1837 over his own name.

There are about fifty articles of varying length. They are clear and well-argued papers: there is common sense in the conclusions and moderation in the language, but they are highly critical. 'Suppose a few African merchants received permission from the English government to erect a factory somewhere on the South Coast of England,' Shore begins and it is clear at once how the argument is going to develop; the Africans gradually get possession of the whole country, they decide that the English are never to be trusted, that the Africans are the only people fit for the higher posts. 'Of our laws the Africans know little or nothing; . . . we are often left to the mercy of young men of two or three and twenty . . . and the hardship is the greater because the ideas of the Africans are in many points very different to ours . . .' And so on.

Shore does it very well; it is a telling piece of controversy and a useful exercise in fairmindedness. He follows up his opening with papers on the behaviour of the English in India, on the attitude of Indians towards Englishmen, and much more that aroused a good deal of indignation in Calcutta. He assailed the whole system that existed before 1833, when some of his criticisms were met; but his sharpest language occurs when he is assailing the boorishness of those who display contempt for a man because of his colour.

What Shore attacked is hateful, and no honest person could deny that it existed throughout the whole time the English were in India. It is perhaps inevitable that in some people such a feeling should sometimes exist in such a relationship; the question is how widespread the attitude was when Shore wrote. He says himself that it is not universal but he does give the impression that consideration and good manners to Indians were in his day the exception; from Bishop Heber, on the other hand, one would gather that, at least among the Company's civil servants, it was bad manners that were less usual. The truth, no doubt, is that on the whole bad manners were due to ignorance and that as a rule British soldiers, subalterns in royal regiments on first arrival, and Calcutta traders were the worst offenders because they knew the least. Shore speaks of young officers using such expressions as: 'I hate the natives,' or 'I like to beat a black fellow,' which they would certainly not have dared to do in the presence of Malcolm or Elphinstone; nor can one imagine such words used before Bird, Thomason, Trevelyan, or the Lawrences. The odious thing seems on the whole to have been rather worse in the 'forties and 'fifties than in the 'twenties and 'thirties, perhaps because the Company's position was growing steadily stronger and confidence increasing; perhaps because Indian character was deteriorating in subjection or the English becoming intoxicated by power; perhaps because Indians were beginning to forget how uncomfortable anarchy had been and to show signs of thinking it preferable to regimentation. But the deepest reason was perhaps a dislike — sometimes subconscious — among the less educated English for the official doctrine of trusteeship and for the increasing education and employment of Indians.

The point for the moment, however, is that Shore not only disliked this attitude, as the most orthodox would have done, but that he discussed it openly and also criticized every aspect of English rule. He wrote for instance of 'a harassing and vexatious system of miscalled justice'. His remedies, however, were not revolutionary. He wanted smaller districts, with one Englishman to supervise and inspect a number of courts in which Indians would preside — much what Metcalfe would have liked to see; he wanted every Englishman to know more of the language and customs of the people and the idlest to work as hard as the most conscientious — sentiments that every Member of Council would have shared. He wanted more employment and better pay for Indians — Munro, Malcolm, Elphinstone and Metcalfe agreed, and the act of 1833 went far to meet him.

2. ROBERT BIRD

I am trying to say what Haileybury men were like. Perhaps one piece of work, stretching over many years, will give a better idea than a patchwork from a dozen men's lives and tastes. The work in question was complicated and highly technical. Victor Jacquemont once asked Holt Mackenzie to explain in five minutes the revenue systems of India; Mackenzie replied that he had been studying the subject for over twenty years and was not yet sufficiently expert to say he understood it. No doubt the answer was meant as a snub, but it was in a sense true; any attempt to condense must lead to some statements not quite accurate and to some misunderstanding. Nor should it be forgotten that this was only one task of many; it was all the same the backbone without which the rest of the bony structure would become a jumble of useless appendages.

Akbar had seen that the problem for any ruler of India was to settle what was the King's share of the produce of the soil, to take enough to provide a solvent treasury, to leave in the peasant's hands enough to keep him on the land, at work and reasonably content. The English in Bengal had seen the same and they too had put land revenue first, letting criminal and civil justice follow. Like Akbar, the English needed money; like Akbar, they perceived that a ruined land was against their true interest. Their first attempts at settling the King's share were, however, confused by an exaggerated idea of the wealth of India and still more by their puzzled search for property in land. Parliament, it will be remembered, had on the advice of Cornwallis cut short the controversy by a simplification; he who paid the revenue was the owner. He might be a hereditary chief, a yearly contractor, the descendant of a Mogul official; it was all one, he was now the proprietor.

This caused some injustice in Bengal; it was worse when English rule spread to what were at first called the Upper Provinces. The terms kept changing and it is confusing to read in succession of the Upper Provinces, the Province of Agra, and the North-Western Provinces. It will be simplest for the rest of this chapter to speak of the North-Western Provinces and to understand that this meant the Gangetic plain between Benares and Delhi, what later still became the United Provinces. But it must be remembered that Oudh was still a feudatory state.

Here, in the plains on which lie Allahabad, Cawnpore, Agra, Muttra, Bareilly and Meerut, there were villages in which something like the original village brotherhood survived, where the land was cultivated by a kind of co-operative society, the shareholders doing the work and the King's share being paid by the society as a whole. Here too there were wide stretches in which the name of farmer or contractor was unknown; village brotherhood or hereditary chief was the rule.

There seem to have been three main kinds of injustice done unwittingly by the English in the North-Western Provinces. An example of one of these is told well by Kaye, who had the story direct from 'a zealous and intelligent civil officer'. The magistrate was fixing the position of a line of police-stations to protect the highway; it was evening and he rode past a village scene familiar enough to him and to those who came after. One may picture the shadows long on the ground, the light rich and golden, with lines of smoky blue drawn in smooth bands above the thatched huts. He rode on, leaving behind him the village, the sound of men's voices and the confused cries of the peafowl going to roost among the tree-tops. By the side of the track rose a mound, a coral atoll in the plain built from the bones of dead houses. At the foot of the mound, dividing it from the green sea of crops, there would be a beach of broken shards of red earthenware and fragments of brick not yet ground back to the dust from which they had been made.

The officer paused at the foot of this mound, then his horse clattered over the potsherds and up the ascent. At the top, he paused, perhaps to enjoy the sunset, perhaps to observe how the line of the Jumna lay in relation to his police posts. 'While thus engaged an old and respectable-looking Hindoo crawled out from a hut'; with him the officer entered into conversation, and at last asked him who he was. 'Who *am* I, do you ask?' he answered. 'I *am* the owner of this wretched hut. I *was* the Chief of all your eye can see.'

He had been the hereditary chief; when the English came, he did not know how to approach these strange folk, who for all he knew might breathe fire and smoke, sport sharp claws and a tail. 'The Collector is a tiger, do not go near him,' advised Nasar Ali, the collector's chief assistant. 'Pay me the land revenue and I will see he gets it.'

So he paid the land revenue to Nasar Ali until one day the whole of his estate was sold by auction because he was a habitual defaulter and had never paid a penny to the Treasury. At the auction no one cared to bid against Nasar Ali's cousin's brother-in-law, who became possessed of the whole estate.

That was one simple way that things went wrong. Another was due to experience in Bengal. There the descendants of the Mogul assignees were on the whole a degenerate crew; they usually sold to someone else the troublesome business of collecting their dues. When the English came to the North-Western Provinces, they sent out low-paid Indian officials, who had been told to write down in the first column of the forms the owner of the land and in the second the name of the contractor who actually collected the revenue from the tiller of the soil. But here there was no such person. A man collected from his own peasants. 'Are you the one who collects the dues?' was all that Nasar Ali would ask. 'Yes?' And down would go the name in column two — 'contractor'. Ask him if that word described his position and he would wonderingly agree. Why not? He had never heard it before

The first column, the place where the owner's name should be, would be blank for a year or two and then unobtrusively a new name would appear but no one in the village would see the owner or know of his existence. Then Nasar Ali would retire and soon afterwards the fictitious owner by a deed of gift or sale would transfer the village to Nasar Ali. 'Yours is a strange rule,' said the people. 'You flog a man for stealing a brass pot and reward him for stealing half a district.'

Much the same thing would happen where there had been a brotherhood holding the village jointly. Their names would go down in the third column, they were cultivators and no more, for years they would know nothing of how they had been entered. Then one day they would discover that for a long time there had been a name in the first column, the name of someone they had never heard of, who had become their overlord and the owner of land that had always been theirs, and from which they would now perhaps be ejected if they did not pay what he asked.

All this happened to a people who were not only simple and illiterate, but who had been used to expect very little of either Heaven or man. They were accustomed to the vagaries of absolute power, so that it did not occur to them that there was much to be gained by complaining and they usually said nothing.

During the first ten years of British rule in the North-Western Provinces, there were three settlements, each of which was meant to settle the King's share and to bring the Government a stage nearer knowing who owned and who tilled the land. In fact, however, each of these settlements probably carried things a little further from the truth; probably in each settlement in each district a few more fictitious names made their appearance. Most English judges and collectors saw little of what was going on or if they did see could find no way of putting it right. But there were always one or two more clear-sighted than the rest. Newnham, for instance, Collector of Cawnpore in 1813, sent in many reports of careful inquiries into these injustices, but they were not easy to put right, and it would be easy at headquarters to persuade oneself that on the whole it was fairer not to interfere with the record.

Four years later, in 1817, Mr. Robertson, as Judge of Cawnpore, was more successful. Being Judge and not Collector, he could give a decision in favour of the man he thought wronged. But the Court of Appeal in Bareilly was not convinced; its members felt that once they departed from the records, such as they were, there would be no solid ground beneath their feet. They reversed Robertson's decisions one after another. There were further appeals, of course, to Calcutta and some inclination there to take Robertson's side, but he was not content to wait. He wrote to the Government, sending as enclosures copies of the Bareilly Court's decisions. This, of course, was highly irregular, but he was a man, says Kaye, with an 'eager sense of justice'. A Commission was appointed to inquire into all transfers of property during the first ten years of British rule. It did not achieve very much; it cannot have been easy to put things back as they had been at a time of flux and transition. But steps were taken to prevent anything more of the same kind. The principles for a new settlement were clearly stated in the Commission's report in 1822 and were never to be substantially changed.

It would be tedious to go one by one through the Regulations and instructions that toiled one after another in pursuit of the truth, a hurried and always slightly belated procession. Here, as in Madras, the men on the spot had to fight the intention of the Government in Calcutta to introduce the Permanent Settlement from Bengal. Cox and Tucker protested and fortunately Tom Munro had been in London recently and the Directors knew something of the dangers of permanency. It is to Holt Mackenzie that most of the credit must go for devising a method of settlement that took some account of northern conditions. His plan was for settlement for long periods with whoever was found in possession of a *mahal*, that is, an estate, whether the possessor was one man or a brotherhood. And Holt Mackenzie, 'a man of large and liberal views', perhaps did more than any regulation when he told the collectors to take their guns and bring back information with their game. But in spite of this Robert Mert-tins Bird in 1832, when he first went to the North-West, still found the law 'wholly distinct' from the facts. The truth was that Mac-kenzie's instructions were too detailed and too painstaking; it would have taken hundreds of years to complete a settlement on his directions.

Bird was told to put things right himself and carried out between 1833 and 1840 operations which affected twenty-three million people and an area about the size of England. They were not confined to settling the King's share; he set out to do far more than that. It was his task to decide where the boundaries lay between one village and the next, and having decided to mark them; to define and record 'the separate possession, rights, privileges and liabilities of the members of those communities who hold their land in severalty . . . and the several interests of those who hold their land in common'; to prepare a record of the fields and of the rights of every cultivator possessing rights; to reform the village accounts; and also to provide a 'system of self-government for the communities'.

There was as a matter of fact nothing new in the principles of the settlement of 1833; they were the principles stated in 1822 as a result of Robertson's irregular zeal. What was new was the method and the speed with which the work was done. This was achieved partly by making full use of the village accountant, one of the original servants of the village brotherhood. He had sometimes become a servant of the zamindar but he was now to enter into the time of his glory. From now on he was a government servant; he was the basis of the whole fabric. The settlement proceeded just seven times as fast as before, and it was partly because he, the village accountant, was now used to the full. His records were taken as a starting point or basis by the staff of the settlement officer, who made a new record, based on the accountant's, and on what the villagers told them. The new record was checked by the assistant settlement officer; and every villager was given an opportunity to see it or ask questions about it; if he objected to anything he could without cost file a complaint. A percentage of the entries was checked by the settlement officer himself.

Sleeman, who had himself accomplished the impossible, wrote only a few years earlier that 'we might almost as well attempt to map the waves of the ocean as field-map the face of any considerable area in any part of India . . .' But this is what Bird did in the North-Western Provinces. A trigonometrical survey fixed certain points, from those points there spread a simpler field survey by triangulation, a system for which the only absolutely essential instruments are a measuring chain and a pair of compasses. It is a system that would no doubt breed error over many miles of country but the professional survey with theodolites corrected that, and within a village it is surprisingly accurate.

Even with the help of the village accountant, the survey was not going fast enough and it looked, at an early stage, as though it would be so slow and expensive that it would have to be given up. Bird had a conference with Henry Lawrence, one of his surveyors; Lawrence asked for an increase in his low-paid staff, whom he would train and with whom he would undertake to survey 3000 square miles in a season instead of one thousand. So the speed was trebled at a trifling extra cost.

The survey and the field maps Bird completed; he made a record of the rights he believed to exist which was far from perfect, but a great advance on anything there had ever been before. It cannot be said that he succeeded in providing the villages with a system of self-government; he was fighting a losing battle there. For just as a bad coinage, which everyone is eager to be rid of, will drive out of circulation a good coinage which men bury under the hearthstone, so an intimate system of justice, in which everyone concerned knows the facts, can hardly stand side by side with one formal and remote, by which the malefactor has a good chance of winning his case. A man who knows he is in the wrong will always take his case to the formal court.

Nor can it be said that Bird was entirely successful in his first task of settling what share of the produce of the soil should be the King's. It had always been the intention to settle leniently. The new rulers had come up 'still damp from Bengal', where the zamindar had wrung from the peasant what he could get and the Company had taken 90 per cent, leaving the zamindar 10 per cent for the trouble of collection. It was proposed in the North-Western Provinces to take between 60 and 70 per cent instead of 90; this, it was believed, would be less than one-third of the total produce of the soil and would leave about one-sixth for the zamindar and one half for the cultivator. It had been recognized now that the King's share was a tax, to be levied not on the whole crop but on the surplus left over when the tiller of the soil had met his expenses for the year and had put aside his seed for the next year.

This was meant to be lenient, and by Mogul standards, considered on paper in the study, it was moderately lenient. But English collections were more regular than in Mogul days, and much more regular than in the anarchy of the eighteenth century, when revenue collection was a series of punitive raids. It was no use hiding part of the crop now, and not only was collection more certain than in the past, but the estimate of what was available for taxation was still much too high. As in Bengal, it had often happened, when the English first came into the country, that two claimants would bid against each other for the right to pay revenue and would bid much too high.

Bird then found an assessment that was too high; this, incidentally, was one of Shore's criticisms. He set out to lower it; he believed — as everyone did who had practical experience of the subject — that it was sound policy to be lenient and after much discussion and some opposition he got his way. But he did not yet go far enough. The proportion taken was still too high; two-thirds of the available surplus — one-third of the whole — was really too much to take. The proportion was reduced in the 'fifties by John Russell Colvin to half of the surplus — one quarter of the whole; it came down eventually to about one-third of the surplus — one-sixth of the whole.

Again, the estimate of what the soil would produce was too high in districts fully cultivated. Any waste land brought into cultivation after the settlement paid no revenue for thirty years and this meant that where there was still land to be brought into cultivation — and that was in most districts — thirty years of peace and order were enough to make the settlement a fair one. It was too high to start with, but on the whole, it worked. By 1852 it was possible to write: 'This year the rains crops have failed entirely and of last year's winter crop very little had been sown. Yet the revenue has been paid up without a balance and has occasioned no perceptible distress. This is the effect of firm rule and a light assessment. Mr. Bird (all honour to his name!) insisted on a considerable reduction of the assessment. The consequence is that land which before was worthless now bears a high value and a people who before were lawless now yield implicit obedience to the laws.'

Bird directed this settlement but he could not be in every district at once; he worked through district officers and settlement officers. He chose young men. 'Where he reposed his confidence, he did so without reserve. He received the opinions of those employed under him with respect; looked after their interests, defended their proceedings and fought their battles as if they had been his own.' His young men speak of him each 'with the faith of a disciple and the love of a son, and seldom mention his name without an inward genuflexion'. Of the life they led, one of them wrote an account, some ten years later in 1849:

'We look back . . . and see the white camp rising in the long aisles of the mango grove. We see the fair-haired Saxon youth opposing his well-trained intellect to the new difficulties that crowd upon him. We see him exerting daily . . . all his faculties of observation, of research, of penetration, of judgment. It is a strange sight . . . to watch the respect and confidence evinced by grey-headed men towards that beardless youth. We see him, in the early morning mist, stretching at an inspiring gallop over the dewy fields . . . He is on his way to some distant point where measurements are to be tested, doubts resolved, or objections investigated. This done, he returns to his solitary breakfast . . . The forenoon is spent in receiving reports from the native officers employed under him; in directing their operations; in examining, comparing, analysing and arranging the various information which comes in from all quarters. As the day advances, the wide-spread shade begins to be peopled with living figures. Group after group of villagers arrive in their best and whitest dresses and a hum of voices succeeds to the stillness before only broken by the cooing of the dove and the scream of the perroquet. The carpet is then spread in the open air; the chair is set; the litigants and spectators take their seats on the ground in orderly ranks; silence is proclaimed and the rural court is opened. As case after case is brought forward, the very demeanour of the parties and of the crowds around, seems to point out on which side justice lies. No need here of *ex parte* decisions or claims lost by default. All are free to come and go, with little trouble and at no expense ... In such a court was justice everywhere administered in the childhood of the human race. ...

'Strange must that man's character be, and dull his sympathies, who, in the midst of occupations like these, does not find his heart accompanying and lightening his labours. He sees the people in their fairest light; he witnesses their ceaseless industry, their contented poverty, their few and simple pleasures, their plain sense of justice, their general faithfulness to their engagements. He finds them as a nation sober, chaste, frugal, and gifted with much of that untaught politeness in which the rustic classes of colder climates are so often deficient. For months together he uses no language, enjoys no society, but theirs. ...'

After two wars, we are less sure than our great-grandfathers of the virtues of the fair-haired Saxon; we are also suspicious of the idyllic. And no doubt this is a picture of what every assistant settlement officer would wish to be. All the same, it is not far from the truth. Disputes really were decided before a settlement officer without cost; there were no court fees, no pleaders, no recording of evidence and no expensive witnesses, no underlings to be tipped. The whole affair was settled as a rule after discussion with both parties in the presence of the villagers; it was a method which even in the twentieth century did not often go far wrong.

It is true too that almost every settlement officer did find that his heart accompanied his labours. Many a man kept carefully till his death the settlement report that he wrote in his 'thirties, a printed volume as long as an ordinary novel, even without the tables of crops and soils, of average output an acre, of rent and revenue reduced to percentages of gross assets and net assets. But his heart would be in the introduction, describing in loving terms the country and people where he had been so happy, turning joyously aside into long dissertations on race, language and custom, dwelling on the angle of a jaw-bone, on a phrase or a sacrificial rite recalling Homer or the Bible — labours thrown in from sheer exuberance.

All this — it must be said again — is an over-simplified account of what happened in the plains of the North-Western Provinces. In the hills — Mr. Traill's hills — settlement was with the village brotherhood in its purest form. In Madras and Bombay, thanks to Munro, it was direct with the peasant; in Bengal it was with the zamindar, which there meant a large land-owner. Behar was still part of Bengal and in the whole of Bengal the settlement was permanent while in the North-West it was for thirty years.

There were a hundred local variations, but they could, if there were world enough and time, all be described in terms of difference from the kind of settlement that happened in the North-West.

3 . JAMES THOMASON

It was John Thornton who in 1849 described the settlement officer's life in such rapturous terms. He had been one of Bird's young men; he had served for a short time in Azamgarh under James Thomason, who followed Bird and was mightier than he; when he wrote he was Secretary to Thomason's government, engaged in perfecting Bird's work.

Thomason had come from Haileybury to Bengal with many introductions; his father had been a chaplain of the East India Company, a man of outstanding character who had been deeply loved. For the first years of his service, James Thomason was employed in or near Calcutta; he was a secretary to government before he had been ten years in the country. But he decided that he must know for himself what happened in a district; he resigned his secretarial appointment and the flesh-pots of Calcutta and no doubt many shook their heads and said he had ruined his career. He went to be Magistrate, Collector, Opium Agent and Settlement Officer of Azamgarh, which is in the eastern part of the North-Western Provinces, about a hundred miles from Benares.

In Bird's operations, there was usually a settlement officer distinct from the district officer; Thomason, however, with several European assistants, was both and he clearly enjoyed it. Every man loves the first district in which he serves and the first of which he has charge;

with Thomason, the two were one, for he learnt his district work as head of the district. He was happy in his married life in Azamgarh — almost for the last time, for his wife died not long afterwards — he was fresh from the Turkish bath of Calcutta to the sparkling winter climate of the North-West, he was six months in camp every year, hard at work on his settlement; it would have been strange if he had not been happy at Azamgarh. 'It was to me,' he wrote to one of his children, 'a field of victory, where such repute and status as I had in the service was founded; but how far short have I fallen in the fulfilment of God's will!' And on another occasion, more succinctly: 'Hurrah, hurrah, for old Azamgarh!'

Thomason succeeded Bird in charge of settlement affairs; he went on to be Lieutenant-Governor of the North-Western Provinces, succeeding Robertson whose eager sense of justice had been aroused at Benares twenty years before. Thomason was ten years Lieutenant-Governor, dying suddenly and while still in office at Bareilly in 1852; he had written a few days earlier: 'I have no specific illness but loss of appetite, loss of strength, loss of power for any exertion whatever . . .' He was worn out, worked to death, and it is not surprising.

Thomason belongs clearly to another generation than the great quartet and in nothing more clearly than in his religion. To Munro, Malcolm, Elphinstone and Metcalfe, each in his own way, religion was something deep in the heart, far below the surface, a private view of the universe, essentially undogmatic. Theirs was, in short, the religion of the eighteenth century. But Thomason and those who followed him were evangelical; their doctrine was explicit and exclusive; there was one truth only, eternally revealed, it was a matter of intense conviction, never far from the conscious mind. Thomason did not read Theocritus in his spare time. When he was not at his official work, he was usually either writing to his motherless children in England or copying out for them extracts from devotional works. He read Hooker, Jeremy Taylor, à Kempis, Herbert, and Quarles; he read the *Christian Year* and *In Memoriam*; the sermons of Melvill of Haileybury, and many other sermons. Convinced that the secular power must not be used for the spread of Christianity, he still always felt his conscience challenged by the millions of heathen who surrounded him.

Religion must be stressed, for it is the key to the man and the mainspring of all he did. Thomason was a delicate man, very tall but slight, and his back had been injured in a riding accident while he was still young. He had none of Malcolm's abounding physical energy;

it was religion, a belief in God's purpose and a sense of his duty to God, that drove him to wear himself out. To a friend in England he wrote of 'the high and responsible duty to which we are now called to address ourselves, with regard to this great country which God has placed in our hands. For its right performance, we no less require the best wishes and prayers of our fellow countrymen than for protection in the day of battle. . . .'

Thomason lost his wife before he became Lieutenant-Governor; all who knew him during those ten years seem to have been impressed by his selflessness and by that tenderness for others that sometimes follows loss. He carried it into official work; those whose departments had come to expect what in India is called stepmotherly treatment found sympathy and consideration when they went to Thomason. Each came to believe that Customs or Opium or Stamps was the special interest of His Honour's life. He was the father of public works; more than any other one man he was responsible for the achievement of two great projects, the Grand Trunk Road and the Ganges Canal. Like his great predecessors, he was anxious to employ Indians in more responsible positions, but this was now official doctrine and he was more successful than they had been in getting his way. In order to train young Indians for the posts he created for them, he founded the Engineering College at Roorkee which bore his name.

But it is as a trainer that Thomason was greatest. He was unfailing in energy and continually travelling about his province; every officer was aware of a friendly personal interest and an acute knowledge of every detail of a district officer's work. There was no chance of glossing over the fact that things were behindhand. His praise was generous and his condemnation was felt to be deserved; he knew exactly what were the special interests and what was the right post for each officer. The sheer goodness of the man was overwhelming. 'He received a ready and devoted service, the fruit of a loving and admiring spirit . . .' wrote Sir William Muir. His success as a trainer received the most sincere and painful recognition; when the last great wave of conquest took the English forward into the Punjab, it was to Thomason that the rulers of the Punjab turned for men. 'It has been a heavy tax,' he wrote to his brother-in-law, Montgomery. 'Nineteen men of the best blood! I feel very weak after so much depletion.'

For ten years he was able to give his undivided attention to internal progress — an opportunity given to no one else; Warren Hastings had had thirteen years but Thomason did not have to concern himself with diplomacy or war, he had no dissenting council to dispute every action he took. He improved every branch of the administration, giving to each a special degree of care that a less whole-hearted man could hardly have found even for one; to him, however, the first was that which had always been first with every great Indian ruler, the settlement of the land revenue.

He brought an extraordinarily acute and clear mind to the completion of Bird's work. He saw that those who had argued about where proprietory right lay were arguing about something unreal. 'Whoever may be in theory the proprietor of land in India', he wrote, 'the absence of all restriction on the supreme power . . . left all property in the land virtually dependent on its will.' In other words, so long as the King took as much as he could get, the estate had not much value for anyone else. 'But when the Government limits its demand to a reasonable amount and fixes that demand for a term of years, a marketable property is thereby created . . .' It is only at this stage that property really comes into existence; the next task is to say whose it is. The usual test is to ask who pays the Revenue; whoever is responsible for the revenue has the right to sell.

But in practice it was not so simple; it was seldom that one person was responsible for the revenue; more often it was one leader on behalf of a group with a common ancestor. The right of sale must accordingly be limited; when one man defaults, both custom and public policy would give a preference to the other members of the group, who must be given the first chance to buy at a concessional rate. There is in short a right of pre-emption.

These are samples of the kind of principles which Thomason embodied in a code of instructions. They are samples only, from a subject obscure, technical, fascinating to a few, of vital importance to millions. Thomason made the principles clear. His instructions remained the handbook for settlement officers for many years and was the basis for all later work; local conditions were different in the Punjab but it was possible even in the Punjab to start where Thomason left off. 'There are evidently', he wrote, 'two distinct operations in the formation of a settlement. The one is fiscal, the determination of the Government demand — the other is judicial, the formation of the record of rights. Ordinarily the two operations are performed at the same time and there are many reasons which render such an arrangement very desirable.' But there is no reason why it should always be so and bringing the record of rights a little nearer perfection was made by Thomason a continuous process. He believed that nothing else, except a just assessment, would contribute so much to the happiness of the people; it was one of his main objects, always in the forefront of his mind, clear in the forefront of his instructions to Collectors.

Thomason's work continued Bird's; it was not final, it was still far from perfect, as both knew. 'How far short have I fallen in the fulfilment of God's will . . .' But in the fifty years between the British entry into the North-Western Provinces and Thomason's death at Bareilly — just the length of Akbar's reign — land tenures that were in a state of highly fluid chaos had been analysed and sorted; there was to be no more argument about principles or definitions. A field by field survey had been made and against every field had been entered the name of the cultivator, the crop sown, the rent paid, and the name of the person, or more usually group of persons, who took the rent and paid the Land Revenue. What were believed to be the village rights and customs had been put in writing. As well attempt to map the waves of the ocean, Sleeman had written, but it had been done, at least over one great arm of the sea and the network was spreading over the whole.

CHAPTER X

BEFORE THE DELUGE

IT is time to pause, to look at the map, to consider what has happened in the first half of the century. The year 1842, when Thomason took office as Lieutenant-Governor, is a convenient point to choose for a political summary; during the fifteen years that follow, events crowd thick and fast and there will be no time to stand still. But in thinking what improvements have been made in administration and what changes have been made in the way the English in India live and work, it is the half century with which we are concerned and not the single year 1842.

The map has changed since 1798. There were seven years of conquest and annexation under Wellesley, a withdrawal immediately afterwards under Cornwallis and Barlow. Then Lord Hastings completed Wellesley's work and put an end to the Maratha empire; since then, there has not been much increase of territory in India proper. It has been a time of consolidation. Apart from Burma, the map has shown no real change since Lord Hastings left India in 1823, twenty years ago. And Burma is a by-product, something like the subsidiary plot in a Victorian novel, something separable from the main story. Burma can come in a separate chapter. So far, Assam, Arakan and the Tenasserim coast had been taken from Burma and added to India; nothing of Burma proper was annexed till 1853.

Up to the Sutlej, then, there is either the red of British districts or the lumps of undigested pink which stand for protected states. There is one large undigested lump in the south — Mysore — entirely surrounded by red; another larger lump in the centre of the peninsula, the dominions of the Nizam of the Deccan. There are remnants of the Maratha Empire, untidy viscera sprawling from West to East; above them the feudal States of Rajputana cut off by their deserts from the world; there is Oudh, completely encircled within the North-Western Provinces; there is the cluster of Sikh states in Sirhind, between Delhi and the Sutlej, the states which Metcalfe had so clearly told Ranjit Singh to keep his hands off; east of the Sutlej, these Protected States were all that remained of native India.

Beyond the Sutlej lay the Sikh empire. It had been built up by

Ranjit Singh alone; he had begun as the chief of one of many warring clans which one by one he had overcome, by battle, cunning or bribery, until his empire stretched from the Khyber to the Sutlej and northwards over Kashmir. The Sikhs are a sect of converts from Hinduism; they profess a rule of life which rejects the many castes and the many gods of the Hindus, which is more like Islam in seeing life in terms of black and white, right or wrong. Sikhism is a military order as much as a religion; it may be looked at as a weapon developed by Hinduism in answer to the challenge of Islam. It is the nature of the Sikhs to fight; they had fought the Moguls at first and latterly they had fought each other with almost as much enthusiasm. Ranjit Singh brought them together and held them together and, when he died in 1839, the Punjab began to seethe and boil; soon it would boil over and there would be war. For the moment, the disintegrating empire of Ranjit Singh confronted across the Sutlej the new empire of the English.

This empire, an agglomerate mass of districts directly ruled and states indirectly guided, was governed by three groups of Englishmen who were chosen in three different ways. There were less than a dozen who came to India for the first time in middle life after a moderately successful career in England as politicians or judges. The rest of the rulers, who did not yet number a thousand, were either civil servants of the Company, usually educated at Haileybury, or had been educated at Addiscombe, Haileybury's military counterpart, had come to India as young officers in the army and had only then been specially selected for civil employment.

Some care had usually been taken to nominate Haileybury men and more to educate them; about one in twenty were 'too idle or too stupid' to survive the Haileybury course and went to the cavalry, but once appointed Writer, it was exceptional to be rejected. The case, however, was quite different with the military civilians. They were nominated for military service in the same way as Writers and educated at Addiscombe. But selection for civil employment came only to those above the average; they were chosen by good luck, good report and good manners, or, to put it differently, by favouritism, when they had had a few years' service. Not one in ten had a chance of being chosen, and if he was not suitable he could be sent back; he was less secure than the civilian, more apt to live in a state of competitive tension.

Those who began as civilians had usually shown some aptitude for their books and at Haileybury they had received an abridged and concentrated university education. Those who began as soldiers came to India less well equipped in this respect, but were subject to far sharper competition; they supplied most of the men employed in the States on semi-diplomatic duties and most of the men for special tasks, such as the suppression of Thuggee. There was as yet no separate police service and there were barely enough trained civilians for the regular posts as district officers, judges and secretaries, so that for any special task it was a matter of downright necessity to call on the army. And again, whenever new territory came under British rule, men were needed not boys; new men could only come from the army. The soldiers strike one as less liable than the pure-bred civilians to fall into a rut or become pedantic; perhaps fewer of them took the broad detached view that was common to the best of both kinds. Neither side could claim a monopoly of courage or ability, of hard work or devotion to duty.

The civilian — like young Trevelyan — spent much of his early life alone. Even if he was fortunate enough to be posted to a large station, he spent a good deal of the winter in much the same kind of way as the young settlement officer. The soldier did not as a rule come to civil employment till he was older; his youth had been passed more gregariously, he was more used to society and as a rule much better versed in the agreeable art of talking about nothing without embarrassment or fatigue.

The civilian was encouraged from the first in a sturdy independence. No Colonel would see that he did not run into debt; no one would guide him in the first case he tried. He would simply be told to try it, with no more help than the law he had learnt at Haileybury, the Hindustani he had picked up at Fort William, and an Indian clerk who spoke no English. That first case would be a very slow and puzzled affair; the wretched litigants would be kept at headquarters while the young man slowly mangled his way through evidence that two years later would not keep him an hour. It is a slow way to learn, but perhaps the best. It taught not only the way to try a case but a sovereign contempt for all professional mysteries. It had been said of the eighteenth-century civilians in Madras that 'no member of Council would hesitate, at a pinch, to take command of a company of foot, to read a sermon, or administer a dose of physic'. That was still true of almost everyone in the service, but to the list should now be added: 'to lay out a road or a canal, design a jail or build a house'. Every district officer was his own engineer as well as his own policeman.

Independence of outlook often took the form of impatience of control. Almost everyone betrayed it in some degree when he was away from headquarters; in those who were district officers all their lives it was endemic. It was occasionally carried to extreme lengths, as in the indefensible behaviour of an anonymous Collector mentioned by Sleeman, who with his peons pursued a criminal across the border into Oudh, an allied State. There was an affray and several people were killed; the Collector, who seems to have known the way Oudh was governed, sought out the newswriter for the district and persuaded him to say nothing about it. And neither Government heard a word of the affair.

The idea that personal power can be limited by law was still strange to India; the English had brought the idea with them but they would have been superhuman if individuals had not sometimes disregarded it — and indeed the success the English achieved was due to their readiness to compromise, their lack of pedantry. They compromised with the oriental; they modified the rule of law by a kindly personal despotism. Even in the twentieth century there was to be one district officer who after carefully reading through a new Act promulgated by the Government of India was to write clearly and decisively in the margin: 'This Act will not apply in this District.' And it did not.

The district officer then was accustomed to give orders. Not so the political officer, whose more difficult task was to keep his head among the splendours and the barbarities of an oriental court; to judge when he must, and how far he might, interfere; to persuade and advise; to know when to ignore and when to stand firm and not budge. Tod of Rajputana was as successful as anyone in gaining the confidence of Indian rulers:

'Here,' he writes, 'the Raja's vassals were numbered and he placed me by his side on the throne. There was not a point of his rural or domestic economy on which he did not descant and ask my advice as his adopted brother. I was also made umpire between him and my old friend the baron of Bednore regarding a marriage-settlement . . . I had besides to wade through old grants and deeds to settle the claims between the Raja and several of his sub-vassals . . . All these arbitrations . . . were forced upon me merely by the claims of friendship, but it was a matter of exultation to be enabled to make use of my influence for the adjudication of such disputes and for restoring individual as well as general prosperity. My friend prepared his gifts at parting; I went through the forms of receiving but waived accepting them; this may be done without offence to delicacy.'

And again Tod writes:

'Even Ameer Khan . . . has commanded his governor of Neembaira to consult me in everything and has even gone so far as to beg I would consider the place as under my own authority. Already, following our example, he has reduced the transit dues nearly one-half and begins to think the English notions of economy better than his own, his loss having proved a gain.' Tod again, called in to help a Raja to decide between the claimants to a barony, gives his decision and then extracts a promise from the successful candidate not to use opium — just as the Governor-General takes every chance he can to extract a promise about the burning of widows.

Tod felt for the Rajputs an affection and an admiration that were far from unusual; he was in fact only one of many Englishmen who have given a generous championship to the people in whose country they have served. But even where no such affection existed, there was respect, there were appeals to the Resident as the one authority whose word could be relied on. In some degree, more or less, every political officer was a Tod.

In the larger states, Oudh, Gwalior, Hyderabad, the Rajputana group, the Resident lived like a small king with his family, that is to say, his two or three assistants, a surgeon, the commander of his escort. As a rule, there would not be much other European society, though at Delhi, Lucknow and Hyderabad there were British officers in command of troops close by. There, life would follow the same pattern as in the headquarter stations of the districts of British India.

There was a family likeness between all stations where troops were posted. Troops in those days were more widely scattered than later; at the headquarters of even quite small districts there might be a company of native infantry; at the headquarters of the larger districts there would almost certainly be at least a battalion. The social life of the Company's servants in such places was, it must be admitted, not very exciting; as Maria Graham had said forty years before, it was very like small town life everywhere.

People in these small stations were, however, more isolated than in small towns in England. It would be seventy, eighty or a hundred miles to the next station; the railway was being talked of in the 'fifties — indeed, work had begun — but in Northern India, travel was mainly by horse-drawn vehicle, though palankeens were still used at night. There were transport agencies which arranged stages; when you 'travelled dawk', or by stages, it seems to have been common for the pony to refuse to start. Its belly is slapped, a twitch is applied to the nose; it remains obstinate. Then a wisp of straw is lighted and suddenly its resistance breaks and it rockets off at a fiery canter, the trap swaying wildly behind. The stages were nine or ten miles; you might get through to the next station in a day, travelling 'dawk', but it would be a day of discomfort.

For a longer journey, those who valued their comfort travelled in their own carriage with riding horses in attendance to vary the monotony. Charles Crawford Parks was posted in 1826 from Calcutta to Allahabad as Collector of Customs; he had never before been away from Calcutta and he and his wife heard such terrible stories of life 'Up the Country' that they felt a good deal of trepidation about the move. However, they started, on November 22nd; they travelled about fifteen miles a day and reached Benares, some four hundred miles from Calcutta, five weeks later on Christmas Day; Charles went on at once the ninety miles to Allahabad, 'travelling dawk', while Fanny stayed on a few days in Benares to pay off the Calcutta bullock-carts and to visit the temples and the city.

It is Fanny who leaves an account of the march; the journal she wrote for her mother, with sketches, paintings, recipes, oriental proverbs, accounts of suttees and of visits to the *zenana*, is surely the cream of all such books. Like Miss Eden, she is constant in nostalgia, thinking often of the ecstatic day when she will be again in England among her family, but unlike Miss Eden she is interested in what is round her. Sometimes, one suspects, she is a trifle too interested for Charles; he is not mentioned much in the journal but emerges from a stroke or two as a placid figure, intelligent but not ambitious, a pious Old Harrovian, regarding with mild amusement the enthusiasms of his wife, as she turns from Hindu mythology and Persian proverbs to the draping of a *sari*, from botany to ice-making or the strange ways of the servants. Always excellent company as a writer, in the flesh there were perhaps moments when she allowed a glimpse of the blue stocking to appear below the riding-habit.

'Our marching establishment consisted of two good mares for the Stanhope, two fine saddle Arabs for ourselves, two ponies, and nine hackeries [bullock-carts] which contained supplies and clothes, also a number of goats . . . We travelled by the Grand Military Road, riding the first part of the stage and finishing it in . . . the Stanhope.' The heavy luggage went by boat up the Ganges.

After the first hundred miles, Fanny wrote that they had so far proceeded 'very much to our satisfaction. The change of air and change of scene have wrought wonders in us both. My husband has never felt so well in health or so desennuyé since he left England'. How different from Lord Auckland! They travelled in the early morning, as most people do in India, resting in the middle of the day at a dak bungalow. 'They are built by government and are all on the same plan; at each a *khidmutgar* and a bearer are in attendance.' In the evening, Charles took out his gun after quail and partridge, snipe and pigeon; Fanny as a rule went too and 'enjoyed it very much'. At Hazari Bagh she became 'possessed of the first pellet-bow I had seen and found it difficult to use'. Anyone else who has tried to use a pellet-bow will have found the same; it looks like an ordinary long-bow but the sun-baked clay pellet strikes the novice painfully on the knuckles of the left hand.

A horse runs away from a bear sleeping in the road; a servant at a dak bungalow steals a silver spoon; there are suttee-tombs and temples; it is all interesting. There are *fakirs* with withered arms and nails growing through the backs of their hands — but Fanny is something of an expert in religious mendicants; she knows the difference between those who follow Shiv the destroyer and the disciples of Vishnu; she even knows the composition of the ashes with which they smear their bodies.

Posted to Cawnpore and thence back to Allahabad, they come by river, taking eight days, and bringing with them everything except the horses, which go by road; the farmyard animals all go in one boat and 'on top of all was a great thermantidote'. This was an arrange-ment of fans, worked by two men, which drove air through a mois-tened screen and lowered the temperature of a room by ten degrees or more in hot dry weather.

This was travel up the country in the eighteen-thirties; it had hardly changed at all in the 'forties or 'fifties. In the South, roads were on the whole rougher and to 'travel dak' usually meant to be carried in a palankeen by teams of men who were relieved every hour and kept up almost as good a speed as the ponies of the North.

Nor did twenty years make much change in station life. There was as yet no club. At such places as Allahabad, Benares, or Bareilly, there would be Assembly Rooms, where sometimes there would be dances and private theatricals. In the smaller stations these festivities would occur less often, while where there were no troops of course they were out of the question. That meant in about half the districts where a civilian might be sent; the soldier's small station is large to the civilian. In a station small by civilian standards there would be the Judge, the Collector, who was also the Magistrate, his junior the

Joint Magistrate, a doctor — and that would be all. The engineer and the policeman were still to come; the Collector performed their functions for himself. The padre would come perhaps once a month, and there would be other peripatetics, but those four would be the station. It was necessary to endure each other, even in the hot weather.

Journals and letters are as a rule inclined to rosy colours; most people prefer the flesh of their relations not to creep too much. Satire should provide a useful antidote, though the samples from India tend to hover between the facetious and the sentimental. The pencil, less self-conscious, usually beats the pen; the drawings in *Curry and Rice*, for instance, are incomparably better than the text.

It is worth pausing over *Curry and Rice*; its picture of a station of the medium size in the middle of the century has some universal application. The people in it are types, but on the whole they are well-chosen. The judge, old-fashioned in his clothes and untidy, 'so desperately absorbed with his official duties that we see but little of him' — him we have met. 'Niggers — no, ten thousand pardons, not niggers, I mean natives — sons of the soil — Orientals — Asiatics — are his source of happiness', writes the more up-to-date soldier author, lapsing into a vulgarity which constantly spoils his letter-press, though his pencil can catch an Indian face as well as an English, can even convey some of the wondering boredom of an Indian servant at the trivial activities of his master. The judge plays the violoncello in a quartet — his only recreation; he has been in India thirty-two years and does not want to go back to England at all. But he is hospitable and kind to subalterns; everyone likes him.

The Collector, too, talks shop; give him a chance and he will lecture on 'settlements — revenues — land-tax — decrees — jails — crops — remissions — duties — salt — police — ' and much more. He is particularly proud of his skill as an engineer, although if his bridges and houses stand up they were really designed by the foreman; if he did design them himself, they fall down in the rains. He is a snob in the modern sense and by a kind of inverted snobbery, 'the military are his aversion, being an inferior caste — inferior in emoluments and in the classified scale of precedence . . .' All the same, he is 'a zealous, indefatigable magistrate' and, like the Judge, he is hospitable; 'if he is dull and heavy, his Moselle is sparkling and light'.

The Joint Magistrate, his junior, fancies himself as a sporting man and is knowing about horses and dogs; 'he is a bit of a dandy, curls his hair, cherishes the rudiments of a moustache'; he listens to complaints with the *Delhi Gazette* in his hand, he has a poor opinion of his seniors; 'nothing comes amiss to him . . . he would with equal willingness preach an extempore sermon at a moment's notice, undertake a Protestant discussion with the Pope and all his Cardinals, or with equal promptitude and despatch, prepare a work for the press on heresy and schism, heavy gun drill and the plurality of worlds'.

The Joint Magistrate is a type that was perennial, at least in the North. In the South, where there were fewer soldiers and where the horse was usually a conveyance rather than a social fetish, I suspect that the young civilian was inclined to be more often a solitary intellectual than a knowing young cub. But 'nothing comes amiss to him'; he despises technicalities and is confident he can master all trades; that is common to North and South. The Collector is not quite so happy a hit but both he and the Judge are fair pictures in one way; both appear as men who are busy and absorbed in their work among people who have much less to do.

If life in an Indian station appears from such a book to be trivial and silly, why, so it was, though not much more so than at Handley Cross or the houses where Mr. Sponge stabled his horses in the same middle decades of the century. Women who have not to do the housework and who live in small towns or small stations do very often talk of not much but clothes and children, recipes and match-making. There were not many who were as unfailingly busy as Fanny Parks, preserving the skins of birds in arsenical soap and setting butterflies; keeping up her archery and riding horses too spirited for the gentleman who last owned them; making vocabularies from the thieves' slang of the Thugs and lists of Indian trees with their Latin and vernacular names and the uses of their wood; spending a week at a Muslim wedding, going to fairs, sketching and learning to play Indian musical instruments.

She at least was never short of something to do and her only complaint was that she was far too often interrupted by eruptions from the farmyard; a horse was ill, a cow was ill, a pet deer had run away; one man wanted an advance of wages to make a feast for his wife's death, another a plaster for his fingers, which had been gnawed by rats as he lay asleep. But it was her own fault; she had brought this on herself by learning the language. There were not many like her but there were always a few; in everyone's list of English ladies in India, there will be one or two who at any rate approached her in unflagging interest and activity.

Bungalows up the country were more elaborate than the thatched tents run aground of Roberdeau's day. One-storied houses as a rule, mostly thatched, but a few with flat roofs of brick and plaster, they were still usually built on a platform of plaster or brickwork. The most common kind was a square building, with a deep veranda on each side; it had a central room, with a dining-room and three or four bedrooms opening on to the verandas. The arches of the veranda in a married house were guarded from sun and hot winds by curtains of split bamboo, or in May and June by screens of scented grass on which water was poured. In those hot dry months, the house was a fort against the sun, every opening closed; outside there were half a dozen coolies, almost naked, drowsily throwing water on the screens, turning the fans of the thermantidote, or pulling the cord of the swaying punkah. Inside, it was dark; in the drawing-room of the Colonel's lady you must pick your way carefully between the occasional tables.

But there would be no difficulty about picking your way in the Joint Magistrate's house or the bungalow shared by four subalterns near the mess. Here everything is severely functional: in the central room, the keep of the fortress, there are half-a-dozen hammock-like chairs with arm-pieces prolonged so that weary legs can be propped up on them as the weary body reclines; there is an attachment screwed on to the right-hand arm-piece which swings out to hold a glass. Not much else, unless perhaps a tiger-skin, a few panther skins on the floor, a few horns on the wall, a rack of hog-spears. In the bedroom, the bed is a wooden frame on four legs, with no headboard or footboard, strung with coarse tape. There is no mattress, but a cool reed mat to lie on; a brass bowl on three bamboos, a metal uniform case and a wooden chest bound with metal, a folding table, a straw chair, a small mirror — that is the bedroom furniture. No pictures, no curtains, no drawers, bare whitewashed walls; a striped cotton mat on the brick floor. It is not the thing for a young man to find money for comfort or decoration; anything he has should be spent on horses, a gun or a rifle.

The bungalow stands in a compound, which may be as small as one acre or as large as fifteen; it includes a garden near the house, irrigated from a well by a pair of bullocks who haul up water in a leather bag. There may be room in the compound for a field of oats for the horses; if not, perhaps a field is hired somewhere else. There must be room for the stables and the untidy Indian village of the servants' quarters. The Parks at Allahabad had fifty-seven regular servants besides twelve or fourteen extra in the hottest weather for punkahs, thermantidotes and keeping moist the grass screens. The list includes a man to wash and another to iron: two tailors; a lady's maid and assistant; eight bearers, originally meant to carry the palankeen, but since palankeens are now seldom used, one is a valet and the rest dust the furniture and pull the punkahs. There is a cowman, a shepherd, and a man who looks after 'the fowls, wild ducks, quail, rabbits, guinea-fowl and pigeons'; a gardener and two assistants; a coachman, eight grooms, eight grass-cutters, and a woman to grind grain for the horses. There are even two carpenters on the permanent establishment; the total of fifty-seven cost about two hundred and ninety pounds a year. 'We, as quiet people, find these servants necessary.' A still quieter family, friends of Honoria Lawrence, manage with less, but mainly because they have fewer horses.

This then was the home where the new rulers of India lived a life not much less sumptuous and uncomfortable than in Hickey's day. The hookah is hardly used now, having given place to the meerschaum and the cigar; no *hookah-burdar* and only two table-servants accompany the diner-out. The list of servants for a married couple is slightly less formidable than Hickey's for a bachelor; bungalows are improved; there is soda-water; in the larger stations, there is ice. It is made, up the country, on a still night in the cold weather, with elaborate organization and much labour, on the principle of the dew-pond, in shallow pans insulated from the ground by straw; it is stored in pits till May and June and then doled out to the members of the ice-club at the rate of twenty-four pounds every other day; in Calcutta it is imported from America, but in the South and in the remoter parts of Bengal, ice is still to come.

But take it for all in all, it is a life which to English eyes was a strange mixture of inconvenience with luxury. Luxury no doubt for a man to have the socks rolled on to the feet with no effort on his own part, for a woman to have her hair brushed for half an hour every evening; but was it worth the dust, the cholera, the lack of privacy, the heat and its effects? 'Oh! Western shore! what would I not give for your breezes, to carry away this vile Indian languor and re-brace my nerves! . . . this heavy unnatural atmosphere overpowers me', writes Fanny Parks on May 10th in Allahabad.

But languor or no, a good deal had been done in the half-century. The immense territories acquired had been assimilated; they had become part of the system. They were no longer preyed on by bands of roving horsemen; Pindari loot and Maratha blackmail were no more; suttee was forbidden, thuggee finished, gang-robbery reduced.

The country was settled and the peasant knew what he had to pay. And the Company was no longer a group of traders but a corporation for the purpose of governing India under the direction of Parliament. They had lost their monopoly of trade in 1813 and in 1833 ceased altogether to be a trading concern.

Something else of great consequence had happened in 1833. The policy of employing Indians in positions of trust had been proclaimed as a matter of principle. Clive and Warren Hastings had tried to continue the English and the Mogul system of administration side by side; Cornwallis had decided that this was impossible and had rigorously excluded Indians from all positions of responsibility. It had not worked and there had been Indian Deputy Collectors since Lord Hastings's time. In a minute of November 5th, 1829, Butterworth Bayley pointed out that of every twenty original suits instituted in civil courts, nineteen were settled by Indian officers. Now the facts were admitted and the policy announced of associating Indians with Englishmen in an administration based on English law and a Christian ethic. There was implicit in this an assumption that Indians today would find arrogant; it is no use pretending, however, that our ancestors had any doubts about the superiority of the Christian religion, English character and English standards of honesty and industry to anything in India.

What was now recognized and encouraged was the employment of Indians in positions that were responsible and important although subject always to supervision. Civil causes were now tried in the first place by *Munsifs*, that is, subordinate Indian judges of various grades; in the North-Western Provinces in 1849, over forty-five thousand suits were tried in the first instance by Munsifs, only twenty by European judges. There were appeals from the lower grade of Indian judges to the Company's covenanted civil servants or to higher grade Indian judges; from the higher grade of Indian judge, the only appeal was to the Calcutta court of appeal, generally known as the Sudder, which heard appeals from the English judges too.

This was for civil disputes, that is suits about property. Indians were not yet judges in criminal cases, but as deputy magistrates they might have power to sentence to three years' imprisonment, which was the limit of the Englishman's powers as a magistrate too. But there was no question yet of equality; they could not be members of the covenanted service.

Who should administer justice was one question; another was its impact on the toad beneath the harrow. It was once customary to extol British justice as a priceless gift to India; recently it has become the fashion to write of it with disparagement. To be clear about it, a distinction must first be made between public order and private justice. There was almost universal relief in the early days of British rule when peace and order replaced anarchy; there was nothing but praise for the suppression of the Thugs and the eventual reduction of gang-robbery. That feeling of relief wore away; there is no cause for surprise in that, rather that it had been there in the first place.

Justice to individuals is not at all the same as public order. But here, too, at first there was usually satisfaction. Mogul justice is best illustrated by a tale told by Bernier in the seventeenth century. The traveller called on a Mogul officer of state whom he already regarded as a friend; he found him sitting cross-legged with a number of letters held between his toes, answers to which he was dictating in turn to a secretary. He apologized for having some business to finish; Bernier sat and waited.

Two criminals were brought in. The officer took no notice but continued his dictation. After some time, he raised his head and addressed them each with a simple statement of fact: 'You committed highway robbery with violence at such a place on such a date.' There was a pause but no reply. One was sentenced to have his hands and feet lopped off, the other to be disembowelled, both to be left in a public place to bleed to death. They were taken away; dictation continued.

This kind of justice was admired, mainly because people felt so strongly the need for public order. Their complaint had been that there were so few who did administer justice as swiftly and ruthlessly as this. When the English first came to a district, their methods were usually milder than the Mogul's but less intermittent, swift enough and sufficiently informal. An inquiry was held, usually in the village of the crime; it was held by the ruler — the Indian word means the man who gives orders. When he was satisfied, he gave an order and it was carried out. There was not much dissatisfaction in those first years with British criminal justice.

But in the regulation districts, criminal justice had already grown more formal; there were lawyers and men were encouraged to plead innocent even when all knew they were guilty, the law of evidence had been introduced and gradually the business of producing witnesses had become a contest, a trial of strength and cunning between the police and the friends of the accused, with little reference to actual happenings.

What was even worse, up till 1833 in the districts ruled by a judge-magistrate there was no time, with the best will in the world, to deal with cases properly. F. J. Shore describes the day of a conscientious judge-magistrate with a vividness that accords with experience a hundred years later. There is the ride before breakfast, combining exercise with inspection, perhaps of the scene of a crime, perhaps of the state of the roads; on return, there are interviews with police-officers and informers. There was, it must be remembered, still no superintendent of police. Breakfast, and the magistrate rides to court at nine, forced to ignore 'all sorts of people, calling for justice'. He finds his court 'as crowded as the court of justice would be during the assizes of a large English county'. He first hears more formal reports from police-officers, and dictates orders, which are written down in Persian or Urdu; he then hears cases of felony, which had been 'prepared', the depositions having been taken down previously in another room. These are now hastily read over to the witness, who 'receives a bob on the hand from a Koran or a bottle of Ganges water' to give sanctity to his oath and is asked to confirm his statement.

But even to this scamped way of doing business, the unfortunate judge-magistrate cannot give his undivided attention; 'The sheriff of the civil courts begs in the right ear for an order on one case. The criminal sheriff whispers on the left for another. An attorney . . . begs for one minute's attention . . . which will save his unfortunate client from ruin . . . The judge-magistrate listens perhaps to what he has to say . . . by which time the officer reading the depositions has galloped through another page . . .' and so it goes on, while 'the crowd, the pushing, the squeezing, the Babel of tongues, formed altogether such an approximation to a bear-garden. . . .'

That is how business was still done in an Indian court a hundred years later; Indian magistrates seem able to listen to half a dozen disputes at the same time. One may guess, however, that if Shore had taken the trouble to enforce order for a few days he could have ended all this. But he must have been right in believing that the burden of business was such that until the offices of judge and magistrate were separated, no one could get through it. From 1833 onwards, however, there was a great improvement in criminal justice and most people acquainted with the working of criminal justice in India would agree that in the great majority of cases the person prosecuted actually was guilty. In more than half the cases prosecuted he would be found guilty, while not once in ten cases was an innocent person convicted. This was much better than anything that had happened before. There is no harm in wondering all the same, what the result would have been with a system more like the French, with a *juge d'instruction* who made an inquiry on the spot and was permitted to record his own opinion as part of the evidence.

All this refers to cases officially prosecuted for felonies; there were also private prosecutions in which there were greater delays and more frequent miscarriages of justice. Such cases were often hardly criminal at all; a man does not become a criminal because he has a quarrel with a neighbour over cattle straying into his sugar-cane. From the start, far more of them might well have been left to village committees — as Munro had hoped they would be.

By 1842, then, true criminal or police justice was reasonably well established; it was far from perfect and was still to be improved, but it did achieve some degree of security for life and property. For disputes about property, nothing like so much could be claimed. The proceedings were slow and expensive, nor was the result always one that could be recognized as just.

Roads were in their infancy, but palankeens were giving place to wheeled vehicles and progress was being made. The next few years were to show great advances — the Grand Trunk Road from Calcutta to Peshawar; the Bombay-Agra road; the Bombay-Calcutta road — over three thousand miles of metalled surface, a thing new to India, all these were in progress. There were minor roads, too, in varying stages of completion by the middle of the century; in one district, the scheme would be for three or four hundred miles, in another for as much as eight hundred. They were everywhere the work of district officers; they were, it may be added, almost everywhere planted on either side with a double avenue of trees.

One example may be mentioned from the South, Salem, once known as the Baramahal, Munro's first district where he served under Read. Here by the middle of the century, seven hundred and twenty-six miles of 'excellent road' had been 'completed, planted, guarded by ditches and with few exceptions marked by milestones'. There are eighty-four bridges . . . one being a noble structure of twenty-six arches, each with a span of sixty feet, 'chiefly built by bricklayers and artificers of Salem district'. Yet sixty years ago Read — a most careful man — had found after long inquiry that there was no such person as a bricklayer in the whole district.

Canals for irrigation were needed even more than roads; canals could reduce the area devastated by drought while roads and the railway could bring grain from outside. In canals, too, there had been fitful efforts ever since the beginning of the century; the momentum had grown slowly and now the Western Jumna Canal, four hundred and fifty miles long, was watering five thousand villages, the smaller Eastern Jumna was complete, and work was in progress on the Ganges Canal, which was to be twice the length of the Western Jumna and irrigate four times the area. The canal system was already far ahead of anything done by previous Indian governments and when the Ganges canal was finished would be the most extensive in the world.

These were the main achievements of the half century. But in spite of progress it is no use pretending that the Government of the Company was really liked. Sleeman, who spent most of his early life either in Indian States or on their borders, believed the Indian States should always be kept in existence. The contrast between their confusion and ill-government and the orderly administration of British India would serve, he thought, as a reminder of past anarchy. He also believed that the States made provision for the ambitious Indian, who might become Chief Minister or Chief Justice under a Prince, while in British India he could rise no higher than subordinate judge or leader of a band of robbers. Sleeman was therefore against the annexation of Oudh, though he reported at great length on its chaos and lawlessness and the misery of the people. He was, however, in a minority. 'Look but on this picture and on this'; it seemed obvious to the English that everyone would prefer law to whim, order to chaos.

But few people are governed by reason. As soon as they had forgotten the bad old days when a man could not step out of his house with any expectation of finding the thatch still on the roof when he came back, men in the British districts began to look regretfully across the border at the turbulence, the confusion and the excitement of the state. They found life dull in British India, where the Company provided no fireworks and no sanguinary contests between wild beasts when anyone married or came of age, where the business of collecting revenue was a dull monotonous grind, with nothing to alleviate the misery of parting with hard-won cash. In a State, now, revenue collection combined the excitement of a sweepstake in reverse, a militiaman's field-day, the Eatanswill election and a bull-fight in a small Spanish town. An officer travelling in Oudh one day found some villagers busily repairing the parapet of a small fort. They expected a visit from the revenue collector, they explained. 'And you will resist?' 'Of course. We will offer him a thousand rupees and he will demand ten thousand. Then we shall go into the fort and he will fire his guns and we shall fire our muskets. Then we shall parley and then there will be more firing. In the end, after two or three days, we shall give him three thousand, which is what we always do give.' 'But would it not be quicker to give him three thousand in the first place?' 'Quicker, yes, but that is not how we do it' — and the implication is clear that it would be much less fun.

This is the reverse to the well-known story from the Governor-General's camp on the borders of Oudh; hearing a heavy cannonading from across the river, Lord Hardinge made inquiries from the district officer and was told: 'Oh, that is only our neighbours in Oudh collecting their revenue.'

A half-century of progress, then, with material developments in the shape of roads, bridges and increasing cultivation; there was more ground gained — far more — in the establishment of public order and in the general process of tidying up, reducing to principle, writing down what men should pay the government, what dues and rights they owed each other. There had been moral progress too. Certainly some horrors had been ended; certainly the servants of the Company were now almost all honest, conscientious and able, probably already, as they believed, the best civil service in the world; certainly it was a moral step to have adopted the official doctrine that India was to be governed in trust for Indians, to have begun once more to employ them in positions of trust.

Most Indians would today agree so far with that verdict on the half-century; most would have agreed in 1850 — but in each case with a reservation entered by the heart rather than the brain. No Indian, surely, of warm intelligence and lively ambition could fail to be aware of something a little chill and clammy near his heart when he regarded the conquerors who were bringing his countrymen so marked a progress in things they would hardly have chosen for themselves. The colour and danger of the old fierce, merciless India, the intoxicating possibility of jewels and slave-girls beyond counting one day and on the next of death, pashed to bloody rags at the feet of an elephant — all this was being filmed over by a viscous monotony of precedents, regulations and law-suits, against which it was as useless for him to struggle as for a fly to swim in treacle.

And indeed there was a deep and subtle danger in the attitude of his new rulers to such men as himself. The earlier of the great Englishmen in India had taken the country, its people and their ways with a noble openness of mind; a gentleman of the eighteenth century was at least a man of the world. Warren Hastings had been content 'to leave their religious creed to the Being who has so long endured it and who will in his own time reform it'. That, too, was the attitude of Munro, Elphinstone and Metcalfe; it could not be the attitude of Thomason. Honoria Lawrence, a woman whose human love was deep, whose religion was warm, ever-present and living, spoke for the best men of her generation when she wrote: 'There is something very oppressive in being surrounded by heathen and Mahommedan darkness, in seeing idol-worship all around, and when we see the deep and debasing hold these principles have on the people, it is difficult to believe they can ever be freed from it. . . .'

No doubt there were still many district officers who talked to the peasant as easily as Sleeman did, to the Raja as frankly as Tod; Colvin even, by no means a district man, speaks of 'my old crony the ryot'; but it is hard to believe there can be real freedom of talk between those they regarded as pagan and men who ruled their own lives so rigorously, who were so sure of the truth and of its exclusiveness, as Thomason and Henry Lawrence. And if there seems a coldness in the attitude to Indians even of men so great as these were — men whose lives were literally given up to service and who fervently believed that all they did was for the good of Indians — it is not surprising that something worse should have arisen among lesser men, that there should have been people who talked about niggers and danced quadrilles on the platform before the Taj Mahal. But among these I do not think there were many civil servants of the Company.

In the 'forties, then, an observer from another planet, looking at the settled districts, might have been inclined to suppose that an alien, bureaucratic greyness was settling on the gorgeous Orient, that adventure and expansion were at an end, that revolution and cataclysm were over. But if his eye turned from the trough to the crest of the wave, if he looked forward to the frontier and forward in time, it was another story, and he would see at once that nothing could be further from the truth.

CHAPTER XI

THE TITANS OF THE PUNJAB

I. THE FIRST SIKH WAR AND THE REGENCY

Now comes a generation of titans, living in a time of swift heroic action. It is the decade and a half of the Sikh wars and the Mutiny, when giant figures move in the North-West of India, in the Punjab and beyond, when two or three dozen men toil with fierce nervous energy at tasks more than mortal.

Speed and an unnatural tension are the notes of all they do; there is no pause for rest, no thought of ease, no time now for such prophetic meditation as had nourished Elphinstone's brain. All is struck off at white heat, as in the press of battle. 'His mind and body', wrote Kavanagh of Henry Lawrence, 'were always in a state of tension and both alike were denied proper rest.' 'We have agreed,' wrote John Lawrence, 'not to recommend any leave unless men are sick. There is still much to do ... Every day is of value and the best officer cannot work too hard or too long for the public interest.'

And indeed these men were in the press of battle, enlisted in a Holy War and fighting beneath the watchful eye of a Heavenly King. Theirs was a simple faith; they did not ask questions. 'We are told to pray, and that our prayers will be answered,' said John Lawrence when someone argued with him on the propriety of public prayers for rain, 'and that is enough for me.' They did not doubt that the hand of God sustained them in all they did; they ignored rather than defied danger, certain of divine guidance, knowing that God would call them in his own good time, sure that His Will was active around them. To Edwardes, the Mutiny seemed a national punishment because the English had withheld Christian principles from the people. 'All human advantages were as nothing,' wrote John Lawrence, 'without the support of the everlasting arm of Almighty God.' 'It was not policy,' wrote Montgomery, 'that saved the Indian Empire to England and England to India. The Lord our God, He it was.'

There was warm love between these men of more than mortal stature; they were knit together into one family by their work, by their fierce restraint and by their puritanical religion. 'Next to his mother, his thoughts turned towards you!' wrote Chamberlain to

324

Edwardes of John Nicholson, lying on his death-bed, shot through the chest at Delhi by a sepoy's musket-ball. 'Let me advise you as a friend to curb your temper and bear and forbear . . . I think you have done much towards conquering yourself and I hope to see the conquest completed,' wrote Henry Lawrence to John Nicholson. 'What a loss have we sustained in our ever dear friend [Sir Henry Lawrence]' wrote Edwardes to Nicholson . . . 'how his great purposes and fiery will and generous impulses and strong passions raged in him . . .' 'Tell him I love him as dearly as if he were my son . . .' said Honoria Lawrence to her husband of John Nicholson as she lay dying. 'May Gold bless what you have said to him . . . Tell him I love him very much . . .' 'Daily and nightly she talks of you and the others of the Punjab as of her sons and brothers,' wrote Henry.

Few of these men were married; they speak constantly of their mothers in terms as emotional as they use of their religion. Passion blazed in them and was harnessed to work and to bodily rigour. A man who wished for marriage before middle-age was frowned on: it was an infidelity to the ideal of work. Still there were marriages; there were deaths too among the wives and many among the children. Even those who lived paid a price. A woman who married into the Punjab Commission had taken a step as decisive as entering a convent. She and her children became camp equipment, jolted in bullock-carts and on the backs of camels, exposed to dust, sun, heat, cholera, malaria, moving always from tent to bungalow and back again, gypsies without a home beneath the stars. They must expect hard wear and a short life and in the end, if they survived, years of deadening, anxious separation. To accept such a life without some sense of spiritual dedication would almost inevitably mean a coarsening of the fibres, but the wives of the Lawrences and their followers were vowed to God just as definitely as their husbands, were as far from humanity, as closely knit in a community of work and religion.

We who live today are better acquainted with subtleties, more aware of how other people feel than the titans of the Punjab a century ago. No doubt they were hard men to live with, sometimes a torture to themselves and to those near them. But they were dynamic; there is a size and force to them we lack. Without their taut strung emotions they would not have achieved what they did. What that was can perhaps never wholly be understood because there was something about it miraculous. Even an imperfect understanding is only possible against swiftly-moving political events which began with Lord

Auckland's unrighteous Afghan War of 1839 and did not end till the Queen's proclamation after the Mutiny.

The Afghans rose and drove the English back from Kabul and for a little it seemed as though the star of the Company had set. But Pollock carried British arms back to Kabul and there was a second retreat, but this time it was voluntary and it was possible, if not very convincing, to sound the trumpets as though it were a triumph. It is not a war that anyone can think of with pride, but there are all the same some names to be remembered.

Sir William Macnaghten might have been regarded as an armchair fire-eater if he had not redeemed his errors of judgment by his courage and paid with his life for the mistake of pleading for the expedition. Eldred Pottinger travelled through Afghanistan, disguised at first as a Cutch horse-dealer, later as an Indian Muslim, and by his gallantry inspired the Afghans in Herat to stand a Persian siege for the best part of a year. Connolly went calmly to his execution in Bokhara, refusing to purchase his life by abjuring his religion; Alexander Burnes was murdered in Kabul by an angry mob although he more than anyone had advised against the policy they hated. There is material for a dozen stories of adventure; two characteristics are common to these men, courage and a restless devotion to a duty of which no one perhaps considered very clearly the ultimate object. And one other point is worth making. We were engaged in a war less defensible on moral grounds than any in our history in India — and not only that but less successful. Yet even at such a time, the signature of an Englishman promising to pay the bearer in India would pass as currency in an Afghan bazaar, though the writer might be shut up in a dungeon, his one shirt soaked in dried blood and lousy with vermin.

The Kabul war came to an end and Lord Ellenborough annexed Sind, in the mood, said Elphinstone from England, of 'a bully who has been kicked in the streets and goes home to beat his wife in revenge'. The conqueror himself, Sir Charles Napier, rough-tongued and hot-tempered, dogmatic, cynical, shrewd and honest, a man who put an edge on all he said, called the annexation, 'a very advantageous, useful, humane piece of rascality'. He was right; its only justification was the belief that the inhabitants would be better off under British rule than under their Amirs. 'You cannot, my boy, understand the question of the conquest of Sind by Sir Charles Napier,' wrote Honoria Lawrence to her son, 'but I wish you to know that your parents consider it most unjust.' 'It grieves me to say,' wrote Outram, 'that my heart and the judgment God has given me, unite in condemning the measures we are carrying out for his Lordship as most tyrannical — positive robbery. I consider that every life which may hereafter be lost in consequence will be a murder . . .' The Ministry in England — Peel, Wellington and Gladstone — acquiesced in a conquest of which they had disapproved; the best opinion of the amateur statesmen in England was for once at one with the best among the professionals in India.

Napier governed Sind through soldiers untainted by experience of politics or administration. Between Outram and himself, in spite of bitter differences, there was liking and respect; both were honest and outspoken, both were brave. For other frocks, even when they had begun as soldiers, Napier had in general little but contempt, while the pure-bred civilians 'have worn out originally vigorous appetites and feeble minds while enjoying large salaries and the adulation of black clerks . . .' But even when Napier's condemnations were most sweeping, they were based on impatient desire for something good. He wanted the people's welfare and could not bear to wait for it. He wanted swift justice — and his subjects certainly got it. He would have no red tape or formalities, and he had a gift for convincing repartee that multiplied by ten the moral effect of a hanging or a flogging. Everyone knows his answer to the Brahmans who pleaded that suttee was a national custom:

'My nation also has a custom. When men burn women alive, we hang them . . . Let us all act according to national customs.'

And when it was argued that a man had a perfect right to kill his wife — why should he not? he had after all been angry with her — Napier replied: 'Well, I am angry. Why should not I kill him?' — which he did.

Napier's 'advantageous, humane rascality' has a warm and lovable side to it but it is not true that his 'Hands off Sind!' campaign set the model for the Punjab and for the swift practical administration of all the non-regulation provinces. That had been set long ago by Elphinstone and Metcalfe. And when an officer who had experience in Sind under Napier was sent to John Lawrence in the Punjab, it was with an audible sniff that he was received; 'a man may make a good many mistakes and still be a better ruler than an Ameer of Scinde,' wrote John.

After Sind came the two Sikh wars, and these could by no English act have been avoided. Ranjit Singh had died in 1839; he left no son of undoubted legitimacy, sound mind and mature age. There followed an interlude of murder and intrigue, one wretched assassination following another, the army becoming a kind of Praetorian Guard, greedy, irresponsible and powerful, who acclaimed the highest bidder Chief Minister or Regent. The final move, long feared and anticipated, was an attempt to unite the Sikhs by war; without the formality of alleging a grievance, in 1846 they crossed the Sutlej, advancing into country known since Metcalfe's day to be under the Company's protection.

The Governor-General was Lord Hardinge, who had distinguished himself as a soldier in the Peninsula and at Waterloo; he had the best soldierly qualities, a man direct, honest, free from vanity and self-seeking. His thoughts were simple and sensible, he expressed them clearly; he sought the public good rather than his own glory. He was in short a man of the school of Cornwallis rather than Wellesley; his utterances are a pleasure to read after the peacocking of Lord Ellenborough. He was as ready for the Sikh incursion as it was possible to be without giving provocation.

There was hard fighting; the Sikhs were beaten and the British forces — mostly the Company's sepoys of the Bengal Army — moved forward to Lahore. By European standards, the terms were hard; if Germany had imposed such terms on France, we should have been indignant. By Asiatic standards, however, they were moderate and the Sikhs themselves were astounded at our forbearance in leaving them a kingdom at all. It was Lord Hardinge's intention to preserve a Sikh state that would be a buffer but not a menace; the bulk of the Punjab proper was to remain under the sovereignty of the boy Maharajah, Dhalip Singh.

There was also to be an indemnity of a million pounds, but there was no money in the treasury at Lahore to meet it. A tributary chief, Gulab Singh of Jammu, offered to pay the indemnity in return for Kashmir. 'We admit that he is a bad man,' said Henry Lawrence, and Edwardes thought him 'the worst native' he knew; but to Lord Hardinge it seemed that what was in question was not his private character but the likelihood of his remaining faithful to his alliance; the offer was accepted and the throne of Kashmir was sold. No one supposed that a million was the true price of the province; it was a forbearance on the Company's part to let it go, one that has often since been regretted. It is absurd however to judge the action by political standards not yet accepted by any government in Europe and to imply that Lord Hardinge should have held a plebiscite among the Kashmiris. This after all was 1846. Nor should the act be condemned because Kashmir is now troubling the peace of the world; Lord Hardinge could hardly have foreseen the cynicism of 1947.

In the Punjab proper, a situation developed which the practice of suttee was perhaps designed to avoid. The Maharajah Dhalip Singh's Mother was a woman of low caste who had entered Ranjit Singh's harem at a stage in his complicated maladies which made it unlikely that she would bear him a child. With the assistance, however, of a water-carrier — or so it was rumoured — she had produced Dhalip Singh; she now proposed to govern the Punjab through her paramour.

This was prevented for the moment but when the terms of the treaty had been carried out the time came for the English to withdraw. The Sikh army and the mother of the Maharajah no doubt exulted but the elders, the leaders of the Sikh tribes, felt deep apprehension. It would mean a return to the lawless days of dictation by the army, of intrigue and assassination. They begged the British to remain.

Lord Hardinge was not anxious to stay. The disadvantages of a divided responsiblity were obvious but so, too, were the dangers of a Sikh state plunged in anarchy. In the end he replied that British bayonets could not stay to enforce the orders of such people as the Queen's favourite. We would stay to keep order on behalf of a Council of Regency, provided that they agreed to act in everything of importance with the concurrence of the Resident; otherwise, we would go.

This was an advance, surely, in public morality since the days when we left troops in Oudh and Hyderabad to enforce just the kind of irresponsible orders we now took precautions to avoid. The offer was accepted, and now the rule of the titans began. Sir Henry Lawrence as Resident kept a guiding hand on Sikh affairs on behalf of the young Maharajah, while his young men — Herbert Edwardes, John Nicholson, James Abbott, Lumsden, Reynell Taylor, George Lawrence, Vans Agnew and Arthur Cocks — scoured the country, advising, exhorting and from time to time firmly and without any authority taking things into their own hands and administering. 'The protection of the people against the oppression of the Sikh Collectors will be your first duty', wrote Lawrence to Nicholson. But the doings of Edwardes in Bannu will give a better idea of these men and their work than any number of generalizations.

2. EDWARDES AND BANNU

Bannu is a wide valley, high up among the hills. It is not easy to reach nor is it a comfortable place to spend the summer; no foreign ruler had made any serious attempt to administer Bannu. The Afghans had suffered a loss of nothing but pride when they ceded it to the Sikhs; nor had the Sikhs found it a profitable possession. They had never posted a Sikh official in the valley, but had demanded an impossibly high revenue of which not a penny was ever voluntarily paid. Every three or four years, a Sikh army was sent to the valley to collect arrears. It marched by the only route the Sikhs knew, one shown them years ago by a Bannuchi; it was a way that involved rivers, quicksands, and mountain passes in bewildering profusion and the heavier guns usually had to be left behind. Long before the army reached the valley, the old men, women and children of Bannu had fled to the surrounding hills with the more valuable herds and flocks and the fighting men were safe in their forts.

In the Bannuchi dialect one word served for a fort and for a village; the inhabitants knew nothing of villages that did not need fortification. Every man went armed; vengeance, the blood feud, and the price of blood were the only forms of justice. There were four hundred village forts; each was protected by a mud wall. The soil of the valley was so tenacious that a cannon-ball fired at the thick lower part of such a wall buried itself and stuck; where the wall tapered at the top a ball would go straight through and you might shoot it 'as full of holes as a colander' but it would still be a wall. There was no making a breach and it was not an easy matter to get into a Bannuchi fort.

The Sikhs would quarter themselves on the country, destroy all the crops they did not eat and round up any cattle they could find. They would sit down before one or two of the forts and occasionally in a fit of bad temper assault one with heavy loss; by the end of the season they might have taken two or three, but they did not stay in the burning windless air of the valley after April. They lost men and went back in the end with not a third of one year's revenue, the main advantage to the Lahore Treasury being that they saved the state their keep for six months. As a method of administration, it involved the maximum loss to the subject with the minimum gain to the king.

Soon after the new protectorate system began in the Punjab, the council of elders suggested to Henry Lawrence that it was time to send an army to Bannu. Sir Henry would agree only on condition that a British political officer went with them, to settle a reasonable revenue and to get the Bannuchis to pay it without coercion. The Sikh elders smiled in their long grey beards. A political officer was welcome to try.

Herbert Edwardes, the political officer chosen, was still a lieutenant, not yet thirty years old. He was used to working for Henry Lawrence; even so, it seemed to him that what he was now asked to do was difficult. He was expected to reach a settlement with a people utterly untamed, a thing neither Greek, Afghan nor Sikh had done, and in barely six weeks. He was in the valley from March 15th to May 1st, when the sun 'burnt them out', but even on this first brief visit he achieved a good deal.

He was the only Englishman with an army of Sikhs, people with whom we had been at war only a year before. The Sikh armies had always been accustomed to live on the country; Edwardes, their political adviser, forbade them to plunder. They must pay for everything. When the driver of an elephant cut standing corn to feed his beast, Edwardes had him flogged and then as a warning made to pass, displaying his lacerated back, before a parade of the whole army. Within a fortnight pillage and looting were stopped.

Word went round the countryside that here was a new kind of Sikh army and that with it there was a real Englishman. Chiefs came to pay their respects; reconnaissance could now safely be undertaken and revealed a far easier route than that the Sikhs had always used. The fierce Wazir tribesmen of the hills round Bannu had never come into a Sikh camp, but to Edwardes they came, bringing a note written twenty-five years ago by Moorcroft. He had been entertained by a group of the Wazirs to supper and had left them a note to say so; they had saved it as an amulet against any harm from this strange new race and now they produced it, confident it would be honoured. And it was; Edwardes at once gave them a warm invitation to stay in the camp as his guests for as long as they liked. 'Swan Khan', the bearer of the note, became Edwardes's staunchest ally.

The Bannuchis were astonished at the spectacle of Sikh soldiers living in their lines, leaving the corn of Bannu untouched. They came to parley; 'they flocked into our camp and bought and sold with our soldiers and sat and talked in our assemblies as friends instead of enemies'; they discussed the idea of agreeing to a reduced land revenue. Forty thousand rupees was the offer Edwardes made them; if they agreed to that, he would take the army away and for so long as they paid no army should come back and there should be no Sikh official quartered on them. Refuse, and he would come again next year and make Bannu a Sikh district with a Sikh official permanently contracting for the revenue.

Night after night they came and talked it over in Edwardes's tent. In the end they refused, but that they should even have discussed the question was an achievement. Edwardes had only had six weeks. He did as he had said; he came back again next year. He knew the way now and he was firm friends with Swan Khan and the Wazirs. This year he stayed three months.

During these three months, the Bannuchis were induced to pull down the fortifications of their villages. They did this themselves; they did it because Edwardes had told them what the consequence would be if they did not, and assured them of protection if they did and because already they believed that he would do what he said. There was no fighting. The Sikh army were meanwhile ordered to build a fort which would replace all the village forts and would dominate the valley; they showed signs of mutiny — as Indian troops who are not well officered sometimes do if ordered to work as coolies — but the mutiny was quelled and the fort was nearly finished when Edwardes left. By then, all the Bannuchi leaders but one — who had fled the country — had submitted and agreed to pay land revenue; a survey had been begun which would produce an accurate assessment, and it was settled that in the meantime the ordinary Bannuchi should pay one-fourth of the year's produce, while ecclesiastics who held lands bequeathed in charity should pay one-sixth.

More wonderful still, the Wazirs had agreed to pay. They were pastoral nomads who had wrested some land on the fringes of the district from the Bannuchis and had begun to cultivate; fierce men, their hands against every man, reckless of human life, but strangely like children. They thought Edwardes's watch was a bird, put it to their ears and listened entranced to its song. Was it true, as they had heard, that the English suffered from a strange affliction which made them unable to lie? Revenue? Revenue from Wazirs? They were wild folk from the hills who had hardly even heard of revenue. That a Wazir should pay taxes was flat against the ordinance of God. Neither Kabul nor Lahore had taxed them, and in any case, they urged, they had bought the land from the Bannuchis who had agreed that they would themselves continue to pay the land revenue for ever. Edwardes replied that this was obviously nonsense; they could pay the revenue or leave the land, that was all they had to decide. They agreed to pay.

Edwardes decided that since they were now paying taxes the people of Bannu deserved a legal code. He sat down one night and wrote them one. Next day he turned it into Persian and it was then published. In eighteen brisk clauses it ran over the field of the Napoleonic and Mosaic codes, dealing with carrying arms and private defence and the punishments for crime, adding to the calendar suttee, infanticide, slave-dealing and the diversion of irrigation channels, summarizing land tenures, forbidding forced labour and internal customs dues and concluding with a standard for weights and measures. And he made a beginning of administering his code single-handed. The Political Adviser became judge as well as financier, tax-gatherer, commander-in-chief, engineer and legislator.

'The assistants of Colonel Lawrence in the Punjab,' wrote Edwardes, 'at no time had ever to complain of too little to do, the work during 1846, 7 and 8 varying from ten to fourteen hours per diem, but I look back to these months in Bannu as the hardest grind I ever endured.' But 'the peace that ensued came home to so many and the cultivation it permitted sprang up and flourished so rapidly under that genial sun, that one's good wishes seemed overheard by angels and carried out upon the spot before charity grew cold. And, indeed, this is the great charm of civil employment in the East'. He adds a few days later in another mood that he viewed the progress made in knocking down their forts by the Bannuchis, 'with equal shares of satisfaction and contempt'. 'Had my proclamation been sent back to me as gunwadding . . . the valley might have been free at this moment. To be sure, it would have been a hell; but what of that? the Bannuchis liked it.'

Edwardes here put his finger on the crucial paradox of British rule in India, but he does not dwell on it. During his three months he very seldom had an English companion. He was alone among these people who obeyed him because of the certainty with which he spoke to them, because of the intensity of his moral fervour. Yet he had not troubled to think where this tremendous outpouring of energy and goodwill would lead. He was saving lives and bringing peace and order, whether the Bannuchis liked it or not. He was sending revenue to the Treasury at Lahore — for Maharajah Dhalip Singh. Sometimes in an agreement with a chief he would slip in the phrase: 'So long as our alliance with the Sikhs lasts.' But the Wazirs and the Bannuchis did not pay much attention to that. They spoke of what was happening as British rule.

To the Sikhs, too, there was something unreal about the Regency.

The Sikh — at any rate the Jat Sikh — is perhaps less able than any-one else in India to understand a compromise. He could respect a master or an enemy who would treat him with the uncompromising harshness he himself dealt out to his subjects. He could not under-stand these victors who held their hands in the moment of victory, these allies who interfered with his customs. The Second Sikh War was a rebellion headed by the Sikh Army, supported by dissident barons. It interrupted Edwardes's work in Bannu and the work of a dozen more like him, Abbott in Hazara, Lumsden among the Yusufzai, John Nicholson at Rawalpindi. It interrupted John Law-rence in the Jullundur country, where with the help of Cust, Scott, Barnes, Lake and Christian a summary assessment that 'added from fifteen to twenty per cent to every man's income' had been made within six weeks of annexation. It was an interruption, but a short one that cleared the air.

3. THE RULE OF THE TITANS

The rebellion began with the murder of two of Henry Lawrence's young men, Vans Agnew, a civilian, and Anderson, a political lieu-tenant. There was again some very hard fighting; when it was over, there were no more compromises that the Sikhs would find difficult to understand. In 1848, the Punjab was annexed and ruled.

In this second phase in the Punjab, government was by a board of three members. They were served by a commission of seventy-nine covenanted and commissioned officers, among whom were all Sir Henry's young men, mostly military politicals with a sprinkling of civilians, while John's preference on the whole was for civilians from the North-West. But there was not much feeling between Haileybury and Addiscombe. There was too much to do.

Sir Henry Lawrence was the President of the Board, his brother John as the second member had revenue and finance in his portfolio; the third member, who at first was a civilian, Charles Mansell, was responsible for judicial affairs. Mansell was succeeded by Robert Montgomery from the North-Western Provinces, Thomason's brother-in-law, who described himself as 'a regular buffer between two high-pressure engines' — and it was not a bad description.

The Lawrences had much in common. Both were men of immense energy, of strange controlled passion, both were deeply religious. Both were essentially rulers of men, each, though in a different degree, inspiring warm affection among his subordinates, each, though again there is a difference, naturally master of that mixture of a kind manner, a fundamental goodwill and a controlled ferocity that is the best receipt for governing an emotional peasantry. But there were great differences between them which were increased by education.

Both had wished to be soldiers, like their father. But when the chance of a quicker way to fortune came their way, the family could not afford to neglect it and John, the youngest brother, did not follow Alexander, George and Henry to Addiscombe but went instead to Haileybury. John had the clearer and the harder head; plunged almost as soon as he arrived in India into the tangled responsibilities of district administration in Delhi and the surrounding districts, he acquired the ruthlessness of a conscientious busy man who has more work than can be done properly every day and must deal with the most important things first. His mind too was essentially practical and he would not debate a proposal for long without thinking of what it would cost. Cost on the other hand would be one of the last things to occur to Henry. In Henry there was a romanticism, an introspective quality, that had perhaps been encouraged by long periods as an artillery subaltern when he had not enough to do. And later, he had been a survey officer observing the habits and feelings of the people without responsibility for the revenue.

Whether the difference was innate or acquired, two men who might have been thought alike found that in practice each put the emphasis on a different end of the balance. John's emphasis was on fear, Henry's on love; John's on what you must pay for what you want — Henry's on the ideal whatever it costs; John's on the rule of law, Henry's on the rule of the individual. But it cannot too often be said that it was a difference of emphasis only, not of principle. Ferocity and kindness alternate in John Lawrence's famous proclamation to the people of Kangra when they showed signs of joining in the Second Sikh war:

'. . . what is your injury I consider mine: what is gain to you I consider my gain . . . If your lands are heavily assessed, tell me and I will relieve you: if you have any grievance, let me know it, and I will try to remove it . . . if you will excite rebellion, as I live I will surely punish you. I have ruled this district three years by the sole agency of the pen and if necessary I will rule it by the sword . . . Tell those who have joined the rebellion to return to me, as children who have committed a fault return to their fathers, and their faults will be forgiven them . . . In two days I shall be in the midst of you with a force which you will be unable to resist'.

That is John's voice, clear and resonant; it rings with the language of the Bible and plays on the primitive emotions of the Old Testament, fear, fatherhood, forgiveness. To Henry, the same emotions were native. Ten years later, on the eve of the Mutiny, Henry wrote: 'Time is everything just now. Time, firmness, promptness, conciliation and prudence.' He wrote to the Governor-General asking for a field survey of Oudh and a light settlement of the revenue; 'I look on a survey as equal to a couple of regiments,' he wrote. And again: 'Until we treat natives, and especially native soldiers, as having much the same feelings, the same ambition, the same perception of ability, and imbecility as ourselves, we shall never be safe.' But while he was constantly expressing sentiments of this kind, he could be as bold and as ferocious as John. The long-awaited outbreak came at last; as Sir Henry sat at dinner with his friends, they heard from the lines the sound of musketry which they had been expecting. Sir Henry went out on to the steps and stood waiting for his horse; the Indian officer commanding his escort of sixty sepoys came and asked if he should load. 'Oh, yes, load of course,' said Sir Henry without a moment's hesitation. The escort stood in line, facing the group of officers on the steps. They loaded and brought up their muskets; 'every heart but his beat faster'. He cried out: 'I am going to drive those scoundrels away: . . . take care to remain at your posts and allow no one to enter my house else when I return I will hang you.' And with that he rode off, without a glance to see if he was obeyed.

There was kindness and ferocity in both, but the difference in emphasis showed itself most clearly over a question which had long divided the Company's servants, who seemed naturally to become either protectors of the poor or protectors of the noble. John, like most civilians, was a protector of the poor; he saw the peasant wringing a hard life from the soil and believed the Government should care for him alone and should not trouble a tender heart about nobles who had done little more than collect revenue. The country could not afford two systems of government; it could not support both busy European officials and idle Asiatic chiefs.

Henry felt this was unfair; he felt no man should lose because we had entered the country. He was always tender for pensioners and those who had been granted estates free from revenue in return for some service to the state. 'Independent of feelings of humanity, I look on the manner in which these people are treated as most impolitic,' wrote Henry. 'He thinks we treat these classes harshly,' said John. 'I think we have been very kind. I cannot see the political value of such allies as these.'

Sir Henry's policy was summed up by Sir Richard Temple: 'In revenue, . . . very light assessments; . . . in judicial matters, to do as much justice as possible under the trees before the people; . . . In material improvements, to go ahead at a tremendous pace and cover the country with roads, bridges, etc. In policy to be very conciliatory to the chiefs in our own territory, very friendly and non-interfering with neighbouring courts . . . Sir Henry would soon have had to close the Treasury . . . and John would have had a full revenue but a mutinous country. . . .'

And here are Henry's own words:

'. . . promptness, accessibility, brevity and kindliness are the best engines of government. To have as few forms as possible; . . . to be considerate and kind, not expecting too much from ignorant people; to make no change, unless certain of decided improvement; . . . light assessment — ' and up to this point the sentiments are those of either brother; John had written to George Christian: 'Mind you assess low; if you don't, I shall be your enemy for life and indeed, what is worse, you will be your own . . .' But Henry's instructions, alas, continue in words John would have contested: '. . . . light assessment, considering the claims and privileges, even where somewhat fantastic, of the privileged classes, especially where they affect Government, not ryots.'

No one can doubt that John was the abler man and that Henry must have been trying to his superiors, almost morbidly eager for praise, quick to detect an implication of censure where none was meant. But while both were leaders, each with the power of inspiring a band of devoted followers, it was Henry, hot-tempered till the end, quick to lose his temper and to ask forgiveness, Henry, warm-hearted, passionate and inconsistent, who inspired a love warmer and more widespread. There is a brooding look on Henry's face; something of the saint, the poet and the prophet burned behind his eyes. 'Sir Henry looked to Heaven and stroked his beard and then he knew what to do,' said the Indian. When he left the Punjab, his progress was like a funeral procession. All who knew him and worked for him loved him; at the end, in Lucknow, the English soldiers of the 32nd (the 1st Duke of Cornwall's Light Infantry) broke into cheering whenever he came near them and the four who were to carry out his body for burial at the last uncovered his forehead and kissed it one by one. It is a tribute that cannot often have been paid by English soldiers.

There was nothing of the poet about John. Plain John Lawrence was a man of facts, of immensely hard work, of detailed knowledge. His ideal was 'a country thickly cultivated by a fat contented yeomanry, each riding his own horse, sitting under his own fig tree and enjoying his rude family comforts . . .' In his early days in Delhi, he had seen the last of the Mogul emperors and where some men would have mused on the fallen splendour of the house of Tamburlaine the Great, on Alexander and Charlemagne and the downfall of majestic empires, John saw what was before his eyes, vice, empty pomp, debauchery, a senseless maintenance of something utterly outworn. He saw human misery that could be made easier by immediate action. He believed in keeping the peace and lightening taxes. 'One lakh given in the reduction of assessments and making people comfortable in their homes is better than three lakhs given to Rajas,' he said.

Among many hard workers and generous givers, no one gave himself so utterly to his work. From the 'vehement, swift-riding man' of his first days in Delhi to his last days as Viceroy, he was, as he said himself, an old bullock for work. All his time was given to it and he was impatient of time wasted. He was intolerant of discussion or argument; he wanted the facts, briefly; he would understand them quickly and make up his mind at once. A line scribbled in the margin of a paper usually conveyed his orders. Charles Aitchison has left us a glimpse of John Lawrence as the first Lieutenant-Governor of the Punjab, seen by chance, through an open door, in 'his shirt sleeves sitting in a chair with an Indian clerk squatting on the floor on either side, dictating orders in short, swift sentences' first to one and then to the other.

There is another glimpse of him, seen fifteen years later through the eyes of John Beames, who had heard the revellers come home so late to Haileybury. Beames was a hard-headed and sensible young man who married early and displayed no strong passion. He did not care for what he heard of John Lawrence in the Punjab, nor later for all he saw of him as Viceroy. He wrote:

'The signal services rendered by this great man have caused him to be regarded as a sort of popular hero and it will seem almost blasphemy to say a word against him. But . . . by those who served under him he was intensely disliked . . . He was a rough, coarse man, in appearance more like a navvy than a gentleman. His ideal of a district officer was a hard active man in boots and breeches, who almost lived in the saddle, worked all day and nearly all night, ate

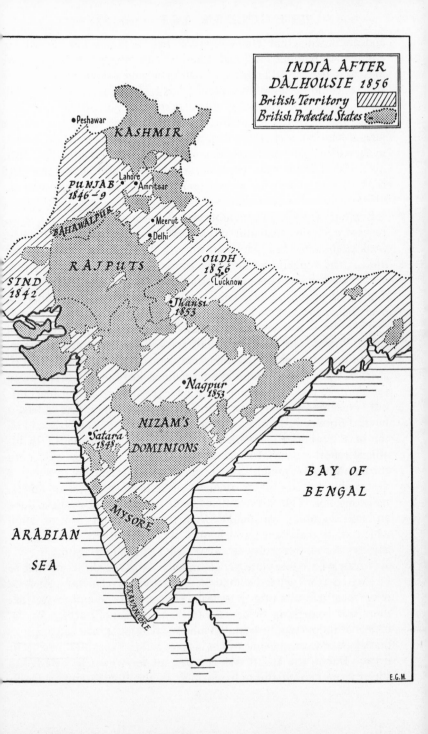

INDIA AFTER
DALHOUSIE 1856
British Territory
British Protected States

• Peshawar

KASHMIR

PUNJAB
1846-9
Lahore •
• Amritsar

BÁHAWALPUR

• Meerut
• Delhi

RÁJPUTS

OUDH
1856
Lucknow

SIND
1842

Jhansi
1853

• Nagpur
1853

NIZAM'S
DOMINIONS

• Satara
1848

BAY OF
BENGAL

MYSORE

ARABIAN
SEA

TRAVANCORE

E.G.M.

and drank when and where he could, had no family ties, no wife or children to hamper him, and whose whole establishment consisted of a camp bed, an odd table and chair or so, and a small box of clothes such as could be slung on a camel . . . Personal government was the only form of rule which the rude and simple Punjabis could understand, therefore the ideal Magistrate must show himself to all his people continuously, must decide cases either sitting on horseback in the village gateway or under a tree outside the village walls, write his decision on his knee, while munching a native chupatty or a fowl cooked in a hole in the ground and then mount his horse and be off. . . .'

Some civilians, however, objected to 'being turned into homeless vagrant governing-machines. To wean them apparently from their weak effeminate liking for clean shirts, a decent house, and a settled life . . .' he kept them constantly on the move. He 'effectually prevented anyone from being comfortable, but also effectually prevented them from acquiring local knowledge of their districts and influence over their people'.

That was a view not taken by many when John Lawrence was still in the Punjab, and those who did take it did not usually stay long. A tradition that made such inhuman demands and was based on so sharp a tension was bound to be modified in time and there was a reaction. It was true perhaps that he seemed a governing machine, but a machine is driven by stored energy and there was indeed a banked furnace in John Lawrence. The doors were shut fast and all the heat went into his work but the heat was tremendous. In his official report on the Mutiny, he writes; 'There is a judge over both them and us. Inasmuch as we have been preserved from impending destruction by His mercy alone, we should be merciful to others, reflecting that if He were to be extreme to mark what we have done and still do amiss, we should forfeit that protection from on High which alone maintains us in India.' Therefore there should be an amnesty for all not guilty of murder who had fought against us.

A man who wrote state papers in such words as those was not to be shifted from what he thought right by any clamour. And he never was. He was utterly honest. He came in the end to see that there was something to be said for some Indian Princes. To the Chiefs of Rajputana, he said: 'Of all fame that great men can acquire, that alone is worth having which is accorded to a just and beneficent ruler.' But to the end it was the peasant for whom he cared. As Viceroy, he carried through rent acts in the Punjab and in Oudh protecting the tenant against the landowner, and started action which eventually gave the Bengal peasant the same sort of protection. In the case of Oudh, this was done in the face of bitter opposition but it hardly occurred to him to consider it.

Dalhousie believed that the Punjab was ruled the better for the difference between the brothers, but a time came when a choice had to be made between them. Dalhousie unhesitatingly chose John, who all along had been much more in his confidence, being of a temperament much more like his own. Henry went as Resident to Rajputana, to him a backwater after the Punjab. Before he left Lahore, he and his wife knelt together in prayer for John's success in the Punjab; the brothers became better friends once more, but Henry in spite of many good resolutions never quite forgave Dalhousie.

Things were not so bad that they could not sign a unanimous report on their administration. It is an official document, couched in deliberately moderate language; there is much left unsaid. Edwardes's doings in Bannu are barely mentioned, nor is there much about Nicholson's administration of Bannu, a golden age when there was less need to punish for theft or murder than for paying divine honours to a ruler who did not care for them. He could not prevent his apotheosis and a religious community known as the Nikal-Seyni Faquirs lasted at least ten years after his death. But there is none of this in the report. There is so much to say that eloquence is not needed, though here and there the plain words cannot help themselves and break into a glow. Hear for instance the Board's idea of justice:

'The Board desire that substantial justice should be plainly dealt out to a simple people, unused to the intricacies of legal proceedings. Their aim is to avoid all technicality, circumlocution and obscurity; to simplify and abridge every rule, procedure and process. They would endeavour to form tribunals which shall not be hedged in with forms unintelligible to the vulgar and only to be interpreted by professional lawyers but which shall be open and accessible Courts of Justice where every man may plead his own cause, be confronted face to face with his opponents, may prosecute his own claim or conduct his own defence.'

There was to be no running from one official to another. One man was magistrate and policeman, collector of land revenue and civil judge. 'With good Officers,' wrote the Board, 'good Rules are almost superfluous; with bad Officers, they are almost ineffective.' 'The burden of the Board's injunctions with regard to civil suits' — that is disputes about property — 'has always been this, that the

Presiding Officer should throw his whole mind into the case and should thoroughly realize to himself the position and feelings of both the plaintiff and defendant, the credibility of the witnesses, the authenticity of documents and the probabilities of the case.'

The report recounts the disbanding of the Sikh army, the disarming of a war-like population and the establishment of a regular police force. '. . . With a force of 11,228 men, a difficult Frontier has been guarded, 500 miles long, inhabited by a semi-barbarous population, and menaced by numerous tribes of hostile Mountaineers . . . With a police force of 14,000 men, internal peace has been kept from the borders of Sind to the foot of the Himalayas, from the banks of the Sutlej to the banks of the Indus, and this when a disbanded army of 50,000 men had mingled with the ranks of society. . . .'

From this note, the report descends to the building of jails, courthouses and treasuries, the planning, surveying and commencement of roads and canals. Of roads built and finished, there were 1349 miles; there were 8612 miles more of main roads — excluding cross and branch roads — on which work had begun. There was the Bari Doab Canal, which was to irrigate 654,000 acres, and others projected. Jails were a special interest of Sir Henry's, for the characteristic reason that if you shut people up you become entirely responsible for their welfare; jails therefore come in for a little more mention than might have been expected. But one may guess from the sections on revenue and finance that in the administration and in the report John was the one who had his way most often.

Land revenue was as always the backbone of the whole administration. The Sikh rulers in two-thirds of the country had collected direct. The crop was in theory divided, the most primitive form of collection, the state usually taking from one-third to one-half. In practice, the grain was not piled up in separate physical heaps; the Sikh official looked at the growing crop, appraised its quantity, stated his share in maunds, that is roughly hundredweight, and sold it back to the peasant at a price slightly above market rates.

For this system, a cash revenue was to be substituted. Throughout the province this was fixed at between twenty and thirty per cent below the Sikh rates. The first assessment was hasty; it was capable of much greater refinement, to allow for differences in the quality of land, in the expense of irrigation and much more, but on the whole it was not a bad one. More of what was collected reached the Treasury than in Sikh days and there were fewer exemptions; for the first two years after annexation John was able to show a surplus of revenue over expenditure of one hundred and sixteen lakhs, or well over a million sterling. He expected a smaller surplus during the next ten years as the building programme got under way and then a yearly surplus of half a million. It may be added that the Punjab was still run as a separate state which paid for its own Punjab Irregular Force and for frontier defence.

It might have been supposed that the peasant would be delighted at a reduction of his land revenue by nearly thirty per cent — and with fewer indirect taxes too — but peasants are not easily delighted. A fixed cash rent instead of a grain rent brings with it an element of risk and is always viewed with suspicion; it was unfortunate that just as the cash rents were introduced peace and prosperity increased the area under cultivation and three good harvests came in succession. There was too much food and prices fell. It was hard with such prices for the peasant to pay his new cash rent; next year he would put more land under cash crops, sugar, tobacco, cotton and indigo, less under wheat and the millets; in a year or two things would right themselves, but for the moment he was not much better off for the reduction in what he had to pay.

There is a murmur of the controversy between the brothers in the last paragraph of the report — no doubt a passage drafted and re-drafted. It runs:

'A great revolution cannot happen without injuring some classes. When a state falls, its nobility and its supporters must to some extent suffer with it; a dominant sect and party, ever moved by Political ambition and religious enthusiasm, cannot return to the ordinary level of society and the common occupations of life, without feeling some discontent and some enmity against their powerful but humane conquerors. But it is probable that the mass of the people will advance in material prosperity and in moral elevation under the influence of British rule. . . .'

That essential point on which Edwardes had put his finger in Bannu — whether the people would really like their advancement — was not a matter the Board discussed in their report. The test, however, was to come. The Board was ended and John Lawrence ruled alone, but there was little change. Tireless energy and deep good will were part of his being; he demanded the same from all his subordinates. Prompt reward, swift punishment, low taxes, peace, roads, canals — those were the stones with which he built — with which the Board had built. And when the flood rose and the stream beat vehemently, the building stood.

CHAPTER XII

THE MUTINY

I. THE SEPOY ARMY

I N the tale of English rule in India there has so far been more reason for pride than for shame. What has been surprising — when one considers the history of other conquests — has been not so much the lapses into corruption or harshness as the speed with which they have been put right, the speed with which it has become an established principle that the country must be governed for the good of its inhabitants. But an interlude comes now at which no Englishman of intellectual honesty can look without embarrassment and unhappiness.

It is a matter for unhappiness that the thing should have happened at all; any rising of the ruled is a failure by the rulers in their essential art. It is, too, a matter for shame that when the tide turned the revolt should have been suppressed with such indiscriminate ferocity. This last can be understood though in this case to understand is not to excuse. The English were in the proportion of one to four thousand, and their lives were in danger; it was not a situation in which anyone was likely to be discriminating. In the truest sense, the story is tragedy, proceeding from weaknesses deep in the characters of English and Indian, exasperating the reader into an angry misery as chances are missed of bringing the waste to an end, as things are done in the passion of the moment which will not be forgotten.

This is no place to recite all the confused and often sickening events of 1857; they are redeemed here and there by acts of noble heroism and touching fidelity, but on the whole they make a picture from which one might well wish to be reprieved. But some must be recounted. There was a time when English historians wrote of the Mutiny as though all the horrors should be debited to the Indian account; Edward Thompson in his eagerness to be just has not only displayed the other side of the medal but in his summing-up has judged the English guilty by the highest moral standards and convicted the Indians of no more than a failure in revolutionary technique. That is one reason for saying clearly what happened; another is that I believe the psychological effect of the Mutiny has been overstated. If that point is to be made good, there must be no shrinking from the facts; it is necessary to say what the Mutiny was, why it happened and why it took the form it did.

It would be easy to argue that the Mutiny was a national rebellion, widely and cunningly planned, or that it was a purely military rising with no more political significance than the naval mutinies at Spithead or at the Nore. Outram thought it was one, John Lawrence the other. The truth is somewhere between the two and to understand exactly what happened it is necessary to consider the curious nature of the sepoy army and the strange paroxysms which did occasionally — though much less often than might have been expected — convulse its members.

It was an army that to Caesar or Frederick the Great would have seemed very strange indeed. The Bengal Army — and it is not the armies of Madras or Bombay with which we are concerned — was recruited mainly from Hindus of high caste, usually Brahmans and Rajputs and usually coming from Oudh; their caste rules were on the whole respected by their officers with scrupulous tenderness. There is surely something paradoxical about a professional soldier in a mercenary army who will not eat meat, yet there were whole battalions who were vegetarians. It is surely strange to find a soldier who will go to death at his officer's order, who will rescue him under fire, but who will throw away his food and starve if the same officer's shadow falls on his cooking-pot. All this was true of the Bengal army; indeed, it was only in 1919 that a regiment was disbanded whose soldiers could not eat when they were contaminated by contact with any form of leather. Nor could they eat anything they had not cooked themselves; it was necessary in the middle of the morning to halt and to allow the men to remove their belts, boots and all their accoutrements, to light seven hundred separate little fires and cook fourteen hundred separate little cakes of wheat.

The rules for Rajputs were only slightly less elaborate than those for Brahmans. And caste is infectious; even Europeans after long residence in India became tainted. Indian Muslims are subject to restrictions for which there is no authority in the Koran while even to canonical ritual they are often much more enslaved than an Arab would be. But all three — Brahman, Rajput and Muslim — could in an emergency be induced by good officers to forget a great many ritual absurdities which in peace and idleness would be elevated by competitive sanctimoniousness until one by one they became necessary to salvation.

It was a mercenary army. It was not from patriotic motives that the sepoy enlisted, but because the army — as a rule — was his hereditary profession, because it brought him an adequate livelihood together with social position, consequence, and honour. The sepoy was a middle class man, much more akin to D'Artagnan and Porthos than to Thomas Atkins. He went on leave with a man to carry his bundle; even on a campaign there were five followers to one fighting man. He was proud of himself and of his profession. He had a fierce pride in the colours of his regiment, which — if he was a Hindu — he worshipped yearly with the same rites the peasant used before his plough, the smith before his tools.

When Lord Lake in 1805 was twice repulsed before Bhurtpore, a battalion of Rajputs had their colours shot to pieces in a particularly bloody assault. The colours could no longer be used; after the campaign, they spent a last night in the guardroom before the day when they were to be ceremonially destroyed and new colours dedicated. In the morning the old colours had disappeared. Not a shred was to be found; no questioning threw any light on what had happened. Thirty years later, the same battalion was at the taking of Bhurtpore. They led the assault. They stormed the breach. In the hour of victory, the old colours reappeared; they had been taken from the guardoom and cut in pieces thirty years before, the fragments saved, each carefully preserved as a religious amulet and secretly handed down from father to son. Now the disgrace was wiped out; the fragments reappeared and the strips were united and tied to the new colours on the spot where the repulse had occurred. Of all this, the officers had known nothing; the men of the regiment formed a close hereditary corporation, knit together by blood, religion and a deep emotional feeling for their colours.

It was a mercenary army, officered by foreigners. That must not be lost sight of. They were not only foreigners but of another faith and the personal habits of officers and men were so widely different that each regarded those of the other as disgusting. Perhaps the Brahman's disgust at his officer's use of beef and brandy was as great as either felt at the toilet and sanitary arrangements of the other. All the same, between those foreign officers and their Indian soldiers there sprang up — much more often than not — a confidence and affection of which both English and Indian may well feel proud. It was something that could survive long marches through burning deserts and icy mountains, sieges on starvation diet, torture and the threat of instant death. Indeed, it throve on such fare as this. But forget that the army was a living organism, treat it as a dry skeleton, sit at a desk and look at returns of strengths, tables of ranks and rations, send away the officers he knew to other regiments — and the sepoy's confidence would wither. And once his affection was gone, once his confidence had withered, his fidelity to that far extravagance, that shadow of a name, that abstract nothing the Company, was liable to shatter to brittle fragments at a breath, at a whisper, at a hint from the bazar of some imagined peril.

So far, however, his fidelity had on the whole been something for wonder and admiration. The sepoys had fought and died for the Company — whatever that might be — because it had fed them and paid them in peace and because they trusted and admired their officers. But mutinies had been known. Before Buxar, the battle that settled the fate of Bengal and Behar in 1764, Hector Monro had had to settle a mutiny and blow away a score of men from guns. It was then that the men of the grenadier company pleaded for the same honour in death as they had enjoyed in life, asking to stand on the right of the line and be the first to be bound over the muzzles of the guns and blown to fragments. It is said there were no eyes dry among the English soldiers and seamen who carried out the sentence. There had been the mutiny at Vellore in 1805, and the affair at Barrackpore in 1824, when the 47th Native Infantry refused to go to Burma and for three days continued in refusal to obey orders. Their mutiny was not complicated by murder or by intention to murder, or even to resist; it was strangely peaceful. But when they refused to lay down their arms the Commander-in-Chief, a Horse Guards soldier, opened on them with grape at short range, and there was an end of that.

There had been a group of mutinies twenty years later, when Sind was declared a British province. These arose from a characteristic piece of financial pedantry; the sepoy's reward for victory was the loss of his foreign service allowance. The Company's flag flew over Sind instead of the Amir's; foreign service allowance, no doubt they wrote in the Secretariat, was 'wholly inappropriate'. But Sind was no closer than it had been to the sepoy's home in Oudh, the air and water were as strange and harsh as before. The sepoy was always particular about air and water; he did not after all ask for very much of anything else.

The sepoy had on the whole been astonishingly and often movingly faithful to a cause he did not understand. But when from time to time he lost his confidence, then indeed there was no telling what he might do. In almost every such case, from Buxar to 1946, it was possible to trace the same pattern. There were usually the same two predisposing factors and then some immediate occasion, which might be quite trivial.

There was almost always something from outside, nothing to do with the regiment. It might begin with a feeling in the villages; men would come back from leave with news of a bad harvest or perhaps a revenue assessment that was too heavy; then there would come a rumour that the Company's armies had all been slaughtered in Burma, that the English had all been killed in the Crimea; then would come another rumour, something more sinister, sometimes something so manifestly silly that in normal times the sepoy would not have listened to it for a moment. The troops were all going to be forcibly converted to Christianity, they were all going to be blown sky-high by a mine below the parade-ground, they were going to be forced to eat cow's flesh; this kind of thing came almost always from some source deliberately malicious. At Vellore it had been an agent of the house of Tippoo Sahib; at Cawnpore, it was an agent of a prince dispossessed by Dalhousie; a century later at Meerut, it was a Communist cell. But some discontent outside the regiment or some political agitation, and often both, there was always.

With good officers whom the men knew, none of this would matter. The officers would hear the tale, talk to the men and do what they could do to put things right. But if there was no one with the regiment but subalterns fresh from Addiscombe and senior officers transferred from another corps, or if the seniors had become too idle and self-indulgent to keep the men's confidence, then the thing would fester and the men grow more and more ripe for mutiny until a touch would set it off. They might be ordered to carry out some new fatigue or wear some different dress; an allowance might be reduced or the quality of the flour altered, something quite trivial. If there was influence at work from outside, and poor officers within, almost anything would be enough.

2. THE CAUSES OF THE GREAT MUTINY

For the officers of the sepoy regiments and for the occasion of a military rising, the civil servants of the Company were hardly responsible but they were much concerned with the political background and with the talk the sepoy heard in the bazar and at home in his village. And here is perhaps the place to emphasize that India was held more by bluff than by force.

The agitators of the nineteen-thirties used to say that if only every Indian would make water at the same time, the stream would wash the English into the sea. It is not an elegant metaphor, but the meaning is clear and it contains a truth. In a district of a million Indians there would often be one English magistrate only, but there were Indian officials who would do as he told them, there were other Indians, private persons, on whose support he could rely. He could hold the district because most people did not find English rule intolerable and because they believed that there was English strength somewhere in the background. That strength was always light. In the 1850s, the total of the Company's armies was usually rather less than three hundred thousand fighting men, of whom as a rule some forty-five thousand or a few more were English troops. There were some two hundred million natives of India. There might then be one English soldier to every five Indian soldiers — and one soldier, fair or dark, to every six hundred civilians. There were a few thousand less English soldiers in the 'fifties than there had been recently; I do not believe this was in any way a cause of what happened. The balance was kept, so long as there was general confidence in the star of the Company, and in particular so long as the sepoy's confidence was preserved. But the sepoy's confidence was unlikely to survive that of the general population for long.

In the years before 1857 much had happened to shake the confidence of the civil population. There were also malicious agents at work. It had been Lord Dalhousie's sincere belief, as it had been Wellesley's, that 'the British Government is bound not to put aside or neglect such rightful opportunities of acquiring territory . . . as may from time to time present themselves'. He acted in accordance with this belief. Whenever a ruler died without direct male heir of the body, his state, if truly dependent, was annexed. There were therefore plenty of disappointed heirs, bitter against the Company, ready to pass on any lying and malicious rumour. And there were other rulers who feared that their turn would be next. Dalhousie's annexations could hardly have been better chosen if it had been his object to destroy confidence. The Sikhs had been the last people to be truly independent; Satara was the seat of the ritual heads of the Maratha confederacy, Nagpur was one of the four remaining great Maratha powers; the King of Oudh, the largest Muslim state in the North, had been our most consistently faithful ally.

There were also chiefs from the North-Western Provinces, once large landholders, who felt themselves aggrieved by the policy of Thomason and his men, who were mostly protectors of the poor. There were men of the same class from Oudh, nobles and landowners who feared the future. There were the disbanded armies of the King of Oudh. And everywhere there were the Brahmans who began to scent that danger to their ascendancy that Macaulay and others had seen so clearly a generation earlier.

Education in western science and particularly western medicine, even railway trains and telegraph-wires, seemed to the Brahmans at this time to presage a reign of reason which they thought might be fatal to their system. And to the insidious assaults of reason, the English had now begun to add legislative interference. It had been made legal for Hindu widows to re-marry; now a convert who had changed his religion was to be allowed to inherit property. Convicts in the jails were being made to feed in messes instead of each man separately. No one knew what might come next. In part, at least, the Mutiny was the reaction of obscurantists against social change.

There were plenty of enemies then, all people who did not like social progress, but it takes a good deal of effort to overcome the inertia of the peasant mass. In Central India and the Punjab, the peasants had been relieved when peace put an end to rapine; throughout the North-Western Provinces and Behar no doubt they grumbled, no doubt they sighed for the colour and excitement of the good old days, but there were protests if any rectification of a boundary involved transferring a village to a State. Confidence, however, was shaken by the Kabul disaster; the news went round as swiftly as the news of Lake's repulse before Bhurtpore in 1805. Kabul had been partly lived down by the 'fifties, but now came garbled news from the Crimea and the resentment of princes, nobles and priests began to spread in an unease among the people.

When it was over, in the 'sixties, some Englishmen saw the Mutiny as the last blow of the Moguls; more recently some Indians have seen it as the last struggle of the Marathas. Both are true, neither — it seems to me — is true to the exclusion of the other. There is no need to suppose an elaborate organization, and good reason against it. A wind began to blow; stories began to pass, tales of prophecy, of the resurrection of old thrones and of disaster to the English, some maliciously invented, others born of some vague wish or half-forgotten memory.

There was unease among the civil population, there were malicious enemies to whisper. And in the regiments good officers who knew their men were few. For years, it had been the aim of every ambitious man to get a staff appointment, and this meant every better paid post. It was a staff appointment to command a Remount Depot or to be a political assistant. And who would not be Edwardes in Bannu — King, Prime Minister, Commander-in-Chief and Lord Protector — rather than a subaltern in cantonments, inspecting cross-belts and ammunition pouches for two hours before breakfast, and yawning away the rest of the day beneath a ragged punkah in a shabby bungalow with the plaster peeling off the walls? For years there had been a drain of the best men to other posts, and they did not even come back periodically for short spells. They were lost to the regiment and those who stayed behind felt themselves mediocrities. To complete the picture, promotion was far too slow, senior regimental officers far too old, a steady reduction was taking place in the powers of the regimental commander, and there was a growing tendency to centralize, to transfer, to reorganize. Battalions were amalgamated, officers reshuffled.

With this weakening of the regimental officer went something common to all the English in India. Religion had become intolerant and dogmatic, racial pride more exclusive. Macaulay had written as a matter of course of 'the hereditary aristocracy of mankind' and everyone felt the same. There had always been social aloofness, but now it was the right thing to be as English as possible in taste and outlook. The overland mail brought letters only a month old; the steam navigation companies brought out young ladies for the cold weather; there were station book clubs and amateur theatricals as well as hog-hunting, polo and shooting; altogether, there was plenty to do that was more amusing than 'listening to the garrulous old subadar'.

And among the sepoys themselves there were reasons for discontent. There was a feeling that now there were no more worlds to conquer; everything in India belonged to the Company and so no doubt the army would soon be disbanded. With this went an idea which perhaps hardly one sepoy could have put into words but of which all were vaguely aware. In the old days, the Company could have asked Ranjit Singh or the King of Oudh for help; now they had struck down their last supports, and they were alone. No one would prop them up if once they were off their balance; no one but the sepoy could give the first push.

Then came something more specific, the General Service Enlistment Act of 1856. This meant that in future all recruits must swear on their enlistment that they would cross the sea, the dark water, in ships if they were ordered. To cross the sea was pollution to an orthodox Hindu; no Indian soldier could eat salt pork and ship's biscuit. Up till now, the sepoys had been bound to serve in India only; they were within their rights if they refused to sail, while to send them by land to, say, Rangoon was a matter of much expense and organization. No general straight from England could be expected to regard such a situation without impatience; the wonder is that it had gone on so long and that even now the reform applied only to recruits. It was not, however, sufficiently considered that the new recruit was usually the son of the serving soldier.

In the same year, 1856, came the annexation of Oudh, the chief recruiting ground of the army. The country had been grossly misgoverned for years; for years the Company's Government had been threatening, persuading and exhorting the King to mend his ways; they had on the whole shown great patience and it can hardly be disputed that the thing had to be done. But there were unfortunate results; it was not so much that every Prince in India felt himself unsafe when he learnt that fidelity was not enough, that he must also be enlightened and public-spirited, a kind of glorified municipal commissioner; it was not so much that the wrong man had been sent to succeed Outram at Lucknow. More important than all this was the sepoy's loss of prestige in his village.

He had been the servant of the Great Company in a state where no one else expected justice; if he had a boundary dispute or a question of succession, he would tell his tale to the Resident or his Assistant. The Resident need not hear the other side — in fact, he must not; the other party was a subject of the King of Oudh. God had given the Resident one ear only; he would go to the King or his minister and demand justice for the oppressed sepoy. The sepoy would get justice — his own idea of justice. No minister would quarrel with the Resident over anything so easy to grant as the decision in a village quarrel. But when Oudh became British territory, the Resident turned into a Chief Commissioner with the normal equipment of ears; he must listen to both sides now and the sepoy's consequence fell away.

The sepoy had, then, already sufficient causes for anxiety when the greased cartridge story began to spread. Cartridges for the new Enfield rifle had to be heavily greased; they had to be bitten to open the end and release the powder. The Company's army was now to be re-equipped with these rifles. It had all been arranged in England

and India by specialists of the Ordnance department, to whom it had naturally never occurred — why should it? — to think of the sepoy army. The grease was half of it tallow, which came from animals of all kinds including no doubt both pigs and cows. The grease was plentiful; the muzzle of the weapon was smeared with it after loading. On the lips of a Hindu cow's fat would be an abomination for which there is no parallel in European ways of thinking; it was not merely disgusting, as excrement would be; it damned him as well; it was as bad as killing a cow or a Brahman. To a Muslim pig's fat was almost as horrible.

The cartridges were in the ordnance depots. They were being prepared for issue to the troops when the news broke. Even in those days it did not take long to reach the officers; on January 24th, 1857, the danger was reported to the Government of India — direct, not through Army Headquarters. The 25th was a Sunday. Orders went out on the 27th; the greased cartridges from the ordnance depots were to be kept for British troops and the sepoy was to grease his own with beeswax and vegetable oil; the rifle drill was changed and the greased cartridges were now to be broken with the fingers.

It was too late. The tale had spread quickly and grown in the telling. There is no reason to suppose any organized conspiracy. Letters passed, of course; there were plenty of enemies, there may well have been agents of the King of Oudh and of the other dispossessed princes who helped, but on the whole the thing spread because there was a favourable soil. The English had planned to break the sepoy's caste, thinking they would then find it easy to make him a Christian as the only refuge left him. They had not only greased the cartridges, they had mixed the ground bones of bullocks with the flour; they had polluted the sugar. It was no use telling the sepoys they could grease their own cartridges; they believed now that the paper of the original cartridges, which they had bitten for years, had been impregnated with the same offensive grease.

None of this would have been believed thirty years ago. No one in his senses would then have thought the English could possibly plot to convert their soldiers to a creed they hardly seemed to hold themselves. All that was changed now. Some indifference there was still, no doubt, but the prevailing tone among the Company's servants was earnest and evangelical. All who have left any clue to their beliefs seem to share an emotional and unreasoning acceptance of the Bible as literally inspired in every word — and the Old Testament was quoted more often than the New.

And more and more of them had begun to feel it a duty to convert others. An officer who in 1857 commanded a regiment of native infantry spoke of his 'conviction that every converted Christian is expected, or rather commanded, by the Scriptures to make known the glad tidings of salvation to his lost fellow-creatures . . .' 'As to the question whether I have tried to convert sepoys to Christianity . . . this has been my object . . .' The Commissioner of Fatehpur at his own expense had put up four pillars at each entrance to the city, inscribed in pairs in the Urdu and Hindi characters with the Ten Commandments. Lord Canning and his Council debated an act to forbid polygamy; a missionary society had recently circulated to the Europeans of Bengal a circular suggesting that 'earliest consideration should be given to the question whether or not all men should embrace the same system of religion'. There was plenty of ground for the sepoy's alarm. It would not, of course, have occurred to any of these proselytizing zealots to set about converting him by fraudulently defiling him in his own eyes. But he could hardly be expected to understand that.

There were mutinies in Bengal in the early part of the year; there was no general attack on officers. The regiments concerned, the 19th and 34th Native Infantry, after much debate and delay were disbanded and the men scattered to spread discontent among the rest. In May, as everyone knows, eighty-five men at Meerut refused cartridges — not the offending variety. They were sentenced to long terms of imprisonment; a punishment parade was held at which the sepoys were drawn up in lines, commanded by the guns of British artillerymen and the sabres of a regiment of British dragoons. The eighty-five were stripped of their uniforms and the irons were fastened on them by smiths on the parade-ground.

It was a long business, taking several hours. It seems to have filled the remaining sepoys with a burning sense of injustice and convinced them that they really were to be forced to use something they believed was against their religion. They dared not move in face of the guns but on Sunday evening three regiments broke open the jail — which, with inconceivable folly, had been left in charge of its usual guard — murdered as many as they could of their officers, their wives and children, and made for Delhi. Here there were no British troops. Here too the Indian troops rose and massacred their officers, their wives and children. The Mutiny had begun.

3. THE SAVAGERY ON BOTH SIDES

Ninety years later something very similar happened among the same people. There were whispers and rumours; the Hindus had killed all the Muslims in Behar, the Muslims had killed all the Hindus in Noakhali; a frenzy of panic would come to a village where the two faiths had lived peacefully side by side for centuries and suddenly fear would flare into hate and the stronger party would massacre the weaker. A moment would be carefully chosen when there was the best chance of complete success; there might be twenty-four hours or more during which the murderous plan was secret, when as they met in the fields or village lanes, men would greet those they meant to murder with friendly nicknames they had used since childhood. Then with inconceivable savagery it would begin; houses would be set on fire, children torn from their mother's arms and the brains dashed out, women slaughtered and left bleeding.

But although it was planned and deliberate it was not done in cold blood. It was done in panic fear, in an irrational frenzy. So it was in the Mutiny. Meerut was in all India the station strongest in British troops. If the thing had been thought out, it would have started anywhere but there. It was done in panic fear, brought to a head by the parade on Saturday morning. They had long been primed by whisperers, they had long talked in the lines at night of what plots had been hatched against their religion, of what they might do to defend themselves, but that Saturday night they must have planned in stammering haste, fright and anger contending for mastery. Their decision must have seemed to themselves, if they had stopped to think, suicidal. There was a regiment of British cavalry, there was a battalion of infantry—riflemen, an important point, for the sepoys still had muskets — and there were guns; the English in Meerut were in numbers almost as strong as the Indian, they were better armed, and they had immense prestige when it came to fighting. No use of reason could have revealed that the English would be so ineptly commanded. No one could have foretold that the mutineers would be allowed to complete their forty-mile march to Delhi without being brought to battle — and to a battle they would not have hoped to win — without even a semblance of pursuit.

They were beyond reason, they were desperate. And once a jail had been broken and an officer killed, there was no turning back. They knew there was little mercy to be expected and, to make sure there should be none at all and that every man should be bound to his leaders by fear of the rope, those who were in the thing most deeply incited the rest to spare no one, to root out the unbelievers, to make an end of the unclean, to destroy any life that might remind them of their own guilt.

There were no British troops in Delhi. When it was realized there was no pursuit from Meerut, the officers in Delhi too were attacked and murdered, usually with their wives and children. But some women and children were preserved for a few days, perhaps with some idea of using their lives in a bargain. Then, when there was still no move in the flat sandy country beyond the Jumna, they too were slaughtered.

The other risings did not follow instantaneously. The news spread and in almost every station where there were Indian troops there came a period of tense waiting; English and Indian alike were frightened and furious. The sepoys waited, tense or sullen, for some further threat to their religion or some sign of distrust that meant they were to be disbanded or imprisoned; the Commissioner or Collector met the military officer commanding the station every day in anxious debate. The English authorities were in the position of the parent who finds a cobra coiled on a child's chest with hood ominously swollen and head upreared. The slightest movement may precipitate the attack and yet to do nothing may be fatal. Between Barrackpore — which is near Calcutta — and Agra, a distance of nearly eight hundred miles, there was only one British regiment. At a hundred stations in between, a handful of English, sometimes one or two, sometimes a score, sometimes a hundred, watched Indian squadrons and battalions. Except in Simla and Calcutta, where there was disgraceful panic, there was an almost uniform courage; men and women went calmly about their affairs and showed smiling faces.

In many stations, there was conflict between civil and military, the civil officer being in almost every case distrustful of the sepoys and anxious to take at once such precautions as collecting food in a defensible position, while the officer of the sepoy army was more often sure — sometimes noisily sure — that he had the confidence of his men, that he could trust them to the death. Sometimes the civilian had his way; sometimes precautions were taken which convinced the sepoys that they were about to be attacked and which provoked them to rise, anticipating what might in any case have happened a few days later; sometimes the soldier went on trusting until he was shot in the back.

Sometimes the men went about with sullen looks and averted eyes;

sometimes there was no sign of disaffection. The Sixth at Allahabad showed no sign; they were a regiment whose officers had always taken a friendly care of their men and a keen pride in their fidelity. The men seemed to return the officer's feeling; they reported strangers from the bazar who made seditious approaches to them, they demanded to be led to Delhi against the rebels. A model regiment, they received the thanks of the Governor-General at a special parade; they greeted the Commissioner's praise with ringing cheers. That same night they rose and murdered their officers.

This was one reason for the relentless fury with which the English waged this war, if it can be called a war, a fury for which there is no parallel in their long history. The sepoy had been a friend — a friend to whom some were indifferent, over whom others had been sentimental. But everyone had taken him for granted. There was not a lady in India, says Kaye, who did not feel safe to travel long distances alone with a sepoy guard, who did not feel happy to see her child playing with the sepoy whom he treated as a fellow-child. Suddenly the friend had become a murderous and irrational enemy and the English too ceased to reason.

It was partly the suddenness of the treachery, partly the murder of English women that roused such a frenzy of hatred in the avenging forces. Men of any race would wish to punish the slaughter of their women, but the English were roused to a special pitch of passion. It was years, indeed generations, since English women had been exposed to the attack of foreigners in war and the Victorian Englishman had raised for himself an ideal picture of womanhood. His creed towards women was based in part, if you like, on poetic convention and no doubt there was often something in it that was false and sentimental, but it was held with all the force that could be banked up by sternly repressed instinct. It sprang, too, from something true, the truth that women are weaker than men and more often in pain and that to treat women with consideration and respect is more noble and more truly human than to treat them with cruelty and contempt. In this matter if in no other, the ethics of the West were far ahead of both Hindu and Muslim. To hear then that the women of his own race, to whom he himself gave so chivalrous a precedence, had been at the mercy of barbarous and immoral ruffians reached the centre of the English officer's being, the very heart of his emotions.

And, in a different way, the man in the ranks felt the same. A child was born in a wagon in the camp before Delhi and a soldier was heard to say to another: 'This force was formed to avenge the blood of innocents — and the first reinforcement we get is a new-born infant . . .' With all their fierceness, there was always a rough chivalry in the ranks. 'No fear, Sir,' came in muttered protest when the men of the 75th Foot, listening to their orders for the assault on Delhi, were told to take great care not to harm women or children.

Inevitably there arose stories that Englishwomen had been violated and mutilated. There was no truth in these stories; most careful inquiry afterwards indicates only one case, that of Miss Wheeler, the Eurasian daughter of General Sir Hugh Wheeler, who was carried off from Cawnpore as the wife or mistress of a sepoy. But the stories were believed. That was why John Nicholson wrote to Edwardes:

'Let us propose a Bill for the flaying alive, impalement or burning of the murderers of the women and children at Delhi. The idea of simply hanging the perpetrators of such atrocities is maddening.' He wrote again, reminding Edwardes: 'You do not answer me about the Bill for a new kind of death for the murderers and dishonourers of our women . . .' And in a third letter: 'If I had them in my power to-day and knew that I were to die tomorrow, I would inflict the most excruciating tortures I could think of on them with a perfectly easy conscience.'

Yet after the battle of Gujrat, it had been Nicholson who wrote: 'I have allowed all the prisoners made after the action to go quietly to their homes.' He was normally a merciful and chivalrous man, but in the Mutiny he forgot what he had been, he and many others. A few kept their heads and exercised some restraint — Canning, John Lawrence, John Peter Grant — but many thought as Nicholson did, not only in India but in England. Trevelyan quotes a young man at the Cambridge Union who used this language: 'When the rebellion has been crushed out from the Himalayas to Comorin; when every bayonet is red with blood; when every gibbet creaks beneath its ghastly burden; when the ground in front of every cannon is strewn with rags and flesh and shattered bone — then talk of mercy . . .' 'This peroration', continues Trevelyan, 'was received with a tumult of applause.' And apart from rhetoric, actual instructions, officially approved, were grim enough; here are General Neill's to Major Renaud, who led the force which was intended to relieve Cawnpore: —

'The villages of Mubgoon and neighbourhood to be attacked and destroyed; slaughter all the men; take no prisoners. . . .

'All sepoys found without papers from regiments that have mutinied who cannot give good accounts of themselves to be hanged forthwith. . . .

'Futtehpore to be promptly attacked, the Pathan quarters to be destroyed, all in it killed; in fact, make a signal example of this place....'

These instructions were grim; they were carried out with a thoroughness that some even then regarded as unnecessary. 'An officer attached to Renaud's column told me that the executions of Natives were indiscriminate to the last degree . . . a batch of twelve men were executed because their faces were "turned the wrong way" when they were met on the march . . .' Those who followed Renaud and Havelock found that 'human beings there were none to be seen . . . the blackened ruins of huts . . . the occasional taint in the air from suspended bodies upon which the loathsome pig of the country was already feasting . . . all these things combined to call up such images of desolation and blackness and woe as few . . . would ever forget....'

Nor was this exceptional. At Allahabad, at Cawnpore, at Delhi, when at last British troops did get back, there was not only much swift rough justice, there was also indiscriminate massacre. For mutineers there was no mercy; they were hanged or blown from guns and not much time was wasted on trial — sometimes none at all. The mutineers, however, were guilty in law of an offence punishable with death; there was no sniff of legality about the slaughter of many males of the civil population at Allahabad, Cawnpore and Delhi. Both at Cawnpore and Delhi there is good evidence that the bazars had had quite enough of the mutineers and of sansculotte anarchy. They wanted the rule of law again and were glad to see British troops. But not for long. The English soldier has never made much difference between one brown skin and another; he was in no mood at all to discriminate now. Nor were the Punjabis. 'To the troops (Native and European alike) every man inside the walls of Delhi was looked upon as a rebel worthy of death,' wrote Roberts, describing how he saved a group of money-lenders. At Calcutta, double sentries were posted on Fort William to keep British soldiers from going out at night to avenge the murders in Oudh and Rohilkand on the tonga-drivers of Chowringhee. In Bombay it was with difficulty that troops arriving from England could be prevented from fixing bayonets the moment they landed and killing every male Indian they saw.

Part of the feeling was due to tales of crimes the sepoys had not committed. What they had done was bad enough, though on their side too it was strangely mixed with instances of chivalrous devotion. At Shahjahanpur, for instance, the garrison rose on a Sunday morning; a dozen troopers rushed into the church with drawn swords and cut down the Collector, Mr. Ricketts, and half-a-dozen others at their prayers. Some troopers intervened and the rest of the English were able to escape, only to fall eventually into the hands of another party of mutineers. After much debate, the mutineers agreed to send them into Lucknow with an escort; but they had not gone far when the escort decided to kill them after all. There were eleven military officers and a sergeant, Charles Jenkins, Assistant Magistrate, eight ladies and two children; one man, Captain Orr, survived. 'We all collected under a tree . . .,' he writes. 'Shots were firing from all directions. The poor ladies only joined in prayer, coolly and undauntedly awaiting their fate. I stopped for about three minutes among them, but thinking of my poor wife and child, I endeavoured to save my life for their sakes. I rushed out towards the insurgents and one of my men . . . called out to me . . . that he would save me . . . Poor Lysaght was kneeling out in the open ground, with his hands folded across his chest . . . but the cowardly wretches would not go up to the spot till they had shot him; and then rushing up they killed the wounded and children, butchering them in a most cruel way . . .' Orr himself was taken to Lucknow and killed there.

That story is an example of what happened in a score of stations. Cawnpore was on a larger scale; the tale is well known but it influenced opinion so much that it must be told again. The garrison had after a long and gallant resistance surrendered to the Nana Sahib — the adopted son of Elphinstone's old antagonist, Baji Rao, the last Peshwa. The Nana Sahib, long known to the Engish of Cawnpore as an amiable nonentity of great wealth who occasionally asked them to parties, had now ascended the forfeited throne of his father by adoption and called himself the Peshwa. It was to him the surrender had been made — and on the clear condition of a free passage to Allahabad by boat for all the survivors. When the garrison reached the landing-stage, they were surrounded and shot down. It was no accident; it was carefully and skilfully planned.

Many women were killed there, but some were saved, making, with other captives, some two hundred all told. They were kept in privation and great discomfort; every day must have been torment to their modesty; they wese humiliated by being made to grind corn for the Nana's household, but they were not actively ill-treated till the last. When, however, Havelock's column drew closer, when the mutineers had been beaten in battle and the Nana knew that he must fly, then he gave orders that the two hundred English women should be killed. The mutineers who formed their guard were ordered to fire on them through the windows of the room where they were confined. They refused to obey, aiming instead at the ceiling. Butchers were sent for, who went in with knives. Next morning the bodies were dragged out and thrown in the well.

Neill, left in charge by Havelock, saw the room where this massacre had taken place. Before he had seen it, when he had only heard what had happened, he had written: 'I can never spare a sepoy again. All that fall into my hands will be dead men.' Now he saw the room. 'Ladies' and children's bloody torn dresses and shoes were lying about and locks of hair torn from their heads. The floor of the one room they were all dragged into and killed was saturated with blood . . . Who could be merciful to one concerned? . . . I wish to show the natives of India that the punishment inflicted by us for such deeds will be the heaviest, the most revolting to their feelings, and what they must ever remember.' He passed orders that: 'every stain of that innocent blood shall be cleared up and wiped out previous to their execution, by such of the miscreants as may be hereafter apprehended, who took an active part in the mutiny . . . Each miscreant, after sentence of death is pronounced upon him, will be taken down to the house in question under a guard and will be forced into cleaning up a small portion of the blood-stains; the task will be made as revolting to his feelings as possible and the Provost-Marshal will use the lash in forcing anyone objecting to complete his task. After properly cleaning up his portion the culprit is to be immediately hanged. . . .'

It will be noticed that the men Neill caught he tried; he tried them for mutiny. 'Unless he can prove a defence, he is sentenced to be hanged.' Neill always set his face against indiscriminate vengeance on a whole nation, but he appears to have assumed that all mutineers must be held guilty of the massacre of the women; it was an assumption fair enough for those rough times as regards the massacre of the men at the landing-stage, but the only mutineers concerned had refused to massacre the women. This was not known till later.

To understand his fierce certainty that he was doing right, it is necessary to add that Neill was as sure as Elijah of the guidance of God. 'I will hold my own, with the blessing and help of God. I cannot help seeing his finger in all this — we have been false to ourselves so often,' he wrote. And to Henry Tucker, Commissioner of Benares: 'I fear in your case your natural tenderness . . . The magistrate bears not the sword in vain. The Word of God gives no authority to the modern tenderness for human life which would save even the murderer. . . .'

It was the natural outcome of strong passions combined with a slavish reverence for the Old Testament. It was an attitude shared by most of Neill's contemporaries. The rising at Meerut, the murders at Delhi were enough for them; the reprisals at Allahabad, Renaud's blackened villages, took place before the Cawnpore massacres.

Fear of a stronger people whom they did not understand had turned in the sepoys to hatred, panic and murder. Deep hidden in English hearts too had glowed a tiny spark, never revealed or admitted, fear of a people far more numerous; that too had flamed up in uncontrolable hate when the despised and feared rose treacherously and laid beastly hands on English women. Against this sombre background shine many strange and deeply moving acts of tenderness and fidelity, such as that of the sepoys who stayed true to Henry Lawrence and defended Lucknow for eighty-seven days. There were many more but all the same these were exceptions. Merciless savagery on both sides became the general rule.

4. THE CIVILIAN'S PART IN HINDUSTAN

In the South, all was quiet. The Madras and Bombay armies — with a few trifling exceptions — did not mutiny. There was no disturbance among the people. In Bengal proper and in the Punjab, a grip was maintained and the country never wholly lost. Indeed, from the Punjab came strength; the work of the Lawrences and their men had been such that they could not only hold the country but spare armed men for Delhi. But Hindustan — that is Behar, Oudh and the North-Western Provinces, roughly from Patna to Delhi, that long stretch which contained only one British regiment — Hindustan was lost.

Even here there was no general rising of the people, nothing purposeful or disciplined. When the troops had killed their officers and looted the treasury, it sometimes happened that some local chief would put himself at their head, as the Nana had done at Cawnpore. Kunwar Singh in the country East of Benares, Khan Mohammad Khan in Rohilkand, made themselves Viceroys for the Emperor in Delhi. Some landowners joined them, some believed the star of the English would rise again. Most believed that English rule was ended and scrambled for what they could get. There was much indiscriminate massacre and confused fighting between chiefs and villages. The peasants were often, but not always, in sympathy with the mutineers; they could hardly be expected to resist them, but on the other hand, Kunwar Singh could raise a local army of no more than eight thousand men to back the mutineers who came to him. Perhaps most often the peasants were indifferent, as they usually were to a change of ruler. Most of them regretted that anarchy had come again, many no doubt felt some malicious pleasure at disaster to the English. Sometimes they despoiled and murdered English fugitives, perhaps for gain as often as for hatred; sometimes they slaughtered to destroy the evidence of their guilt; just as often, villagers and landowners saved lonely English families, fed them and hid them, sometimes to their own danger.

Eighty years later men would come with grubby fragments of yellowing paper, falling apart along the folds, perhaps jealously pasted on a new sheet: 'June, 1857: This is to say Nubbee Bux of village Ajnore gave water to me to-day when I was escaping with two children from the mutineers at Bareilly. Mary Smith, wife of Captain Henry Smith, 89th N.I.' He risked his life to do it. A mutineer would have shot him without scruple. And it would seem to the great-grandson of Nabi Bakhsh in 1937 a betrayal to keep his son out of the clerkship for which there were fifty applicants.

But though the rising was never general, the country from Patna to Delhi was lost because the key points were lost. There was a treasury at the headquarters of each district; everywhere in Hindustan the mutineers made sooner or later for the treasury, the civil administration ceased to work, and the people took to fighting among themselves. But the mutineers did not always come at once. There was first a time of waiting.

Henry Tucker, Commissioner at Benares, will stand for those who had to wait and watch troops who might still be saved from rising. He was fortunate in his companions, Frederick Gubbins, the judge, and Lind, the magistrate, two who 'exerted themselves with great skill to maintain the peace of the city, now patrolling with parties of troopers, now persuading Bunyas to lower the price of corn, now listening to the tales of spies, who reported clearly the state of feeling in the city and told the minds of the sepoys far more truly than the officers in command'. 'Mr. Gubbins and Mr. Lind agreed with me,' wrote Henry Tucker, when certain soldiers suggested retiring to a fort eighteen miles away, 'that to show any open distrust would cause a panic, the bazaars would be closed, and both the troops and the city would be up against us. We therefore determined to face the danger without moving a muscle.'

He carried the policy of not moving a muscle to unusual lengths. He did not possess any weapon but a riding whip and rode every evening, with his daughter, to the most exposed places, 'fearless and confident, saying to himself: "The Lord is my rock, my fortress and my deliverer; the God of my rock, in Him will I trust. He is my shield and the horn of my salvation; my high tower and my refuge; my Saviour." ' It was rather against his own wish that arms were served out to the European residents, but in this he gave way to the advice of Gubbins and Lind. He found time to remember these two in all his reports, begging the Governor-General to thank them, 'for beautiful police arrangements and general exertions'. He kept his head when not many were kept, writing early in June for power of life and death for every civil magistrate, adding that he would prefer this to martial law. 'I do not think,' he said, 'that the greater proportion of the military can be entrusted with the power of life and death. The atrocious murders have aroused the English blood and a very slight circumstance would cause the Natives to be shot or hung. I would therefore much prefer retaining the powers in the hands of those who have been accustomed to weight and value evidence.' But already in Calcutta the acts had been passed which made possible just that outbreak of lynch law which he had foreseen and feared.

Tucker held things together at Benares until some tiny reinforcements arrived; they were hurried on with noble unselfishness towards Cawnpore but more took their place and at last Tucker was strong enough to disarm the most dangerous elements; there were no scenes of horror at Benares.

Herwald Wake at lonely Arrah, between Patna and Benares, had another problem. There were no troops at Arrah, the headquarters of Shahabad district; the question was whether mutineers from elsewhere would march on the station and as it was the district of Kunwar Singh it seemed probable that they would. A few hours' march away at Dinapore were three battalions of native infantry; all through June and July, the general who commanded them refused to take any precautionary action. On July 25th, he at last ordered them to return their percussion caps to store 'by four o'clock this afternoon', thus giving them 'nine hours in which to pack their clothes, ammunition, and wives, cook their rice, and get a wash, and march out of the station . . .' They marched for the Treasury at Arrah.

Here were Wake, the Magistrate, James Colvin the younger and two other civilians, Littledale and Combe the railway engineer; the civil surgeon, two subordinate opium officers, a schoolmaster, five Englishmen of subordinate grades, two Indian deputies, fifty Sikh military police, sixty-six men all told. They had already sent away the women and children to a place comparatively safe; there was still time to leave the station and ride for Buxar where there was a company of English soldiers. They decided, however, to stand fast. Wake was not the senior but he seems to have taken command; he and his sixty-five moved on the evening of Sunday, July 26th, into a small bungalow, used normally as a billiard-room, which had been lightly fortified during the last few weeks by the railway engineer. Here for eight days they defended themselves against several thousand men who had artillery.

A record was kept; it was written by Wake over the mantelpiece on the wall 'with a stump of Pencil at any moment that could be Spared in case we should be Scragged'. The attacking mutineers were the men of three battalions, reinforced by the guards on the Arrah treasury and jail and by many of Kunwar Singh's volunteers; they had a four-pounder gun and a two-pounder and plenty of powder, but not many cannon-balls. During the eight days of the siege, the besieged were under fire from muskets almost continuously and inter-mittently from the cannon; they went through every experience of a regular siege; they dug a well eighteen feet deep in twelve hours, made a sortie and captured some sheep, heard the enemy sapping towards them and dug a counter-mine. There were many attempts to persuade the Sikhs to betray the English, all of which failed.

On the third or fourth day, a force of three hundred and fifty English soldiers of Her Majesty's 37th Foot with sixty Sikhs and some young civilians left Dinapore by boat. They landed at evening near Arrah, but they were badly led. Refusing, against all advice, to wait till morning, their commander, Captain Dunbar, advanced in the dark, through unknown and hostile country, against enemies greatly outnumbering him, without scouts, flankers or any reconnais-sance. He marched into a narrow defile which had been carefully prepared; after very heavy losses, the force fell back on the boats.

One of the volunteers with this force was Ross Lowis Mangles, Assistant Magistrate at Patna, only four years from Haileybury, a young civilian whose father was this year Chairman of the Court of Directors. He was foremost in keeping a knot of men together in the retreat; they supplied him with loaded muskets and as he was 'a dead hand at bear and antelope', he contrived to keep the sepoys at a distance for six miles, for which distance he carried a wounded soldier of the 37th. Every now and then he laid him down, took aim and fired; then he must pick him up and stagger on. Another volunteer was William Fraser McDonell, of ten years' service, Magistrate of Saran, who, when the boats were reached, when the survivors were aboard and crouched below the gunnels, when the mutineers had crowded close and were firing their muskets at pistol range, climbed out over the stern and loosed the rope that made the last boat fast. Both McDonell and Mangles were awarded the Victoria Cross, but Dunbar had lost his life and the expedition had failed. Herwald Wake and his men continued their defence until they had nothing left to eat. The time came when they could perhaps hope to last forty-eight hours without food but hardly more.

Another column had, however, already started to the rescue. This was less than half the strength of Dunbar's; Major Eyre had a hundred and fifty-four English bayonets, three field-pieces with crews to man them, and a cavalry troop of a dozen volunteers, planters and joint magistrates, young men each with a hog-spear, a rifle and a pony. This force, about two hundred all told, advanced against Kunwar Singh with his two thousand five hundred sepoy bayonets and his eight thousand volunteers. Battle was joined and the first onslaught of the sepoys beaten back; the enemy took counsel and without closing again developed from cover a heavy fire of musketry. Being more than fifty to one, it was not hard for them to work round both flanks and enfilade Major Eyre's small force. He began to lose men fast and it was not a process he could survive for long. With the same insolent contempt for probability that had won so many English battles, he charged the centre of the mutineers' position. They scattered and fled; next day, Herwald Wake completed the inscription on the mantelpiece with the words: 'Major Eyre defeated the rebels and on the 3rd we came out. Vivat Regina!'

The defence of the little house at Arrah is one story from one district: there were half a hundred districts in the North-West and Oudh and Behar from which came tales of death and danger and escape; there can hardly have been one civilian whose life was not in peril a dozen times that summer. Most had to leave their districts; sometimes they found in another district work that had a civil smack about it, organizing supplies or restoring some kind of order if there was enough strength available. More often they became moss-troopers. Bax-Ironside, Joint Magistrate at Ghazipore, rode with Vincent Eyre's troop of twelve hog-spears; Richard Oldfield, an

THE MUTINY

Assistant Secretary to the Government of the North-West at Agra, and Phillips, Joint Magistrate at Etah, were with Prendergast's Mounted Volunteers when a troop of twenty charged three hundred rebel cavalry, losing five killed and nine wounded. Wallace-Dunlop, Magistrate at Meerut, founded and led the Khaki Risala, the Dusty Squadron, a force in which Commissioners rode knee to knee with Assistants, with officers who had lost their regiments, plate-layers who had lost their railways, faithful Indian troopers and clerks from the Divisional Headquarters. They patrolled the district, keeping it clear of mutineers and keeping the road open to the Ridge at Delhi.

These were the cavaliers, moss-troopers. There were some who made themselves tasks entirely their own. John Cracroft Wilson, for instance, Judge of Moradabad, showed no less confidence and courage than Henry Tucker in that first anxious period when the loyalty of the sepoys still hung in the balance. When all was lost at Moradabad, he made for Meerut and there organized a small force of former native officers of Irregular Cavalry, with whom he roamed the country rescuing English fugitives — and incidentally, when he could, collecting a little revenue. He had, said Lord Canning, 'the enviable distinction of having by his own obstinate courage and perseverance saved more Christian lives than any man in India. He did this at the repeatedly imminent risk of his own life'.

Another was Arthur Cocks, in the summer of 1857 judge at Mainpuri. As a young man, he had been in the Punjab with Vans Agnew, whose murder began the Second Sikh War; Cocks himself had been wounded at the battle of Gujrat in hand-to-hand encounter with a Sikh trooper; now he was back in his own province. There was a detachment of the 9th Native Infantry stationed at Mainpuri; they rose and Cocks with most of the officials succeeded in escaping to Agra, where he joined the Mounted Volunteers and soon afterwards, with Watson, Magistrate of Aligarh, and Watson's assistant, young Outram, and eight others of the Volunteers, returned to Aligarh. Here for some weeks they encouraged the peasants, and patrolled the district, rescuing fugitives and harassing the mutineers when they could, keeping alive the idea of British rule. 'This party', wrote a contemporary, 'would appear never to have slept.' Hearing of the approach of a body of mutineers, they moved out to attack them, though 'the enemy's Advance Guard numbered at least five hundred'. The eleven charged and cut down fourteen, the rest fled. But in the end the eleven had to fall back on Agra, where they arrived just in time for the battle of Shahganj and the charge with Prendergast's Volunteers.

Another kind of service was performed by such men as Galloway, an Assistant, who when the mutineers arrived in Delhi went to his post at the Treasury. A chance came to leave with a party of officers, but he refused it. He stayed on, the sole guard, and died sword in hand on the threshold he thought it his duty to defend. Cockerell, with four years' service, had independent charge of the sub-division at Karwi; he refused to obey the summons of his District Magistrate to come in to headquarters at Banda until it was too late and he was murdered.

Loyd, Magistrate of Hamirpur, and Donald Grant his Assistant, were also invited to come into Banda and join a stronger party there but they refused. Loyd had no illusions about the one company of Indian troops in Hamirpur who were, he said, 'as ready to cut our throats as they can be' and if mutineers come from elsewhere 'will turn on us like wolves', but he raised some local auxiliaries of whom he had hopes and the people of Hamirpur 'are all for us though if a shot was fired they would keep to their houses'. He wrote a letter to his wife, who was in England, on May 28th, saying that it 'truly, unless God in his mercy interferes, may be my last!' Cawnpore, further North, had gone; Allahabad went on June 6th. Loyd was still in Hamirpur on the 13th, when mutinous sepoys from outside arrived and his one company rose. He and Grant escaped across the river under a heavy fire of musketry but on the 15th went back to their district and were fed by friendly villagers, until they were betrayed by a goatherd, brought bound to Hamirpur and shot, Loyd's last words to his executioners being: 'Are the English not back yet?'

Ten years later an officer on tour in Hamirpur found Loyd's name still remembered. Men pointed to wells, steps down to the river, banks to store water for irrigation, as the work of Loyd Sahib. He had been a good district officer. He wrote before he died a paper, which survived, noting the few rupees he owed his Indian landlord for his bungalow and directing that his watch should be given as a present to his head reader. 'My Father's snuff-box to be dear little Archie's and the little cross and chain dear little Annie's and all the other little things that may escape to be divided among my dear children whom with my dearest Wife may God preserve . . .' In his last letter he had written: 'Kiss my dear Babes for me and tell them how necessary it is for the youngest as well as the oldest to live daily to God . . .' There is more, but there are things that even after a hundred years should not be published.

Mention must be made, too, of Jenkinson, an Assistant with two years' service, who, as he rode round Benares with Gubbins, saw a sepoy raise and aim a musket at the judge; he reined back at once to cover Gubbins with his own body. Mackillop, Joint Magistrate of Cawnpore, volunteered during the siege for the supremely dangerous task of fetching water. There was no cover at all near the well and there were besiegers always posted, by day to watch it and by night to listen for the creaking of the tackle; there were always guns trained on the well and loaded with grape. Mackillop was Captain of the Well for a week, which was longer than anyone had hoped; as he lay dying, he asked that the lady to whom he had promised a drink for her children should not be disappointed. And to the same company belongs Robert Tucker, Judge of Fatehpur, brother of Henry Tucker, Commissioner at Benares. It was Robert Tucker who had put up the tablets inscribed with the ten commandments; when the sepoys rose, plundered the Treasury and let loose the prisoners, Tucker refused to leave with the other officials, but stayed on alone. He went in the end to the roof of his house and fought it out till he was killed. There had been Indians in Fatehpur who had felt respect, admiration and affection for Tucker; two Hindus stood out and cursed in public the slayers of so good a man, and lost their lives for their pains.

That is a handful of names. It would be easy to find many more, easy, too, if there was room, to give many examples of Indians who risked or lost their lives for Englishmen. I have said nothing here of those on the lonely heights, Colvin the Lieutenant-Governor at Agra, Henry Lawrence in Lucknow and his Financial Commissioner, Martin Gubbins, brother of the Gubbins at Benares, nothing of Spankie who held Saharanpur and Keene who held the Doon. There are many more left out. The civil servants of the Company were picked men, a corps of officers, and they lived in a time of national greatness, of strong and simple emotions. It is not surprising that they should have displayed a high sense of duty and unselfishness, some of them outstanding powers of leadership, all of them unflinching courage. It is not surprising; they would have put it themselves, I think, that they were unprofitable servants, they had done that which was their duty to do.

5. THE CIVILIAN'S PART IN THE PUNJAB

In the Punjab, things were different. The Punjab held. It was a new province, still appreciative of benefits received; there had been a good harvest; it had been brilliantly administered by men specially chosen from the North-West and the Army — and not only brilliantly but with painstaking, self-destructive energy; it was, besides, much less under Brahman ascendancy than Hindustan. Perhaps most important of all, the Punjabis hated the Hindustani sepoys who had conquered them.

It was a natural enough feeling. In physique and personal habits, the Punjabis, whether Sikh, Jat, or Muslim, were the most virile men in India; their armies had made the British fight harder than anyone else. They had been beaten, and as a whole felt no resentment against the English, whose prowess in battle and subsequent generosity they recognized. But they did resent the swaggering airs of sepoys from Oudh, men they felt they could have eaten alive if it had not been for British leadership. The Punjabis had been disarmed; the sepoy dared to ruffle it in the streets of Lahore and they dared not drive him out. But they did not like him.

The rulers of the Punjab shared some of these feelings. Tod's devotion to the Rajputs was an extreme example of a common phenomenon; almost all good officers felt, like Mr. Pattle in the eighteenth century, 'a degree of partiality' for the people of their own district, and insensibly absorbed some of their dislike for neighbours who were hereditary enemies. 'Pandy' was the Englishman's nickname for a mutineer, Pande being a common caste termination among the Oudh Brahmans; there was an extra ring of contempt to it in the mouth of a Punjab civilian and in the Punjab there was no hesitation about dealing with Pandies with an iron firmness.

There were certain unwritten rules in the Punjab service. There must be no hesitation. Show a bold front, take the offensive at once, a blow in time saves nine — that was the first commandment. And the second, supplementing it, was this; because the junior must not wait for support, the senior must back him up. With confidence, one can rule a million. Every officer must be sure he will be supported.

The news of the rising at Meerut reached Lahore on May 11th; next day came a telegram which gave some idea of what had happened at Delhi. John Lawrence was at Rawalpindi and Robert Montgomery the Judicial Commissioner was in charge. At Lahore were one royal regiment of British infantry and two troops of horse artillery manned by 'the Company's Europeans'. These were the 'reliable' troops and there were also three infantry regiments of the line and one of cavalry from the Company's native army, all with proud records and colours heavy with battle honours. Montgomery discussed what had happened with the leading civil officers and went at once to the Brigadier commanding the station. All agreed; on the morning of the 13th all four sepoy units were disarmed. They were taken completely by surprise and made no sign of resistance — indeed, they could not for they were drawn up in column gazing straight into the muzzles of the guns.

That was the pattern for the Punjab. It was followed up by disarming parades at Ferozpur and Peshawar and 'before the sepoys had time to recover from these blows, . . . all outlying treasure had been brought under proper custody and temptation thereby removed. All letters' — that is, all addressed to sepoys — 'had been waylaid; the Hindostani element in the executive and detective force gradually fell into disuse; the cupidity of the villagers was excited by rich rewards for the capture of mutinous sepoys dead or alive; the great forts of Lahore and Govindghar had been abundantly stored . . .' wrote Cooper, Deputy Commissioner at Amritsar, who had himself been instrumental in securing Govindghar.

John Lawrence was a little doubtful about Montgomery's swiftness, though of course he supported it in public; he was joint father of the Punjab Creed. But he wrote privately to Edwardes: 'The misfortune of the present state of affairs is this — Each step we take for our own security is a blow against the Regular Sepoy. He feels this, and on his side takes a further step, and so we go on until we disband or destroy them, or they mutiny and kill their officers.' Not all in the Punjab perceived that tragic dilemma.

That Lawrence saw it so clearly did not, however, make him hesitate. He made it a matter of policy to replace men from Hindustan by Punjabis and to raise local levies. But though the Punjabis had no love for the Hindustani sepoys and would be glad of service with regular pay, they waited to see whether the star of the English would rise again. 'Men remembered Kabul,' Edwardes wrote of those first days. 'Not one in a hundred could be found to join such a desperate cause.'

Very soon — on May 21st, only eleven days after Meerut — the Hindustani troops mutinied at Nowshera, twenty-four miles from Peshawar, and it became necessary to decide whether it was possible to spare British soldiers for Nowshera while five battalions of sepoys under suspicion remained at Peshawar unguarded. Edwardes consulted Nicholson and Cotton; they had to think of an external danger, too, for they held the gate of India. Dost Mohammed at Kabul had been heavily subsidized, but he might die or prove faithless and in any case he did not control the border tribes. Edwardes and Nicholson took the risk; they disarmed four of the five Hindustani corps, many of whose English officers in profound shame and misery threw their own swords and spurs upon the muskets and sabres of their men. 'As we rode down to the disarming', said Edwardes, 'a very few chiefs or yeomen of the country attended us and I remember judging from their faces that they came to see which way the tide would turn. As we rode back, friends were as thick as summer flies and levies began from that moment to come in.' It was a triumph for the policy of the risk taken by the throat.

That policy was continued. It was necessary to control those who had been disarmed and to prevent their attempting to desert to the hills, where they might have started fresh trouble. Among the first batch of deserters recovered was the Subador-Major, the senior native officer, of the 51st Regiment; he was hanged in the presence of all the troops in Peshawar, including his own corps. The 55th mutinied at Hoti Mardan and fled, with their arms, colours and treasure. Nicholson hunted them ruthlessly down; he killed a hundred and twenty, captured a hundred and fifty and scattered the rest.

Even Nicholson wrote: 'I must say a few words for some of the Fifty-fifth prisoners.' Lawrence concurred. 'They were taken fighting against us and so far deserve little mercy. But on full reflection I would not put them all to death. I do not think we should be justified in the eyes of the Almighty in doing so. A hundred and twenty men are a large number to put to death. Our object is to make an example to terrify others. I think this object would be gained by destroying from a quarter to a third of them . . . These should be shot or blown away from guns . . . The rest I would divide into batches, some to be imprisoned ten years, some seven, some five, some three. I think that a sufficient example will then be made . . . the sepoys will see that we punish to deter and not for vengeance. . . .'

A parade was held of armed and disarmed troops. In the presence of all, forty men were blown to fragments at the mouth of guns. 'Thousands of outsiders had poured in from the surrounding country to be spectators of the tremendous ceremony.' Every form of ceremonial pomp was used; guns boomed a salute as Brigadier Cotton rode on to the parade-ground. Every deliberate detail of inspection and review, every peal of trumpets and rattle of arms, made the conclusion more weighty, more considered and more terrible. After that parade, the people of Peshawar had no more doubts; the handful of men who at such a moment and in the face of such odds had dared to do that, and with such imposing, such insolent calm, would assert their iron will on Hindustan.

It was an essential part of the Punjab creed that severity at the beginning saves lives in the end. There were five thousand six hundred and twenty European troops to fourteen million Punjabis and eighteen thousand nine hundred and twenty sepoys from Hindustan. Every officer in the Punjab believed that, as Edwardes had written ten years earlier, the only freedom of which the people of the country had been deprived was freedom to murder and oppress each other, to burn widows and torture peasants. Every officer believed that the English would in the end restore their rule; if the Punjab stood fast, it would not be long before that day came; if the Punjab went, the whole country would have to be reconquered slowly and bloodily. Therefore the Punjab must now be held at all costs. And if you are one to two thousand, you cannot be particular.

It is in this light that the reports of the Punjab Deputy Commissioners must be read. Perhaps some of the casual asides are most revealing; in one month, wrote Mr. Roberts, Commissioner of Lahore, 'with the exception of . . . the summary execution of a Meerut butcher who . . . made a very dubious and threatening speech to the Bazaar Sergeant, nothing of moment occurred'. 'No stirring events occurred here in September', wrote Mr. Cooper of Amritsar, 'with the exception of the hanging of a native doctor of the 35th Infantry for seditious conversation in denying the fall of Delhi.'

There were cases, too, when civil officials, jail warders or revenue collectors, even officers of Sikh police battalions, were hanged for 'having failed in their duty to the State', not for a positive act but for being lukewarm. 'The Punjab authorities adhered to the policy of overawing, by a prompt and stern initiative, . . . and would brook nothing short of absolute, active and positive loyalty. Government could not condescend to exist upon the moral sufferance of its subjects,' wrote Cooper of Amritsar, a claim more insolent, more superb, than perhaps any made in history.

A local officer did not often refer to central authority; when he did, not much time was wasted on minuting. Mr. Hawes, assistant commissioner, having caught ten men of the 14th Native Infantry, wrote:

'I intend proceeding to try these mutineers immediately on their arrival. Their conviction is beyond doubt. The only thing is are they to be hanged here or blown away from the guns elsewhere . . . I hope to receive your authority to my punishing these mutinous dogs as they deserve by return of post.'

On this the Judicial Commissioner, Montgomery, wrote:

'I have ordered them all to be hanged — R. M.'

To which had been added:

'All right. J. L.'

One more tale must be told, partly because it is the most extreme example of severity I have found, partly because it has been told with scrupulous partiality in two books by Edward Thompson. It is not a pleasant tale, but if it is to be told surely the attempt must be made to understand feelings on both sides.

Until Delhi was recaptured from the mutineers — which was not till September 14th — it was touch and go in the Punjab. Very few Sikhs from the Punjab proper came to the colours till Delhi had fallen. In July, the sepoys of the isolated station of Sialkot, having risen and murdered some of their officers, were so convinced that English rule had ended that they offered their commanding officer, whom they held prisoner, two thousand rupees a month, with leave to the hills every year as a make-weight, if he would command them again as an independent mercenary force. No one on the English side was sure how long the Punjab troops and police would hold fast; there were large numbers of Hindustani troops disarmed who could not be in a happy state of mind and who if they escaped would no doubt increase the strength of the mutineers in Delhi.

At Delhi, a small British force on the Ridge watched — they could not be said to besiege — an army of mutinous sepoys of at least five times, and sometimes nearer twenty times, their numbers. The great states on either side the Punjab; the Bombay army; Nepal, Hyderabad, Dost Mohammed in Kabul — all watched Delhi for the result. Still Delhi did not fall. John Lawrence had seen from the first the importance of Delhi; at last he decided it was Delhi or nothing. He 'shut up his telescope'. Taking the Frontier on trust, holding the Punjab and his own mutinous regiments with his left hand only, John Lawrence shifted all the strength he could muster to the Ridge. He sent every man and gun. He held the Punjab by a shred of faith that a stray shot might sever.

This was the English side. The left hand had to hold. On the other side, it is not hard to imagine the calculations of the disarmed sepoys in Lahore; their brothers were fighting in Delhi, but they had no arms and it was hardly safe to move. But every now and then such a rational reckoning-up as this would be blown to the winds by some gust of fear. And it was not irrational that they should be frightened; they had committed no fault but they were not trusted with arms. Sooner or later the Company would get rid of them — and in the Punjab the phrase 'disposed of' when applied to Pandies had come to have a sinister meaning.

Early in July, the disarmed 26th Native Infantry broke from Lahore and fled. They had made preparations to go; it may not have been by design that they killed a Major and two warrant officers in the going. It was expected they would go to Delhi and in that direction the pursuit followed, but in fact they had turned north, as if they meant to hide in the hills and make their way gradually eastward to their homes. They entered Amritsar, Cooper's district, the central nursery of the old Sikh armies; they were attacked by a force of Sikh villagers under the *tahsildar*, a revenue official and subordinate magistrate. Being unarmed, they were driven back into the river; weak from the want of food and tired by a march of over forty miles, about a hundred and fifty were killed by the quarter-staff of the Northern peasant or drowned. About two hundred and fifty took refuge on an island in the river; others were scattered in small parties among the villages.

Cooper arrived as the sun was sinking. He had ridden hard for the twenty-six miles from Amritsar; the country was very wet and the going slow; the air must have been heavy with the steamy heat of July. He brought with him a force of about sixty troopers, of whom rather more than half seem to have been Muslims from Hindustan, while the rest were Sikhs. He was joined by a few Sikh villagers, but most of them had dispersed to their homes. In the fading light, he could see the mutineers crouching on the island 'like a brood of wildfowl', wet, hungry and dispirited.

His first task was to get them to land without their escaping. He had only two rickety boats, which would not hold more than sixty men apiece; he was afraid that unless carefully watched his Muslim troopers would help the prisoners to escape. He thought at once of the old problem of the fox, the goose and the bag of corn; this he told privately to the Sikhs, who were amused. He kept as many of the Muslim troopers as possible on the bank holding horses; and this done, he put across to the island, the boats bristling with muskets, two Sikhs to one Muslim. The mutineers came down to the water's edge with joined hands — the attitude which Europeans reserve for prayer to the Almighty, but which is used in India as a gesture of thanks or submission and to accompany a request. They allowed themselves to be tightly bound and they were ferried across sixty at a time.

Now came the task of getting them across country six miles to Ajnala, the nearest police-station. This was accomplished, in the dark and with light rain beginning, and the men were locked up, still without an escape. It was a considerable achievement, a triumph of Cooper's personality. He had been the only Englishman present. During the night, more were captured from the surrounding country and brought in.

Cooper had arranged to be met at Ajnala by men with a sufficient supply of rope, in case there should be trees enough to hang his prisoners, and by a Sikh firing-squad in case there should not. He had meant from the start to finish them off. Nicholson, a few days earlier, had made a tremendous march from Amritsar with his Movable Column, had beaten the Sialkot mutineers in the battle of Trimmu Ghat and hanged or shot every man he had taken in battle. Cooper meant to do what Nicholson had done — but the circumstances were not quite the same. He postponed the execution on account of the rain and darkness till next day, and it then occurred to him that as it was the Mohammedan festival of Id he could give his doubtful troopers leave and do what he had determined on while they were away.

'Ten by ten the sepoys were called forth. Their names having been taken down in succession, they were pinioned, linked together, and marched to execution, a firing-party being in readiness. Every phase of deportment was manifested by the doomed men after the sullen firing of volleys of distant musketry forced the conviction of inevitable death; astonishment, rage, frantic despair, the most stoic calmness . . .' The number executed had arrived at two hundred and thirty-seven when the remainder refused to come out of the bastion where they had been imprisoned. It was supposed that they were planning a rush, but 'behold! they were nearly all dead. Unconsciously, the tragedy of Holwell's Black Hole had been re-enacted. No cries had been heard during the night in consequence of the hubbub, tumult and shouting of the crowds of horsemen, police, *tahsil* guards and excited villagers. Forty-five bodies, dead from fright, exhaustion, fatigue, and partial suffocation, were dragged into light. . . .'

Cooper had been no more aware than Suraj-ud-Daula that his prisoners were dying, but Suraj-ud-Daula has never been regarded as a model ruler and more, surely, was to be expected of a Haileybury man and a Christian. Cooper had deprived these men of liberty and was responsible for their lives. They had surrendered 'in the insane belief' that they would be given a trial. He made sure, one may assume, that his horse was fed that night and even a condemned prisoner is entitled to as much care as a newly bought litter of pigs. As to the executions, Cooper says that the assembled natives considered the act righteous but incomplete, because the magistrate did not also destroy 'the rabble of men, women and children, who had fled miserably with the mutineers; they marvelled at the clemency and justice of the British'.

It is difficult to believe that even Cooper wholeheartedly believed this kind of flattery, and, what is far more important, British rule in India became meaningless if we were to accept the Asiatic standards of that day. Cooper adds that 'had the 26th Native Infantry escaped, or even had their punishment been less terrible and instantaneous, the whole of the disarmed regiments would of a certainty have followed their example . . . their extermination probably saved the lives of thousands . . .' There is an ominously prophetic ring about these words; so spoke Dyer seventy years later. The answer is surely that the man on the spot is concerned with the local situation and with that only. He is entitled to take a wider view if he cannot communicate with higher authority. He is not entitled to act on his own authority from mere impatience or because he wishes to force higher authority into something he suspects would be refused sanction.

John Lawrence, true to the Punjab creed, wrote that night briefly to congratulate Cooper on what he had done and proclaimed:

'It is fervently hoped that the signal and summary punishment which has overtaken this corps may deter all others from committing the atrocious and wanton murders which have disgraced the name of the Bengal sepoy.'

It is all very well to pass judgment on this from an armchair a hundred years later; the outstanding fact was that some six or seven thousand English had to keep their hold on fourteen million warlike people and yet find strength to recover Delhi. Lawrence, Montgomery, even Canning, at the time thought the act was justified. They knew how narrow was the balance of safety, yet it is impossible today to feel they were right The men were technically mutineers and their lives were technically forfeit, but when before has every man of a mutinous regiment been executed? As to expediency, what Lawrence had written of the 55th at Peshawar was still true; ten men executed at Lahore in the presence of the troops would have had a more deterrent effect than two hundred in an obscure village.

Cooper had, of course, practical difficulties to contend with; these he mentions among noisy protestations of pride in what he had done, as though he felt the need of some further justification. But he had surely broken the back of the problem when he got his men to Ajnala. He was only twenty miles from Amritsar and forty from Lahore; to have waited two days for orders or an escort would not have changed history. His true defence was the hubbub, the excitement, a tense and dangerous situation. If he had defended himself on those lines, there would be no answer, but in his self-justification as it stands there is a tone of gloating triumph that would have been impossible to Lawrence or Edwardes. He told the story for years; one at least of his hearers, though believing him to have been justified in his act, sickened at the manner of its telling. Canning and Lawrence delivered the same verdict and to the end of his life Lawrence spoke of Cooper's account of what he had done as nauseous.

One must feel pity for those two hundred and fifty men, starving, wet and exhausted, hunted and terrified, dragged out to death. One must feel shame that an Englishman could have fallen to the depths of flippant brutality that Cooper displayed. But it remains true, when one stands back to get a clearer view, that if there had not been such men as Lawrence and Montgomery in the Punjab, if they had faltered or shown fear, the bloodshed would in the end have been far greater. Their task was harder, if their immediate perils were less, than in Hindustan; they were no less faithful to their duty than those other unprofitable servants. They saved India; Delhi fell in September, and from that day onwards everyone in India knew what the end would be. The bluff held good; men began to come over to the winning side and now, 'friends were as thick as summer flies' once more.

EPILOGUE

IT is not often that there is a true end in history. There is, of course, in one sense an end to the episode of the British in India but that did not come till 1947, and even then much that was English stayed behind. The Mutiny was neither an end nor a beginning but an interruption. It was inspired by people for whom progress was too fast, by priests and princes who did not like to see their old world melt. But those who supplied this inspiration were not organized; they acted dispersedly, and as far as they could, on the one organized source of power, the Bengal Army. And in that there were already at work just those ingredients which were always to be found when there was trouble in that Army, officers who did not know their men, discontent at minor incidents of military life, the soldier's loss of prestige at home in the village. The result was a reactionary outbreak of force, defeated by force, but symptomatic of a deeper disorder that was not to declare itself frankly for years to come.

The Mutiny then was an interruption. There was nothing new about the direct assumption of responsibility by the Crown which followed it; more than seventy years earlier Warren Hastings had written indignantly: 'All the arts of policy cannot conceal the power by which these Provinces are ruled.' And Lord Granville in 1813 had said in Parliament that 'the British Crown is *de facto* sovereign in India'. Each of the great Government of India Acts, in 1813, 1833, 1853, had brought theory a little closer to the facts and asserted a little more clearly the sovereignty of Parliament. All that happened in 1858 was the final extinction of a corporation through whom sovereignty had once been exercised, but over whom parliamentary control had been progressively strengthened and whose field of independent action had been progressively reduced. That Corporation was indeed an Honourable Company which had done what it had to do usually with dignity and sometimes with a certain nobility. But the place to assess its value is perhaps when the whole story has been told.

Still, 1858 is a place where one can pause to look back and see what has happened. The first English in India were petitioners for leave to trade. But they found it necessary to have cities of refuge in which they could be secure from the absolute power of Indian monarchs who tended to impose from time to time a capital levy on merchants in their dominions. This necessity, together with an obstinate determination not to play second fiddle to the French, led to the astonishing twenty years between 1740 and 1760, by which date the English had ceased to be petitioners and it was the Mogul who came to call on the English Governor. This had been achieved because the servants of the Company, like the sergeant at the siege of Arcot, had been resolute 'to maintain the character of Britons in a clime so remote from their own'.

Presented with absolute power there were, of course, many among these merchants who used it as a cynic might expect merchants to do. But even while Messrs. Johnstone, Hay and Bolts were scraping together every penny they could by arrogance, bullying and chicanery, Vansittart became Governor-General, a man brilliant, imaginative and fair-minded but lacking in the obstinacy, the fire, the sense of the practical of Warren Hastings; he was succeeded by Verelst, himself the first District Officer, first too in enjoining his new District Officers to be patient, accessible and sympathetic. And there were soon such District Officers as Pattle, confessing with some embarrassment his 'partiality' for the people of his district.

Hastings himself has no peer; as statesman, administrator, scholar, his ardour, his patience, his pertinacity, above all his sympathy, combine in a whole which has no rival. But his successors are not wholly unworthy. By the 1780s there was Shore, conscientious, deeply religious, able if a trifle dull, and Clevland, first among the long series of men who have befriended and loved the aboriginal tribes. And in another twenty years we have such men as Roberdeau, already superbly claiming to be 'minutely just, inflexibly upright' members of a Service without rival for integrity 'in the whole world'.

Then came the fine flower, the golden age of Elphinstone, Metcalfe and Munro, men who used absolute power for the good of those they ruled, who rejoiced in a battle or a hog-hunt and yet could meditate on philosophy and think of the past and the future as part of history, who already looked ahead to the end of our rule. The pace increased and there came in their stead Thomason and the Lawrences, and their followers such as Edwardes or Taylor, who wrote that 'there was a glow of work and duty round us in the Punjab such as I have never felt before or since', unresting men who worked at white heat, who gave all they had to their work and who yet by the side of that earlier generation seem humourless and too dogmatic in their sympathy. It was in their time that the interruption came, cutting across the steady record of progress.

EPILOGUE

In the time that was to come there would be a problem to be faced that would grow in importance day by day until it over-shadowed all others. It had been foreseen by Elphinstone and Munro, whose prophetic meditation had turned constantly to the question of what would happen when 'the Natives were so far improved' as to be capable of self-government. In the generations before and after the interruption, it was forgotten in the absorbing task of perfecting the system of rule by Guardians. Then, as the system became technically more and more efficient, the problem of how it was to end became more and more insistent. It was now to be settled what form self-government should take and by what process the English should take the glory of their achievement as their reward and leave this Empire which they had built with so much blood and so much expenditure of vital force. That question, how it was answered by the men who ruled India, and the effect it had on them, is the theme of what remains of the story.

NOTES ON THE AUTHORITIES

This does not profess to be a work of research and for the student there are voluminous bibliographies in the *Cambridge History of India*. The list that follows is meant only to indicate the books I have used most and to acknowledge the original manuscripts and notes lent to me:

PART I

The First Letter Book of the East India Company, 1600-1619: Letters Received, 1602-1613: Early Travels in India, 1583-1619, ed. W. Foster, Humphrey Milford: *The Embassy of Sir Thomas Roe*, Hakluyt Society: *Travels in Mogul India*, Bernier, Humphrey Milford: *Rise and Fulfilment of British Power in India*, Thompson and Garratt: *A History of England from the defeat of the Armada to the death of Elizabeth*, Edward P. Cheyney: *India at the death of Akbar, From Akbar to Aurangzebe* and *Agrarian Systems of Moslem India*, W. H. Moreland: *The Economic History of England*, Lipson: *Travels of Peter Mundy*, Hakluyt Society: *Akbar*, Vincent Smith: *Akbar*, Laurence Binyon: *Albuquerque*, Rulers of India series: *Early Records of British India*, Talboys Wheeler: *Keigwin's Rebellion*, Ray and Oliver Strachey: *The History of India as told by its own Historians*, Elliott & Dowson: travels of de Mandelslo, Fryer & Hedges: unpublished papers of the 1680 volume of the English Factories series: *New Account of the East Indies*, Hamilton: Diary and Papers of Streynsham Master: *The Life of Lord Clive*, Sir George Forrest, also lives by Sir J. Malcolm and G. B. Malleson: *Military Transactions*, Orme: D'Urfey's *Pills to Purge Melancholy* for songs about the two East India companies: *The Indian Civil Service*, L. S. S. O'Malley: *History of Hindostan*, Orme.

PART II

The Siyar-al-Muntakherin, tr. Raymond: *Echoes of Old Calcutta*, Busteed: *Memoirs of the Revolution in Bengal*, Printed for A. Millar in the Strand, 1760: Letters of the Court of Directors: Scrafton's letters: Letters of the Select Committee: Verelst's *Government of Bengal*: the Cambridge *History of India*: *William Bolts, A Dutch Adventurer under John Company*, W. L. Hallward, Cambridge University Press, 1920: *Hastings' Letters*, ed. Sydney C. Grier: *Warren Hastings and the Making of British India*, Penderel Moon: *Warren Hastings*, G. R. Gleig: *Life of Lord Teignmouth* by his son, Lord Teignmouth: *Studies in the Land Revenue History of Bengal*, R. B. Ramsbotham: *Memoirs* of William Hickey: *Journal* of Bishop Heber:

Roberdeau's sketch is in *Bengal, Past and Present* No. XXIX, Jan. —
June 1925: *The Indian Police*, J. C. Curry: Dodwell and Miles's Civil List,
1780-1836: *Wellesley*, P. E. Roberts.

For the inscription on Clevland's monument I am indebted to Mr. R. M.
Lines, I.C.S. Kipling altered, and improved, the inscription on Clevland's
monument and advanced its date. He transplanted Clevland to the C.P.
and grafted him on to a family tree very like that of the Outrams, among
whom there is a tradition that some of the material in Kipling's story was
told him by an Outram.

The Nabobs, T. S. P. Spear is immensely learned and most carefully
documented, but I think misleading in one respect. Professor Spear
believes there was a golden age when Englishmen and Indian met as friends
and equals and that this ended when political power brought racial
arrogance and contempt. My own impression is that from the earliest days
most of the English kept to themselves, more from idleness than anything
else. The attitude to Indians of the gently-mannered, the *sharif* as the
Indian says, was always aloof but not I think usually contemptuous. But
the Englishman who was not *sharif*, Hastings's 'European of the Lower
Sort', was often extremely ill-mannered to Indians. I cannot find any
evidence for the view, often expressed, that when Englishmen had 'sleeping dictionaries' they spoke better Hindustani. I believe the women, like
Jemdanee, spoke a mixture of nursery English and kitchen Hindustani;
certainly there are plenty of examples of ludicrous mistakes by Englishmen
who had Indian mistresses.

Denis Kincaid's *British Social Life in India* is brilliantly written, but I
cannot help regretting that he — whose family were servants of the Company
and the Empress four generations at least — should give no hint that his
ancestors had any work to do or any reason for being in India. And as he
gets nearer to modern times the tendency to satire without indignation
grows stronger.

To my mind, the best book of social history is H. H. Dodwell's *The
Nabobs of Madras*, which is well written and readable, well documented,
and grinds no ideological axe.

There is a wealth of light material on social history, such as d'Oyly's
Tom Raw the Griffin, and for a later generation, *The Chronicles of Budge-
pore*.

The chances of retiring on a pension were poor in the eighteenth and
early nineteenth centuries. In 1784, the figures given in Parliament were
508 appointed during the 22 years since 1762, of whom 150 were dead,
320 were alive and serving in India and 37 had returned. Taking 250
names at random from Dodwell and Miles's Civil List of 1838 — it begins
with appointments in 1780 so covers nearly 50 years — I find 112 are serving, 85 died in India and 48 retired or died in England, while about a dozen
are unaccounted for. From the same 250 taken at random, the bag was
seven Hons and Barts.

Life of Sir Thomas Munro, Gleig: The Cambridge History, J. T. Gwynn on the *Ryotwari Settlement*: *The Fifth Report* of the Select Committee: *Life of Malcolm*, Kaye: *Life of Elphinstone*, Colebrooke: *Elphinstone*, J. S. Cotton, in the Rulers of India series: *Annals of Rajasthan*, Tod: *Rambles and Recollections*, *Journey through the Kingdom of Oudh* and Reports on *Thuggee*, Sleeman: *Oriental Memoirs*, Forbes: *Journal of a Residence in India*, Maria Graham: *Suttee*, Edward Thompson: *India's Cries to British Humanity*, Pegg: *Confessions of a Thug*, Meadows Taylor: *Memoirs of Old Haileybury*, Sir Monier Monier-Williams and others: *Malthus and his Work*, James Bonar: *Notes on Indian Affairs*, F. J. Shore: *James Thomason* in the Rulers of India series by Sir Richard Temple: *The Journal of a Pilgrim*, Fanny Parks: *Curry and Rice*, Atkinson: John Lawrence, Bosworth Smith and the smaller life in the Rulers of India series: *Henry Lawrence*, Edwardes: *Honoria Lawrence*, Maud Diver: *A year on the Punjab Frontier*, Edwardes: *Lives of Indian Officers*, Kaye: *Sepoy War*, Kaye: the Reports on the Punjab for 1852 and 1853.

I speak of the King of Oudh, before Lord Hastings permitted him to adopt this title. But it is a much simpler expression than 'Nawab-Vizier'. On the same principle, I call the elder Wellesley by that name, though he was Lord Mornington when he arrived in India. Lord Moira too became Marquis of Hastings, and it is easier to call him that throughout.

The quotations in Chapter IV which are mentioned as typical are from *Henry Crawford, H.E.I.C.S.* with notes by R. G. B. and from *A memorial of three generations of the Urmiston family* — but there are many parallels. The words about the Devonshire home are from *The Tomb of His Ancestors*.

CHAP. V. There is no biography of Jonathan Duncan; the D.N.B. refers to Higginbotham's *Men whom India has known*, but the account of him there is even shorter than in the D.N.B. He is referred to in the Cornwallis Correspondence, in Wellesley's dispatches, in the lives of Elphinstone and Malcolm, in Heber and indeed in almost any book that mentions Bombay in the first ten years of the century. His struggles with infanticide are described in Kaye's *Administration of the East India Company; A History of Indian Progress*.

Charles Williams Watkins Wynn, the President of the Board of Control to whom Bishop Heber wrote, was the brother of Sir Watkins Wynn and because of the way they spoke the elder brother was known as Bubble and Charles as Squeak. Charles, who was fifty-four years continuously in the House of Commons, once stood for election as Speaker; the only reason Canning could think of for voting against him was that one might be tempted to address him as Mr. Squeaker.

On Mr. Traill I have included some hearsay remembered a century and a quarter later; it has not been easy to keep this chapter within bounds since

384

Shahi, where Mr. Boulderson waited for Bishop Heber, was a favourite camping-ground in my first subdivision, and part of Mr. Traill's kingdom — the best part, Garhwal — was the district of which I held charge.

The travel books of Lord Valentia and Moorcroft though interesting and readable do not help much for my present purpose. Nor do Forster and Buchanan.

CHAP. VI. *Narrative by Major-General John Campbell* of operations for suppressing Human Sacrifices and Female Infanticide mainly about the Meriah sacrifices, is a straightforward account of the kind of thing many people did. But Campbell's predecessor, Macpherson, had been involved in controversy, having been probably too respectful to the instructions he received. Neither Macpherson's pamphlet nor Campbell's narrative tell the whole story. Kaye seems to have read Macpherson and not Campbell, Thompson, I suspect, Campbell and not Macpherson. The proceedings of the three Governments, Madras, Bengal and India, were published by authority in 1854 and restore the balance.

There is a good deal about human sacrifice in India under the head 'Human Sacrifice' in the Encyclopaedia of Religion and Ethics published in Edinburgh in 1920.

CHAP. VII. Kaye's *Life of Metcalfe* is a good solid Victorian biography with plenty of letters and minutes quoted in full. Edward Thompson's is much more likely to appeal to the general reader, but there is a tolerable deal of Thompson to every pennyworth of Metcalfe.

I have quoted from Miss Eden's *Up the Country*; Captain Trotter's *Lord Auckland*, in the Rulers of India series, professes to be a biography but is a scathing indictment of Lord Auckland's foreign policy. The Cambridge History discusses the first Afghan War at length and where a point can be made for Auckland makes it. But I do not see how he can be absolved. In his famous minute discussing the three courses open, he does not write like a man to whom binding instructions have been issued, but like a free agent. He chose what was morally the worst of the three courses — which was to encourage the Sikhs to march on Kabul — and then let Ranjit Singh manoeuvre him into adopting the worst from the point of view of expediency — a British march to Kabul with the Sikhs cheering on the touchline. He had meant it to be the other way round!

All this was brought about while he was 'Up the Country', his Council being in Calcutta. The Council did formally concur with him in the end but there was no round-the-table discussion. It is argued that Macnaghten, first Foreign Secretary and then Envoy to Kabul, and Colvin, Private Secretary, were responsible; I can only reply that a Governor-General who knew what he was about — Metcalfe, for instance, or Elphinstone — would have left no doubt in anyone's minds who was responsible. The controversy is discussed at length in Sir Auckland Colvin's *John Russell Colvin*.

And if anyone still thinks I am unfair to Auckland, there remains the whole business of his dishonest manifestoes and the lying Blue Book.

CHAP. VIII. The memoirs of John Beames have not been published; I am indebted for them to his grandson C. H. Cooke. And see also passim *Mr. Verdant Green*, *Tom Brown's Schooldays*, and Trevelyan's *Lord Macaulay*. Incidentally, my publisher has shown me a treatise on mathematics for use at Haileybury by the Rev. Jonathan Cape, and the log of an East Indiaman, the master being another Jonathan Cape. In one way or another, India has touched the lives of most English families in the last two centuries.

CHAP. IX. F. J. Shore is a useful antidote to Victorian complacency and to too much of 'the fair-haired Saxon youth'; it should be remembered that on the subject of land revenue he is usually writing of the time before Bird's settlement. Even so it takes a strong head to read him and keep a firm grasp on the point that Thomason, Bird, Henry Lawrence and fifty others talked to Indians as much as Shore, were as conscientious and as intelligent and formed different impressions.

CHAP. XI. The story of Napier's telegram — *Peccavi*, I've Sind — seems to be apocryphal. Sir Hugh Dow, last Governor of Sind but one, traced its origin to *Punch* in 1846; it was capped ten years later, on the annexation of Oudh, by the couplet:

> '*Peccavi*, I've Sind,' said Lord Ellen so proud;
> Dalhousie, more humble, said '*Vovi*, I've Oudh.'

For political perspective, the Cambridge History, as usual, is dull but reliable, Thompson and Garratt readable but biased. The latter excel themselves in efforts to show that even the First Sikh War was the fault of the English. There was a strong expanding Empire on one side of the river, a smaller Empire disintegrating on the other; in such a situation, war was obviously a danger and it is legitimate to argue that it was inevitable, though the argument involves a political determinism that to me seems misleading. To say however that we provoked the war by frontier incidents is merely perverse. Lord Hardinge did not want war, nor did the Court of Directors, nor the Cabinet. It is untrue to imply that after the first Sikh war we kept power in the Punjab from greed and that the retention of Dhalip Singh as Maharaja was hypocritical pretence. All the evidence I have seen is to the effect that Hardinge was most reluctant to stay.

All this is easier to forgive than sneers at individuals. Edwardes, for instance, whose achievements in Bannu would seem to most people almost miraculous, is described as an infallible Greatest Common Intellectual Measure; what times those must have been! He saved India ten years later, being right when Lawrence was wrong about Peshawar and the

Afghans. That the giants of the Punjab were all a little mad and certainly cannot have been comfortable to live with I would admit. But it is the kind of madness without which there would be no history.

CHAP. XII. The Mutiny: There is nothing so good on the causes of the Mutiny as Kaye's *Sepoy War*. G. O. Trevelyan's *Cawnpore* and *The Competition-Wallah*, for the defence of the little house at Arrah, provide excellent back-ground: so does Cooper's *The Crisis in the Punjab*, and Lord Roberts's, *Forty-one Years in India*. There are the official reports of Deputy Commissioners in the Punjab and a record of the services of Haileybury men in the Mutiny is included in Monier-Williams's book. Edward Thompson's *The Other Side of the Medal* should be read; it does not profess to be impartial but it is definitely untrue to say that the greased cartridges were forced on the mutineers at Meerut. The only case I have found of Indian soldiers using the greased cartridges was in Sind; the men were mutineers who had looted the cartridges from an Ordnance Depot. It is worth repeating for its priggishness and its strange perversity the conclusion of Thompson's chapter on the Mutiny in *The Rise and Fulfilment of British Power in India*. He writes:

'On the British side, the valour and endurance of soldiers and civilians were marred by crude racial passions and by gross ingratitude to many Indians who assisted them. Indians must also recognize certain failings in the conduct of those who took arms against the Government; the indecision which kept large numbers inactive when they might have been most effective, the selfishness and lack of national pride which prevented leaders working together or sacrificing their own personal ambitions.' The English, it will be observed, are judged by high moral standards, the Indians are condemned for failure in revolutionary technique.

The regiment mentioned at Bhurtpore was later to become the 1st Battalion, 7th Rajput Regiment (Queen Victoria's Own Light Infantry). I am grateful to Lieut.-General Sir E. Wood for the story. It was Sir E. Paget who opened on the sepoys with grape at Barrackpore. He was a cornet in the Life Guards at 17, and Lieutenant Colonel in command of 28th Foot at 19. He was 49 at Barrackpore, having had thirty years in command.

I do not think the Sepoy's loss of prestige at Oudh has been given enough weight as a cause of the Mutiny. Having been Secretary of one district soldiers' board, president of another, and secretary of the Indian Soldier's Board, I may be inclined to lay too much stress on this but I do not think so. Nor has the religious attitude of British Officers been sufficiently stressed, while I am inclined to think that too much weight has been laid on the reduction in the number of British Troops. The total reduction in the seven years before the Mutiny was three thousand. Twenty thousand more might have prevented the Mutiny, but I find it hard to believe that three less caused it.

NOTES ON THE AUTHORITIES

For the Cooper story, Cooper's official dispatch is published as well as his book; both are nauseating. They need to be checked with the account given in Bosworth Smith's *Life of Lawrence*. Thompson must have read this but differs from it without saying why.

★

For the period from 1784 to 1834 I am indebted for much help to Mr. B. B. Misra of the Patna University whose scholarly work on the administration of the East India Company is not yet published at the time this goes to press. I am also very grateful to Mr. F. N. Crofts for his generosity in compiling the index.

INDEX

ABBOTT, CAPT. JAMES, 329, 334
Aboriginals, 148, 184, 249-52
Accountant-General, 178, 189
Achin (Sumatra), 21, 58
Adam, John, 225, 272, 273, 276
Addiscombe College, 283, 307, 334, 335, 348
Afghanistan, 215, 275, 277, 326
Afghans, 41, 98, 172, 173, 215, 330, 331; wars with, 277-8, 325
Agnew, Patrick Vans, 329, 334, 367
Agra, 23, 24, 26, 32, 35, 40, 45, 47, 50, 105, 173, 231, 267, 293; factory, 54; presidency, 273; province, 293; in Mutiny, 356, 367, 369
Ahmadabad, 47, 51
Ahmadnagar, 259; Raja of, 259
Aitchison, Charles, 338
Ajit Singh, Raja of Jodhpur, 258
Ajnala, 376-8
Akbar Shah, Emperor
  British debt to, 13-14, 36-8, 51, 141; reign, 37-47, 122, 305; revenue policy, 37-45, 103, 120, 135, 137, 184, 292-3; religious tolerance, 45; Civil Service, 45, 71; successors, 48-9; suttee, 257; greatness, 122, 269, 277
Albuquerque, Affonso d', 30
Aligarh, 367
Ali Vardi Khan, Nawab, 94
Allahabad, 293, 311, 312, 315; in Mutiny, 357, 359, 360, 362, 368
Allard, General, 236
Almeida, Francisco d', 30, 34
Almora, 226, 301
Ameer Khan, Nawab of Tonk, 310
Amritsar, 371, 373, 375, 376, 378
Amyatt, Peter, 108
Anderson, David, 115, 131
Anderson, Lieut., 334
'Anglo-India', 151-62, 163-5
Anijdiv Island, 57
Arabic, 45, 148
Arabs, 30, 51
Arakan, annexed, 306
Archdekin, Mr., 158
Arcot, 81, 83, 175; Nawab of, 81, 175-6, 177, 185, 272; siege of, 84-9 South Arcot, 194
Armagon, factory at, 64
Armenians, 28, 32, 41
Arrah, in Mutiny, 364-6
Asaf Khan, 28, 32, 33
Asiatic Society, 162
Asoka, King, 37
Assam, annexed, 306

Assaye, Battle of, 200, 202, 214, 216, 218
Assessment of rent and revenue by Moguls, 37, 39-41, 43-4, 137, 184-5, 292-3 (see Revenue: Settlement)
Auckland, Lord, Gov.-Gen., 276-8, 312, 324
Aungier, Gerald, 55, 57, 58, 60, 73, 74
Aurangzebe, Emperor, 36, 43, 49, 57, 62, 71, 73, 74, 79, 80
Aylmer, Rose, 152, 169
Azamgarh, 301-2

BABER, EDWARD, 109, 115
Baji Rao (Peshwa), 216-8, 360
Bakir Khan, 50, 51, 54
Balasore, factory at, 70
Baluchis, 51
Banda, 368
Bang (bhang), 79, 101
Banias (Banians), 55, 56, 122, 128, 363
Banjaras, aboriginals, 252
Bannerman, Mr., 252
Bannu, 329, 330-4, 341, 343, 351
Bantam (Java), 22, 23, 24
Baramahal (now Salem), 186-9, 191, 193, 270, 320
Bareilly, 228, 293, 295-6, 302, 305, 312; in Mutiny, 363
Bari Doab Canal, 341
Barlow, Sir George, 153, 167, 209, 276, 306
Barnes, Mr., 334
Barnwall, Mr., 225
Baroda, 131, 231; Gaekwar of, 131
Barrackpore, 356; mutiny at, 347
Barwell, Mrs., 159-60
Barwell, Richard, 160
Bastar, 253
Bateman, N., 140
Bax-Ironside, Mr., 366
Bayley, William Butterworth, 273, 284, 317
Beames, John, 282, 285, 338
Beard, Governor, 79
Becher, Richard, 115
Bednore (Mysore), 309
Behar (Bihar), 42, 71, 94, 95, 101, 103, 108, 111, 112, 120, 173, 227, 258, 301, 350, 355; in Mutiny, 347, 362, 366
Bell, Andrew, 235
Benares, 109, 145, 177, 179, 212-13, 227-8, 234, 239, 240, 256-7, 267, 293, 301, 302, 311, 312; in Mutiny, 361, 362, 363-4, 368, 369; Rajah of, 125, 126, 131

INDEX

Benfield, Paul, 176
Bengal, factories, 70, 73; life in, 71, 76,
143; E. India Co. in, 78, 93, 94;
Governors, 79, 106, 107, 288; Viceroys, 93; Clive and, 97, 103, 120;
acquired by E. India Co., 101-3;
Council, 107, 117, 125, 141; revenue,
110-12, 116, 185; Hastings and, 115,
127, 128, 131, 132; Bombay and,
130-1, 146, 177; revenue settled, 133,
293, 298, 301; administration, 133-4,
194; climate, 134; Permanent Settlement, 140-1, 163, 176, 178, 192-4,
238, 271, 301; *Gazette*, 158, 160, 161;
district life, 163-71; Marathas and,
173; progress, 175, 177-8; compared
with Madras, 176-7, 192; and Bombay, 177; suttee in, 257-8; dacoity in,
289; rent reform, 341; Mutiny and,
345, 354, 362
Bengalee, character of, 94, 128, 178;
language, 104
Beni Ram Pundit, 160
Bentinck, Lord William, Gov-Gen.,
236, 257, 260, 275, 276
Bernier, François, 35, 44, 318
Best, Capt., 31
Bhawani, Goddess, 262-3
Bhils, aboriginals, 211
Bhonsla, The, 131, 214
Bhurtpore, Battle of, 346, 350
Biderra, Battle of, 118
Birbhum, 170
Bird, Robert Mertins, 228, 291, 296-9,
301-2, 304-5
Black Hole of Calcutta, 78, 96, 104, 108,
376
Board of Control, 146, 147, 153, 179,
232, 276, 280
Board of Revenue
    Bengal, 135, 141, 178, 288; Madras,
    193
Board of Trade, Bengal, 159
Bogle, C., 115
Boglipoor, 148
Bokhara, 326
Bolts, William, 104-10, 112, 116, 145,
149, 179, 185, 272
Bolts, Mrs. Anne, 109, 110
Bombay, life in, 57-63, 64, 245; sup-
plants Surat, 57-8; Keigwin's re-
bellion, 61-2; Deputy Governor, 56,
58; Governors, 57, 177, 221-2, 238-47;
council, 130, 177; Bengal and,
130-1, 146, 177; compared with
Bengal, 177, 245; progress, 177,
238-47; suttee in, 257; settlement,
301; Mutiny and, 345, 362, 374
Loughton, Dr. Gabriel, 70
Boulderson, Mr., 228
Bowcher, Mr., 56, 60

Bowcher, Mrs., 60
Box-wallahs, 156, 179
Brahmans, 212, 227, 253, 256, 260, 265,
345-6, 350, 353, 370
Bramport (*see* Burhanpur)
Bristow, John, 159
Bristow, Mrs. (*see* Wrangham, Emma)
British, qualities, 28, 74, 112, 169-70,
180, 231, 232, 233-4; debt to Akbar,
13-14, 36-8, 51, 141; power spreads,
47, 93, 101, 172-3, 198, 238; death-
rate, 54, 76, 81, 104, 114, 122, 161-2,
178; religious tolerance, 57, 59, 242,
249; and intolerance, 351; compared with Indians, 101, 241, 310, 357;
compared with French, 233-4;
treatment of Indians, 104, 117, 124,
128, 179, 291-2; standoffishness,
160-1, 166, 232, 233, 245, 351;
friendship with Indians, 196, 310;
administration, 210, 218-19, 344;
benefits of rule, 11, 229, 234, 236,
275, 299, 303-5, 316-17, 321, 337,
341-2; avarice, 112, 245; love of
compromise, 309, 334; confidence in,
326; paradox of rule, 333, 349; pride
in rule, 344; ruthlessness in Mutiny,
344, 357-9, 361-2, 372-8
Broach, 47, 239
Brooke, M. H., 227, 232, 257
Brown, Mr., 185
Brydon, Dr., 278
Buckland, Mr., 284
Budh Singh, Raja of Bundi, 258
Bulkeley, Lieut., 89
Bundelkhand, 173
Bundi State, 258
Bungalows, 165, 314-15
Burdwan, 102, 119, 139, 157, 161, 233,
257
Burhanpur (Bramport), 26, 27, 32, 47
Burke, Edmund, 112, 145, 146, 176
Burma, 253, 306, 347, 348
Burnes, Alexander, 326
Bushire, 239
Bussy (Marquis de Bussy-Castelnau),
99
Buxar, 365; Battle of, 118; mutiny at,
347, 348

CABUL (*see* Kabul)
Calcutta founded, 73; death-rate, 76;
fortified 78; Black Hole of, 78, 96,
104, 108, 376; siege of, 95; acquired
by E. India Co., 102; recapture,
119, 238; revenue, 120; Hastings and,
128-9, 178; Shore in, 134; council,
138; private trade, 144; life in,
151-6, 158-62, 163, 165, 245, 301;
courts, 157, 167, 246; religion in, 169;
compared with Madras, 176-7, 192;

INDEX

Calcutta *(cont.)*
and Bombay, 177, 245; manners in, 291; Mutiny and, 356, 359, 364
Campbell, Capt. John, 251-2, 253
Canals, 303, 321, 342
Cannibalism, 46-7
Canning, Lord, Gov.-Gen., 353, 358, 367, 377-8
Capital punishment, 65-6, 78-9, 126, 174, 220, 270
Carew, Lord, 34
Carnatic, 73, 82, 83, 173, 175; Nawab of, 81, 94
Castlereagh, Lord, 280
Cawnpore, 293, 295, 312, 348; in Mutiny, 358-9, 360, 362, 364, 368, 369
Ceded Districts (Madras), 173, 186, 191; land tenure, 186-8
Central India, 195-211, 220, 225, 238, 252, 350; Agency, 210, 221; Malcolm's history of, 215
Chait Singh, Rajah, 125, 126, 127, 131
Chamberlain, Major Crawford, 324
Chandah, dancing-girl, 205
Chandarnagar, 72, 97, 98, 99, 256
Chanda Sahib, 82, 83, 85, 87; his son, 86, 87
Chandu Lal, 273
Charles II, King, 57, 61
Charles II, S.S., 62
Charnock, Job, 71-4, 76, 102
Charter of Elizabeth I, 1-2; of Charles II, 65
Cherry, G. F., 213
Child, Sir John, 60-2
Child, Sir Josiah, 56, 59-62, 67, 68, 73, 75, 77-8
China, 13, 111, 112
Chinna Patanam (Madras), 64
Chinsura, 256
Chittagong, 73, 102, 119, 140, 141, 161
Cholera, 161, 196, 316, 325
Chota Nagpur, 148
Christian, George, 334, 337
Christianity, 11, 27-8, 242-3, 248, 257, 264-5, 302, 317, 324, 348, 353-4
Churchill, Sir Winston, 82, 164
Civil cases, 317, 320, 341-2; Judge, Bengal, 142, 166
Clevland, Augustus, 148-9, 179, 226, 251
Climate, 55, 133, 134, 161, 169-70, 232, 237, 250
Clive, Robert (1st Baron), 77; at Arcot, 83-9; character, 95, 118, 122; Suraj-ud-Daula and, 96-100, 110, 160; Plassey and after, 100-2, 116, 117, 238; Revenue Minister, Bengal, 103, 120; reforms, 108, 177; Vansittart and, 116; dual system, 120, 128, 178,

317; compared with Hastings, 122; chaos after, 133; and trade, 143; India under, 172; Malcolm's life of, 215
Clive, 2nd Baron, 207
Close, Sir Barry, 213, 225
Clothes of British in India, 151, 176, 224
Club, The (Social centre), 154, 312
Cochran, Mr., 197
Cockburn, Mr., 196
Cockerell, Mr., 368
Cocks, Arthur, 329, 367
Colebrooke, H. T., 212
Collector of customs, 169, 311
Collector of revenue
Mogul, 44, 51; Bengal, District Officer, 51, 119, 142, 168, 170, 171; revenue powers only, 128, 164, 166, 168; 'supervisors', 129, 135; case-work, 134; liability in law, 168; Madras, 192, 193, 194; Bombay, 220-1; malpractices, 152, 188; finally District Officer, 180, 271; military, 143, 186, 235; caricatured, 313-14
Collings, Mr., 158
Collins, Colonel, 267-8
Colour bar, 160-1, 291-2
Colvin, James, 364
Colvin, John Russell, 299, 323, 369
Combe, Mr., 365
Commercial Department, 169, 179, 204
Communal riot, 227-8, 355
Company *(see* E. India Co. and Hon. do.)
'Competition-wallahs', 284-5, 288
Connolly, Capt. Arthur, 326
Consent, S.S., 21
Cooper, Frederick, 371, 373, 375-8
Coote, Sir Eyre, 169
Cope, Capt. John, 89
Cornwallis, Lord, Gov.-Gen., 145, 152, 200, 209, 275, 306, 317; Permanent Settlement, 141, 192, 293; salaries under, 144, 169; 'school' of, 148, 179, 220, 239, 271, 328; code, 153, 166, 167, 168, 192, 220, 271; Bombay and, 177, 238; Madras and, 186
Coromandel, 64, 66
Corporation, Madras, 68, 70; E. India Co. as, 10, 317
Coryat, Tom, 45
Cossimbazar (Kasimbazar), 70, 73, 99, 118
Cotton, Brig., 372
Courts
of Pleas (Bombay), 58; in Madras, 65; Mayor's (Madras), 70; Revenue, 134, 142, 166, 300; of Appeal, 166, 295, 317; of Circuit, 166; Supreme, 245-7; Sudder, 317

INDEX

Covenants of H.E.I.C.S., 108, 317
Cox, Mr., 289, 296
Crimean War, 348, 350
Criminal law
  Bengal, 166-7; Maratha, 174; trial of cases, 317
Criminal tribes, Delhi, 271
Croftes, Charles, 115
Cruttenden, Miss, 158-9
Cuddapore, 185
Culpee (Kalpi), 157
Cuddalore, 78
Curry and Rice, 313-14
Cust, Mr., 334
Customs and dues
  exemption from, 33, 55, 73, 96, 105, 107, 118, 119, 139; Mir Kasim and, 107-8; Collector of, 169, 311; transit dues, 288, 310
Cutch, 225, 326

DACCA, 70, 71, 226
Dacca Jelalpore, 226
Dacoity (gang robbery), 226-7, 289, 290, 316, 318
Dacres, P. R., 140
Dak (dawk)
  travelling by, 310-11; bungalow, 312
Dalhousie, Lord, Gov.-Gen., 259, 341, 348, 349
Danes, 20, 99, 256
Davis, Samuel, 212
Day, Francis, 64
Debauchery of Indian rulers, 28, 79, 93, 101, 172, 216-17, 269, 338
Deccan, 36, 45, 52, 96, 97, 99, 183-4, 210, 220, 222, 242, 246, 253; Nizam of, 83, 306
Delhi
  under Moguls, 79, 98, 118, 135, 137, 172; British society in, 158, 310; Marathas and, 173; Jacquemont at, 235; Metcalfe and, 236, 268, 270-1, 273-4; suttee in, 257; Trevelyan and, 289; Mutiny and, 325, 354, 355-9, 362-3, 368, 373, 374-5, 377-8; J. Lawrence at, 335, 338
Dhalip Singh, Maharaja, 328-9, 333
Dig, Battle of, 268
Dinajpur, 140
Dinapore, 227, 364-5
Directors, Court of (*see* East India Company)
District Judge, Bengal, 170 (*see* Judge-Magistrate)
District Officer (Magistrate)
  (*a*) Bengal. Collector as, 119, 168, 170, 171; in abeyance, 142; Judge-Magistrate as, 143, 164, 166-9, 171; powers, 142, 166-8
  (*b*) Maratha, 174

(*c*) Madras, 191, 193, 194, **195**
(*d*) Bombay, 220
(*e*) Delhi, 271
(*f*) All-India, 180, 271; intrigues **and,** 126; importance, 133, 141, **237;** and roads, 320
Districts, life in, 163-71, 224, **226,** 308, 310, 312-14
Doon, The (Dehra Dun), 369
Dost Mohammad, Amir, 278, 372, **374**
Downton, Capt. Nicholas, 32
D'Oyly, Sir Charles, 227
D'Oyly, Sir John, 157, 227
Drake, Roger, 95, 115
Drunkenness, 75, 151, 155, **226, 232,** 249-50, 252, 269, 282
Dual system of Clive, 120, 178, 317; Hastings and, 128-30, 178, 317; in Madras, 175
Ducarel, G. G., 140, 141, 147, 192
Dunbar, Capt., 365-6
Duncan, Jonathan, 112, 115, 177, 179, 186, 238-40
Dundas, Henry (Lord Melville), 153
Dupleix, Joseph, Marquis de, 83, 89, 93, 131, 173, 175
Durga (Doorga), Goddess, 253, 262
Dutch, 20, 21, 23, 24, 30, 48, 49, 51, 57, 62, 69, 118, 256
Dyer, Brig.-Gen., 377

EAST INDIA COMPANY
  Trade (*see* s.v.); Service of (*see* Hon. East India Company's Service); Charters, 19-20, 65; early voyages, 21-22; Indian dialects, 26, 56; direct rule by, 49, 178, 198; lease Bombay, 57; nepotism, 60, 153, 157, 212, 267, 307; officials and, 68, 77, 108-9, 135, 141, 143, 176, 270; courts and, 66; on taxation, 68-9; war with Aurangzebe, 73; attacked in England, 77, 94; compensation after Black Hole, 100; Empire and, 103, 120, 130; out of touch, 107, 117, 138; Hastings and, 125; patronage, 129; policy unreal, 135; nomination by, 145, 179, 283-6; Parliament and, 146-7, 276; interference by, 152; Oudh and, 172; evolution, 179, 317; Munro's advice to, 196; Malcolm and, 205, 247; Lord Wellesley and, 209, 221; Bombay judges and, 247; Metcalfe and, 273, 274, 275; Haileybury and, 279-86; on Permanent Settlement, 289, 296
Eccentrics, 231, 237, 267, 281
Eden, George (*see* Auckland, Lord)
Eden, Miss, 269, 277, 311
Edmonstone, Mr., 206, **269**

INDEX

Education of Indians, 13, 240-3, 288-9, 292, 303; effect, 350
Edwardes, Sir Herbert, 324-5, 328, 329, 330-4, 341, 343, 351, 358, 371-2, 373, 378
Elizabeth I, Queen, 19-20, 37
Ellenborough, Lord, Gov.-Gen., 326, 328
Elliot, Gibby (*see* Minto, Lord)
Ellis, Sir Henry, 225
Ellis, William, 117-18
Elphinstone, James, 212, 257
Elphinstone, Mountstuart, 13; on Munro, 197; and Marathas, 204, 211, 212-22, 238, 271; character, 205, 225, 237, 244, 266, 277, 279, 302, 323, 324; writings, 213; on punishment, 220-1, 270; at Kabul, 236, 268; Gov. of Bombay, 240-4; and Indians, 245, 287, 291, 292; policy, 245-6, 247, 327; on Sind annexation, 326; mentioned, 190, 208
Empire
  first steps to, 103; Elphinstone on, 221; Lord Wellesley on, 279; trusteeship, 12, 196, 234, 288, 292, 322
England jobbery in, 75, 112-13, 129, 145
English
  in H.E.I.C.S., 152-3, 204, 266; language, 234, 241; law, 245-7, 317
Erskine, H. N. B., 259
Etah, 367
Europeans
  jurisdiction over (Madras), 65; (Bombay), 245-7
Ewer, Walter, 258
Eyre, Major Vincent, 366

Factories
  failure over, 23, 28; established, 47, 55; Surat, 47, 53-6; Agra, 54; Madras, 64, 73; Bengal, 70, 71, 73; records, 65, 66-8
Factors
  life of, 53-6, 63, 64-6, 76; salaries, 65, 76
Famine, 46, 54, 138, 178, 277
Fateh, Hyder, 189
Fatehpur (Futtehpore), 359, 369
Faujdar, 168
Ferozpur, 371
Finch, William, 24
Fitzroy, Hon. Frederick, 152, 179
Flogging, 65, 220, 295, 327, 331; abolished by Metcalfe, 270
Food eaten by British, 53-4, 151, 165, 176, 214, 234-5, 345; prices, 165, 177
Foote, Samuel (playwright), 154
Forde, Colonel Lionel, 118

Fort St. David, 78, 83, 84, 87
Fort St. George, 64, 68, 73, 176, 185, 238
Fort William, 79, 93, 107, 116, 213, 238, 359; College, 279-80
Fox, Charles James, 145
Francis, Sir Philip, 125, 127, 130, 135, 136, 141, 144, 154, 155, 158, 159
Fraser, Mr., 67
Fraser, William, 236-7
Freedom of the Press, 276
French, 81-5, 89, 94, 97, 99, 100, 116, 130, 131, 175, 233-4, 256
Fryer, Dr. John, 55, 58, 59, 66

Galloway, Mr., 368
Ganges, River, 73, 99, 108, 183, 227-8, 256, 260; Canal, 303, 321; water, 319
Ganjam, 251, 252
Garhwal, 229, 230
Gary, Mr., 58
Georgians, 41
Ghazipore, 366
Ghulam Husain Khan, 100
Gladstone, W. E., 327
Glass, Ensign, 89
Gleig, Rev. G. R. (author), 223
Goa, 24, 28, 30, 49
Goddard, Col. William, 131
Golconda, 45, 67, 68, 70, 73
Governor-General
  appointment of, 275-6, 278; acting, 209, 272, 273, 276, 306; Private Secretary to, 206, 271; Council and, 257, 277, 289
Governors
  appointment of, 289; of Madras, 65-6, 77, 177, 185 195, 207, 222, 276, 288, 289; of Bengal, 106, 107; of Bombay, 177, 221-2, 238-47 (*see also* Lieut.-Govs.)
Govindghar, 371
Graham, Maria (quoted), 245, 310
Grand, Mr., 154
Grand, Mrs., 154-5
Grant, Charles (Lord Glenelg), 112, 115, 141, 179
Grant, Donald, 368
Grant, James, 179
Grant, Sir John Peter, 358
Grant, Mr., 225
Gray, Mr., 106
Grote, Harriet, 154
Gubbins, Frederick, 363-4, 369
Gubbins, Martin, 369
Gujerat (Bombay), 50, 239
Gujrat, Battle of (Punjab), 358, 367
Gulab Singh, buys Kashmir, 328
Gulston, Mr., 108
Gupta dynasty, 37

393

INDEX

Gurkhas, 229, 230; war with, 231
Gwalior, 131, 173, 208-9, 310
Gya, 153

HAILEYBURY COLLEGE, 12, 280-6, 287-8, 289, 292, 301, 302, 307, 308, 334, 335, 338, 365, 377
Halhed, N., 162
Hall, Major Henry, 236
Halliday, F. J., 288
Hamilton, Captain Alexander, 59, 76
Hamirpur, 368
Harding, Charles, 256
Hardinge, Lord, Governor-General, 322, 328, 329
Hare, Dr., 161
Harkaras, 214
Harwood, W., 140
Hastings, Màrquis of, Governor-General, 124, 200, 202, 204, 209, 273, 306, 317
Hastings, Warren, 152, 159, 162; and Vansittart, 106, 107, 108; virtues, 112, 115; career, 115, 122-32; compared with Vansittart, 118; compared with Clive, 122; compared with Marlborough, 122-4; attitude to Indians, 124, 130, 132, 160, 323; charges against, 125; and Council, 125, 135, 146, 304; policy, 128-9, 146, 178, 287, 303, 317; verdict on, 132; impeachment, 125, 132, 139
Havelock, General Sir Henry, 359, 360
Hawes, Mr., 373-4
Hawkins, Mr., 228, 232
Hawkins, William, 21-9, 33, 34, 35, 36, 42, 62
Hay, William, 104, 107, 108, 112, 116, 145, 149, 186
Hazara, 334
Hazari Bagh, 312
Heath, Captain William, 73, 74
Heber, Bishop Reginald, 148, 204, 223, 226-33, 237, 239, 290, 291
Hector, S.S., 21, 22, 24
Hedges, William, 70, 135
Henckel, Tilman, 179
Herat, 326
Hervey, Mr., 71
Hickey, William, 114, 130, 139, 145, 151-62, 163, 167, 172, 224, 267
Hickey, Charlotte, 114
Hicks, Mr., 252
Hicky, Augustus, 158, 159
Higginson, Nathaniel, 68, 77
Himalayas, 36, 183, 229, 230, 235, 252, 342, 358
Hinde, Mr., 83
Hindus, 245, 346, 355-7; and caste, 170,

239-40, 345; law, 166, 212-13; Hinduism, 241-2, 248, 253-5, 258-60, 262, 265, 307, 350, 352, 353; *Vedas*, 253; *Shasters*, 254
Hindustani, 104, 215, 227, 236, 274, 280, 288, 308, 314, 353
Hodgson, John, 193
Hog-hunting, 164, 240, 247, 287, 289, 315, 351
Holkar, 131, 214, 218
Holwell, J. Z., 78, 95, 96, 97, 116, 376
Hon. East India Company's Service, 114, 152, 223; virtues, 9, 11-13, 49-50, 74-5, 150, 169-70, 179, 247; paternalism, 9, 152, 194, 195, 225, 231, 300, 309, 323, 336, 339; evolution, 11, 47, 49, 62, 120, 132, 133, 179; death-rate in, 54, 76, 104, 114, 122, 161-2, 178; nepotism, 60, 145, 153, 157, 179, 212; life in, 64-6, 76-7, 114-15, 122, 134, 151-62, 163-6; salaries, 65, 76, 133, 169, 188, 223, 272; linguists, 68, 104, 115, 116, 121, 147-8, 153, 154, 157, 162, 186, 188, 195, 196, 205, 212-13, 215, 227, 236, 239, 240, 274, 279-80, 284-85, 288, 292, 300, 308; qualifications, 68, 283-6; promotion, 76, 133; conditions in, 76, 89, 145-6, 147; trade, 77, 104-5, 109, 143-4, 152, 176, 177, 178; malpractices, 104-13, 175-6, 179, 185, 188, 196, 239, 240, 272-3, 288; covenants, 108, 317; avarice, 112, 245; seeds of I.C.S., 120; under W. Hastings, 132; compared with Whitehall, 133; worship of, 149, 179, 225, 341; religion, 149, 166, 169, 170, 233, 244, 302-3, 323, 324-6, 336, 353-4; composition, 152-3, 307; snobbery, 153-4, 313; versatility, 162, 166-8, 195, 210, 213-14, 218, 220, 230, 235, 240, 271, 284, 289, 292, 303, 308, 314, 333, 341, 351; district life, 163-71; ideals, 169-71, 179, 180, 190, 196, 197, 225, 231, 232, 287-8, 292, 303, 324-5, 337; extravagance, 157, 170, 178, 232, 234, 236, 245; careers, 179; training, 179, 196, 213, 279-86, 303, 308; integrity, 179, 180, 322; types in, 223-37, 313-14; isolation, 226, 233, 274, 287, 300, 308, 333; eccentrics in, 231, 237, 267; independence, 287-90, 308-9; security, 290, 307; pensions, 290
Hoogly (Hugli) River, 66, 72, 122, 145, 232; Town, 70, 71, 73
Hoti Mardan, 372
Human sacrifice, 242, 248-53, 260 (see Infanticide: Suttee)
Hunt, Mr., 140
Hyder, Ali, 131, 205

INDEX

Hyderabad, 97, 205, 206, 213, 272, 310, 329, 374; Nizam of, 131, 172, 173, 185, 191, 198, 200, 213, 272-3

ICE-MAKING, 316
Id festival, 376
Idar, 259; Raja of, 259
Imperial Service (Mogul), 14, 41-5; avarice, 23, 28, 51; salaries, 27, 35, 41, 42; extortion, 44, 51, 72; corruption, 45; Viceroys, 71, 79-81, 93, 94, 102
Impey, Sir Elijah, 159, 246
Income-tax, 169, 272
India
  first British voyages to, 21-2; under Moguls, 23, 26-9, 35-6, 45-7, 79-80, 168, 185; comparison with England, 101, 241, 270; perjury in, 111, 125-6, 226, 246, 264; law, 115; England and, 144, 145, 178, 179; Acts, 145-7; in 1798, 172-80; under British, 204, 226-37, 248, 274-5; superstition, 249, 353; overpopulated, 265; consolidated, 306; in 1842, 306-23
Indian Civil Service, seeds of, 120
Indians
  employment of, 68, 128-9, 195, 243, 271, 287, 303, 317; views on power, 101, 309; treatment of, 104, 117, 124, 128, 179, 231-2, 291-2, 323; W. Hastings on, 124; intrigues, 125-7; Shore on, 133; no social contact with British, 160-1, 166, 232, 233, 245; views on law, 178, 219-20, 230; Sir A. Wellesley on, 190-1; Munro on, 191, 194-5; friendship with British, 196, 310; Lord Wellesley on, 200; education, 240-3, 288-9, 292, 303, 350; views on British, 241, 284, 291, 295, 346; fraud by, 294-5; dislike of British rule, 321-2, 333
Indus, River, 236, 275, 278, 342
Infanticide, 179, 232, 239-40, 242, 248, 259-60, 333
Infidels, taxation of, 49, 71
Innes, Lieut., 87
Irish in H.E.I.C.S., 204, 215
Islam, 37, 43, 307

JACQUEMONT, VICTOR (quoted), 223, 226, 233-7, 273, 292
Jagir (District), 185, 192, 193
Jagirs, 136
Jahangir (Je-), Emp., 23-4 27-9, 32-3, 36
Jails, 342
Jains, 213
Jalalabad, 278

James I, King, 22, 23, 32, 33
Jammu, 328
Janam Asthami, festival, 227
Japan, 111, 112
Jats, 51, 333, 370
Jenkins, Charles, 360
Jenkinson, Mr., 368
Jeremie, Rev., at Haileybury, 281, 286
Jessore, 140, 168, 170, 179
Jesuits, 24, 27, 28
Jodhpur State, 258
Johnson, Rev. William, 160
Johnson 'Begum', 160
Johnstone, John, 104, 107-8, 110, 112, 116, 145, 149, 186
Joint Magistrate, 313, 314, 315
Jones, Sir Harford, 209
Jones, Richard, at Haileybury, 281, 286
Jones, Sir William, 162, 212
Jowett, Prof. Benjamin, 285
Judge-Magistrate (head of district)
  Bengal, 143, 164, 166-9, 171, 178, 194, 205, 212, 237, 271, 319; Bombay, 220
Judges (*see* Civil Judge, District Judge, Judge-Magistrate, Registrar)
Judicial Department, 204, 267; life in, 163; and Executive, 143, 166-9, 171, 271
Jullundur, 334
Jumlabad, 189
Jumna, River, 294, 356; Canals, 321
Justice
  administration of, Surat, 58-9; Madras, 65, 70; Bengal, 78-9, 120, 142, 166-8, 170-1; executive and judicial combined, 143, 166-9, 171, 271, 319; procedure, 163, 212-13, 317, 318-19; simple law preferred, 178, 219-20, 230, 341; delays, 194; flaws in, 292, 298, 317-18; (*see* Law)

KABUL (Cabul), 215, 236, 268, 277, 278, 325, 332, 350, 371, 372, 374
Kali, Goddess, 262, 265
Kanara, 189-91
Kangra, 335
Karwi, 368
Kashmir, 235, 307, 328-9
Kasimbazar (*see* Cossimbazar)
Kathiawar (Kattewar), 225, 239, 240
Kavanagh, Mr. (quoted), 324
Kaye, Sir John (quoted), 223, 240, 266, 272, 273, 277, 293, 296, 357
Keeling, William, 21
Keene, Mr., 369
Keigwin, Captain James, 56, 61-2, 66, 74
Kennedy, Mr., 214
Kennedy, Captain, 235
Kenny, Col., 214

INDEX

Khafi Khan (quoted), 62-3
Khandesh, 220
Khan Mohammad Khan, 362
Khonds, aboriginals, 249, 251, 265
Khyber Pass, 307
Kilpatrick, Captain James, 89
Kipling, Rudyard, 149, 158, 170, 289
Kirkpatrick, Mr., 206, 213
Koum, River, 66
Kumaon, 229-31
Kunwar Singh, 362-3, 364, 366

LAHORE, 42, 215, 236, 268, 328, 330, 332-3, 370; in Mutiny, 370, 371, 373, 375, 378
Lake, Edward John, 334
Lake, General Gerald, 200, 268, 346, 350
Lakhipur, 119
Land Revenue (see Revenue)
Land Tenure
  under Moguls, 35, 38, 43, 47; in Ceded Districts, 187-8; in N.W.P., 304-5; pre-emption, 304
Langhorn, Sir William, 66
Lashkarpur, 142
Laswari, Battle of, 200
Law
  Indian, 115, 219-20, 270; Hindu, 166, 212-13; Muslim, 166-7; Maratha, 174, 219-20; effect of rule of, 178, 230, 263, 292, 321; codification in Bombay, 240-1; and Bannu, 333; English, 245-7, 317 (see Civil Law: Criminal Law: Justice, Administration of)
Lawrence, Alexander, 335
Lawrence, Sir George, 329, 335
Lawrence, Sir Henry
  Punjab policy, 271; and Indians, 291; as surveyor, 297; character, 323, 324-5; and Kashmir, 328; Resident in Punjab, 329; President of Punjab Board, 330-1, 333; compared with John, 334-8; in Oudh, 341; Punjab reforms, 341-3, 360; in Mutiny, 336, 362, 369; death, 325
Lawrence, Honoria, 316, 323, 325, 326
Lawrence, Sir John (Lord)
  and Indians, 291; character, 324-5, 338, 340; member Punjab Board, 334; compared with Henry, 334-8; in Delhi, 335; Lieut.-Governor Punjab, 338; Viceroy, 338; Punjab reforms, 341-3, 362; in Mutiny, 345, 358, 370-2, 374, 377-8; mentioned, 327
Lawrence, Stringer, 83, 89
Le Bas, Mr., at Haileybury, 286
Legislative Council, 288
Lepers, murder of, 260

Lewin, Thomas, 154, 186
Liberalism, 143, 167, 266, 276
Lieutenant-Governors
  N.W.P., 276, 302, 303, 306; Bengal, 288; Punjab, 338 (see Governors)
Lind, Mr., 363-4
Lindsay, Hon. Robert, 152
Littledale, Mr., 365
Liverpool, Lord, 160
Loyd, Mr., 368
Lucknow, 154, 158, 159, 310, 337, 352; in Mutiny, 360, 362, 369
Lumsden, Sir Harry Burnett, 329, 334
Lushington, C. M., 258
Lushington, Henry, 108
Lushington, Mr., 231
Lysaght, Mr., 360

MACARTNEY, LORD, 177
Macaulay, Hannah (Mrs. Trevelyan), 288
Macaulay, Lord
  quoted, 13, 79, 94, 111, 125, 130, 276, 350, 351; employment, 179; writings, 215, 223; Haileybury and, 284-5; family, 288-9; Trevelyan's life of, 288
McDonnell, William Fraser (V.C.), 366
Mackenzie, Holt, 292, 296
Mackenzie, Mr., 158
Mackillop, Mr., 369
Mackintosh, Sir James, 221, 240
Mackintosh, William, 155
Macleod, Donald, 227
Macleod, Duncan, 227
Macleod, Hugh, 227
Macleod, Norman, 227
Macnaghten, Sir William, 326
Macpherson, Captain, 252
Maddock, Mr., 235
Madras
  founded, 64; early administration, 64-70; council, 64, 66, 70, 73, 97, 175, 185, 188; independent spirit, 64-6, 151-2; Charnock at, 73; Governors, 65-6, 77, 177, 185, 195, 207, 222, 276, 288, 289; Dupleix and, 82-4, 86, 93, 175; help for Calcutta, 96; Vansittart at, 116; Bengal and, 131, 146; life in, 151; religion, 169; spread of, 173, 185-6; revenue, 175; malpractices in, 175-6; compared with Calcutta, 176-7, 192; settlement, 192-4, 238, 296; human sacrifice and, 250-1, 256, 257; Mutiny and, 345, 362
Maharashtra, 174
Mainpuri, 367
Makhua, 72
Malaria, 161, 325

396

INDEX

Malcolm, Sir John
and Munro, 189; character, 190,
205-6, 207, 212, 216, 225, 237, 266,
302; in Central India, 200, 204,
210-11, 216, 219, 236, 238, 239,
270; in Hyderabad, 206; in Mysore,
207; in Persia, 206-7, 209, 268; and
Lord Wellesley, 208-9, 214; as
soldier, 210, 218; writings, 215;
passed over, 221; on Red Tape,
224; Governor of Bombay, 240,
244-7; on Indians, 291, 292
Malda, 106
Malthus, Prof., at Haileybury, 281, 286
Malwa, 210, 236, 239
Mamlatdars, 174, 220, 221
Mandelslo, Albert de, 53
Mangles, Ross Lowis (V.C.), 365-6
Mansell, Charles, 334
Marathas
oppression by, 47, 316; wars with
Moguls, 55, 59, 81, 94; E. India Co.
and, 64, 70, 78, 87, 150, 173; wars
with British, 130-1, 195, 200, 204,
207, 209, 214, 216, 238, 239;
strength, 172-5; administration,
174, 184, 219-20; decay, 177, 238,
266, 306; war with Rajputs, 202,
210; civil war, 213; in Bombay,
245-6; under British, 271; Mutiny
and, 349, 350
Marlborough, 1st Duke of, 122, 124
Marlowe, Captain, 23
Marriott, Mr., 109
Martin, Mr., 235, 273
Massacres
of Patna, 108, 110, 118; of Calcutta
(*see* Black Hole of Calcutta); in
Mutiny, 354, 357, 360, 362, 374
Master, Gilbert, 226
Master, Streynsham, 66, 70-1, 73, 74, 77
Masulipatam, 47, 76
Meerut, 293, 348, 354-6, 362, 367, 370,
371
Melbourne, Lord, 276
Melvill, Mr., at Haileybury, 281, 302
Merchants
life of, 53-6, 63, 64, 66, 76; salaries,
65, 76
Meriahs, human victims, 249-52, 253
Metcalfe, Sir Charles (Lord), 13; and
Sikhs, 215, 268-70, 306, 328; in
Delhi, 236, 268, 270-2, 273; on suttee,
257; member of Council, 257, 273;
character, 266-7, 274-5, 278, 279, 302,
323; Life of, 266; in Agra, 267-8; in
Hyderabad, 272-3; Lieut.-Governor
N.W.P., 273, 276; policy, 275, 327;
and Governor-Generalship, 275-6;
Press Act, 276; subsequent career, 276;
and Indians, 287; mentioned, 284, 288

Meverell, Mr., 72
Mhairwara (Merwara), 236
Middleton, Sir Henry, 31
Middleton, Samuel, 139, 159, 170
Midnapore, 102, 119, 178
Miles, Mr., 225
Military Collectors, 143, 186, 235
Miller, Mr., 252
Mills, Mr., 252
Minchin, Captain, 74
Mint, at Madras, 66, 74
Minto, Lord, Governor-General, 209,
215, 267, 268
Mir Jafar, Nawab, 93, 100-2, 106, 110,
115, 116
Mir Kasim, Nawab, 93, 102, 103, 106-8,
116-18, 119
Mirzapur, 212
Mixed marriages, 28, 160, 176, 213, 237,
269
Moguls
India under, 23, 26-9, 30, 35-6, 45-7,
168, 185; presents to, 23, 51, 71,
93, 99; and trade, 22, 23, 30; justice,
35-6, 79, 318; land ownership, 35,
38; decay of empire, 36, 43, 47, 49, 79,
93, 118, 168, 178, 238; Akbar, 37-47;
land revenue, 38-41, 43-6, 136,
298; intrigues, 48; and E. India Co.,
55, 58, 64, 75, 178; war with
Marathas, 55, 57, 59, 60, 61; and
with E. India Co., 57, 73, 93;
Bengal grants, 78, 173; ex-Emper-
ors, 172-3, 226, 268, 270, 338;
suttee, 257; Sikhs and, 307; Mutiny
and, 350 (*see* Imperial Service
(Mogul))
Mohammad Ali, Nawab of Arcot, 83,
84, 87, 175-6, 177
Moharram (-um) festival, 88, 227
Moira, Lord (*see* Marquis of Hastings)
Molony, Edmund, 257
Monier-Williams, Sir Monier, at Hailey-
bury, 283, 285
Montgomery, Robert, 303, 324, 334,
370-1, 374, 377
Moon, E. P. (quoted), 126
Moorcroft, Mr., 235, 331
Moradabad, 367
Moreland, W. H. (quoted), 45
Morse, Mr., 159
Mubgoon, village, 358
Muhabbat Khan, Nawab, 73
Muir, Sir William, 303
Mukarrab Khan, 23, 24, 27, 28, 31
Mundy, Peter, 46, 50, 51, 53-5, 105, 151
Munro, Major (Sir) Hector, 93, 347
Munro, Sir Thomas, 13; on Moguls,
185; settlement work, 186-90, 191;
policy, 190-1, 194-6, 222, 320; views
on revenue, 192-4, 220, 296, 301;

INDEX

Munro, Sir Thomas (*cont.*)
    Governor of Madras, 195-6, 222; death, 196; character, 197, 205, 212, 266, 302, 323; administration, 204, 259; Indian view of, 225; on Indians, 292
Munsifs, 317
Murshidabad, 93, 94, 95, 98, 100, 120, 134, 139, 145, 157, 227
Muscat, 207
Muslims (Mussulmans), 245, 269, 345, 353, 355, 370, 375; law, 35, 43, 166-7; Koran, 82, 319, 345
Mutiny
    earlier examples, 347-8; Great Mutiny, 324, 326, 336, 340, 344-78; its causes, 348-54
Muttra, 293
Mymensingh, 163, 166, 169, 170
Mysore, 131, 172, 173, 186, 207, 306; wars with, 185, 186, 189, 206, 239

'NABOBS', fortunes of, 110, 112, 116, 121, 144, 145, 154, 155-6, 176, 177, 223, 234, 276
Nagpur, 214, 225, 349
Najm-ud-Daula, Nawab, 110
Nana Sahib, 360-1, 362
Nanda Devi, mountain, 230
Napier, Sir Charles, 326, 327
Napoleon, 81, 83, 84, 209, 215, 268-9
Native States (*see* Protected States)
Neembaira, 310
Neill, General, 358-9, 361
Nepal, 231, 374
Newnham, Mr., 295
Nicholls, Captain, 58
Nicholson, John, 325, 329, 334, 341, 358, 372, 376
Nilgiris, mountains, 252
Noakhali, 355
Nobkissen, Raja, 160
Non-regulation Provinces, 143, 271, 327
Norris, Mr., 225
North, Lord, 145
Northern Circars, 173, 185
North-Western Provinces, 248, 273, 276, 292-305, 306, 317, 334; Lieut.-Governors of, 276, 302, 303, 306; settlement, 292-305; land tenure, 301, 305; and Mutiny, 350, 358-64, 366
North-West Frontier, 225, 237
Nowshera, 371-2
Nuncomar, 125-7

OAKLEY, HENRY, 258
Ochterlony, Sir David, 231, 272
Oldfield, Richard, 366
Oman, Imam of, 207
Opium, 22, 36, 39, 104, 269, 310; Agent, 227, 301; Department, 303
Orissa, 94, 95, 103, 173, 249, 258

Orr, Captain, 360
Oudh, Kingdom of, 118, 129-30, 159, 173, 213, 228, 239, 293, 306, 309, 310, 321-2, 329, 336; annexed, 352; and Mutiny, 345, 347, 350, 359, 366, 370; King (Nawab) of, 93, 172, 198, 200-2, 349, 350, 351, 352, 353, 366; Rent Act, 340-1
Outram, Mr., 367
Outram, Sir James, 326-7, 345, 352
Oxenden, Sir George, 55, 57, 74
Ozeander (Osiander), S.S., 31

PALMER, WILLIAM, 272-3
Panchayats
    Madras, 195, 320; Marathas and, 219; Bombay, 220
Papillon, Mr., 60
Paramountcy, 239, 258
Parks, Charles Crawford, 311-12, 315
Parks, Mrs. Fanny, 311-12, 314, 315-16
Parliament, 9, 10, 12, 132, 144, 145, 147, 152, 176, 194, 275, 288, 293, 317
Parsees, 345
Partabghar, 253
Parvati, Goddess, 262
Patels, 220
Pathans, 24, 202, 359
Patna, 66, 70, 71, 74, 108, 109, 110, 117, 118, 140, 362, 363, 364, 365-6
Patronage of E. India Co., 129, of Parliament, 275-6
Pattle, Thomas, 142, 370
Patwaris, 141, 297
Paull, Mr., 154
Peacock, Mr., 72
Peasants
    under Moguls, 37-47, 49, 136-8; in Bengal, 120, 140, 142, 179; rent of, 136, 137, 141; character, 171, 264, 300; settlements with (Madras), 187-8, 190-1, 301; settlements with (Bombay), 301; under Marathas, 210, 238; and British, 210-11; opinions, 219; in Delhi, 271
Pedda Naik, 65
Peel, Sir Robert, 327
Penang, 270
Peons, 189, 191, 251, 259, 263
Pepper, Mr., 207
Permanent Settlement of Bengal, 140-1, 163, 176, 178, 192, 238, 271, 289, 296, 301
Perron, Monsieur, 231
Persia, 206-7, 209, 215, 239, 275, 326; Agent of, 56
Persian
    language, 27, 104, 115, 116, 124, 147, 153, 162, 205, 212, 213, 227, 236, 240, 280, 282, 311; Gulf, 49, 207, 209, 238

Peshawar, 158, 320, 371-3, 378
Peshwa, The, 130, 131, 173, 214, 215-18, 246, 360
Pettit, Mr., 56, 60
Phillips, Mr., 367
Pigot, Lord, 177
Pig-sticking (*see* Hog-hunting)
Pindaris (-ees), 47, 225, 316; war with, 204, 210, 216
Piracy, punishment for, 66
Pitt, Thomas, 66, 74, 77
Pitt, William, 84, 125, 145-6
Place, Lionel, 192, 193
Plassey, Battle of, 100-1, 102, 110, 118, 119
Police, 167, 168-9, 170, 213, 220, 308, 313, 341; Supt. of, 170, 319
Poligars, 185, 191, 192
Political Department (Service), 204, 205, 213, 235, 260, 267, 308, 309, 334
Pollock, Major-General Sir George, 326
Pondicherry, 85, 233
Poona, 174, 211, 213, 214, 215-18, 220, 222, 234, 253
Popham, Captain, 131
Portuguese, 19, 23, 24, 28, 30, 31, 33, 34, 49, 51, 57, 60, 61, 65, 70, 75, 97, 176, 242
Pott, Robert, 145, 156-8, 179, 227
Pott, Mrs. Emily, 157
Pottinger, Eldred, 326
Pottinger, Henry, 225
Prendergast, Mr., in Mutiny, 367
Prendergast, Mr., of Calcutta, 154
Presents
  to Moguls, 23, 51, 71, 93; to officials, 108, 110, 112; in Political Department, 206-7, 309
Press Act, 1835, 276
Prince Regent, The, 145
Privateering, E. India Co. and, 20
Protected States
  paramountcy in, 239, 258; suttee in, 258-9; administration, 275, 306, 308; compared with British India, 321-2
Public Schools, 114, 153, 170, 266-7, 269, 273, 274, 281, 282, 284, 285, 311
Punishment
  Elphinstone on, 220-1; Metcalfe on, 270-1
Punjab
  under Moguls, 40, 78; Jacquemont on, 235, 236; Sikhs and, 268-9, 306-7, 328; Lawrences and, 271, 324-5, 327, 337-8; Commission, 303, 325, 333, 334, 338, 340; settlement, 304, 342-3; after first Sikh war, 328-9, 330; after second Sikh war, 334; Lieut.-Governor, 338; Rent Act, 340; reforms, 341-2;

  revenues of, 343; Mutiny and, 362, 370-8
Punjabis, 340, 359, 370, 371, 373
Purnea, 107, 140

Qanungo, 137, 138, 141, 179
Qazis, 166

RADCLIFFE, LORD (quoted), 11
Railways, 310, 321, 350
Rajputana, 40, 50, 173, 231, 306, 310, 340, 341
Rajputs, 202, 210, 239-40, 248, 254, 345, 346, 370
Ram Charan Das, 107
Ram Mohun Roy, 258
Ram Narain, 101, 108, 116, 117, 119
Ranjit Singh, 47, 236, 268-9, 306-7, 327, 329, 351
Rattray, James, 168
Ravenshaw, Mr., 197
Rawalpindi, 334, 370
Raymond, François de, 116
Read, Col. Alexander, 186-7, 189, 192, 193, 194, 270, 320
Read, Mr., 197
Recorder of Bombay, 221, 240
Red Dragon, S.S., 21-2, 31
Red Sea, 31, 238
'Red Tape', 224, 237, 271, 347
Registrar, Bengal, 164, 166
Regulation Provinces, 143, 205, 237, 318
Regulations, 224, 237, 238
Religion
  intolerance of Portuguese, 30, 49, 57, 242; intolerance of Aurangzebe, 49, 57; tolerance of Akbar, 45; tolerance of British, 57, 59, 242, 248-9; tolerance of Ranjit Singh, 269; climate and, 55, 134; in H.E.I.C.S., 53, 149, 166, 169, 170, 233, 244, 302-3, 324-6, 336, 340
Renaud, Major, 358, 359, 362
Rent reform, 340-1 (*see* Assessment: Settlement)
Residents
  administration by, 207, 215-16, 239, 259, 270, 309-10, 329, 341; Commercial, 169
Revenge, S.S., 60, 74
Revenue
  originally rent to King, 39; collection by Moguls, 37, 39-41, 43-5, 184-5, 292-3; collection by E. India Co., 103, 110, 120, 138, 166, 175, 298; collection by Marathas, 174; collection by Sikhs, 342; Minister (Bengal), 120, 134; cases, 134, 142, 165, 300; Board of, 135, 141, 178, 193 (*see* Assessment: Settlement)
Rickets, Mr., 252

Ricketts, Mr., 360
Rider, Jacob, 268
Roads, 191, 247, 320, 322, **342**; Grand Trunk, 303, 320; Grand Military, 311
Roberdeau, Henry, 163-71, 172, 179, 315
Roberts, Lord, 359
Roberts, Mr., 373
Robertson, Mr., 295-6, 297, 302
Roe, Sir Thomas, 32 6, 45, 47, 79
Rohilkhand, 173, 228, 359, 362
Rohillas, 228
Roorkee, Thomason Engineering College, 303
Rowlandson, Mr., 156, 227
Royds, Sir John, 161
Russell, George, 250-1, 252, 253
Russell, Lady, 152
Russell, Mr., 272
Russell, Sir Henry, 152
Russia, 119, 209, 215, 275, 277
Ruttledge, Hugh, 230
Ryots (*see* Peasants)

SADALLO, 109
Sage, Mr., 109, 110
Saharanpur, 290, 369
St. John, Dr. John, 59
Salbai, Treaty of, 130, 131, 200
Salem, 186, 320
Salsette, 60, 239
Sanderson, Governor, 131
Sanderson, Miss (Mrs. Barwell), 159-60, 169
Sanskrit, 148, 162, 212, 239, 280, 283, 284, 285, 287
Saran, 366
Satara, 220, 225, 349; Raja of, 173, 253
Saunders, Thomas, 84, 87, 89
Scindia of Gwalior, 131, 173, 208, 217, 231, 267
Scots in H.E.I.C.S., 153, 197, 204, 205, 215, 266
Scott, Mr., 334
Scrafton, Luke, 97, 98, 99, 115, 118
Sealy, Cudbert, 258
Sea-power, importance of, 30, 31, 34, 73
Secretary to Government, 169, 178, 301
Sedley, Jos., 154, 224, 225, 237
Sepoys
  in Bengal Army, 344-8; causes of unrest, 351-3
Serampur, 256
Servants of officials, 155-6, 313, 315-16
Seton, Alexander, 268, 270
Seton-Kerr, W. S., 287
Settlement
  Bengal, 133, 140-1, 163, 176, 178, 193; Madras, 187-90, 192-4, 296, 301; Malwa, 210; Kumaon, 229-30, 301; Delhi, 271; N.W.P., 292-305;

Bombay, 301; Behar, 301; Bannu, 322; officers, 186-7, 189, 191, 296-7, 299-301, 304
Shahganj, Battle of, 367
Shahi, 228
Shah Jahan, Emperor, 33, 70
Shahjahanpur, 359
Shams-ud-Daulah, Nawab, 226
Sher Shah, Emperor, 37, 38, 43
Sherer, Mr., 268
Shipman, Sir Abraham, 57
Shore, F. J., 290-2, 298, 319
Shore, Sir John (Lord Teignmouth), 112, 114, 115, 133-50, 153, 156, 158, 162, 169, 172, 179, 186, 192, 238, 239, 276, 290
Sialkot, 374, 376
Sidi, The, Mogul Admiral, 59-62
Sikhs, 47, 172, 266, 269, 306-7, 328-31, 333, 342, 349, 367, 370; wars with, 324, 327-8, 334, 335, 367; revenue system, 342; Mutiny and, 365, 373, 374, 375, 376
Sikhism, 307
Simla, 234, 236, 356
Sind (Scinde), 225, 326, 327, 342, 346
Singhiya, factory at, 70
Sirhind, 306
Siva (Shiv), God, 262, 265, 312
Sivaji, 55, 57, 58, 61
Siyar-al-Muntakherin, 100, 108, 112, 139
Slaves, 66-7, 270
Sleeman, Sir William, 202, 204, 225, 254, 255, 257, 260-4, 297, 305, 309, 321, 323
Smith, Cecil, 189
Smith, Courtney, 258
Social life in India, 151-62, 310, 351
Soldiers in H.E.I.C.S., 10, 143, 186, 198, 221-2, 237, 251, 260, 307-8
Sonthals, aboriginals, 148
South India, 225, 252, 312, 316, 362
Spankie, Mr., 369
Spice Islands, 20, 30, 49
Spice trade, 21, 23
Sport, 164, 170, 190, 222, 229, 240, **247**, 282, 287, 289, 312, 351
Sri Ranga Raja Patanam (Madras), 64
Stephen, Sir James, at Haileybury, 281
Stephenson, Edward, 79
Stodart, Mr., 197
Strachey, Edward, 213, 214, 225
Strachey, Richard, 225
Superintendent of Police, 170, 319
Supervisors
  (a) for Indian reforms, 118; (b) to collect revenue, 121, 128, 129, 133; renamed 'Collectors', 135
Suraj-ud-Daula, Nawab, 93, 94-101, 108, 119, 160, 377

Surat
under Moguls, 22, 24, 27, 28, 31, 32, 33, 34, 46, 49; factory, 47, 50, 53-6, 57, 105, 238; supplanted by Bombay, 57-8; extension, 239
Surman, John, 79, 105
Survey, for settlements, 188, 229-30, 297, 332, 336
Survey Officer, 335
Sutlej, River, 269, 306, 307, 328, 342
Suttee, 55, 66, 74, 242, 248, 253-9, 270, 310, 311, 312, 316, 327, 329, 333, 373
Swan Khan, 332
Sylhet, 152

TALLEYRAND, MONSIEUR DE, 208
Talleyrand, Princess (see Mrs. Grand)
Tamerlane (Timur), 37, 81, 112, 277, 338
Tanjore, 193, 253
Tapti, River, 22
Taxation
of infidels, 49, 71; at Madras, 68-9; at Calcutta, 95; tax-gatherers, 41, 43-6, 136, 192
Taylor, John, 159
Taylor, Meadows, 263
Taylor, Reynell, 329
Teignmouth, Lord (see Shore, Sir John)
Telegraphs, 247, 350
Temple, Sir Richard (quoted), 337
Tenants (see Peasants)
Tenasserim, annexed, 306
Terry, Rev. Edward, 34, 54
Thackeray, Mr., 197
Thackeray, William Makepeace, 223-4, 266
Thomas, Mr., 71
Thomason, James, 248, 291, 301-5, 306, 323, 334, 350
Thompson, Edward (quoted), 200, 258, 269-70, 273, 344, 374
Thorburn, John, 61
Thornton, John, 301
Thring, Dr. E., 284
Thugs, 225, 260-5, 308, 316, 318
Thurlow, Lord Chancellor, 145, 157
Tippu (Tippoo) Sultan, 172, 188, 189, 200, 205, 348
Tirhoot, 168
Tod, Captain, 231
Tod, Col. James, 204, 205, 223, 254, 309-10, 323, 370
Todar Mal, 44-5, 71, 103, 137
Todas, aboriginals, 252
Tories, 276
Touring in districts, 141, 144, 170-1, 179, 187, 189-90, 191, 228-9, 264, 299-300, 302, 308
Trade
E. India Co.'s main interest, 11, 19, 20, 27, 33, 34, 47, 49, 74, 103, 169, 179; Mogul apathy, 22, 33; private, 77, 104-5, 109, 143, 144, 152, 176, 177, 178; conditions for, 97; E. India Co. loses rights, 317
Traill, G., 229-31, 232, 237, 301
Traill's Pass, 230
Travel
(a) dangers of in Mogul times, 25-6, 50-1; dangers after Moguls, 226, 261; (b) in nineteenth century, 226-37, 310-12
Treaty
with Mir Jafar, 101, 110; with Suraj-ud-Daula, 96, 119; of Salbai, 130, 131, 200; with Oman, 207
Trevelyan, Charles Edward, 288-9, 291, 308
Trevelyan, Mrs., 288
Trevelyan, George Macaulay, 288
Trevelyan, Sir George Otto, 288, 358
Trevelyanpur, Delhi, 289
Tribute
British to Golconda, 65, 67, 68; zamindars to Moguls, 136; Marathas demand, 173
Trichinopoly, 83, 84, 85, 258
Trimbakji, 215
Trimmu Ghat, Battle of, 376
Tucker, Henry, 361, 363-4
Tucker, Mr., 289, 296
Tucker, Robert, 367, 369
Turkish, the Mogul Court language, 27, 41
Twenty-four Pergunnas, district, 102

UNITED PROVINCES, 293
Upper Provinces (N.W.P.), 293
Urdu (see Hindustani)

VANSITTART, GEORGE, 139
Vansittart, Henry, 93, 106, 108, 112, 114-19
Vellore, 347-8
Verelst, Harry, 110, 112, 115, 116, 119-21, 128, 133, 186
Verelst, Willem, 119
Viceroys (Mogul Governors), 71, 79-82, 93, 94, 101, 362
Vijayanagar, Rajas of, 64
Village
community (brotherhood), 38, 136-7, 168, 174, 184, 193, 293, 295, 301; boundaries, 121, 229-30, 296
Vincent, Mr., 71
Vishnu, God, 312

WAKE, HERWALD, 364-5, 366
Walker, Major, 232
Wallace-Dunlop, Mr., 367
Warner, Mr., 226-7

INDEX

Watson, Admiral Charles, 96, 98, 99, 100

Watson, Mr., 367

Wattel Punt, 208

Watts, William, 98, 99, 118, 160

Wauchope, Samuel, 289-90

Waziris, 331-3

Webbe, Josiah, 196, 225

Wellesley, Sir Arthur (Duke of Wellington), 189, 190-1, 200, 206, 207, 208, 209, 214, 239, 327

Wellesley, Henry, 206

Wellesley, Marquis of, Governor-General, 172; character, 153, 161, 209; and Madras, 192; progress under, 198, 306, 349; recall, 200; on Empire, 200; methods, 200, 202, 206-7; and Oudh, 200, 202, 228; Malcolm and, 206, 208-9; 'the glorious little man', 206, 214, 238, 247; his 'set', 206, 213, 222, 267, 328; and Directors, 209, 221; suttee and, 257; infanticide and, 260; Fort William College, 279-80

Wheeler, General Sir Hugh, 358

Wheeler, Miss, 358

Whigs, 94, 125, 143, 276

Wilkins, Mr., 162

Wilks, General Mark, 225

Wilson, John Cracroft, 367

Winter, Sir Edward, 65-6, 74, 177

Withington, Nicholas, 31

Wrangham, Emma (Mrs. Bristow), 158-60, 169

Writers
life of, 64-6, 76-7, 114-15, 122, 134; salaries, 65, 76

Wynn, Sir Charles, 232, 285

Yale, Elihu, 66

Yusufzai, 334

Zamindars
in Bengal, 78, 136-41, 168-9, 178, 192, 271, 293, 298, 301; in Delhi, 271; in N.W.P., 293-5, 298

402

J. E. NEALE

THE AGE OF CATHERINE DE MEDICI and Essays in Elizabethan History   J.C.P.1

Professor Neale gives a clear and concise survey of the period of the French wars of religion, describing the religious and social conditions which provoked them. THE AGE OF CATHERINE DE MEDICI provides the continental background to Elizabethan history, many aspects of which are discussed in ESSAYS IN ELIZABETHAN HISTORY. Professor Neale shows how the past throws light upon the present, as well as the present on the past.

GARRETT MATTINGLY

CATHERINE OF ARAGON   J.C.P.2

For twenty-four years Catherine of Aragon was the wife of Henry VIII. England loved her; Henry loved, respected and finally feared her. Wolsey hated her. Twice she saved England, once from invasion, once from civil war. Garrett Mattingly has clothed the story of her life—uncovered in years of painstaking research—in rich and vivid prose.
'There is no doubt that he has written what is now the standard work on Catherine.'—OBSERVER

A. L. ROWSE

SIR RICHARD GRENVILLE OF THE *REVENGE*
J.C.P.3

'Herein lies one of the notable features of Mr. Rowse's biography. He knows his sixteenth-century Cornishmen as few or no others do... Mr. Rowse has found an unpublished document in the Spanish archives, describing the battle and written apparently by someone aboard the Spanish flagship. It is an important discovery, both for the intrinsic merits of the description and because the existing evidence about this famous battle is slight and extremely confusing... The picture of Grenville which we now have is the traditional story, a mixture of heroism and heroics; the story of a man who scorned to fly from the enemy or surrender. It is truly Elizabethan... There is no doubt that Mr. Rowse's book will establish itself as the standard biography of Grenville, and he deserves our unstinted thanks for the patient research that he has put into it.'

J. E. Neale in the SUNDAY TIMES

GEORGE BURTON ADAMS

CONSTITUTIONAL HISTORY OF ENGLAND

J.C.P.4

This standard work first appeared in 1921, since when it has gone through fourteen impressions and has been in steady demand. In his original introduction the author wrote: 'I have endeavoured in writing this book to keep constantly in view the needs of the general reader and of the college student.' There is by now ample evidence that he has succeeded.

GAETANO SALVEMINI

THE FRENCH REVOLUTION 1788–1792

J.C.P.5

This book is a study of the break-up of the feudal regime in France, of the early years of the Revolution and of the leading personalities who took part in it. The author makes clear the underlying causes of the Revolution and the political and intellectual forces which sprang from these causes and have, in fact, led to all the great movements of our time.

'His book is evidence that history ... can be exciting as well as scholarly.'—SUNDAY TIMES.

Translated from the Italian by I. M. Rawson.

JOHN BOWLE

POLITICS AND OPINION IN THE NINETEENTH CENTURY

J.C.P.6

The theme of this book is the development of liberal-social-democratic political thought from the Romantic Age to the early twentieth century, the attacks made upon it by doctrines of class war, nationalism and nihilism, and its later reinforcement by the beginnings of modern sociology.

'This is a good book, comprehensive, vigorous and easy to read... The book is a monument to the industry, impartiality and talent for lively exposition of its author.'

MANCHESTER GUARDIAN

DAVID HARRIS WILLSON

KING JAMES VI & I J.C.P.7

Professor Willson has written a biography of James the Sixth of Scotland and First of England which is at the same time a contribution to scholarship and a fascinating, witty story for the general reader. King James was a baffling combination of learning and pedantry, shrewdness and folly, lofty aspirations and contemptible practice, whose interests included theology, natural history, poetry and witchcraft, not to mention hunting. The Scottish part of his life, so dramatic, but so complicated and baffling to the student of English history, here finds its proper treatment.

'A brilliant and fair-minded book.'—THE TIMES

PHYLLIS DOYLE

A HISTORY OF POLITICAL THOUGHT

J.C.P.8

'This is an able and interesting account of the chief theories of government from Plato to T. H. Green... In Miss Doyle's book the analysis of the most famous works on political theory is very well done and the sketch of the political conditions which were the occasions for each theory is vivid and vigorous.'

SPECTATOR

PHILIP WOODRUFF

THE MEN WHO RULED INDIA
Vol. I: The Founders J.C.P.9

This is the story of the men who ruled India for over three centuries. It is a story about men, not about tendencies or policies, an attempt to show what these men were like, what they thought and felt, how they came to rule so many people with so little use of force. And yet, because they were responsible for running the country, an account of what they did must touch at point after point on the whole history of India. The author's method is biographical; he chooses one man who seems representative and gives some account of his life and opinions, leaving out a hundred and passing on ruthlessly to the next, including in his gallery obscure as well as famous men.

'It will take its place as a standard work.'—ECONOMIST

THE MEN WHO RULED INDIA
Vol. II: The Guardians

J.C.P.10

In his second volume, THE GUARDIANS, Mr Woodruff carries the tale of THE MEN WHO RULED INDIA from the Mutiny to the end of British rule on August 15th, 1947.

'As in the first volume, against the background of high policy and administrative problems, its author deftly weaves a glowing tapestry of the lives, personalities, eccentricities and intimate thoughts of some of the handful of men who composed that "impartial and immovable civil service"—the Indian Civil Service.'—DAILY TELEGRAPH